JOE AND MARILYN

This Large Print Book carries the
Seal of Approval of N.A.V.H.

JOE AND MARILYN

LEGENDS IN LOVE

C. DAVID HEYMANN

THORNDIKE PRESS
A part of Gale, Cengage Learning

GALE
CENGAGE Learning·

Farmington Hills, Mich • San Francisco • New York • Waterville, Maine
Meriden, Conn • Mason, Ohio • Chicago

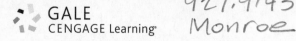

Lg Print
927.9143
Monroe

GALE
CENGAGE Learning®

Copyright © 2014 by C. David Heymann.
Thorndike Press, a part of Gale, Cengage Learning.

ALL RIGHTS RESERVED
Thorndike Press® Large Print Biography.
The text of this Large Print edition is unabridged.
Other aspects of the book may vary from the original edition.
Set in 16 pt. Plantin.

LIBRARY OF CONGRESS CATALOGING-IN-PUBLICATION DATA

Heymann, C. David (Clemens David), 1945-2012.
  Joe and Marilyn : legends in love / by C. David Heymann. — Large print edition.
    pages ; cm. — (Thorndike Press large print biography)
  Includes bibliographical references.
  ISBN 978-1-4104-7213-7 (hardcover) — ISBN 1-4104-7213-2 (hardcover)
  1. Monroe, Marilyn, 1926-1962. 2. DiMaggio, Joe, 1914-1999. 3. Motion picture actors and actresses—United States—Biography. 4. Baseball players—United States—Biography. 5. Large type books. I. Title.
  PN2287.M69H46 2014
  791.4302'8092—dc23
  [B]   2014017371

Published in 2014 by arrangement with Atria Books, a division of Simon & Schuster, Inc.

Printed in the United States of America
1 2 3 4 5 6 7 18 17 16 15 14

To Joe DiMaggio Jr.
October 23, 1941–August 6, 1999

I agree with no man's opinions: I have some of my own.

— CLEMENS HEYMANN, SENIOR QUOTATION, THE ETHICAL CULTURE FIELDSTON SCHOOL, CLASS OF 1962

The history of any public character involves not only the facts about him but what the public has taken to be facts.

— J. FRANK DOBIE

CHAPTER 1

Joe DiMaggio had been thinking about Marilyn Monroe since the early spring of 1951, when he first saw her picture in the gossip column of a local San Francisco newspaper. Later, having retired after a thirteen-year baseball career as the star center fielder for the New York Yankees, he spotted her picture again, this time on the sports page of the same paper. Several major-league ball clubs had set up spring training camps in California, and to publicize their arrival, they asked a number of film studios to send over their most attractive young starlets to pose for press shots with the ballplayers. Twentieth Century–Fox dispatched Marilyn Monroe, whose recent ascent of the proverbial Hollywood success ladder had been characterized as nothing short of meteoric. Wearing high heels, tight white shorts, and a form-fitting blouse, she was handed a bat and told to assume her approximation of a batting stance, while Joe Dobson, the power-hitting left

9

fielder, wrapped a muscular arm around her from behind in a feigned effort to improve her swing. Rounding out the photo, off to the side, was pitcher Gus Zernial, a bemused smile spread across his face.

The newspaper shot of Marilyn Monroe gripping a baseball bat evidently served to reignite Joe DiMaggio's imagination. Hoping to meet the actress, he telephoned Zernial, an acquaintance, who replied that he had no idea how to contact Monroe. He could tell DiMaggio only that she'd been "warm and giggly" — and, "yes, of course," beautiful as "all hell," a "real looker."

Following up on his Zernial inquiry, DiMaggio now called George Solotaire, a well-connected New York City ticket broker and one of Joe's most trusted cronies. During DiMaggio's final years with the Yankees, he and "Gentleman George" had shared a suite at the Elysée, 60 East Fifty-Fourth Street, known to insiders as the "Easy Lay Hotel." About to join Joe in San Francisco for a long-planned two-week trip to Hawaii, Solotaire suggested that the person most likely to know Marilyn well enough to effect an introduction would be a chap named David March. A high-strung, fast-talking Hollywood publicist (and sometime talent agent), March had at one time lived in New York, where one of his hangouts had been Toots Shor's, the Midtown Manhattan tavern popular among sportswriters and professional athletes; it was there that March had befriended both Solotaire and DiMaggio.

As March later recalled the sequence of events, he received a telephone call one evening from Solotaire in his office suite overlooking Sunset Boulevard. "Do you happen to know Marilyn Monroe?" asked the caller. "She's an old personal friend of mine," replied March. "Well then, Joe DiMaggio would like to meet her," said Solotaire. And March said, "I think I can help."

A few days later, March reached the actress at the Beverly Carlton Hotel in Los Angeles, where she was staying. "Marilyn," he said, "there's a nice guy I'd like you to meet." "Are there any nice guys left?" she inquired. To which he said, "The guy is Joe DiMaggio."

At first Marilyn said nothing. And then, "Who's Joe DiMaggio?"

March couldn't quite believe what he'd just heard. Was there anyone — man, woman, or child — who didn't know the name Joe DiMaggio? The Yankee Clipper. Joltin' Joe. The epitome of grace and style. Baseball's greatest living legend. The ballplayer who led the Yankees to nine World Series championships. Three-time winner of the American League's Most Valuable Player Award. Thirteen times an all-star, holder of a fifty-six-consecutive-game hitting streak, a record that would very likely stand until the end of time.

11

"Marilyn, you must be kidding," said March. "You've never heard of Joe DiMaggio? He's the greatest baseball player since Babe Ruth." And she asked, "Who's Babe Ruth?"

Marilyn consented to meet DiMaggio on the condition that David March join them and bring a date of his own along. "I'd be honored," said the publicist. He made a seven o'clock dinner reservation for Saturday, March 15, at the Villa Nova, a trendy Italian restaurant across the street from his office. The Villa Nova's dark wall paneling, cozy cherrywood booths, simple décor, and subdued lighting made it, according to March, an ideal spot for a dinner rendezvous between Joe and Marilyn. "The joint," as he put it, "drips with romance."

Aspiring actress Peggy Rabe, March's date that evening, had met Monroe on a previous occasion during an informal gathering at actor Gene Kelly's house and was looking forward to seeing her again. When she and David arrived at the restaurant, Joe was already sitting in a booth, waiting. The three of them ordered cocktails. Forty minutes later, they ordered a second round. Marilyn hadn't yet arrived. Never a man of great patience, DiMaggio kept peeking at his watch. "I should've warned you, Joe," said March. "The blonde Venus has never been on time for anything in her life." He pointed out that she was presently in production on a film called *Monkey Business,* with Cary Grant and Ginger Rogers. "She probably got held up on the set. I'll give her a ring."

He called from a restaurant pay phone and found the actress in her hotel room.

"Marilyn, we've been waiting for you. Joe DiMaggio's here. Remember? I told you Joe wanted to meet you."

"Please, Dave," she pleaded. "I'm very tired."

"Marilyn, you can't let me down," said March. "We're waiting for dinner. Joe DiMaggio's a wonderful guy. You'll like him."

"But I'm not dressed," she said. "I'm wearing my blue jeans."

"Okay, so you're in blue jeans. Come just as you are. You promised, Marilyn, remember?"

Reluctantly, wearily, Marilyn changed into a blue tailored suit and low-cut white blouse. She walked to her car and drove to the Villa Nova, making her entrance at eight thirty, an hour and a half late. Her date stood as she approached the table. "I'm glad to meet you," he said.

Describing her initial encounter with Joe DiMaggio on that balmy Los Angeles night, Marilyn Monroe would state in her published memoir (as told to journalist and screenwriter Ben Hecht) that she had expected to meet a "loud, sporty fellow" with slicked-back hair and flashy clothes, a guy "with a New York line of patter" who talked a lot about things (and people) that didn't in the least interest or concern her. Despite her earlier denial to David March, Marilyn admitted in her memoir that she'd actually heard of Joe DiMaggio but knew little about him beyond the obvious fact that he'd once been a major-league baseball player. As for baseball, she knew only that it was played with a bat, ball, and glove.

"When I met Joe that night," she confessed, "my first thought was: 'He's different.' " She noticed his hair; it was sprinkled with gray. His fingernails were perfectly manicured. At thirty-seven, twelve years her senior, his six-foot-two-inch frame looked lean and capable. He wore a conservative gray suit and matching tie. "If I hadn't been told he was some sort of ballplayer," she remarked, "I would have guessed he was either a steel magnate or a congressman."

For his part, DiMaggio seemed equally, if not more, impressed. The vision of Miss Monroe in the flesh surpassed even the fantasy he'd conjured from the newspaper images he'd seen of her. As the evening progressed, Marilyn noticed that her blind date barely touched his food. Nor did he speak. He did little more than smile and stare at her. At one point, she opened her blue eyes wide and exhaled breathlessly. Observing Joe's reaction at that very moment, David

March said later, "You could almost hear Mr. DiMaggio going to pieces." It was an understandable reaction. Marilyn had reached her physical peak. Never again would she be as vital and high-spirited. In his quasi biography of Monroe, Norman Mailer would describe her at this time looking as though she'd been "fed on sexual candy."

Other than DiMaggio's polite opening line, the only audible verbal exchange between Joe and Marilyn took place when she noticed a blue polka dot located precisely in the middle of his gray tie knot.

Pointing at his tie, she asked him, "Did it take you long to fix it like that?"

He responded "no" by shaking his head.

Marilyn could readily see her dinner companion was not a man to waste words. "Acting mysterious and far away while in company was my own sort of specialty," she noted. "I didn't see how it was going to work on somebody who was being mysterious and far away himself."

The actress would soon learn that DiMaggio's silence while in the company of others was hardly an act — it was and had always been his natural state. It wasn't that he had nothing to say, only that he chose not to say it. It wasn't that he lacked self-confidence; on the contrary, he had almost too much of it. Thinking back on the evening, Marilyn would have to admit that if his remoteness somehow

15

annoyed her, it also served to pique her interest.

Her awareness was further heightened by the furtive glances of recognition that came from diners at neighboring tables. They were directed not at Marilyn but rather at Joe DiMaggio. It soon dawned on her that this man was not just an ordinary ballplayer — he was evidently an exceptional ballplayer, an idol, perhaps even a hero of sorts. And from all indications, his renown seemed to extend far beyond the male-dominated world of baseball.

Her growing sense of DiMaggio's preeminence reached another plateau when Mickey Rooney sauntered over from the restaurant bar and pulled up a chair. In 1950 Rooney had offered Marilyn a brief role in one of his more forgettable films, *The Fireball.* The veteran actor, however, joined the dinner group not to see Monroe but to talk to DiMaggio. An avid baseball fan, Rooney wasn't about to pass up the opportunity to rub shoulders with one of the game's most famous players. He wanted to hear all about outfielder Al Gionfriddo's spectacular one-handed catch of Joe's towering drive in game six of the 1947 World Series between the Yanks and the Brooklyn Dodgers, a catch that resulted in an uncharacteristic reaction on DiMaggio's part. Rounding first and heading for second, the ever stoic Yankee Clipper had

16

kicked the base path in a rare public display of anger and frustration. But that particular play was only the beginning. Undaunted by DiMaggio's seeming reluctance to engage in conversation, Rooney chattered on for nearly an hour, recalling sundry highlights of the former center fielder's illustrious career.

"Rooney wouldn't go away," said March. "I tried signaling him, but he didn't take the hint. He just kept hanging around, talking baseball."

Unable to disengage Rooney from the table, March began sharing his own recollections of the "good old days" at Toots Shor's, when the great DiMaggio would show up after a game and practically be carried into the establishment on the shoulders of his many admirers. "He was a god!" exclaimed March. "A fucking god!"

March's discourse on the ballplayer caught the attention of two other baseball enthusiasts at a nearby table, and they too came over to partake of the merriment. One of them knew exactly how many hits, homers, and runs batted in Joe had produced during each of his years with the Yankees. A walking, talking baseball encyclopedia, he reeled off a litany of statistics, none of which meant a thing to Monroe.

DiMaggio remained silent. His restraint was not lost on Marilyn. "Mr. DiMaggio," she commented in her memoir, "didn't try to impress me or anybody else. The other men talked and threw their personalities around. Mr. DiMaggio just sat there. Yet somehow he was the most exciting man at the table. The excitement was in his eyes. They were sharp and alert . . . I thought, 'You learn to be silent . . . like that from having millions of people look at you with love and excitement while you stand alone getting ready to do something.' "

In Hollywood, Marilyn would assert, "the more important a man is, the more he talks. The better he is at his job, the more he brags. By these Hollywood standards of male greatness my dinner companion was Mr. Nobody. Yet I had never met any man in Hollywood who got so much respect and attention at a dinner table. Sitting next to Mr. DiMaggio was like sitting next to a peacock with its tail spread."

Although Marilyn considered DiMaggio an intriguing figure, his aloof and standoffish manner confused her. Since her comment to him about his tie, they had said practically nothing to each other. She felt neglected and rebuffed. She wondered why he had wanted to meet her in the first place. Did he even know that she was an actress? And if he did know, did he care? As respectable and celebrated as he appeared to be, he had nevertheless made no effort to get to know her. Rationalizing the situation, she conjectured that DiMaggio was "the kind of egomaniac who would rather cut off an arm than express some curiosity about somebody else."

Convinced that the evening had been a waste of everyone's time, Marilyn ultimately decided to leave. It was nearly eleven o'clock. She said she'd had a hard day at the studio, and she was exhausted. She thanked David March, excused herself, and stood.

Joe DiMaggio also stood.

"May I see you to the door?" he asked.

He followed her through the restaurant to the front entrance, where he broke his silence again.

"I'll walk you to your car," he said.

Marilyn owned a white 1949 Ford convertible, which she'd parked a block from the restaurant. When they reached her car, DiMaggio had more to say.

"I'm not staying very far from here," he said, "and I haven't any transportation. Would you mind dropping me at my hotel?"

"Not at all," said Marilyn, "as long as you don't mind the mess." Sliding into the car, DiMaggio noticed that the backseat was piled high with books, newspapers, film scripts, empty soda bottles, candy wrappers, half-eaten candy bars, and assorted articles of clothing. On top of the slag heap sat a camera and a tennis racquet. On top of the tennis racquet were five or six traffic tickets. When he later described the scene to George Solotaire, Joe said it looked like a bomb had gone off in the backseat.

"Where are you staying?" Marilyn asked.

"At the Knickerbocker. It's on North Ivar."

Marilyn drove for several minutes. Then, as she reported in her memoir, she "began to feel depressed." For some difficult to define reason, she didn't want Joe DiMaggio to step out of her car and out of her life forever, "which was going to happen" as soon as they reached his hotel.

DiMaggio must have experienced a similar sense of impending loss. As they approached the Knickerbocker, he said, "I don't feel like turning in. Would you mind driving around a little while?"

"It's a lovely night for a drive," Marilyn answered.

They drove around for the next three hours, and for much of that time DiMaggio did something he'd almost never done before. He talked about himself. He opened up and didn't stop. He told Marilyn about his days as a baseball player with the New York Yankees ball club. When he arrived in New York in 1936 as a twenty-one-year-old rookie, he wore a new business suit and visited the top of the recently completed Empire State Building, where, by chance, he met Fiorello La Guardia, the city's renowned Italian American mayor. Tony Lazzeri, the veteran Yankees infielder, who also hailed from San

Francisco, took the trouble to show DiMaggio around. Joe found New York intriguing, and he loved baseball; but in truth, the sport had served him primarily as a springboard, a means to an end, a way to avoid having to follow in his father's footsteps as a commercial fisherman. As a young man, he had no particular ambitions. He didn't know what he wanted to do in life; he knew only what he didn't want to become.

His parents, Giuseppe and Rosalie, had come to America from Isola delle Femmine, a Sicilian island adjacent to Palermo in the Golfo di Carini, where the DiMaggios had been fishermen for generations. His father had arrived first and, after saving enough money, had sent for Rosalie. They settled in Martinez, a small fishing village twenty-five miles northeast of the Golden Gate Bridge. It was there, on November 25, 1914, that Joe was born, the eighth of nine children. Less than a year later, Zio Pepe, as his father was known, packed his fishing boat with everything they owned and moved the family into a four-room ground-floor flat at 2047 Taylor Street, a three-story building on the slope of Russian Hill, in San Francisco. The rent on the apartment came to $25 per month.

Overlooking resplendent San Francisco Bay, North Beach ("a tiny town within a large city") encompassed a quarter mile of row houses, bars, restaurants, and coffeehouses. Fisherman's Wharf, with its endless stream of tourists and sightseers, stood at the bottom of the steep, ski-slope-like hill that led to the DiMaggio residence. Hundreds of small fishing vessels bobbed gently in the waters below. Seagulls wheeled above, swooping down for an occasional morsel of discarded food. In the early-morning hours, the old fishermen, most of them Italian immigrants like Giuseppe, could be seen standing in clusters, patching their nets and repairing their boats.

Zio Pepe, a short, robust man who spoke almost no English, rose at four o'clock in the morning six days a week to comb the Bay for crab. He worked hard not only because he had to but also because he believed you were supposed to. He expected his five sons, each of whom bore the middle name Paul (after the family's patron saint), to do likewise. Money was sparse, but pride was plentiful in the DiMaggio household. Until he turned twelve, Joseph Paul DiMaggio wore hand-me-downs and earned his keep at the dinner table by toiling after school on Zio Pepe's fishing boat. Two of his older brothers — Mike and Tom — had withdrawn from school to work with Dad on a full-time basis.

Joe had other thoughts. He'd begun playing baseball at the local Boys' Club. One day he made off with a broken oar from his father's boat and fashioned it into a baseball bat.

Baseball violated Zio Pepe's "code of life," his oft-proclaimed notion that financial independence and self-respect could be attained only by adhering to a strict work ethic. He became infuriated and called his son *lagnuso,* lazy, *meschino,* good-for-nothing. "You a bum!" he shouted in broken English. Rosalie DiMaggio calmed her husband by informing him that Joe had procured an after-school job working in an orange juice plant. In Joe's eyes anything beat having to swab the deck of his father's boat. It wasn't the fishing itself or being out on the open water (unless it was very choppy) that bothered Joe; it was the stench of fish and crab entrails after the boat had been at sea. Cleaning up "that mess" nauseated Joe. Mike and Tom would watch with amusement as their younger brother leaned over the side of the boat and puked his guts out.

To help pay his share of the household expenses, Joe undertook several jobs, none for longer than six months. After leaving the orange juice plant, he went to work on the docks, followed by employment in a cannery and eventually at a warehouse, loading and unloading trucks. When all else failed, he resorted to hawking newspapers on street corners, at the same time perfecting his athletic skills by playing ball in the sandlot leagues of North Beach, not far from home.

Joe recalled the difficult days of the Great

Depression when he and the rest of his family would sit in the Taylor Street kitchen under long strips of sticky yellow flypaper hanging from the ceiling to catch the flies and other insects that flew into the house. In the heat of summer, before the advent of the air conditioner, it was necessary to keep the windows and screen door open. "I felt as if I were stuck to the flypaper," Joe told Marilyn. "I felt utterly doomed, like one of those poor insects. In 1929 I started high school, and I hated it with a passion. I don't think I cracked a single book that year. I wanted to quit school — and all those crazy jobs — and start playing ball full-time. Zio Pepe didn't go for it. Two of my brothers — Vincent, two years older than me, and Dominic, two years younger — had also developed an interest in baseball. The three of us shared a bedroom, and on weekends we would listen to the games on radio. It was our mother who finally went to bat for us. She confronted Zio Pepe and won the right for three of her sons to eventually become major-league baseball players."

Rosalie DiMaggio appeared to be a well-bred lady, attired in plain, dark clothes, with her hair often fastened in a bun; she seemed to be an old-fashioned, old-world woman who would never question the opinions of her Sicilian fisherman husband. In reality she was much more sophisticated and open

24

minded than Zio Pepe. "This is America," she told him. "Everything is possible. Let the boys pursue their dreams. If they want to play baseball for a living, let them at least try." She made this dramatic proclamation in Italian, her English being no better than her husband's. And she made it, DiMaggio observed, at a time when Italian Americans were still all too commonly referred to as "guineas."

In 1930, having completed the ninth grade, Joe dropped out of school and, two years later, signed on to play minor-league baseball with the San Francisco Seals of the Pacific Coast League. The following year he captured the attention of nearly every major-league scout by hitting safely in sixty-one straight games. His teammates called him "the Walloping Wop." In 1934 the New York Yankees purchased DiMaggio from the Seals for $25,000 and five yet-to-be-named players. In 1936 he got three hits in his first major-league game and wound up the season with a .323 batting average. The Yankees topped the standings in the American League that season and went on to win the World Series. The owners of the ball club attributed the team's success largely to the Iron Horse, first baseman Lou Gehrig, as well as to the efforts of their star rookie. Joe DiMaggio wasn't just a phenomenon at the plate; he was equally adept in the field. Even if he had to say so

25

himself, he possessed an uncanny instinct for the game, a sixth sense, which enabled him to make the most difficult play look easy. It was a skill shared by few. On the Yankees, only Gehrig, fast approaching the end of his career, and catcher Bill Dickey could be compared to DiMaggio.

Two of Joe's brothers also wound up in the majors. Dom, known as the "little professor" because he wore glasses when he played, signed with the Boston Red Sox. Vince played in the National League for no fewer than five teams, including the Pittsburgh Pirates and the New York Giants. All three played the same position: center field.

The DiMaggio siblings garnered an abundance of publicity. They weren't the only brothers playing major-league baseball at that time, but because there were three of them, all playing the same position and all doing well, the attention came in a variety of forms. Hollywood gossip columnist Louella Parsons wrote that the saga of the DiMaggio family would make a "great movie," and inquiries arrived at the Taylor Street homestead from a number of producers and film studios. There were countless articles in newspapers and magazines. There were dozens of requests for radio interviews, television having not yet arrived. Every Italian American group and organization in America invited the brothers to become honorary members. Grantland

Rice, then the nation's most famous sports-writer, got so caught up in the excitement that he penned a poem and ran it in his column: "Out the olive trail they go — Vincent, Dominic, and Joe . . . Who is it that steals the show? Vincent, Dominic, and Joe."

But what most pleased the Yankee Clipper was that Zio Pepe soon became the baseball trio's most ardent fan. He regaled the other North Beach fishermen with daily updates on their latest feats. He scanned the box scores in the newspaper every morning to see how his sons had performed the day before. He adorned his living room with photographs of his offspring in their respective team uniforms. For each son, he compiled a scrap-book of sports page items and articles clipped from the newspapers by his four daughters. He even traveled east one year to watch his boys play in person.

"He never fully understood the game," Joe told Marilyn. "He showed up in a straw hat, then simply stood and cheered with the rest of the crowd. What he liked most were the hot dogs they served at Yankee Stadium, though he complained they were too expen-sive. The next time he came to the stadium, he said, he'd bring along his own food."

The more DiMaggio spoke, the more Mon-roe liked him. He hadn't told her everything about himself, but he'd told her enough. Two and a half hours had elapsed, and they were

27

still driving around Hollywood and Beverly Hills in Marilyn's car. Not yet done, Joe began speaking, in an almost boastful manner, about his relationships with women.

According to Marilyn's memoir, he revealed that he "worried" whenever he went out with "a girl." He didn't mind going out once with her. It was the second time that made him uneasy. As for the third time, that eventuality seldom took place. He had a "loyal friend" named George Solotaire who "ran interference" for him and, when necessary, "pried the girl loose."

"Is Mr. Solotaire in Hollywood with you?" Marilyn inquired.

"Yes," said DiMaggio. "He's staying with me at the Knickerbocker."

"I'll try not to make too much trouble when he starts prying me loose," she said.

"I don't think I will have use for Mr. Solotaire's services this trip," he replied.

They drove on without speaking for a while, but Marilyn didn't mind. She had the feeling that "compliments from Mr. DiMaggio were going to be few and far between," so she was "content" to sit in silence and enjoy the one he'd just paid her.

Several minutes later, he spoke up again.

"I saw your picture the other day," he told her.

"Which movie was it?" she asked.

"It wasn't a movie. It was a photograph of

you on the sports page. You were holding a baseball bat."

Marilyn remembered the photo session with Gus Zernial and Joe Dobson.

"I imagine you must have had your picture taken doing publicity shots like that a thousand times," she said.

"Not quite," Joe answered. "The best I ever got was Ethel Barrymore or General Mac-Arthur. You're prettier."

"Two compliments in one sitting," remarked Marilyn. "This must be my lucky night."

"Here's another compliment for you," said DiMaggio. "I wouldn't have waited at the Villa Nova as long as I did if I hadn't really wanted to meet you. I kept thinking of that sports page photo. I figured you must like ballplayers." Actually, Joe's admission that he found Marilyn attractive had an odd effect on her. "I had read reams on reams of writing about my good looks, and scores of men had told me I was beautiful," she said in her memoir. "But this was the first time my heart had jumped to hear it. I knew what that meant, and I began to mope. Something was starting between Mr. DiMaggio and me. It was always nice when it started, always exciting. But it always ended in dullness."

It did not end in dullness that night. Marilyn returned to the Beverly Carlton and invited Joe to join her. He didn't see George

Solotaire again until the following morning when he took a cab back to the Knickerbocker Hotel. Solotaire was waiting for him.

"How'd it go?" he asked.

"Pretty damn well," said DiMaggio.

Joe had known a lot of good-looking women but none more beautiful than Marilyn Monroe. He phoned her later that morning and in the afternoon sent her a bouquet of roses.

"You know," he told Solotaire, "this is the first time I ever called up a girl the morning after. I had to ask her how she felt."

CHAPTER 2

It goes without saying that Joe DiMaggio and George Solotaire never did get to Hawaii that year. George returned to New York, while DiMaggio spent the next few weeks in Los Angeles with Marilyn Monroe. When David March called Marilyn to find out how she and the ballplayer had fared after leaving the Villa Nova together, she told him, "Your friend struck out." The truth of the matter is that he'd hit a home run, but Monroe hoped to avoid unnecessary publicity so early in their relationship. She knew full well that if she leveled with March, the press would be at their doorstep in no time at all.

Naïve in certain respects but uncommonly savvy in others, Marilyn also understood that in the eyes of the general moviegoing public, a sex symbol is always sexier if romantically unattached. The powers that be at Twentieth Century–Fox, with which Marilyn had signed a seven-year contract, couldn't have cared less how many lovers she took so long as their identities remained a matter of private concern.

During Marilyn's and Joe's time together, she spent her working hours at the studio on the set of *Monkey Business,* while he played golf at the Brentwood Country Club and on other days visited the racetrack to bet on the horses. One afternoon Joe joined Frank Sinatra for lunch at the Polo Lounge. He and Sinatra had known each other since Skinny D'Amato, a former Mob figure turned nightclub operator, had introduced them in New York. In June 1946, accompanied by Toots Shor and Marlene Dietrich, Sinatra and DiMaggio attended a Joe Louis–Billy Conn heavyweight fight at Yankee Stadium. DiMaggio spent the night with Dietrich, who was thirteen years his senior, reporting afterward that while she "wasn't a bad lay, she had the foulest breath I've ever inhaled."

By far the two most recognizable Italian American celebrities of their generation, DiMaggio and Sinatra had formed an immediate bond. A music critic of the day compared Sinatra's vocal style to the sight of DiMaggio swinging a bat. "They both make it look so easy," he wrote. Although they both enjoyed the benefits of their respective fame — and everything that came with it, including financial reward and beautiful women — there were essential differences between them. While Sinatra bathed in the glory of his renown, DiMaggio resisted the attendant intrusions into his personal life. When approached by an aggressive autograph hound at the Polo Lounge that afternoon, Sinatra obliged, whereas DiMaggio refused. "Can't you see we're eating lunch?" Joe snapped. The intruder retreated, pleased to have copped at least one signature for his trouble.

"How do you stand it?" DiMaggio asked.

"It comes with the territory," said Sinatra. "And if publicity bothers you, wait till they hear about you and Marilyn."

To forestall the inevitable, DiMaggio and Monroe spent their evenings hidden away in his suite at the Knickerbocker Hotel. They ordered their meals from room service and paid a bellhop to buy wine for them from a nearby liquor store. Their secret remained intact until Marilyn called her old buddy and confidant, Hollywood columnist Sidney Skolsky, to ask him what he thought of Joe DiMaggio. "He has a big name," said Skolsky. "You could do a hell of a lot worse." The next day he ran an item on Joe and Marilyn in his newspaper column.

DiMaggio didn't know about the item until later that day when he received a telephone call from Toots Shor.

"Is it true?" he asked.

"Is what true, Tootsie?"

"About you and Marilyn Monroe? It's in Sid Skolsky's column."

Although DiMaggio ordinarily might have denied the story, he and Shor had been friends since Joe's earliest days with the Yankees. On one occasion, overhearing a deprecating comment about Joltin' Joe at a Yankee baseball game, the saloonkeeper had punched out the irreverent spectator, thereby proving his everlasting allegiance. On those occasions when the Yanks lost at home, Toots would soothe Joe by taking long walks with him down Fifth Avenue. And when they won, which was usually the case, Toots would stand rounds for everyone in the house.

"It's true about Marilyn," DiMaggio admitted. "We're like a good double-play combination. It's just a matter of two people meeting and something clicks."

Despite the amusing baseball analogy, Joe DiMaggio wasn't amused.

In her memoir, Marilyn described what was to be the first of a number of "frank and often vociferous discussions" between them.

"I don't know if I can take all your crazy publicity," Joe told her. She tried to explain that Sidney Skolsky had betrayed her, that it didn't serve her purpose any more than Joe's to have the story go public. But it wasn't the Skolsky item that bothered DiMaggio. What displeased him was another story about Marilyn that had just surfaced in the press, namely her admission that several years earlier she'd posed in the nude and that one of the resultant photographs had been used as the basis for a calendar that had become a piece of Americana, a frozen image of female sensuality.

In May 1949, when the photo was taken, Marilyn was just another Hollywood hopeful without a studio or a job, a simple but imaginative young woman with small-town good looks and a figure that took one's breath away. Columbia Pictures had dropped her, she claimed, because she'd refused to sleep with Harry Cohn, the studio's tyrannical boss. She later told Truman Capote that though she'd thwarted Cohn's awkward advance, she'd accepted cash from occasional businessmen "who could well afford" her favors. "It made them happy, and it paid the rent," she mused, "so what the hell." But now she was broke and behind on her monthly car installment. Photographer Tom Kelley had once asked her to pose au natural, and she had declined. Recalling Kelley's offer, she called him and asked if the offer still stood. It did. They arranged to meet on May 27 at Kelley's Sunset Boulevard studio. Also present at the studio was Tom's wife, Natalie, who acted as her husband's assistant. The photographer spread a red velvet drop across the floor and put an Artie Shaw record on the turntable. Marilyn disrobed. Over the next two hours Kelley shot two rolls of film, twenty-four shots per roll. He gave Marilyn one of the developed rolls as a gift. Marilyn signed a release form using a pseudonym. Kelley paid her $50. After the session, the three of them celebrated by going to a coffee shop and ordering chili.

Kelley subsequently sold two of the nude shots of Marilyn for a total of $1,000 to John Baumgarth, a calendar publisher from Chicago, who used one of them as the centerpiece of what became known as the "Golden Dreams" calendar. The remaining twenty-two exposures mysteriously disappeared, purportedly stolen from Kelley's file cabinet. The "Golden Dreams" calendar grossed millions of dollars and could be found hanging in nearly every bar, gas station, and barber shop in the States, to say nothing of its prodigious sales abroad. So popular an item was it that FBI Director J. Edgar Hoover, though rumored to be gay, displayed it on the wall of his recreation room in the privacy of his home. By strange coincidence, Marilyn met Hoover in the early 1950s when she attended a Department of Justice reception in Washington with comedian Milton Berle. Marilyn and Uncle Miltie had briefly been lovers in the late 1940s, a period in the actress's life when nearly every man she met became a bedmate, provided he could help advance her career. There were exceptions — such as Harry Cohn — but more often than not, Marilyn allowed herself to be exploited.

Hollywood, she quickly learned, wasn't a place where an ambitious starlet could afford to be a prude.

About the time Marilyn met Joe DiMaggio — with the "Golden Dreams" calendar selling better than ever — a wire service reporter named Aline Mosby received a tip that the nude calendar girl was none other than Marilyn Monroe. Mosby called the publicity department at Fox and asked for a confirmation. In a state of near panic, studio executives contacted Marilyn, who readily admitted that she had indeed committed "the unforgivable sin" of posing in the nude. Darryl Zanuck, head of Fox and instrumental in helping to launch Monroe's career, ordered her to "deny everything." Nice girls, he told her, don't take off their clothes for money. Marilyn told Zanuck she wasn't ashamed of what she'd done and therefore saw no reason to lie. Zanuck threatened to invoke the morals clause in her contract and cut her loose, a course Monroe didn't believe he would pursue. Harry Brand, Fox's publicity director, ultimately supported her decision and arranged a luncheon between Marilyn and Aline Mosby, at which the actress tearfully described the two-hour photo session with Kelley, insisting that at the time she'd been broke and frightened. She made clear the only funds she'd collected for the session were the $50 she'd received from the photographer.

Mosby's scoop became front-page news. The nude calendar shot, airbrushed to comply with censorship requirements, received wide publication in newspapers and magazines. Joe DiMaggio didn't object to the fact that she'd posed for the photo, but rather that she'd admitted it when there was no particular need to do so. "Joe doesn't mind being written about," Marilyn noted in her memoir, "but he is against doing anything to encourage or attract publicity." He applied the same standards to Monroe and condemned her for manipulating the media in order to create a news story. When he told her he didn't know if he could deal with her voracious appetite for public exposure, she replied, "You don't have to be part of it."

"I am," he said, "and it bothers me."

"It's part of my career," Marilyn pointed out.

What irked DiMaggio even more than the Hollywood gossip mongers — the columnists and reporters — were the press photographers constantly in pursuit of Marilyn, waiting for her on every street corner, ready to pounce the moment she appeared.

"When you were a baseball idol," she remarked, "you didn't duck photographers."

"Yes. I did," he answered.

"I can't," she said.

"Don't I know it."

"Do you want me to hide in a basement?" she asked. "Movie stars aren't born, they're created. Publicity is part of the manufacturing process."

"We'll see how it works out," he said.

On April 7, 1952, Marilyn was the subject of a *Life* magazine feature article, making her first appearance on the cover of the periodical. The publication of the *Life* piece only weeks after her nude calendar disclosure indicated that the latter hadn't damaged her reputation in the least. If anything, the "Golden Dreams" calendar shot increased her star power and made her a more valuable commodity. Yet when Marilyn showed DiMaggio a copy of the April 7 issue, he dismissed it with a wave of his hand.

"I've been on the cover of *Life* myself," he said "What does it prove?" Then, answering his own question, he remarked, "Absolutely nothing. It's all vanity."

In April 1952 Joe DiMaggio returned to San Francisco and several days later flew to New York to begin a new job. He'd ended his thirteen-year baseball career in 1951, due to the grind of the road and an accumulation of injuries, not least of which was a surgically removed three-inch bone spur in the heel of his foot. At the time of his retirement, he'd been making $100,000 per year, one of the first major leaguers to reach the six-figure plateau. The Yankees currently had a new center fielder, a kid from Oklahoma named Mickey Mantle. Neither as graceful nor as polished a ballplayer as DiMaggio, Mantle would nonetheless develop into a great outfielder in his own right. He would also remain a source of ongoing annoyance to DiMaggio, who too easily became jealous of any ballplayer whose skills rivaled his own. Even Boston Red Sox star Ted Williams, often said to have had the "best eye" in baseball, would refer to Joe as "the Prima Donna of Prima Donnas."

DiMaggio's new job, which paid just about the same salary he'd earned during his last years with the Yanks, seemed at odds with his personality. He'd become the host of a television talk show that was broadcast from a cramped studio located in the basement tunnel behind the home-team dugout at Yankee Stadium. The show involved five minutes of pregame commentary on his part, followed by a post-game interview with either a Yankees player or a member of the visiting team. The producers of the show were responsible for choosing the interviewee and writing out the postgame questions. DiMaggio hated doing the show almost as much as he'd despised working on his father's fishing boat. He felt insecure about appearing before the cameras and was convinced he wasn't doing a good job. He was right.

Richard Ben Cramer, one of DiMaggio's biographers, reported one instance when the Yankee Clipper threw an absolute fit, spewing curses and refusing to go on, because somebody had misplaced the first cue card. The program director eventually calmed him down and saw to it that they wrote out a new cue card in block letters:

HI, I'M JOE DIMAGGIO.

WELCOME TO THE JOE DIMAGGIO SHOW.

He was once again sharing a suite with George Solotaire at the Elysée Hotel in Manhattan. Also staying with them was Robert Solotaire, George's twenty-two-year-old son. "Joe would rush back to the hotel after his TV spot and call Marilyn Monroe in Hollywood," recalled Robert. "He was nuts about her. Following their daily phone conversation, the three of us would head out for dinner, either at Toots Shor's, where Joe had his own table, or the Stage Deli, on Seventh Avenue. Although Joe usually let others do the talking, these days he'd blabber nonstop about Marilyn. From the very beginning, he wanted to marry her. He'd construed an image of her that seemed totally unrealistic. I remember one night at Toots Shor's when he told sports reporter Jimmy Cannon that 'Marilyn's nothing but a fun-loving little kid.' She'd give up her acting career if he asked her, he said. She'd quit making movies to start a family, have babies.

"My old man never said anything to him, but he thought Joe misunderstood Monroe. Like, here's this young, beautiful woman on the verge of becoming one of the most successful and famous actresses in the world, an international superstar, and she's going to give it all up to make lasagna for Joe and spend her days changing diapers. It didn't compute. The main problem was that Joe's triumphs belonged to the past, and he lived on them, while Marilyn's great success lay just ahead of her."

To be sure, Joe DiMaggio had a very "old school" view of women: a woman should be reserved and, it went without saying, should respect and honor her man. Proud of Marilyn's beauty, he loved that she was admired but preferred that she be admired from afar. According to Joe, there was no better career for a woman than being a homemaker and mother. He and Marilyn had discussed this issue during their time together. And while she had refused to promise anything concerning her own intentions, she had assured Joe that starting a family was her dearest wish. DiMaggio convinced himself that he would prevail in the end and would convince her to give up her acting career in exchange for the sanctity of a domestic partnership. Until that time was at hand, he would help her attain the public acclaim she so desperately sought.

On April 27, some three weeks after DiMaggio's departure from Hollywood, Marilyn suffered an appendicitis attack. Taken to Cedars of Lebanon Hospital, she had her appendix removed the following day. "If I die," she told Joe DiMaggio over the phone prior to the surgery, "I want you to put roses on my grave every week, just as William Powell did for Jean Harlow." Actually, Marilyn wasn't afraid that she would die — it wasn't a dangerous surgical procedure — but that she would be left with a lower abdominal scar. "You never know when I might want to pose for another nude calendar shot," she joked with Shelley Winters, who'd shared an apartment with her when both actresses were first breaking into the film business.

"When it came to surgery," said Shelley, "Marilyn's greatest fear was that some doctor would accidentally remove her ovaries, eliminating the possibility of having a child. I learned later that prior to her appendectomy, she'd taped a note to her abdomen reminding the surgeon not to tamper with her ovaries. When I heard this, I told her an appendectomy has nothing to do with a woman's reproductive organs. 'I know,' said Marilyn, 'but when they have you strapped to an operating table, they just love to carve you up.' I believe her fear stemmed from the fact that she suffered from a condition that had been diagnosed as endometriosis, a gynecological disorder that caused extremely painful menstrual periods, for which she underwent some half dozen surgical procedures during her life. I have no idea why, but her gynecologist, Dr. Leon Krohn, was also in the operating room when she had her appendectomy, so perhaps she thought he might remove her ovaries."

Unable to join Marilyn after her operation because of his television commitment, Joe telephoned her at all hours. He sent letters and telegrams and several bottles of champagne, which the head nurse confiscated for the duration of her stay. He arranged for a local florist to deliver a fresh bouquet of roses twice a day until she left the hospital. He also asked David March, who'd introduced them, to visit her after the surgery. To DiMaggio's dismay, March brought along a reporter. DiMaggio never spoke to the publicist again.

After Marilyn's release from Cedars, Joe telephoned her nonstop at the Bel Air Hotel, where she'd rented a suite to convalesce. He dispensed advice and counsel on how she should handle the public relations aspect of her profession. He'd gone through it in his own career, he said, and he'd learned from bitter experience how to deal with "all those vultures," most of them only too willing to take advantage of her. Nobody in Hollywood could be trusted. They were all fakes and charlatans. She must be wary of reporters

44

and agents, producers and photographers. And among the worst were the studio executives. They were using her. They were exploiting her beauty and talent for their own purposes. It was because of this, he told her, that the only film role they would ever offer her would be that of the bombshell, the buxom blonde, the wiggling, giggling, ass-grinding sexpot, a fantasy figure whose inclusion in the script was solely a moneymaking proposition. And the only bank accounts they were interested in enriching were their own. They were about to make millions off Monroe, and they were paying her thousands. The only way to fight them, insisted DiMaggio, was to do what he'd done with the New York Yankees: hold out. "Hold out," he said, "until they pay you what you're worth."

Joe would continue to offer Marilyn this kind of frank, earnest, fatherly guidance for the rest of her days. It was one of the traits she most admired in him, which drew her to him as both a friend and a lover. He became one of the few devotees who gave her more than he took, a man who, in his own way, came to love her unconditionally. Yet somehow, even his all-abiding love couldn't begin to heal all the wounds she'd suffered in her childhood, a period so dark and dismal it had left her emotionally scarred for life.

Chapter 3

Several weeks after Marilyn Monroe's appendectomy, an event ensued that proved eerily similar, in a number of respects, to the recent "Golden Dreams" nude calendar affair.

Based on what Marilyn had told Twentieth Century–Fox about her childhood and upbringing, the studio's publicity department had portrayed her in various press releases as a "disadvantaged orphan" whose formative years had been spent shuttling back and forth between a desolate Los Angeles orphanage and a collection of foster homes, some better than others. Investigating the actress's past and present, a reporter discovered that Marilyn's mother was still alive, suggesting that either the studio or Monroe (or both) had lied. "Just who is the real Marilyn Monroe?" the journalist asked in a widely distributed UPI (United Press International) article. It was a question Marilyn herself would pose many times in her life and to which there was no single or simple response.

In search of an answer, Marilyn had begun therapy in 1950 with Dr. Judd Marmor, a prominent West Coast psychiatrist (analyst), whose patient roster included an assortment of movie stars, studio executives, and Beverly Hills housewives. Discussing Marilyn, Dr. Marmor acknowledged seeing her only once or twice in 1950. "One of my patients was Shelley Winters, Marilyn's friend and former roommate, and she sent her to see me. Another person who recommended that Marilyn begin therapy was director Elia Kazan, with whom Marilyn had an on-again, off-again three-year affair. The problem was that Marilyn lacked the funds at this point to commit to any long-term program. So we really didn't get into anything. I think she'd seen one or two other therapists in Los Angeles, but, again, only for a session or two. It wasn't until she moved to New York in 1955 that she began therapy in earnest."

Marilyn had actually attempted a form of therapy prior to 1955. The doctor's name was Rose Fromm, a German Jewish refugee who arrived in New York in 1937 and settled on the Upper West Side of Manhattan. "In 1951," said Dr. Fromm, "I spent six months in Los Angeles. I knew journalists Jim Bacon and Sidney Skolsky, and they introduced me to Marilyn Monroe. I'd known both columnists since 1948. I have to stress that I'd worked as a psychotherapist in Europe but not in the United States, and I made that perfectly clear to Marilyn. My doctorate in clinical psychology had been awarded abroad, and I had no interest in going through the process all over again, beyond what I needed in order to do psychiatric research in the US. In any event, Marilyn and I got along famously, and she visited my Los Angeles apartment at least a dozen times during 1951. I think at this point in time she actually preferred the kind of informal setting I provided, as opposed to the more traditional and regimented psychoanalytic sessions she underwent later in life. Basically, I think she just wanted to have somebody help her make sense of her troubled past and very turbulent childhood."

The circumstances surrounding that "turbulent childhood" took shape well before June 1, 1926, the date of her birth in a charity ward at Los Angeles County General Hospital. Her mother, Gladys Pearl Monroe — she claimed to be related to James Monroe, the fifth president of the United States — came from a working-class family with a considerable history of emotional disturbance. Gladys's maternal grandfather, Tilford Marion Hogan, committed suicide in 1933, and her mother and father both spent time in mental institutions. Gladys, red haired, fair skinned, and attractive, married businessman Jack Baker in 1917, when she was only fifteen. They had two children, Hermitt and Berniece, but Jack terminated the marriage after several years and took the children with him when he moved to Kentucky. Gladys never saw her son again. He contracted tuberculosis and died at age fifteen. Meanwhile, a succession of men followed Jack in Gladys's bed, including an unemployed merchant named Edward Mortensen. Gladys and Mortensen were wed on October 11, 1924, and were divorced seven months later. Despite the irrefutable fact that Gladys and Mortensen never spoke again following their divorce, he is identified as Marilyn's father on her birth certificate, a designation that is biologically not feasible considering the date of their last meeting. The same certificate listed Marilyn's baptismal name as Norma Jeane Mortenson, a misspelling of Edward's last name, which her mother later changed (though not legally) to Norma Jeane Baker.

At the time of Norma Jeane's birth, her mother was employed as a film cutter at Consolidated Film Industries in Hollywood, where she'd worked since 1923. In the early fall of 1925, she had an affair with C. Stanley Gifford, a salesman in the same firm. Gladys became pregnant, and Gifford, unwilling to assume responsibility, cut off the relationship. He offered her money, which she proudly refused to accept. According to Dr. Fromm, Marilyn, or Norma Jeane, "never doubted the true identity of her birth father. Nor did Gladys Baker, for that matter. It was Stanley Gifford. Why Gladys wrote "Mortenson" on her daughter's birth certificate is anybody's guess. My guess is that she was in love with Gifford and felt terribly hurt that he'd abandoned her. And at least she and Mortensen had been married, which conferred the newborn infant with some vague sense of legitimacy."

Gladys Baker had turned twenty-four when she gave birth to Norma Jeane. Gladys's mother, Della Monroe Granger, urged her to retain her full-time position at Consolidated and to place the infant with a foster family. Norma Jeane was turned over to Wayne and Ida Bolender, Christian Science adherents, who lived on East Rhode Island Street in Hawthorne, California, the same street as Della, an overzealous follower of the same religious ideology. Gladys paid the couple $5 a week to look after her daughter. "Aunt Ida," as Norma Jeane knew her, served as her foster guardian and substitute mother. Although Ida objected to being called "Mommy" by the child, Wayne didn't mind being referred to as "Daddy." He thus became the first in a long line of elusive father figures that Norma Jeane/Marilyn Monroe would look to for protection and guidance in years to come.

"With the exception of Joe DiMaggio and perhaps one or two others, the pivotal truth is that few of these so-called father figures offered her anything even close to guidance," said Dr. Fromm. "And the surrogate mothers even less so. There's that horrific anecdote she related to me involving her grandmother, who frequently visited her at the Bolender house when she was a baby and sometimes took her across the street to her own home. The story has it that one day Della tried to smother the infant with a pillow because she wouldn't stop crying. They committed the woman to Norwalk State Hospital, in Norwalk, LA County. It wasn't her first stay in a mental institution. After several weeks at Norwalk, she suffered a manic seizure and died the following day."

Even the most mundane of Norma Jeane's childhood activities had a phantasmagoric edge to them. On weekends her mother sometimes took her on outings, mostly by trolley, to the beach at Santa Monica. But on those occasions Gladys seemed nervous and preoccupied, barely capable of relating to her daughter. Wayne and Ida Bolender took her to religious pageants and sent her to Sunday school, an experience, she told Dr. Fromm, that gave rise to a recurring childhood dream wherein she stands up in church without any clothes on, and all the people there are lying

51

at her feet on the floor of the church, and she walks naked, with a sense of freedom, over their prostrate forms. Another dream, also involving nudity, resulted from a visit she paid with the Bolenders to a country cemetery. In this dream she races naked around a cemetery at dawn trying to find a way out, getting lost, tripping over a headstone, then finally exiting the cemetery through high steel gates.

Norma Jeane attended kindergarten and then first grade with Lester, a boy her age who'd been adopted by the Bolenders. The two children were given private piano lessons at home, but Lester, as Marilyn Monroe recalled, constantly disrupted the lessons by throwing temper tantrums. She additionally remembered (how could she not?) that the Bolenders would discipline both youngsters by beating them with a belt, a practice that forever instilled in her a fear of violence. Her favorite "household member" turned out to be Charlie, a pet collie that accompanied her on treks through a clump of piney woods several blocks behind the house. One morning she awoke to find that Wayne Bolender had given the dog away the night before. No explanation for this action was ever provided. "Charlie simply disappeared," Marilyn would tell Dr. Fromm, "like so many others in my life."

In June 1933 Norma Jeane's mother, currently working as a film cutter at both Columbia Pictures and RKO Studios, suddenly decided to reclaim her seven-year-old daughter from the Bolenders. For a brief period, they resided in a small rental apartment in North Hollywood, while Gladys put the finishing touches on a six-room bungalow she'd acquired on Arbol Drive, a short distance from the Hollywood Bowl. To help with the monthly mortgage payments, Gladys rented out one of the bungalow's three bedrooms to an English couple, George and Maude Atkinson. Among the items she acquired for Norma Jeane was a white lacquered baby grand piano (and matching bench) that had once belonged to actor Fredric March. She also gave her daughter a set of Glenn Miller records and a windup portable Victrola. At the beginning of September, Gladys enrolled Norma Jeane in the Selma Street Elementary School. Determined to succeed in her new role as a doting parent, Gladys altered her work schedule so that she could take Norma Jeane to school in the morning and retrieve her in the afternoon. She used a small inheritance from her mother's estate to hire a part-time housekeeper to help with chores and prepare meals. But by the end of 1933, Gladys had run out of cash and had to let the housekeeper go. It was the same year that Tilford Hogan, Gladys's grandfather, committed suicide by hanging himself, some said, with a shower curtain.

For all Gladys Baker's noble intentions, her plan to create a home for her daughter soon went awry. As the months passed, her behavior grew increasingly erratic. She took a medical leave of absence from her job and began spending more and more time in bed. At night, Marilyn would tell Dr. Fromm, she could hear "the lady with red hair" weeping in the other room. Gladys no longer bothered to change her clothing. On the rare occasions she went out, she always wore the same baggy black dress. Her hair was matted. She had stopped bathing. For hours she would stand at the window of her bedroom, staring out, motionless. One night Norma Jeane lay next to her in bed, clasping her hand. Not knowing what to do or say, she told her mother she loved her. It was the night she realized Gladys wasn't well and wasn't going to get better.

Returning home from school the next day, Norma Jeane found her mother in bed, her nightgown hiked up to her waist, her legs coated with a patchwork of urine and feces. A foul odor filled the room. Gladys addressed her as if in a trance.

"I saw God this morning," she said. "He's a little old man, lives in a cabin in the woods. Seems like a nice guy. He's a vegetarian. Grandpa Til and Mama Della were with him. Mama had flowers in her hair and seemed happy to see me. 'It's not so bad here,' she said. 'It really isn't. You ought to stay for a while. You'd like it. And next time bring Norma Jeane. I want to see her again.' "

"There's something almost comical about the situation, but it isn't difficult to imagine how frightening all this must have been for a young child," remarked Rose Fromm. "It made her realize just how alone she was in the world. Nobody, not even Gladys, ever treated her like a real daughter. Nobody had ever held her. No one kissed her. Nobody."

In January 1934 Gladys Baker was carted off to a rest home in Santa Monica. From there she went to the psychiatric ward at Los Angeles County General Hospital, where Norma Jeane was born, before being transferred to the Norwalk State Asylum, where Della had perished in 1927. At Norwalk, Gladys was diagnosed as having paranoid schizophrenia — the same mental illness that had led to the deaths of her parents and grandfather. Marilyn Monroe feared, not without cause, that the dreaded disease would one day invade her own mind and destroy her life as surely as it had wrecked the lives of so many others in her family.

The baby grand that her mother had bought for her — a token of what Gladys had hoped would be a prolonged period of familial bliss — was sold following Gladys's institutionalization. Years later, Marilyn tracked down the piano, purchased it, and had it installed first in an apartment she leased in 1953 in Beverly Hills and then in her New York apartment on East Fifty-Seventh Street, a sentimental reminder of the woman who had originally given it to her.

Another item in the Arbol Drive house that didn't go unnoticed by Norma Jeane was a small framed photograph of a man with dark hair, even features, and a mustache, which had been mounted on the wall over Gladys's dresser. "When I asked her who he was," Marilyn would tell Dr. Fromm, "she said, 'He's just an old friend.' I later learned it was a picture of my father, Charles Stanley Gifford. He resembled Clark Gable. One day I came across an eight-by-ten-inch photo of Mr. Gable in a memorabilia shop and bought it. I'd look at it now and then and say, 'That's my father — that's him!' "

So that she could complete the year without having to switch schools, it was decided Norma Jeane would continue living with the Atkinsons at the same address. Gladys's boarders undertook the task of looking after the child, which they did for several months until a death in the family forced the Atkinsons to return to England. Once again Norma Jeane found herself in transition, going from one foster home to another until finally she was taken in by Mr. and Mrs. Harvey Giffen, former friends of Gladys Baker. Harvey, a sound engineer with the Radio Corporation of America, gave her tennis and sketching lessons. The living arrangement appeared to suit everyone until Harvey's employer reassigned him to a new position in Mississippi. Preparing to leave, the Giffens offered to adopt Norma Jeane and take her along. The prospect of staying with a family she had quickly grown to like appealed to the child, but Gladys, presently undergoing electroshock therapy, wouldn't allow it.

The Arbol Drive bungalow was repossessed and put up for sale, and, in a sense, so too was Norma Jeane. Grace McKee, a film librarian at Columbia Pictures when Gladys Baker worked there, had become friendly with both Gladys and her daughter. Not that Gladys and Grace had always gotten along. Allegedly, Gladys once accused Grace of trying to poison her. In retaliation for this imagined misdeed, Gladys attacked Grace with a butcher knife. The police were called, and Gladys was led away in handcuffs.

Nevertheless, insofar as she had no children of her own, Grace McKee volunteered to become Norma Jeane's legal guardian. Because she wasn't married at the time and because the guardianship papers hadn't yet been processed, she decided to place the child with the Los Angeles Orphans Home Society (now Hollygrove), at 815 North El Centro Avenue in Los Angeles, not far from

57

the same RKO Studios where Gladys Baker had previously worked. Norma Jeane entered the orphanage in September 1935 and remained until the end of June 1937, a total of twenty-one months. She was assigned bed number 27 (of sixty-five beds) and told that her mandatory chores included scrubbing the latrine and waiting on tables in the dining hall. She called the facility "the child factory" and later claimed that being there had been the worst experience she'd ever had to endure.

"They taught her how to swim at a nearby public swimming facility," said Dr. Rose Fromm, "and that's the extent of it." The child's only respite from the dreariness of the institution came when she attended day school during the week and on occasional Saturdays when Grace McKee would take her out for the afternoon, typically to Hollywood Boulevard for a matinee at Grauman's Chinese Theatre or Grauman's Egyptian Theatre. Afterward, they'd have ice cream cones and watch the caged monkeys in front of the theater.

The girls at the orphanage were required to wear a prisonlike uniform consisting of a formless skirt and faded gray blouse. Whenever one of them celebrated a birthday, the orphanage provided a birthday cake. After the birthday celebrant blew out the candles, the cake would be taken away only to reappear on the occasion of the next girl's birthday party. In other words, they didn't get to eat the cake; they only got to look at it. What made this cruel exercise seem even more extreme was the ordinariness of the food they did get to eat: oatmeal for breakfast, hot dogs for lunch, and broiled chicken for dinner. The menu rarely varied. To escape the orphanage's stultifying atmosphere, Norma Jeane would often retreat to a deck on the roof of the building and peruse Hollywood fan magazines that Grace would bring her whenever she visited.

Marilyn recalled for Dr. Fromm the process whereby couples hoping to adopt an orphan would drop by the administration offices to browse through a catalogue containing photographs and descriptions of the girls. When they came across a photo that interested them, the child would be delivered to the office for a personal meeting. If all went well, the prospective adoptee would spend a trial week or two with her new family. As often as not, the child would be rejected by the couple and returned to the orphanage. Because Norma Jeane had already been "spoken for" by Grace McKee, she was ineligible for general adoption and therefore spared the indignity of what she called "the dog pound" experience. "It's bad enough to live in a dog pound," she told Rose Fromm, "but it's ten times worse to be thrown back in."

■ ■ ■ ■

On the tenth of August, 1935, Grace McKee married Ervin "Doc" Goddard, a failed actor then working as a technician in a precision instruments company. Ten years younger than Grace, Goddard had three children from an earlier marriage. He also had a drinking problem, and as Marilyn assessed it, "was drunk more often than he wasn't." Doc's alcoholism notwithstanding, Norma Jeane felt a burden had been lifted when she moved out of the "child factory" and in with the Goddards, who had set up some semblance of a household at 6707 Odessa Avenue in Van Nuys, California. She felt comfortable enough with Grace and looked forward to the prospect of becoming the newest member of a close-knit family.

But if one burden had been lifted, another would soon take its place. "Daddy Doc" — Norma Jeane's nickname for Grace's husband — complained that the eleven-year-old daughter of his wife's "insane friend" represented nothing more than "another unnecessary mouth to feed." Grace subsequently applied for and received a fairly substantial court-mandated monthly foster family stipend to cover the cost of Norma Jeane's room and board. Doc Goddard withdrew his objection.

Eleanor "Bebe" Goddard, one of Doc's three children, described her foster sister as "kind and fun-loving — she had a good sense of humor and liked to laugh." Eighteen months younger than Norma Jeane, Bebe freely admitted that her father spent his evenings hanging out in the taverns and bistros of Van Nuys, and that Grace too had become a heavy drinker. "Aunt Grace considered herself my substitute mother," Marilyn told Dr. Fromm, "but I never recognized her as such. When it came to Doc, Grace was overly indulgent. She let him get away with murder."

It wasn't murder, but it was serious enough. In late 1937, following a usual nightly stopover at a local watering hole, Doc Goddard stumbled home, barged into Norma Jeane's bedroom, and proceeded to abuse her sexually. Although he didn't rape her, he evidently molested her. Norma Jeane said nothing at the time, but Grace Goddard must have sensed something because she arranged for the child to move in with Ida Martin, Norma Jeane's great aunt. A strict, evangelical Christian, Ida had a house in Compton, on the outskirts of Los Angeles. To help cover expenses, Grace Goddard paid Ida Martin $30.

Doc Goddard wasn't the only sexual predator Marilyn Monroe encountered while growing up. An elderly male boarder had accosted her during her stay with the Bolenders and had given her a nickel in exchange for her silence. Although she reported the incident to Mrs. Bolender, the woman refused to believe Norma Jeane, insisting the boarder was "a nice gentleman" who "wouldn't harm a flea" — if Norma Jeane repeated her lie, she would have to be punished. And then there was her teenaged cousin, Jack, the son of Gladys Baker's brother, who also apparently took liberties with the child. But the Doc Goddard affair was the most upsetting, because Norma Jeane had come to regard him as something of a father figure. Whatever faith and trust she had invested in their relationship had been abruptly and permanently destroyed.

After moving in with Ida Martin, Norma Jeane entered the sixth grade at the Lankersham School in North Los Angeles. A schoolmate, Roxanne Smith, with whom she became friendly, lived within walking distance of the school. Before long, Norma Jeane began spending a day or two each week with the Smiths, sharing Roxanne's bedroom. Despite the best efforts of the dozens of biographers who have written about Marilyn Monroe over the years, the relationship that developed between Norma Jeane and Roxanne has never come to light. Though she herself never mentioned it in her memoir (or anywhere else), that it made an impression on young Marilyn is evidenced by the detailed description she provided Dr. Rose Fromm, replete with recalled snippets of actual conversation.

Roxanne, like Norma Jeane, was pretty and well developed for her age. Roxanne's favorite pastime, as Marilyn remembered it, entailed "staring at herself in the mirror." That she was attracted to Norma Jeane became evident by virtue of the effusive compliments she lavished upon her. Roxanne's bedroom contained twin beds, but one night that winter she said to Norma Jeane, "It's cold. Can I just climb into bed with you for a minute?" Without waiting for an answer, she slid into Norma Jeane's bed. "It's freezing," she said, hugging Norma Jeane tenderly. Norma Jeane pulled away.

"I'm just trying to warm myself," Roxanne remarked.

Not certain what her schoolmate wanted of her, Norma Jeane twisted herself so that her back faced the girl. Roxanne persevered. "Do you want a back rub?" she asked. She began massaging Norma Jeane's shoulders in soft, soothing movements. She continued in silence, her fingers inching their way down Norma Jeane's back, and up under her pajama top, then down again until they reached the upper part of her backside.

"Why are you doing this to me, Roxanne?" Norma Jeane asked.

"Relax," whispered the girl, "just relax."

Norma Jeane moved away until she reached the edge of the bed and could go no farther. Without breaking her rhythm, Roxanne followed and snuggled even closer.

It became clear to Norma Jeane that Roxanne, a year older and far more experienced, had overcome the objections of other visiting girlfriends. Norma Jeane was no match for her seducer. Yet she was determined to make one final effort. She turned around and faced her bedmate. "I want you to go back to your side of the room," she insisted in as officious a tone as she could muster.

"I guess my voice had no conviction," Marilyn would tell Dr. Fromm, "because she not only didn't budge, she proceeded to unbutton my pajama top and her own as well. She then rolled me onto my back and out of my bottoms. She began to kiss me and didn't stop until I began to cry." Marilyn told Dr. Fromm she couldn't recall exactly how she felt about the experience, only that she never returned to Roxanne Smith's home and in addition cut off all further contact with her in school.

"If anything," said Marilyn, "I probably felt betrayed."

In the fall of 1938, Norma Jeane went to live with (Edith) Ana Lower, Grace McKee Goddard's fifty-eight-year-old aunt, at her two-family Nebraska Avenue home in Sawtelle, at the time a lower-middle-class section of Los Angeles. A divorcee, "Aunt Ana," more than anybody else, became Norma Jeane's true surrogate mother. "She was the first person in the world I ever really loved, and who in turn loved me," Marilyn told Dr. Fromm. "She was a wonderful human being. She never hurt me, not once. She was very spiritual, always consulting Mary Baker Eddy's *Science and Health,* the Christian Science handbook, constantly reading me excerpts from it and, like the Bolenders, forever dragging me to church. But it didn't bother me. Aunt Ana was all light and kindness. I used to tell her all my little dreams and fantasies about wanting to become an actress. 'You're going to be a star, Norma Jeane,' she'd say. She wasn't rich. She rented out the bottom floor of her house to make money. And though she didn't have much, she paid for my voice, dance, and piano lessons. Nobody else ever cared what became of me. She did. The sad thing is she died in March 1948, before I began to make a name for myself, so she never knew whether she was right or wrong about my future. But had she lived, she would've been thrilled for me."

Living with Ana had only one drawback: she refused to install a telephone in her home. She maintained that people would call at all hours, and she didn't want to be disturbed. This made it difficult for Norma

Jeane to have friends over for playdates. Yet Ana's essential goodness and her openness afforded Norma Jeane a sense of security she hadn't felt before. It was Ana who revealed the identity of the man in the photograph Norma Jeane had seen in her mother's bedroom, telling her all she knew about C. Stanley Gifford. It was also Aunt Ana who informed her that Gladys Baker, her mother, had recently attempted to escape from the mental hospital at Norwalk and as a result had been transferred to the more secure Agnew State Asylum in San Francisco.

On June 1, 1939, Norma Jeane's thirteenth birthday, she accompanied Ana Lower and Grace Goddard to San Francisco for a visit with her mother. Recalling the encounter for Dr. Fromm, Marilyn said, "She looked as though she'd been lobotomized. She wasn't there. I mean she was there physically but not mentally. She didn't speak, just sat on the bed, looking frightened and lost."

On the train ride back to Los Angeles, Norma Jeane learned from Ana that she had an older half sister named Berniece, who had similarly just learned of Norma Jeane's existence and had reached out to her by way of a written note. Although Berniece and Norma Jeane didn't meet until 1944 (after Berniece had married and become a mother), by the fall of 1939, they were in touch with each other via telephone and letter. Norma Jeane informed her half sister that she'd enrolled at Emerson Junior High School, where her favorite subjects became English literature and Spanish. Her least favorite: cooking. She enjoyed athletics, especially track and field. She'd joined the staff of the school newspaper and had developed an interest in acting. She looked forward to performing in school plays and thought that one day she might want to be in the movies. All in all, she sounded like a typical, happy-go-lucky teenager without a care in the world rather than a fatherless child whose schizophrenic mother was locked away in an insane asylum and whose foster father had sexually molested her.

Indeed, Norma Jeane was quickly blossoming into an early iteration of the famed actress and personality she would eventually become. Leaner and sporting darker curls than the later Monroe, she exuded a youthful beauty that, if not yet wondrous, was certainly noticeable. Boys her age (and older) had begun to pursue her. "She could be a bit shy and withdrawn at times, but for the most part, she absolutely glowed," said a friend named Susan Ryder. "She was not only pretty but very bright. You could see it in her eyes. She also had great skin; the clearest, pinkest skin I've ever seen. It was silky and flawless. Then in the ninth grade, she began spilling out of her clothes. Not fat, just curves. She wore makeup and sweaters that were a size too small, accentuating her bustline. She couldn't walk down the street without having some jerk in a passing car come to a screeching halt and start yelling and whistling at her out the window."

Barbara Anthony, another playmate from this period, considered Norma Jeane "quite alluring and sensitive but thin-skinned and somewhat secretive. She didn't talk much about her personal life. She did well in school. She was witty, but, as I say, she could be very thin-skinned. If you said something that rubbed her the wrong way, she'd let you know it."

In 1940 Ana Lower suffered a mild heart attack, and Norma Jeane went back to the Odessa Avenue home of the Goddards. Given Doc Goddard's sexual proclivities, the arrangement was far from ideal, but under the circumstances, it remained the most practical alternative. By that fall, Norma Jeane had entered the tenth grade at Van Nuys High School and had met James Edward Dougherty, the son of Edward and Ethel Dougherty, neighbors of the Goddards. At age twenty, Jim Dougherty, truly "the boy next door," cut a manly figure. He had blue eyes, light brown hair, and a muscular physique. A graduate of Van Nuys High, he had been student body president as well as a football star and member of the Maskers Drama Club. In addition, he owned his own car, a blue Ford coupe. Although he'd been offered a partial college scholarship, he had opted for a job at Lockheed Aircraft Corporation, in Burbank, augmenting his income by working at a funeral home embalming corpses. When Lockheed offered to increase his salary, he quit the funeral home job.

At the time that Norma Jeane met him, Dougherty was dating three other girls, among them Doris Ingram, who'd been crowned Miss Santa Barbara. He nevertheless began driving his neighbors Bebe Goddard and Norma Jeane Baker to school every morning and hanging out with them on weekends. Each girl had a crush on Jimmy. In December 1941 Grace Goddard asked Dougherty to take Norma Jeane to a Christmas dance at Lockheed. There she was introduced to the future actor Robert Mitchum, then one of Jim's coworkers. By the end of January 1942, Jim and Norma Jeane were going steady. A month later, Grace informed Norma Jeane that she and Doc, along with his children, would be moving to Huntington, West Virginia, where Doc had procured a lucrative position with an electronics firm. She also told her it would be best if Norma Jeane remained in California, especially now that she and Jim Dougherty were involved.

Looking back, Marilyn would tell Rose Fromm that once again she felt as though she'd been deserted. "It came as a blow," she said. "Not that I necessarily wanted to go with them — rather, that I wasn't given a choice. When I thought about it, I remembered that though Daddy Doc never touched me again, he used to give me suggestive looks. Grace probably surmised it was only a matter of time before he tried something. Maybe she was jealous, or perhaps she just didn't want to chance it."

Having returned to Ana Lower's Nebraska Avenue home, Norma Jeane withdrew from Van Nuys High School and enrolled at University High. She continued to see Jim Dougherty. What she didn't know was that Grace Goddard, no doubt feeling guilty over having left Norma Jeane behind (and so that she wouldn't have to go back to the orphanage), had conspired with Jim's mother to have him propose to her. After they became engaged, Norma Jeane dropped out of University High, and in early June, she and Jim signed a one-year lease on a small cottage in Sherman Oaks. Ana Lower made Norma Jeane's white embroidered wedding gown. The service in the Los Angeles home of friends of Grace Goddard took place on the evening of June 19, 1942, and was led by Reverend Benjamin Lingenfelder of the Christian Science Church. Aunt Ana walked the sixteen-year-old bride to the makeshift altar, where Jim Dougherty, in a rented white

70

tuxedo, took over. Ana Lower paid for a wedding reception for thirty-five guests at an Italian-themed nightclub and restaurant called Florentine Gardens. The Bolenders attended, but Doc and Grace Goddard were conspicuously absent.

In March 1953, long after they were divorced, Jim Dougherty wrote an article for *Photoplay* magazine entitled "Marilyn Monroe Was My Wife," which began: "Our marriage was good . . . It's seldom a man gets a bride like Marilyn . . . I wonder if she's forgotten how much in love we really were."

She evidently had forgotten, because she'd previously told Dr. Fromm that her marriage to Dougherty had been "a sham, a coupling of convenience." On the surface, at the point she married him, she seemed at least moderately content. They didn't go on a honeymoon, but the young couple went on weekend fishing expeditions to Sherwood Lake in Ventura County, California. They took ski lessons together and attended college football games. They saw movies at Grauman's Chinese Theatre, where Norma Jeane had gone as a child. They prepared picnic luncheons and frolicked on the beach at Malibu. And when they weren't making love at home, they would have sex in the backseat of his car on the side streets and back roads up and down the San Fernando Valley.

Their sexual relationship proved to be less

than satisfying for Norma Jeane. "For all the girls he'd supposedly had," she informed Fromm, "he [Dougherty] didn't seem to know very much. He didn't believe in foreplay. It was slam, bam, thank you, ma'am. I knew even less than he did, so I thought it was mostly my fault. He'd fall asleep afterward, leaving me awake, frustrated, and angry. I began to suspect he might still be seeing Doris Ingram, but I kept it to myself. I didn't want to complain. I wrote to Aunt Grace in West Virginia, by then a seasoned alcoholic, extolling the virtues of marriage. I sweetened my letters out of loyalty to Grace and in an effort to please her, which is more than she'd done for me."

The Norma Jeane that Dougherty wed was still an unformed person. She had a beautiful face and figure. She was a mature sixteen-year-old in certain respects but a little girl in others. She'd had no childhood as such. In a way, there were two Norma Jeanes: One was the little girl whose dolls and stuffed animals were propped up on top of her chest of drawers "so they can see what's going on." The other Norma Jeane was a person of unpredictable moods. In her published memoir, Marilyn portrayed herself at this stage as being "divided" into two people: "One of them was Norma Jeane from the orphanage who belonged to nobody, the other was someone whose name I didn't know." In his *Photoplay* piece, Jim Dougherty depicted his former wife as possessing two distinct and very different personalities, which made her "a bit scary at times." He blamed her lack of cohesion on her "impossible" childhood. "Now and again," he wrote, "you'd catch glimpses of someone who had been unloved for too long, unwanted for too many years."

Whatever chance the marriage might have had of surviving ended when Jim, about to be drafted into the army, joined the Maritime Services and went away to a merchant marine training base, finally winding up on Catalina Island, just off the Southern California coast. Norma Jeane, feeling a sense of abandonment, moved in with her mother-in-law and occasionally visited Catalina to be with her husband, but the visits terminated after she began working at the Radioplane Company in Burbank as a parachute inspector and paint sprayer. It was here, at the height of World War II, that she was "discovered" by US Army photographer David Conover, who'd been assigned by his commanding officer (Ronald Reagan, the future US president) to shoot pictures of women working to aid the war effort. Eventually penning a book titled *Finding Marilyn: A Remembrance,* Conover detailed first seeing her at Radioplane and asking if he could photograph her in a tight sweater rather than her work overalls. She obliged, and the die, as the saying goes, was cast. The photo appeared on the cover of *Yank.* Other pictures of Norma Jeane ran in *Stars and Stripes,* the US troop newspaper, which named her "Miss Cheesecake." She was voted "the present all GIs would like to find in their Christmas stocking." Conover's book goes on to document his short-lived but memorable affair with the photogenic model. Norma Jeane, having moved out of her mother-in-law's house and back in with Ana Lower, is depicted by Conover as having "a great body and enormous passion."

In May 1976 Jim Dougherty was quoted in *People* magazine as claiming, "If I hadn't gone into the merchant marine during World War II and been shipped off to the Pacific, Norma Jeane would still be Mrs. Dougherty today." Had she survived long enough to read Dougherty's comment, Marilyn Monroe would probably have deemed it an overblown case of wishful thinking. By the time he returned from the Pacific, his wife had undergone a dramatic change.

She had left her job at Radioplane and gone full-time into modeling, having been signed by Emmeline Snively of the Blue Book Modeling Agency. As a popular pinup and cover model (her image appeared in more than a hundred magazines), she started to meet other photographers, agents, would-be agents, film producers, publicists, advertising executives — in short, an entire crew of Hollywood types, all of them quite different from the people she'd known as Mrs. Jim Dougherty. She had colored her hair a golden blond. The limited contours of domesticity had given way to an exhilarating and expansive new world.

As for Norma Jeane's mother, she had been released from the San Francisco mental hospital and, as of May 1945, was living in a small room on the top floor of a rundown hotel in downtown Portland, Oregon. In December André de Dienes, a fashion photographer with whom Norma Jeane had started a romance, drove her to Portland for a reunion with Gladys, the first time she'd seen her mother since 1939.

"We had little to say to each other," Marilyn would inform Dr. Fromm, recounting the Portland visit. "She looked much older than I remembered her. She emanated no warmth. I tried to maintain a cheerful façade. I unpacked a few presents I'd brought for her — a silk scarf, a bottle of perfume, and a box of chocolates — and placed them on top of a coffee table. She wouldn't go near them, just stared at them. Then, without a word, she lowered her head and buried her face in her hands and seemed to forget all about me. I saw myself to the door and left."

With her modeling career in full bloom,

Norma Jeane was earning enough to rent the bottom floor of Ana Lower's house on Nebraska Avenue. In early 1946 she received a letter from her mother asking if she could come to Los Angeles and stay with her. Against her better judgment — and in spite of the disappointment of her Portland visit — Norma Jeane agreed. Their second attempt at living together as mother and daughter turned out no better than the first. Within months, Gladys Baker reentered the psychiatric ward at Norwalk State Asylum, the same institution from which she had once tried to escape. From there she would in time be sent to the Rockhaven Sanitarium, a virtual country club for the incurably insane, in Verdugo, California, where she remained until 1967, five years after Marilyn's death. Throughout Gladys Baker's lengthy internment at Rockhaven, it was Marilyn who footed the bills.

In 1946 Norma Jeane became involved with Tommy Zahn, a lifeguard and aspiring actor who later described her to a reporter as "tremendously fit, very robust . . . so healthy." Photographs of her taken at this time support Zahn's portrayal. That same summer she hired an attorney, established residency in Las Vegas, and instituted divorce proceedings against Jim Dougherty. The divorce decree was granted on July 5, 1946, in Clark County, Nevada.

Her newfound freedom marked the beginning of an extremely active sexual phase during which Marilyn took numerous lovers ranging in age and experience from a young college student named Bill Pursel to over-the-hill Borscht Belt comedian George Jessel. "Talk about being promiscuous," she told Dr. Rose Fromm, "I can't remember the names of three-quarters of the men I slept with at that time." A name she did recall belonged to Charlie Chaplin Jr., son of the legendary comic, with whom she had an affair in 1947. According to Anthony Summers's *Goddess: The Secret Lives of Marilyn Monroe,* the affair ended when Charlie Jr. caught Marilyn in bed with his brother Sydney. The latter romance ended when she underwent one of several early abortions.

In subsequent years, Jim Dougherty, having remarried and become a patrolman with the Los Angeles Police Department, would tell a journalist: "I never knew Marilyn Monroe. I knew Norma Jeane Baker, but Marilyn Monroe and Norma Jeane Baker were two different people."

By 1952, the year she met Joe DiMaggio, Norma Jeane Baker had grown into the iconic role of Marilyn Monroe both in name and in terms of her career, which, while not yet at its height, was well on its way. Having overcome the "Golden Dreams" nude calendar scandal, she now defended herself against a charge by the press that she'd fabricated her family history, having presented herself to Twentieth Century–Fox and to the public at large as an orphan, when, if truth be told, her mother was still very much alive.

As she'd done in the nude calendar controversy, Marilyn took matters into her own hands, releasing a statement admitting that Gladys Baker was incapacitated, a patient in a mental institution, and that she'd fibbed only to protect her mother from the glare of public scrutiny. She said that although she'd lived with her mother for a brief period as a child, she barely knew her. Nor had she ever met her father. Her childhood, she added, had largely been spent in an orphanage and in the homes of a number of foster families. If the press felt she had misled anyone, she wished to apologize and hoped to be forgiven. She was forgiven.

As Hollywood columnist Hedda Hopper wrote, "Let's give Marilyn Monroe the benefit of the doubt."

CHAPTER 4

In late May 1952, having fully recuperated from her appendectomy and having set the record straight on her Little Orphan Annie past, Marilyn Monroe arrived for a brief stay in New York before continuing on to Buffalo, where, in June, she would star in *Niagara,* a suspense drama with a cast that included Joseph Cotten and Jean Peters. Marilyn's role as a young, sultry, oversexed wife called for her to wear a dress that, in the words of one film critic, was "cut so low you can see her navel." In anticipation of her stay in New York, Joe DiMaggio temporarily vacated his quarters at the Elysée Hotel and moved into a large suite at the Drake. He filled the suite with several bouquets of fresh roses.

Marilyn's first order of business in New York entailed visiting Yankee Stadium to watch DiMaggio — immaculately attired in a pinstripe suit — suffer through one of his pre- and post-game WPIX-TV broadcasts. Yankees shortstop Phil Rizzuto, DiMaggio's interview subject that day, recalled how elated Joe seemed when Marilyn complimented him on his performance. "I don't know whether she meant it or not," said Rizzuto, "but Joe lapped it up. She told him how well he'd done — 'You're doing swell,' she said, 'just relax' — and he broke into an ear-to-ear smile. And whenever Joe DiMaggio smiled, he'd reveal those horse-sized buck teeth of his. Needless to say, they weren't his best feature. In any event, they didn't seem to bother Marilyn. I once read that she felt attracted to men who wore glasses and had bad teeth. Joe didn't wear glasses, but he certainly qualified so far as his choppers were concerned."

Rizzuto remembered how, once the broadcast ended, the tiny TV studio filled up with Yankees ballplayers eager to catch a firsthand glimpse of Monroe "There were maybe a dozen of us in the room," said the shortstop, "all vying to get close to Marilyn, badgering her for an autograph. Even old Casey Stengel, the skipper, shoved his way in. And Marilyn was very accommodating, very sweet about everything, posing for pictures with some of the players and so forth. Everyone knows how glamourous she looked, so I won't go into that. Let's just say that in person she looked even more scrumptious than she did on the silver screen, and I guess some of the guys were maybe getting a little too familiar with her, because all at once Joe began to lose it. He became agitated, no doubt equally pissed off because he was being ignored. He suddenly grabbed Marilyn rather forcefully and started pushing her toward the door. 'C'mon, you fuckers, you've seen enough,' he said. And then a moment later they were gone."

That week, DiMaggio squired Marilyn to all his usual haunts. They visited the Stork Club, the Copacabana, El Morocco, the Colony, the Jockey Club, and Toots Shor's. And wherever they turned up, they were in the spotlight. Fellow diners and drinkers looked and whispered. They tapped each other on the shoulder and pointed with their eyes. Marilyn adored the attention. She told Joe she loved New York and hated Hollywood. "There's no place like New York," she said. At Toots Shor's, they encountered Dario Lodigiani, an old wartime crony of Joe's, a former bunkmate who'd grown up with Joe in San Francisco and then found himself in the same World War II unit as Joe. Dario, who'd played second base for the Philadelphia Athletics and the Chicago White Sox, regaled Marilyn with stories related to DiMaggio's military service, including one about how in 1944 (after Joe had spent time at a number of training bases on the mainland), the Seventh Army Air Forces flew him to Honolulu to play baseball with the troops.

"So here's Staff Sergeant Joseph Paul DiMaggio, without the familiar number five on his back, and the instant he arrives," said Dario, "they pile him into a jeep and drive him to Honolulu Stadium and shove a baseball bat into his paws. His Yankee teammate Charles 'Red' Ruffing is pitching. There are twenty thousand fans, mostly military personnel, in the stands, and he steps to the plate and belts Ruffing's first pitch a country mile, way over the left-field bleachers, out of sight and onto the street, and everybody goes nuts. And the next time up he stretches a double into a triple and slides into third so hard you'd think he was Ty Cobb. But that's how he played the game. I'm glad we were on the same team. I mean, we're not fighting the Nazis, but we're at least entertaining the boys. And then after a couple of months, Joe's duodenal ulcer kicks up, and he spends the rest of the war in and out of military hospitals."

"Right," responded DiMaggio, "and when I'm not playing ball or convalescing in a hospital bed, I'm playing pinochle and poker with four- and five-star generals. It was boring as hell, but it's not my fault they didn't ask me to drop bombs on the enemy. I'd have gladly obliged."

"Like Ted Williams," said Dario. "Now, there's a war hero for you."

"Listen," said DiMaggio, "Pee Wee Reese

and Johnny Mize played exhibition ball for the navy during the war, and nobody said a word. It's not my fault they handed me a bat and mitt instead of a machine gun."

Marilyn liked the give-and-take. And she enjoyed the stream of men that flocked to Joe's table to shake hands with the Clipper and ogle his date. Nor did she mind the autograph collectors with their ever-ready supply of pens and notepads. For them it was a double bonanza: the baseball immortal and the Hollywood glamour queen. Approaching DiMaggio when he sat alone (or with his coterie of followers) would have been out of the question, but in Monroe's presence, he became more serene and more human. Joe took immense pride in having this utterly beautiful woman on his arm, knowing that every man in the room envied him, wanted to be him. It was true. Let them covet their secret dreams of what it must be like to fall into bed with her. Let them gaze upon her and wonder. Look but don't touch. For once he wasn't even distressed by the omnipresence of the press, the loathsome scribes who tailed them from place to place, reporting on their daily doings as if they were the two most vital personages on the planet. He smiled for the paparazzi — as well as the legitimate lensmen — who hovered round like flies at a beach resort. This was the new DiMaggio. It was different from the stardom he'd enjoyed as a ballplayer. It was love, and he loved it.

Given the enormity of DiMaggio's ego, it is easy to imagine the thrill he experienced at the end of the day when he and Marilyn returned to his hotel suite to spend the night together. And she, too, took great pleasure in being with Joe at a point when everything still seemed so simple, so wonderful. She was a person with human relations problems, worries, fears, inadequacies, and insecurities, but everything she was beginning to feel for Joe — trust, gratitude, admiration, even adulation — helped combat her shortcomings and frailties. And then too, as she later informed Truman Capote, DiMaggio, with his amazing physique and staying power, had all the makings of a superb lover. She called him "Daddy" and "Pa" as well as "Slugger," and in extolling his sexual prowess to Capote, she remarked, "Joe's biggest bat isn't the one he used at the plate."

Yet from the beginning of their relationship, there were moments and incidents that must have raised red flags in Marilyn's mind. One of these incidents took place the night they celebrated her twenty-sixth birthday with George Solotaire at Le Pavillon, then New York's finest (and most expensive) French restaurant. On being introduced to Solotaire, whom Marilyn hadn't as yet met personally, she said: "So you're the fellow who runs interference for Joe and pries the girls loose when they become inconvenient."

"I guess that's me," agreed the Broadway ticket broker.

Comparing notes, it developed that Solotaire, like Marilyn, had spent several years of his childhood in an orphange. Their shared experience created an immediate and lasting bond between them. Of DiMaggio's pals, Solotaire remained the one to whom she always felt closest.

During the meal, an elderly gentleman approached them from another table. His name was Henry Rosenfeld. A wealthy clothing manufacturer, Rosenfeld had known Marilyn since 1949, when she arrived in New York to help promote *Love Happy,* a Marx Brothers comedy in which she'd been handed a small role — one of her first — as the dumb blonde. From the way Marilyn and Rosenfeld spoke to each other, it became obvious to DiMaggio that the pair had once been on intimate terms.

Rosenfeld's brief appearance at the table sent DiMaggio into a tailspin. He stopped speaking. Matters grew worse when Solotaire, making idle conversation to fill the void, told Marilyn he'd known Johnny Hyde, the powerful William Morris Agency vice president and agent largely responsible for launching Monroe's film career by landing her roles in *The Asphalt Jungle,* directed by John Huston, and *All About Eve,* directed by Joe Mankiewicz. Her skillful performances in these projects led to a studio contract and more vital roles in future films.

Hyde noticed several minor cosmetic imperfections in Marilyn's face and paid to have them corrected, most notably the removal of a sliver of cartilage from the actress's nose and a slight enhancement of her chin and cheeks to improve her close-ups. It can be said that without Johnny Hyde, whom she'd met at the Racquet Club in Palm Springs in 1949, there would have been no Marilyn Monroe. More than twice her age, he fell passionately in love with her, fled his family (including a wife of long standing), and set up a household with Marilyn on North Palm Drive in Beverly Hills. Repeatedly, persistently, he'd asked her to marry him, but, just as persistently, she declined, insisting she loved him but wasn't in love with him. He nevertheless wooed her by being kind, talking to her openly about his intimate life, and listening to her stories about hers. Above all, she stayed with him because she felt he really needed her. Then in December 1950 Hyde suffered a massive heart attack and died. Once again a father figure had vanished into thin air.

The mere mention of Johnny Hyde's name by Solotaire brought tears to Marilyn's eyes and concomitantly caused DiMaggio to explode in a fit of anger of the sort that was fast becoming all too familiar to Monroe.

"Do we need to discuss all of her fucking ex-lovers?" he yelled. "This Hyde jerk sounds like just another Hollywood vulture out to get laid."

Marilyn had heard enough. Now it was her turn to vent. "Johnny Hyde was a lovely, warm, caring man," she said. "He gave me more than his kindness and love. He was the first man I'd ever known who tried to understand me. How dare you question his integrity?"

Then, with neither malice nor regret, Marilyn embarked on a lengthy account of the men in her life that had played instrumental roles in her personal and professional development. The list — from Joseph Schenck, cofounder and chairman of the board of Twentieth Century–Fox, to Fred Karger, her former vocal coach and lover — seemed endless to DiMaggio, but having been properly and thoroughly chastised by Marilyn for his outburst, he sat there and listened. "He took it like a man," George Solotaire later told his son. "Then again," he added, "what choice did he have?"

As her most intense liaisons — and even some of her nonsexual interludes — demonstrated, Marilyn usually sought out older, stronger, more distinguished, and powerful male figures as opposed to those who were solely interested in debauching her. These were the very qualities she found so appealing in Joe: his quiet strength, his resoluteness, his seeming desire to love and protect her. Equally important, through her association with DiMaggio, she could transport herself to new heights of popular acceptance. The Yankee Clipper, after all, was no ordinary citizen. Even if he hadn't flown bombing missions during the Second World War, Joe DiMaggio was regarded as nothing less than a national hero. That Ernest Hemingway had mentioned him in his latest novel, *The Old Man and the Sea,* only seemed to confirm DiMaggio's status as a notable personage on the American landscape.

Marilyn spent most of June and July commuting back and forth between Buffalo and New York, seeing Joe on nonproduction weekends and shooting *Niagara* during the week. One Saturday night they drove to Coney Island for a dinner of hot dogs, corn on the cob, and clams on the half shell. Another time, when the Yankees were out of town, she accompanied him to a golf club in Cherry Hill, New Jersey, where he rented an extra set of clubs and attempted to introduce her to the game. And then there was the day they visited the Metropolitan Museum of Art on Fifth Avenue. DiMaggio described the latter outing (for George Solotaire's benefit) as "excruciating." "Art," he proclaimed, "bores me to tears."

During one three-day stretch in mid-July, Joe joined Marilyn on location at Niagara Falls. They ate dinner together each night at a corner table in the Red Coach Inn. It was there that Monroe introduced DiMaggio to Natasha Lytess, her personal drama coach. Lytess had initially coached Marilyn in 1948 when she was under contract to Columbia Pictures and had been given a small part in *Ladies of the Chorus.* They had worked together since then and even lived together for several months. Marilyn convinced Twentieth Century–Fox to pay Natasha's salary, a major concession on the studio's part considering that Monroe hadn't as yet attained star billing.

Lytess, an out-of-the-closet lesbian, made no secret of her feelings for Marilyn, more than once letting her pupil know she'd fallen in love with her. "Don't love me, Natasha," Marilyn cautioned her, "just teach me." Lytess voiced her disapproval of Marilyn's personal involvements with men. She particularly disliked Joe DiMaggio, who seemed to be usurping her own role as Marilyn's close advisor. "You'd have been better off with Joan Crawford than the baseball player," Lytess told Monroe, referring to the time in 1951 when Crawford all but propositioned Monroe and got turned down. When DiMaggio and Lytess encountered each other on the set of *Niagara,* they traded insults. It appeared that as Marilyn's relationship with Joe deepened, her bond with Natasha deteriorated. Joe tried to convince Marilyn that her drama coach was living off her — her salary exceeded Marilyn's, and the studio now wanted Monroe to contribute her own money to support Lytess. Like everyone else in the film business (according to DiMaggio), Lytess was using Marilyn, enhancing her own reputation at Monroe's expense. And who the hell is this woman, anyway? What are her credentials? The next time DiMaggio spoke to George Solotaire, he referred to Lytess as a "goddamn bull dyke." "She thinks," he said, "that she's Marilyn's husband. And she's convinced that since they're filming at Niagara Falls, they're on their honeymoon."

In July Marilyn attended the New York premiere of *Don't Bother to Knock*. Portraying a lonely, emotionally disturbed babysitter, Monroe gave one of her best and most underrated dramatic performances. "The role is right up my alley," she told her costar Richard Widmark. "I modeled myself after my mother."

Unfamiliar with Marilyn's familial background, Widmark had no idea what she meant. "I must have given her a blank look," he said, "because she explained that her mother suffered from schizophrenia and had spent years in a mental hospital. I knew Marilyn's childhood had been difficult, but I didn't realize just how difficult it must have been. In any case, she did a first-rate job with her role. I always felt she had talent, but had been misused by Hollywood because of her good looks. I told her I thought she'd do well in a dramatic role on Broadway, and she seemed deeply appreciative of the compliment."

Joe DiMaggio wasn't in town for the premiere, having traveled to Chicago to appear in a magazine ad for the Buitoni pasta company, the sponsor of his television show. In light of his friend's absence — and after clearing it with DiMaggio — George Solotaire offered to take Marilyn for drinks after the movie. They met in the Oak Room at the Plaza Hotel.

Over drinks and a late dinner they discussed Marilyn's future acting obligations. She revealed that she'd been offered the part of Lorelei Lee in *Gentlemen Prefer Blondes,* which would be directed by Howard Hawks and would start shooting in mid-November. Jane Russell had also been signed to appear in the film, and Marilyn had heard good things about her. She could hardly wait to begin.

Not unexpectedly, Solotaire brought up her relationship with Joe DiMaggio.

"Joe's crazy about you, but I suppose you know that by now," he said.

"And I'm crazy about Joe," answered Marilyn.

"Trouble is, he's Italian," said Solotaire. "He's jealous of every man you've ever known — and half the men you never met."

"Do you want to know something?" said Marilyn. "When I lived with Shelley Winters, I made a list one night of the men I most wanted to sleep with. At the top of my list was Albert Einstein. If I ever told Joe about it, I'm sure he'd make Einstein duke it out in an alley someplace."

"Either that or he'd challenge him to a home run hitting contest," Solotaire countered.

"Exactly," said Monroe. And yes, she conceded, she'd availed herself of the casting couch syndrome to further her career. She'd earned her kneepads. "It was part of the job," she explained. "They aren't making all those sexy movies just to sell popcorn. They want to sample the merchandise. If you don't play along, there are a thousand other girls who will."

Changing the subject, Solotire asked Marilyn whether she'd been introduced to "Little Joey — Joe's ten-year-old son."

Monroe looked perplexed. "Little Joey?" she inquired. "I didn't know Joe had a son."

Now it was Solotaire's turn to look perplexed. "How about Dorothy Arnold, the boy's mother? Did he mention her? They've been in and out of court for years quibbling over child support."

"Never mentioned her either," said Marilyn. "But then that's so typical of Joe. Let's face it: he doesn't like to talk about himself."

What wasn't typical of Joe DiMaggio is that late in 1936, following his first year with the New York Yankees, he agreed to accept a small film role in *Manhattan Merry-Go-Round,* a frothy musical designed as a showcase for Cab Calloway and his Cotton Club Orchestra. Playing himself, DiMaggio delivered a self-conscious monologue on baseball and even sang a lyric or two. During filming in Astoria, Queens, the ballplayer happened to meet a young actress, Dorothy Arnold, whose name didn't appear in the credits but who was one of the girls in the chorus line. "The thing I do is never fall in love," DiMaggio had boasted to a reporter for the *New York World Telegram.* "I just talk a good game with women." Despite his claim, Dorothy Arnold soon became Joe's first serious love interest.

She was born Dorothy Arnoldine Olson on November 21, 1917, in Duluth, Minnesota. Her mother, a schoolteacher, was of Norwegian descent. Her father, an official with the Northern Pacific Railroad, was half Norwegian and half Swedish. Eager to make a name in show business, Dorothy was only fifteen when she signed up to travel on the Balaban

& Katz vaudeville circuit as a singer and dancer. At age eighteen, she moved to New York, where she took acting lessons while performing on the radio and in nightclubs, modeling for ladies wear ads, and working at NBC as a staff singer. Her good looks — she was blond and cuddly — attracted a talent agent who suggested the name change and then talked Universal Studios into offering her a stock contract at $75 a week, plus moderate expenses. She made her acting debut in *Manhattan Merry-Go-Round.* Like Marilyn Monroe after her, Dorothy Arnold had never heard of Joe DiMaggio, though when she met him, he'd been in the majors for only two seasons.

Prior to Dorothy Arnold and even while dating her, DiMaggio socialized mostly with showgirls and club hostesses. Dom DiMaggio, his younger brother, recalled how Joe lost his virginity. "There was a brothel in North Beach," he said, "and all of us, all the DiMaggio boys, frequented the place at one time or another. Being de-virginized in this locale became a kind of family ritual. I remember Mike taking Joe the day after his fourteenth birthday. The woman must have been around forty-five, and, believe it or not, was the same one I wound up with two years later. A buxom brunette, her claim to fame was her expertise in the French arts. She could swallow anything in the room, if you

94

know what I mean. After he had her, Joe told me, 'You can be with a million broads, but you never forget the first one.' "

Besides the showgirls and club hostesses he met in New York, Joe DiMaggio's chief source of women were the young ladies he encountered when the Yanks were on the road. When the ball club traveled, Joe roomed with Vernon "Lefty" Gomez, the ace Yankees pitcher. "Lefty had created a name for himself as the team clown," said Dom DiMaggio. "My brother felt comfortable around him. Lefty would act out the goofy things Joe could never permit himself to do. Joe liked to read comic books, for example, and he'd send Lefty out to the newsstand to pick them up for him because he didn't want to be seen buying them. Anyway, Lefty and Joe had this groupie thing going for them. As soon as the team checked into a hotel, the phone would start ringing in their suite. There'd be a couple of girls in the lobby, and they'd want to come upstairs to meet Joe and Lefty. The desk clerk would send them along, and if they were decent-looking, Joe would grab one and Lefty the other. Joe would disappear into the bedroom with his chick, while Lefty entertained his in the sitting room. They were like rock stars. Not that this sort of behavior was unheard of in the world of baseball, but Joe made a science of it. He had a dozen groupies in every port of call. He led the league in groupies. The bad thing is he carried on in this fashion long after he married Dorothy Arnold."

During their two-year courtship, DiMaggio continued to compile Herculean statistics on the ball field while Dorothy Arnold toiled away with little success in her chosen career. Between 1937 and 1939, she appeared in no fewer than fifteen films, the most noteworthy of which were *The Phantom Creeps* and *The House of Fear,* but her roles were often uncredited and always minor. Joe DiMaggio made it known that if she wished to marry him, she would have to give up her present livelihood and agree to become a housewife, his housewife. Unlike Marilyn Monroe, Dorothy was only too happy to comply. It was she, for that matter, who proposed — not the other way around.

The couple married on November 19, 1939, at the Church of Saint Peter and Saint Paul in San Francisco. Dorothy (Joe called her "Dottie") was about to turn twenty-two; DiMaggio was three years older. With fifteen thousand screaming spectators clogging the streets surrounding the North Beach cathedral, and two thousand spectators crammed into the cathedral itself, it was almost certainly the biggest wedding ever to take place in San Francisco. Or so claimed Joyce M. Hadley, the bride's younger sister, in a 1993 account of Dorothy's life. Irene, her other sister, was maid of honor; Tom DiMaggio served as best man. The press turned out in force. Dozens of policemen and security guards patrolled the cordoned-off streets. According to one San Francisco newspaper, the "bride entered the cathedral like a queen. She was so utterly beautiful in her white satin designer wedding gown, it hurt to look at her."

It didn't seem to bother Dorothy that her moment of glory was owed almost exclusively to the renown of the stone-faced man who awaited her at the altar. Nor did it matter to her that she had been brought up Protestant and, in order to marry Joe, had been forced to convert to Catholicism. In her Dorothy Arnold biography, Joyce Hadley describes the groom, North Beach's favorite son, as "tall, broad-shouldered, handsome, rich, and fabulously famous." He was also "uneducated, very insecure, painfully shy, wary of strangers, and practically inarticulate." But Dorothy, Joyce insists, was "going to fix all that."

Joe's parents, his brothers and sisters, Dorothy's parents and sisters, and assorted uncles, aunts, nephews, nieces, and cousins representing both families, to say nothing of friends and associates — nearly five hundred guests in all — gathered for the postceremony reception at the Grotto, an Italian restaurant on Fisherman's Wharf owned and operated by the DiMaggios. (For commercial reasons, the name of the establishment would eventually be changed to Joe DiMaggio's Grotto). Three four-foot-tall ice sculptures of baseball players in midswing celebrated Vince, Joe, and Dom, the ballplaying brothers, all of whom had invested money in the restaurant. The guests consumed twelve turkeys, fifteen chickens, six capons, eight hams, five sides of beef, six pounds of caviar, multiple cases of scotch, bourbon, gin, wine, and champagne. Dessert consisted of gallons of ice cream and six wedding cakes circled by friezes of crossed miniature baseball bats to signify Joe's success with the Yankees.

Dorothy had gone to great lengths to endear herself to Joe's parents, learning Italian so she could converse with them and spending hours with his mother learning how to prepare his favorite food. Joe, on the other hand, showed no such consideration for his parents-in-law. During his single premarital visit to Duluth, he reportedly barely spoke to them. A family friend accused him of being rude to the Olsons, who seemed to the friend to be unsure of what to make of their future son-in-law.

In late February 1940 the newlyweds drove cross-country from San Francisco to Yankees spring training camp in St. Petersburg, Florida, stopping briefly in Duluth for a visit with Dorothy's parents. "On this occasion," recalled an Olson family friend, "DiMaggio seemed totally hostile toward the Olsons. They were all having drinks in the living room when he suddenly rose and bolted out of the house, after telling Dorothy he'd wait for her in the car. As far as I know, he never offered an explanation, never said a word."

Regardless of his personal demons, DiMaggio's cosmos had certain undeniable advantages, and Dorothy Arnold managed to fit in. She never missed a game and was quickly accepted by the coterie of veteran wives who each day sat in the section of Yankee Stadium reserved for the families of players. Her closest ally was June Gomez, Lefty's bride, but she soon also befriended Vi Dickey, the wife of catcher Bill Dickey, and Pauline Ruffing, pitcher Red Ruffing's wife. In a *New York Daily Mirror* profile of Dorothy, the reporter wrote: "Being Joe DiMaggio's wife carries a responsibility all its own. No one in baseball ever demonstrated more grace than Joe. No one ever looked as good in a uniform, his fitting him as if it were a Savile Row suit. In public he is a man of great dignity. He is proud, possessive, and a trifle old-fashioned. In Dorothy Arnold, a former actress and model, he has found the perfect companion."

What the profile didn't say, and what Dorothy Arnold came to see, is that under the public posture there lurked an entire catalogue of less admirable traits, several of which

Joyce Hadley had already noticed. Joe DiMaggio exhibited unaccountable moments of anger and distrust, black moods, idiosyncratic behavior, parsimony, self-adulation, indifference, egocentricity, and an overwhelming urge to control the actions of others.

Several months into the marriage, it became apparent that Joe and Dorothy didn't see domestic life in quite the same way. Whereas she enjoyed playing the effervescent hostess to family and friends, Joe's notion of fun hadn't changed appreciably from what it had been throughout the duration of his days (and nights) as a "gay" bachelor. He would leave home around ten each morning to work out at the stadium before the game. At game's end, he would wend his way to Toots Shor's for drinks and a steak dinner with his pals, a clique that most often included George Solotaire, Walter Winchell, Jimmy Cannon, Walter "Red" Smith, Jackie Gleason (on occasion), and even Toots himself. The group would gather at "Joe's table" — table number one — to pick apart the day's action or to commiserate with DiMaggio on those infrequent occasions when the Yankees lost or Joe happened to go hitless. Attractive women were a welcome addition to the scene but were discouraged from contibuting anything to it other than their looks. Joe would usually return home long after his lonely wife had gone to bed. To add to their growing inventory of problems, he held it against her when she made her own plans for the evening. Dorothy had several friends in the entertainment field, including Bud Abbott and Lou Costello (Abbott and Costello), and whenever she invited them over or went out with them to a movie or for a drink, he became surly. He resented all her friendships, but especially those with men. He encouraged her to appear in a print media ad for Swift's Premium Franks but only because it brought in money with a minimum of exposure.

Such were the vagaries of being married to baseball's leading participant. A fairly inattentive suitor to begin with, Joe was an even worse husband. On those evenings he chose to remain at home, he would gobble down a quick dinner with Dorothy and then affix himself to the television or radio set for a night of cowboys and Indians, detectives and anything else, in which Dorothy took no interest. He would chat with Dorothy only when their talk concerned his profession. Once, for instance, he asked her whether she'd noticed any subtle changes in his swing. She had, in fact, seen something and, being a good athlete in her own right, proceeded to demonstrate the slight shift she'd discerned in his batting stance. He made the adjustment.

Yankees right fielder Tommy Henrich, Bill

Dickey, and Bill's wife, Vi, accompanied Joe and Dorothy to dinner one night. "I remember the occasion very clearly," said Henrich, "because it was one of the few, if not the only time I socialized with DiMaggio. He simply wasn't one of the guys. Except for Lefty Gomez, he kept pretty much to himself. I didn't know him that well on a personal basis, only as a ballplayer, and as a ballplayer he was in a league by himself, very likely the best all-around player in the game. I never knew him to make a mental mistake on the field. To err is human, not to err is divine. Mr. DiMaggio was divine. That, at any rate, was his baseball persona. As a human being — well, that was something else again. The night we all went to dinner — we dined at a small Italian restaurant in Greenwich Village — he behaved like a real prick, particularly toward his wife. I mean, he totally ignored Dorothy — didn't look at her, didn't talk to her, didn't interact with her in any way. Somehow she managed to keep the conversation flowing. She told several amusing stories about her experiences as an actress. Bill and Vi laughed, and I tossed in an occasional aside. DiMaggio looked the other way, never so much as cracked a smile. It made for one hell of an uncomfortable evening."

Henrich recalled an anecdote related to him by Lefty Gomez. That same summer, during an off day when the Yanks weren't playing,

Joe and his wife went to Jones Beach with Lefty and June Gomez. They drove out to Long Island in Joe's car. They'd packed a picnic lunch prepared by the ladies. They spread out their beach blankets, and Dorothy removed her skirt and blouse, under which she wore a black-and-white-striped two-piece bathing suit. DiMaggio took one look at his wife and exploded.

"You can't be serious!" he yelled. "You're not going to walk around in that goddamn bathing suit, are you?"

"But I just bought it," said Dorothy. "It's French, and it was expensive."

"I don't give a damn," answered DiMaggio. "Your midriff's showing. Put on your blouse."

June Gomez came to her friend's defense. "Joe," she remarked, "stop being so puritanical. There's nothing wrong with it. A lot of women are wearing them this summer."

"She's not wearing it without a blouse," DiMaggio thundered.

With tears welling in her eyes, Dorothy slipped the blouse over her shoulders. But it was too late. Still seething, DiMaggio stood, grabbed his belongings, returned to the parking lot, and drove off, leaving all three to ponder how they were going to get back to New York.

The more Mrs. DiMaggio tried to please her husband, the more distant he became. Dorothy went along with the Yankees on a road trip to Chicago, where she'd arranged to meet for dinner at the Del Prado Hotel with her sisters, Irene and Joyce, and Joyce's husband, Les Hadley. Although Joe had promised to join them for dinner, he never showed up. Dorothy carried on without him, but Joyce discerned her sibling's underlying disappointment at what had clearly become an undeniable pattern in a marriage that seemed destined for failure.

Convinced that having a baby might provide a solution to their troubles, Dorothy underwent a delicate gynecological procedure in mid-October 1940. They spent Christmas in Duluth with her family. Les Hadley's boss and a coworker, devout baseball fans, wanted to meet DiMaggio. Les invited them over for cocktails. More aloof than ever, Joe mumbled a few words and after several minutes rose and left the house without excusing himself. Dorothy tried to cover for his rudeness by explaining that he hadn't felt well of late. Les later found him alone in a bar. Joe said, "They were not my friends. They seemed perfectly happy to be entertained by Dottie."

The remainder of their stay went smoothly enough. The town had a minor-league baseball team, and Joe was asked to attend a meeting of the team's owners to discuss their plans to build a new stadium. The manager of the team invited Joe and Dorothy to go ice fishing at a nearby frozen lake. Otherwise the couple played cards and took long drives into the surrounding countryside. One evening the family went bowling, and Dorothy outscored everyone, including Joe. Though not pleased with the results, he managed a good-natured smile. She also trounced him at billiards and ping-pong. On their next-to-last day, Dorothy's mother took her aside and complained that the entire household could hear her and Joe making love at night. "Well, Mom," Dorothy responded, "you know how that works. You get to the point where you don't care. If the bed squeaks and bangs, that's just the way it has to be. We're sorry if we disturbed anyone's sleep. Aside from everything else, we're trying to have a baby."

In April 1941 Joe and Dorothy moved into a penthouse apartment at 400 West End Avenue at Seventy-Ninth Street in Manhattan, three blocks from Lefty and June Gomez's apartment. Graced by a wraparound terrace, which Dorothy covered with houseplants, tubs of flowers, and gilded garden furniture, the three-bedroom flat had a view of the Hudson River, the Palisades of New Jersey, the West Side Highway, and, in the distance, the George Washington Bridge. Dorothy installed a grand piano in the wood-paneled living room. Learning that she was pregnant, she transformed one of the bedrooms into a nursery, purchasing a complete set of matching baby furniture and installing wallpaper adorned with nursery rhymes.

For a while, the couple seemed to get along better than they had in the past. During his wife's pregnancy, DiMaggio spent more time at home and less at Toots Shor's. In the evening, the couple would stroll hand in hand along Riverside Drive. They went to the movies and took in several Broadway plays. They sponsored a party for thirty-five kids from the poorer neighborhoods of New York at which they served ice cream and chocolate cake; Joe was particularly attentive to the children, signing and handing out baseballs and bats that had been donated by the New York Yankees. Dorothy must have begun to believe that having a baby with Joe was indeed the right way to go. He certainly seemed more cheerful than usual. How could he not be? It was the year he hit safely in fifty-six consecutive games, finishing the season with a .357 batting average and leading the ball club to a resounding World Series victory over the Brooklyn Dodgers.

On October 22, 1941, Dorothy entered Doctors Hospital and the following day gave birth to a baby boy, Joseph Paul DiMaggio III (Joey Jr.) — seven pounds, eleven ounces — who, even as a newborn, bore a striking resemblance to his father. Joe celebrated his son's arrival by handing out cigars at Toots Shor's and belting down a couple of drinks with the boys. "Hey, Daig," said Tootsie, proposing a toast, "here's to a second slugger in the house." Photographs of the proud, beaming parents cuddling their two-month-old infant appeared in every major American newspaper. What Dorothy hadn't counted on was that once the initial thrill wore off, her husband would revert back to his former indifferent self.

Emerald Duffy, whose mother Bertha Dorothy had hired as a live-in baby nurse, recalled the events of those days. "We needed the money," she said, "so my mother hired herself out as a nanny. She and I shared a bedroom in the DiMaggio apartment on West End Avenue. I was fourteen. Domestic life in the apartment was anything but peaceful. Little Joey was a crier, and this disturbed the baby's father no end. He claimed he couldn't sleep with the infant wailing away half the night, so he insisted on having the nursery soundproofed. This in turn upset his wife. 'He's a baby, he's supposed to cry,' she told him. 'That's what babies do.' I never saw Joe DiMaggio hold the baby, no less change a diaper. Once when the baby got sick, he checked into a hotel. He couldn't deal with any of the difficulties associated with fatherhood. He had zero parenting skills. The same can be said for his shortcomings as a husband. When his wife did or said something that displeased him, he'd shut down — he wouldn't talk to her for days on end. Or if she started to argue with him about something or other, he'd tell her if she didn't like it, she could move out."

Nothing had changed. With his old-fashioned Victorian view of family and marriage, Joe wanted Dorothy to be his personal cheerleader, his admirer and supporter. He encouraged her to root for him at home games, pack his bags when the team went on the road, cook for him when he felt like eating dinner with her, be his sex partner when he wasn't in bed with someone else, run his errands, manage the household, and look after the kid. It didn't seem to occur to him that Dorothy might have her own list of needs. DiMaggio wanted a hausfrau, an obedient pinup, a mate who would perform on cue and do whatever he asked of her. Instead, he found an intelligent, high-spirited woman who expected him to be a full-time husband and father, whereas he expected her to wait around for him at home while he gallivanted about town and partied with select members of New York's café society. As sportswriter Roger Kahn put it: "The marriage never had a chance."

Tommy Henrich noted that in 1942 DiMaggio batted only .305, his lowest average since reaching the majors and well below his first six seasons. The Yankees center fielder's home run and RBI totals dipped as well, to 21 and 114, respectively. "He blamed it all on his failing marriage," said Henrich, "and on a baby that wouldn't stop crying. Now, there's an explanation for you. Bear in mind that half the guys on the team had little kids, and nobody I knew ever used them as an excuse. And then there was the time Dorothy brought the baby to the ballpark and everyone clustered around them in the clubhouse after the game — everyone, that is, except for the baby's father. DiMaggio flew out of there like a bat out of hell."

The family vacated their West End Avenue residence and moved to an equally spacious apartment at 241 Central Park West. They had just moved in, wrote Joyce Hadley, when Dorothy hired a private investigator to follow her husband. The investigator returned with photographs of Joe checking into a Manhattan hotel with a redhead on his arm. The photos substantiated Dorothy's suspicions. She took Joe Jr. and, after visiting her parents in Duluth and hiring an attorney, checked into the Riverside Hotel in Reno, Nevada, in order to initiate divorce proceedings. Joe followed and begged his wife to try again, promising to amend his ways. Their reconciliation was short lived. With DiMaggio serving in the armed forces, Dorothy took the baby and the nanny and moved into a two-bedroom suite at the Hotel Adams, announcing to the press that she and the Yankee Clipper were terminating their marriage.

On October 11, 1943, Dorothy filed divorce papers in Los Angeles Superior Court on grounds of "cruel indifference." "Joe never acted like a married man," she testified. "I had a child with him, thinking that would make him realize his responsibilities . . . but even the baby's arrival didn't change him. He became ill tempered; refused to talk to me for days at a time. And several times asked me to get out of our home." Dorothy asked for and received a lump sum payment of $14,000 in cash, $500 a month in alimony payments, and $150 a month for "the care and maintenance" of Little Joe, in addition to "any and all future medical and educational fees incurred by the minor." Joe was likewise ordered by the court to create an irrevocable trust in his son's name "for no less than ten thousand dollars," payable "immediately following Mr. DiMaggio's death." The decree of divorce, uncontested on DiMaggio's part, was handed down on May 15, 1944. Dorothy retained full custody of the child. Joe was granted alternating weekend visitation rights, an improbable arrangement considering he was currently in the military and at war's end would resume his baseball career. He was also ordered to pay all legal costs in connection with the divorce, including those accrued by his former wife.

Encouraged by Hollywood talent agent Mort Millman, Dorothy Arnold (having resumed use of her professional "screen" name) decided to reenter the world of show business, not as an actress but primarily as a vocalist. Millman reasoned, not incorrectly, that as "the former Mrs. Joe DiMaggio," Dorothy could draw a crowd — more out of curiosity perhaps than anything else. By mid-1945, she had contracted to appear nightly with Nat Brandwynne and His Orchestra in the Starlight Room at the Waldorf-Astoria.

"My mother had stayed on as Little Joe's nanny," said Emerald Duffy, "and when Dorothy began singing with the band, we all moved into a large residential suite at the Waldorf Towers. Incredibly, Joe DiMaggio was still courting Dorothy, hoping to remarry. He'd come by to retrieve his son and take him back to his own suite at the Hotel Edison or the Elysée, where they'd sit around and watch TV all evening. Then he'd have somebody drop the boy off in the morning. At some point he suggested they try living together again. She had no intention of going back to him. She told my mother that he would never change, that he was immersed in cement, that he had no regard or respect for women. Besides, she'd started dating somebody else, and she was evidently crazy about him."

Her new love interest was George Schubert, a former Wall Street investment broker who soon took over as Dorothy's manager.

They were married on August 1, 1946. As Joyce Hadley saw it, he was more talkative than Joe DiMaggio but otherwise shared many of Joe's characteristics. "Schubert," she wrote, "was stiff . . . and controlled in everything he said and did." Like DiMaggio, he was domineering, demanding, narcissistic, and full of himself. As she'd done with Joe, Dorothy rationalized his behavior, oblivious to the reality of the situation. Life with her new husband consisted largely of dining, drinking, dancing, and attending wild parties — a radical change from her previous life-style. But unlike DiMaggio, Schubert had little of his own money. "I'm afraid," she told her sister Joyce, "I'm attracted to all the wrong men."

"The real victim in all this was Little Joey," said Emerald Duffy. "His mother had nick-named him Butch, though I never knew exactly why. To be honest, his parents simply weren't there for him. After she married George Schubert, Dorothy absented herself almost completely from her son's life. Between her marriage and her show business career, she was never around. And the boy was virtually invisible to his father. Joe DiMaggio appeared to like little kids, con-stantly gave them his autograph and a few kind words, but he seemed oblivious to his own son. Occasionally he'd take him along to the ballpark. I went with them only once. Joey was about six, and he wore his little Yankee baseball uniform, pinstripes and all. And he had his own baseball mitt, the Joe DiMaggio children's signature model. He looked really cute. He kept asking me if I thought his dad would play catch with him on the sidelines before the game. 'I don't see why not,' I told him. But when we reached Yankee Stadium and after DiMaggio suited up, he asked one of his teammates to toss a ball around with his son. He couldn't be bothered."

Emerald recalled the day a sports magazine needed a photo of DiMaggio and Joe Jr. for their front cover. DiMaggio sent a limo to collect Joey and drive him to the photographer's studio, where they posed together for a few shots, after which the boy was driven home. His father didn't say two words to him. He had a dinner date that night with Peggy Deegan, his "girlfriend of the moment." He didn't have time for his son.

Emerald Duffy went on to describe Little Joey's early childhood years as an "abysmal period," during which he had little emotional contact with either parent. In addition, he had few friends his own age. At school, when he told classmates his name was Joe DiMaggio, nobody believed him. "You're full of shit," they'd say. "His best pal," Emerald noted, "was an elderly elevator operator at the Waldorf, whose name was Max. Max had no family of his own, so he kind of adopted

113

Joey. They adopted each other. Joey spent hours riding up and down with Max, chatting away with him, unburdening himself. It seemed sad in a way. My mother tried to be there for Joey, but she was being paid to look after him — it wasn't the same thing."

Then in late 1950, following her divorce from George Schubert, Dorothy Arnold became convinced that her career opportunities would be brighter in California. With Joey in tow, she left New York and moved to Los Angeles. There, once again bereft of companionship and left to his own devices, Joey eventually found a new "best pal." Her name was Marilyn Monroe, and in January 1954 Marilyn would evolve into something far more vital than a "best pal" — she would become Joey's stepmother.

It wasn't that Joe DiMaggio hadn't wanted to tell Marilyn about his four-year marriage to Dorothy Arnold — it wasn't that at all. Rather, it had been a question of finding "the right time and the right place." That, in any case, is how he phrased it when he finally got around to conveying the sordid details, many of which Monroe had already heard from George Solotaire the night they dined together at the Plaza. As a result, Joe's long-awaited "confession" came as no great surprise.

By late July 1952, Marilyn had finished

shooting *Niagara* and had flown to Los Angeles, leaving Joe behind in New York to plod on with his television sports show. But at the beginning of September, she returned to the East Coast to attend the New York premiere of *Monkey Business,* and to serve as grand marshal for the Miss America beauty pageant in Atlantic City, New Jersey. Twentieth Century–Fox's publicity department had arranged Monroe's participation in the pageant and had booked her into a luxury suite at the Ritz-Carlton, directly on the Boardwalk. In conjunction with her appearance as grand marshal, a US Army photographer was deployed to take pictures of the actress for an upcoming recruitment drive.

The day before the pageant DiMaggio joined Marilyn at her hotel. That evening they ate a late dinner at the Merry-Go-Round Bar, off the Ritz lobby, and it was during their meal that he brought up the subject of his previous marriage. The following day Marilyn dressed for the event in a low-cut black chiffon gown, which displayed a good deal more of her than Joe thought it should have.

In his biography of Joe DiMaggio, Richard Ben Cramer refers to Marilyn's comment on the outfit. It was "an entirely decent dress," she insisted. "You could ride in a streetcar in it without disturbing the passengers. But there was one bright-minded photographer who figured he would get a more striking picture if he photographed me shooting down. I didn't notice him pointing his camera from the balcony."

The "bright-minded" photographer in this case happened to be the one sent by the army, and while his pictures revealed too much of Monroe's very ample cleavage to be utilized for recruitment purposes, they appeared (somewhat retouched) in the next day's press. If there were anybody who hadn't as yet seen Marilyn's nude calendar shots, they could familiarize themselves with her body by taking in the Atlantic City pictorials. Letters poured into newspaper offices from church groups and ladies' clubs condemning Monroe for her lack of decorum and good taste.

Predictably, Joe DiMaggio became infuriated when he saw the published photos. For him it was Dorothy Arnold and her "scandalous" Jones Beach two-piece bathing suit all over again. "He was screaming at Marilyn," wrote Richard Ben Cramer. "Like she'd done the whole thing to embarrass him. She tried to explain. It was publicity. It was part of her job. She had to show herself."

They'd been through all this before, and DiMaggio remained as adamant as ever. "You don't need to show them anything. Not a damn thing. You look like a fuckin' whore in that outfit."

But that was the gown the studio had given

her to wear.

"Wear your own goddamn clothes, not theirs."

She didn't have any clothes worth wearing.

"Well then, buy them," he snapped. "Or maybe you do have them, and they're in the backseat of your car along with everything else you own. Can't you see that those Hollywood swine are using you? You're nothing to them but a piece of meat."

Marilyn agreed and Joe calmed down. He apologized for yelling, and she accepted his apology. That was the pattern they'd established. She'd do something that would set him off. He'd scream. She'd retreat. He'd feel contrite and offer an apology. They'd embrace and make up. And then, without fail, something else would come along, and they'd begin all over again.

CHAPTER 5

When the 1952 baseball postseason ended in early October — the Yanks took the World Series from the Dodgers in seven games — Joe DiMaggio flew to San Francisco, picked up his dark blue '52 Cadillac bearing the license plate "JOE D," and drove to Los Angeles to spend time with Marilyn Monroe. The first thing he did was to take her on a shopping spree for a new wardrobe. He sat there patiently while she tried on a variety of outfits. Every dress had a high neckline. That was the deal: he'd pay for the clothes provided they met his sartorial specifications. She agreed to wear them if he promised to be more patient with her. He said he would try.

A few weeks later, Marilyn, wearing one of her new fashion selections, accompanied DiMaggio to Black-Foxe Military Institute on Wilcox Avenue in Hollywood to visit his son. Joe Jr. had just celebrated his eleventh birthday. DiMaggio hadn't seen the school before, though Joey had been a student there since 1951. Because of its location, Black-Foxe (named after its cofounders) catered primarily to the sons of families involved in the movie industry. Ranging in age from seven through nineteen, the "junior cadets," as they were officially designated, were required to wear military uniforms when attending class. One of Joe Jr.'s classmates, the son of a well-known film director, later described the academy as "an overpriced dumping ground for the disaffected male offspring of prominent Hollywood parents eager to rid themselves of their kids for a couple of years, if not longer."

On Friday afternoons the entire student body, in full dress regalia, with a band playing in the background, would march up and down the drill field for the pleasure of the academy's instructors and those parents who were there to pick up their sons for the weekend. The school would break out the rifles for the parade, small stock rifles for the younger students, real rifles for the high school–aged cadets. "That's when you knew you were at a military academy," said Joey Jr. "There was no mistaking it for a regular boarding school."

The day they came to visit, Joe Jr. led Marilyn and his father on a walking tour of the campus. They then took him to Trader Vic's for dinner. Years after first meeting Marilyn, Joe DiMaggio's son would say, "I took to her at once. In many respects she was like a kid herself, not at all like a movie star. Marilyn was neither haughty nor imperious. Quite to the contrary, she was straightforward and down-to-earth. There was a soft simplicity about her. She could be moody, but she was usually buoyant and always generous. She seemed extremely feminine. She tried to encourage me in my difficult relationship with my father, but at the same time, she never tried to supplant my mother, though in fact that wouldn't have been a difficult thing to do. She always asked all the right questions: Did I have any friends at school? What were my favorite courses and why? Which writers did I like to read? It wasn't just idle chatter. I felt she had a sincere interest in getting to know me.

"By contrast, my father's main focus revolved around Black-Foxe's athletic program. He wasn't concerned with me as a person. And I had to be careful how I spoke to him, because the wrong tone or comment would instantly jettison him into a black hole. It was always a matter of living up to his expectations. The only times he seemed pleased with me were when I could report I'd scored a game-clinching basket or won a student tennis tournament, or something of that sort. Attaining a good exam score or course grade didn't mean much to him. You had to excel in sports. That's what impressed him, and that's the reason I never took baseball very seriously. No matter how hard I tried, I would never be good enough. I could never be another Joe DiMaggio."

Joey stressed that his father had a rather superficial view of life. "He concerned himself with image, with how things looked," said Joe Jr. "For example, he was a chain-smoker. I can't remember ever seeing him when he didn't have a cigarette in his mouth. He went through three to four packs a day. But you won't find many photographs of him smoking. He'd see a photographer coming his way, and he'd ditch the cigarette. It wasn't cool in terms of image for an athlete to be caught with a cancer stick in hand. To impress the kids, you had to demonstrate that you were a wholesome guy, even if you weren't."

Joey's mother took advantage of the fact that her son was boarding at Black-Foxe — she was rarely around. Mort Millman, Dorothy Arnold's agent, had found his client work as a lounge singer at the Mission Inn in Carmel, California. When that job ended, she embarked on the dinner club circuit and later performed on the road with the Minsky's Follies. "She was out of town most of the time," said Joey. "I remember taking several short vacations with her, once to Mexico and twice to Las Vegas. And then her family owned a summer cottage on Caribou Lake, in Wisconsin, so we'd hang out there once in a while.

But for the most part I didn't see much of her, particularly during my first two years at Black-Foxe. Because I was by myself most of the time, Marilyn began visiting me at school, sometimes with my father, other times alone. She'd take me out for dinner or invite me back to her place. Within a matter of months she moved from a house rental on Castilian Drive in the Hollywood Hills to a suite at the Beverly Hills Hotel, and then into an apartment on North Doheny. She couldn't sit still. Neither could my mother or father. Consequently, I never had a permanent childhood address. Because Marilyn experienced a similarly nomadic childhood, she understood me better than anyone else."

Joe Jr. readily admitted that he soon developed a "mad crush" on Marilyn. He confessed that she became the "object" of his "adolescent fantasies." Joey went so far as to tell his mother that Marilyn was "a doll" and had "beautiful legs."

"I suppose I was jealous of my father," he admitted. "It was all very Freudian." Joey's Black-Foxe classmates seem to have fostered their own MM fantasies. They couldn't stop talking about her. They demanded to know if Joe Jr. had ever seen her "in the buff." "Yeah," he told them, "I saw her in that nude calendar spread, where she's sprawled across a red velvet sheet." "Not the calendar, asshole! In the flesh!" Even if he had seen her that way, he never would have admitted it. Not to them. They asked if in private she sounded the same as she did on-screen — with that breathy, sexy voice of hers. In fact, she didn't, but he assured them she did. And then there was the time he engaged in fisticuffs with a schoolmate because "the jerk" called Marilyn "a hooker." Busted him in the mouth. Split his lip and broke a couple of teeth. The fight nearly got Joey suspended from school. He told his father about it, and Joe DiMaggio "must've said something to somebody," because in the end nothing came of the incident.

While Joe Jr. never experienced Monroe "in the buff," save the nude calendar shot, he did see her in a bathing suit. "Her Hollywood Hills sublet had an outdoor swimming pool," he recalled, "and when I went over there, mainly on weekends, I'd swim, and Marilyn would sit poolside and read. She always had her nose in a book. I think she felt somewhat insecure because she hadn't completed high school, and this is how she compensated. Then, too, she was perpetually on this self-improvement kick. She wanted to expand her horizons. She had an artistic nature and a quick mind. She was imaginative and creative, but in a sort of childlike way. I can't explain it. She wrote poetry and kept journals. She'd often quote from writers like Walt Whitman and Ralph Waldo Emerson. She'd taken an

123

extension course in art and literature at UCLA and had planned on taking additional courses, but there was never enough time."

One Sunday afternoon Joe and Marilyn picked up his son at school and drove him to the Castilian Drive residence to spend the day. The three of them were sitting around the pool, relaxing, when they heard a clicking sound coming from behind some hedges. A newspaper photographer had hidden out and was taking pictures. DiMaggio jumped up and chased the fellow away, but the damage had been done. The photos appeared in all the papers a day or two later. "And that," said Joe Jr., "is when all hell broke loose."

The news media contacted Dorothy Arnold for a comment. Did she know about Monroe and her former husband? What did she think of Marilyn? And did she mind her son spending time with the couple?

Dorothy claimed she knew of DiMaggio's relationship with Monroe. She said she had nothing per se against Marilyn — she seemed to be "a kind and sweet lady" — but her former husband was a horse of a different color. He never took a fatherly interest in his son. He didn't take his visitations with Butch seriously. All they ever did together was watch television. And eat junk food. Joe never even spoke to Butch. He didn't offer parental guidance of any kind. To be blunt, he was an unfit father. She had taken up golf with Butch, which is more than his father had done, even though Joe was an avid golfer. She'd exposed her son to all sorts of activities. He loved building model airplanes. She'd registered him at Clover airfield (in Santa Monica) for an aviation course geared toward young teenagers. He'd flown in the cockpit of a plane with a private instructor. At her family's lake house in Wisconsin, he'd been given sailing and waterskiing lessons. In Mexico, he'd learned all about the art of bullfighting. She'd done all this for Butch, and what had DiMaggio done for him? Nothing, absolutely nothing!

The Hearst newspaper syndicate picked up the story and ran a follow-up article comparing Dorothy Arnold and Marilyn Monroe, pointing out that both were blond, both were fair skinned, both had "curves in all the right places," and both were performers. The difference between them, read the piece, "is that Marilyn's nine years younger than Dorothy and far more successful in her film career."

Offended by the article, Dorothy went on the warpath, asserting in the press that her former husband was subjecting their son to a "loose, amoral side of life" and to "a person" (i.e., Monroe) with an "unsavory" reputation, "a person" better known for her "sexual conquests" than for her "film roles." (So much for the "kind and sweet" Marilyn.) Dorothy reported that during her son's

125

"quality time" with his dad, Joe would take Butch over to Marilyn's place and let him use the pool while Joe and Marilyn "retired to her bedroom and had sex." And while DiMaggio could do whatever he wished in terms of a social life, she didn't want her son exposed to his father's affair. "He should be more discreet." To this she added that considering Joe's rather substantial income, he was paying far too little in child support. She planned, she said, on going back to court.

She went back to court, but not until Joe DiMaggio offered his own statement to the press. He called Dorothy's accusations "ridiculous" and charged her with using his child support payments to her own benefit, rather than their son's. He stated that her Marilyn Monroe–related comments were vile and untrue. "It's pure jealousy on her part," he observed. "She doesn't even know Marilyn."

It was but one more battle in an ongoing war. Before the end of the year, Dorothy Arnold filed papers with the Superior Court of Los Angeles requesting that the monthly child support payment of $150 be increased to $1,000 so she "could establish a home for our son in keeping with his father's wealth and position." Further, she petitioned the court to suspend DiMaggio's visitation rights because he had exposed Joe Jr. to "a person with an immoral reputation."

Having retained the services of Loyd Wright Jr., a Los Angeles attorney, DiMaggio took the witness stand and pointed out that not only was he paying child support, but he also financed Joey's education, summer camp program, extracurricular activities, and medical needs. As an example of his former wife's "treacherous" behavior, he testified that she had recently sold a piano he'd acquired for Joey and had pocketed the proceeds. And regarding visitation rights, he insisted he was currently negotiating the purchase of a residence in the area, which would give him the opportunity to see his son on a more regular basis. If anything, he felt his visitation rights ought to be broadened, not curtailed. He accused his former wife of "bad-mouthing" him to their son, thereby turning the boy against him. "My son," he said, "has been brainwashed."

Although Judge Elmer Doyle agreed to raise the monthly child support payment to $300, he otherwise ruled for DiMaggio, going so far as to tell Dorothy Arnold she should probably "never have divorced" Joe DiMaggio. As the parties filed out of the courtroom into the outer corridor, a spectator overheard Dorothy mutter to a friend, "I should never have married him — if I hadn't, I wouldn't have had to seek a divorce."

Jane Russell may have been given top billing.

in *Gentlemen Prefer Blondes,* but Marilyn Monroe *was* the blonde, and as the film title suggested, gentlemen preferred them. And while it might have been better for publicity purposes had they become rivals, once shooting began, Jane and Marilyn had become good friends. Five years older than Monroe, Russell had graduated from Van Nuys High, the same school Norma Jeane Baker would attend a few years later. At Van Nuys, Jane performed in the same student theater group as Jim Dougherty, Norma Jeane's future husband. Russell and Monroe also had Howard Hughes in common. Hughes had discovered Jane, and he and Monroe had likewise crossed paths, though to what extent and how intimately Marilyn never divulged.

Like so many other women in Marilyn's life, Jane Russell took a protective, almost maternal attitude toward her. Marilyn turned to her for advice on her relationship with Joe DiMaggio. If anyone could discuss the pros and contras associated with marriage to a career athlete, it had to be Jane Russell. In 1943 she'd married her high school sweetheart, Bob Waterfield, who went on to become an all-pro quarterback for the Los Angeles Rams. Having retired from football the same year Joe quit baseball, Waterfield soon began hanging out with DiMaggio. While Jane and Marilyn busied themselves on the movie set, Joe and Bob went golfing together. Despite their shared interest in all matters athletic, they had little else in common. Bob Waterfield envisioned a future for himself in the business end of the movie industry. In the early 1950s, he and Jane Russell started their own film company, producing four motion pictures over the next ten years. Joe DiMaggio hated the Hollywood jungle and everything associated with it. He remained hopeful he could convince Marilyn to quit making films and start making babies. Bob Waterfield told DiMaggio he couldn't see why she couldn't do both. Jane Russell concurred. She and Bob had adopted three children, and she had always found parenting perfectly compatible with an acting career. Marilyn felt encouraged.

In connection with the premiere of *Gentlemen Prefer Blondes,* Marilyn and Jane were asked to participate in the traditional hand-foot imprint ceremony in the courtyard at Grauman's Theatre. For Marilyn it was the fulfillment of a fantasy she'd entertained since her childhood days at the orphanage. As Marilyn and Jane kneeled on the sidewalk, Marilyn suggested that Russell pull down the top of her dress and press her exposed breasts into the wet cement; she offered to do the same with her buttocks, preserving them for posterity's sake. When informed by the Fox representative that her suggestion was unacceptable, Marilyn came up with another idea.

She thought a diamond should be used to dot the *i* in her name, a reminder of her big number ("Diamonds Are a Girl's Best Friend") in *Gentlemen Prefer Blondes.* Instead of a diamond, Fox sanctioned the use of a rhinestone. A few weeks later, the rhinestone mysteriously disappeared. "Oh well, it's the thought that counts," Marilyn told a journalist. "Frankly, I think if Jane Russell's boobs and my ass had been used instead of our hands and feet, a lot more people would've visited that site."

Long after she and Marilyn appeared together in *Gentlemen Prefer Blondes,* Jane Russell stated that she retained "genuine admiration and affection" for Marilyn. "She was anything but the airhead she so often portrayed in her films," said Russell. "She was very smart and quite unique. Despite her spotty background, she managed to make a grand success of her career. Yet for all her success, she remained neurotically insecure, constantly in search of advice and guidance, and forever in pursuit of a lasting love. I never for a minute believed that she and Joe DiMaggio would last. They were in love, very much so, but they didn't understand each other. They came from different universes. That was the tragedy of their relationship. They couldn't stay together. It was ill fated, written in the stars."

■ ■ ■ ■

One of the many characters who attempted to latch on to Marilyn Monroe was Robert Slatzer, a self-proclaimed screenwriter and producer. Slatzer (he died in 2005 at age seventy-seven) met Marilyn at Twentieth Century–Fox in 1946, when he was a struggling fan-magazine reporter and she a struggling model and actress. Having fallen in love with her, Slatzer proceeded to write countless articles and a book about her, in the course of which he made the incredible claim that he, and not Joe DiMaggio, had been her second husband. It is noteworthy that Slatzer's disclosure of a purported marriage came only after Marilyn's death.

Without a shred of evidence to support his claim, Slatzer contended that their "secret" wedding took place on October 4, 1952, in Tijuana, Mexico, while Joe DiMaggio languished in New York covering the World Series. According to Slatzer, an unnamed lawyer performed the marriage ceremony for a $5 fee. The marriage supposedly ended two or three days later when Darryl F. Zanuck, Marilyn's boss at Fox, coerced her into a divorce. Slatzer later penned a treatment for a proposed film to be titled *Three Days in Heaven,* encapsulating his "three-day marriage" to Marilyn, and submitted it to several independent producers, hoping to elicit interest in the project.

"Slatzer's treatment crossed my desk in New York," said television and film producer Lester Persky, "and while it wasn't particularly well written, the story line, if true, was sensational. On the surface, I found it difficult to believe because at the time Slatzer claimed he married Monroe, she was involved with Joe DiMaggio. Why would one of the world's most alluring and famous women marry a penniless nobody when she had the likes of DiMaggio and Arthur Miller banging at her door? It made no sense, but then again that's what was so intriguing about it."

On Persky's next trip to Los Angeles, he met with Slatzer to discuss the property. "He turned out to be an absolute sleaze bucket," said Persky, "the kind of bloke who'd sell you his soiled underwear if you were dumb enough to make him an offer. After meeting him, I decided to do a little snooping around and soon learned Monroe had been nowhere near Tijuana on October 4, 1952. A Beverly Hills real estate agent I knew had driven Marilyn around during those three days, showing her prospective apartment rentals all over Los Angeles. The agent had business journals dating back to 1950 detailing the names of clients and the addresses they visited. And there in black and white were her notations on Marilyn Monroe covering the dates in question. So much for Mr. Slatzer's little fairy tale. I'm not saying he didn't love her; I'm saying he never married her."

The single Bob Slatzer story that did ring true took place in early December 1952, after Marilyn had moved into a suite at the Beverly Hills Hotel. Joe DiMaggio had told her that he would be going to San Francisco for the day to attend a friend's birthday party, and she had invited Bob Slatzer over for drinks that evening. She had spent the afternoon on the set of *Gentlemen Prefer Blondes* and didn't expect Joe to return until later that night. Catching an earlier flight back to Los Angeles, Joe arrived while Slatzer was still present. Imagining the worst, DiMaggio asked Marilyn's guest to leave. Slatzer stood his ground. He wasn't about to let this dumbass dago toss him out on his can, even if it meant getting the shit kicked out of him. DiMaggio turned on Monroe. The couple became embroiled in a bitter quarrel. With no end in sight and probably feeling embarrassed by the mix-up, Marilyn ordered both men to get out. Outside on the street, DiMaggio glared at his adversary. "Good night, slugger," said Slatzer under his breath as he headed for his car. DiMaggio climbed into his Cadillac and drove off in a huff. He spent the night at the Knickerbocker Hotel. The next day he confronted Marilyn and accused her of "two-timing" him. He told her if he ever saw Slatzer's face again, he'd kill him.

They had a second spat on Thanksgiving Day. Bernie Kamber, a New York press agent and one of Joe's buddies from Toots Shor's, showed up in Los Angeles for a business meeting. While there, he offered to take Joe and Marilyn to the Brown Derby for a late-afternoon turkey dinner. Joe and Bernie arrived first. Marilyn waltzed in nearly two hours late. She'd fallen asleep while taking a bath. DiMaggio refused to speak to her. He spoke only to Kamber, as did Marilyn. Once Joe and Marilyn arrived back at her hotel, he finally let loose. He made such a racket and screamed so loudly that guests in a nearby room called the front desk. A pair of gun-toting security guards knocked at Marilyn's door. She pulled it open. Was everything all right? They were concerned because a guest on the same floor had complained about the noise. DiMaggio sidled into view. He apologized. The security guards left, and so did Joe. He spent the night in Bernie Kamber's suite at the Beverly Wilshire Hotel.

If Joe DiMaggio demonstrated a propensity for violence, he had an altogether different side as well. He was capable of great and unexpected moments of tenderness. On Christmas Eve, Marilyn returned to her suite from a studio party and found Joe standing on a stepladder hanging the last ornaments on an eight-foot-tall Christmas tree. He had placed a magnum of champagne in a silver ice bucket. Logs blazed in the fireplace. On a table, next to a small gift-wrapped box, sat a card that read "Merry Christmas, Marilyn." The box contained a pair of emerald earrings. "The earrings were beautiful," she would tell Joe DiMaggio Jr., "but not as beautiful as the tree. It was the first time in my life anyone ever gave me a Christmas tree. I was so happy I cried."

In return, Marilyn gave Joe a pair of gold cufflinks as well as an eight-inch-by-ten-inch matted and framed photograph of herself reclining on a satin chair, smiling at the camera. The photo was signed across the front in bold blue ink: "I love you Joe. Marilyn."

They celebrated New Year's in San Francisco with Joe's family. Marilyn had visited Joe in the Bay City several months earlier, but only for a weekend. On that visit she had demonstrated her interest in what Robert Solotaire called "the simple pleasures of life" — she and Joe had spent part of the day cleaning and polishing his car. This time, with the Fox Studios closed for the holidays, she anticipated spending a week.

They stayed on the third floor of Joe's three-story attached stone house at 2150 Beach Street, a quiet residential block in the Marina District, one hundred yards from

Marina Green, a picturesque park adjacent to Fisherman's Wharf and the Municipal Boat Basin. DiMaggio bought the house in 1937 (for less than $15,000) as a gift to his parents. After his father's death in 1949 and his mother's in 1951, his widowed sister, Marie DiMaggio Kron, moved in (with her daughter Betty) and lived on the second floor. Following his retirement, Joe DiMaggio made it his home base, a place to hang his hat on the few occasions he wasn't out of town. Marie looked after the house, cooked, cleaned, answered Joe's fan mail, and in general took care of her brother. Practically an obsessive-compulsive when it came to cleanliness, she kept the house dust-free and absolutely spotless. No one could be neat enough for Marie. A small room off Joe's third-floor bedroom contained many of his baseball trophies, plaques, and medals. Another room on the same floor became Joe's walk-in wardrobe closet. A larger-than-life oil portrait of DiMaggio in his Yankees pinstripes covered a wall in the downstairs living room. A den served as the TV room. A patio faced an enclosed backyard, where Joe had set up a telescope to gaze at the stars on cloudless nights. Unbeknownst to most of his cronies, Joe had been interested in astronomy since his teenaged years and had even gathered a tidy selection of books on the subject. It was the only even remotely intellectual pursuit he'd had as a young man.

"Don't read anything into it," DiMaggio had told George Solotaire, one of the few friends aware of his interest. "I don't know shit about astronomy. I just like looking up there at all the lights. It makes me wonder."

Marie, a slim, handsome, dark-eyed woman devoted to Joe's needs, took it upon herself to introduce Marilyn to Italian cooking. Wearing a pair of eyeglasses (she was myopic), Marilyn watched and took notes as she stood next to Marie in Joe's kitchen. They spent hours going over Marie's homespun recipes for both meat and vegetable lasagna. "It was a lost cause," said Dom DiMaggio. Joe's younger brother had been introduced to Marilyn at the Grotto. Older brother Tom managed the eatery, and Vince managed the bar area until he quit to move his family forty miles north of San Francisco. Other family members held various jobs, from cashier to maître d'. The restaurant always became more crowded when word spread that Joe was in town. Celebrities, particularly from the sports world, made it a point to drop in. Ted Williams, Joe Louis, and jockey Eddie Arcaro were among that year's crop of visitors.

"Marilyn radiated great beauty and charm," said Dom DiMaggio, "which is probably one of the reasons she eventually established a name that far transcended the film business. I used to kid her because in truth she couldn't cook her way out of a paper bag. I told her if you're Italian, food is not only sustenance, it's the basis for social gatherings, a way of life. She said she'd been trying to learn to cook for years but couldn't get the hang of it. She accepted her culinary limitations with good humor. 'I guess I'll never be a chief chef at the Waldorf,' she quipped. She mentioned she loved Italian food as well as the people of Italy. 'They're warm, lusty, and friendly as hell,' she said. 'I want to go to Italy someday.' 'Maybe you and Joe can go together,' I responded. She smiled and said, 'I'd like nothing better.' "

Marilyn's favorite dish at the Grotto was lobster thermidor. She also liked the boiled beef dinner. Whenever she and Joe ate at home, he would make a point of dropping into the Grotto kitchen to pick up a healthy serving of each. She complained lightheartedly that since meeting Joe, she'd gained ten pounds and gone up a complete dress size. "If we're together much longer," she quipped, "I'll begin to look like Mae West."

Early one morning, while Marilyn caught up on her sleep, Joe and Tom DiMaggio went duck hunting. Between them, they bagged five birds. That evening Tom and his wife Louise invited Joe and Marilyn to their apartment (four blocks from DiMaggio's house) for a dinner of wild duck and wild rice. They were joined by Tom's grown daughter June

DiMaggio, who was taking voice lessons with the hope of breaking into show business. Marilyn confided in June that she'd never eaten wild duck and doubted she'd be able to tolerate the gamy flavor. But she didn't want to insult Joe, who took great pride in having "hunted down" their dinner with a shotgun. "If you don't like the taste," said June, "turn to me and give me a wink." Marilyn did more than that. After a few bites, she crossed her eyes and curled up her nose. June took her plate into the kitchen, removed the remaining duck, replaced it with chopped sirloin and covered the meat with rice. June placed the new delicacy in front of Marilyn. She tasted it and smiled broadly. "This is wonderful!" she purred. None the wiser, Joe watched Marilyn devour her dinner. He told her he was glad she appeared so taken with wild duck. "Maybe I'll shoot some more for you again soon," he said. "I can't wait," gushed Marilyn.

Another day Tom invited Marilyn to join him on a deep-sea fishing trip aboard the *Yankee Clipper,* a twenty-two-foot Chris-Craft that the New York Yankees had presented to Joe in 1949 in conjunction with Joe DiMaggio Day at Yankee Stadium. Joe had given the boat to his brothers for use as a commercial fishing vessel. The fish served at the Grotto were often caught aboard the *Yankee Clipper.* Joe and June DiMaggio rounded out the crew that went out to sea that morning.

They shoved off at four in the morning. Marilyn wore a pair of June's white deck pants. It was a cold, damp, foggy day. The dark waters of the San Francisco Bay splashed up against the side of the boat as it rolled up and down, up and down with the waves. An hour into the excursion, Marilyn began to feel queasy. Her face had turned ashen. "Got any crackers, Junie?" she asked. June, who was prone to seasickness, produced a box of table crackers. The more they ate, the sicker they felt. To Marilyn's surprise, Joe didn't seem the least bit bothered by the constant rocking of the boat. He and Tom were having a wonderful time, reeling in one fish after another. As they passed under the Golden Gate Bridge, Marilyn leaned over the side of the boat and started upchucking the crackers and the remains of her meal from the night before. June bent over the other side of the boat and did the same. Tom reluctantly turned the boat around and headed back to port. Marilyn spent the rest of the afternoon dashing back and forth between bed and bathroom, vowing that any future fishing endeavors would take place on a lake or off a pier, not at sea.

Yet two days later, she agreed to go deep-sea fishing again, this time in company with Joe and his wartime buddy, fellow retired major leaguer Dario Lodigiani, and to her own amazement, she hooked a big fish after struggling for an hour to reel it in. Dario wanted Joe to help her. "She hooked it," Joe insisted. "Let her bring it in." "And I'll be damned," said Dario, "if Marilyn didn't land that monster."

As for Marilyn and June, their friendship grew each time Monroe returned to San Francisco. When Joe had business to take care of at the Grotto, Marilyn would frequently get together with June. With Marilyn in disguise (black wig, prescription sunglasses, no makeup), they would stroll to the marina and feed the pigeons. Or they'd sit at an outdoor café, sip hot chocolate, and watch the tourists amble by. In *Marilyn, Joe & Me,* June DiMaggio's book on Monroe, she recalled a shopping trip to Sears when Marilyn decided not to go incognito. Easily recognizable, Marilyn soon attracted a large crowd. As they paid and started to leave, they found their way blocked. "Aren't you Marilyn Monroe?" asked an elderly woman in the crowd. Adopting a Scandinavian accent, Marilyn launched into a lengthy diatribe on how she was just visiting the United States. "Everywun sinks I'm Marileen, but my name is Eve Lindstrom." When one of them still wanted her autograph, she signed her name as *Eve Lindstrom.* On the way home, Marilyn and June laughed so hard they almost cried.

And then there was the midday walk they took along the streets of North Beach when they passed the beauty salon Marilyn had started to use during her visits to San Francisco. As they approached the salon, Marilyn gasped and grabbed June's hand. There, hanging in the shop's front window, were tiny packets of blond snippets labeled "Marilyn Monroe's Hair," priced at $100 per packet. Marilyn and June were stunned. They rushed home to June's father's apartment and called Tom at the Grotto, because he'd been the one to recommend the North Beach salon in the first place. Usually "even-tempered and slow to anger," June's father dropped everything, stormed out of the restaurant, and headed straight for the beauty salon. Without a word and ignoring the objections of salon staffers, he grabbed every packet of hair hanging in the window, ripped up the sign, and then, his face a deep crimson, he shrieked at the owner, "How dare you sell Marilyn's hair without her permission?" When Joe DiMaggio heard the story from his brother, he said, "It's good you went in there and not me. I'd probably have burned the place down. In fact, I still may."

Given her interest in show business, June DiMaggio delighted in hearing Marilyn's take on the film industry, "a business," in June's words, "that didn't give a hoot for morals or feelings." At heart a raconteur, Monroe seemed only too glad to oblige, provided June not pass on her stories to "Uncle Joe," whose Sicilian rage tended to flare at the mere mention of Hollywood, or (in Joe's words) "the real pimps of Los Angeles: the studio bosses."

Marilyn had made the mistake one night, having had too much to drink, of thinking Joe might find amusing a Joe Schenck anecdote, namely how she'd allowed the old man to fondle and lick her breasts while another starlet "gave him head, lots of it, tons of it." It had been their combined birthday present to Schenck. "I don't know his exact age," Marilyn had told DiMaggio, "but he was old, take my word for it. He was as ancient as the pyramids of Egypt. And this little game went on for what seemed an eternity, and nothing happened. It wouldn't go up. Or maybe it sort of went halfway up for a few seconds, then down again. So after a while we switched places. He started licking the other girl's boobs, while I did what she'd been doing. And I worked hard at it. I gave it my all, because I liked Joe and wanted to make him happy on his birthday. Nothing. No reaction. Dead as a doorknob. It was kind of sad, not so much for us but for him. I think it depressed him. It reminded him of his age, of what he'd once been and what he'd become,"

Joe DiMaggio hadn't found the anecdote the least bit touching or amusing or anything other than an old pimp exploiting two young girls. It angered him. He refused to converse with Marilyn for the better part of a week. "For God's sakes, Joe," she'd pleaded. "I was a kid at the time, an impressionable young kid. And he was a sweet old man. It meant absolutely nothing." It didn't matter what she said. Here was another example of Marilyn's succumbing to the system, of prostituting herself merely to advance her career. So in talking to June DiMaggio about her past, Marilyn spoke only in generic terms. No names. She said nothing that would shock DiMaggio if it ever did get back to him.

"She told me," wrote June DiMaggio, "how the head honchos at Twentieth Century–Fox chased after her around the office, and she would give in to them quickly just to get it over with. She said that it hurt and that she hated it." According to June, Marilyn added that when she came home exhausted from a day's shoot, invariably "some powerful old geezer" from the studio would call, and just the sound of his voice "made her skin crawl." June surmised that Marilyn "must have learned to turn off her emotions as a very young child. On the casting couch, believing that she had to sleep with wrinkled old men to survive in the business, she continued to turn her emotions off. She protected herself by playing a part there, too."

CHAPTER 6

Returning from San Francisco, Marilyn moved into a three-room, first-floor apartment at 882 North Doheny Drive between Sunset and Santa Monica Boulevards in Beverly Hills. It was small but charming. The living room featured wall-to-wall white carpeting, a wall of floor-to-ceiling mirrors, a working fireplace, and the same white baby grand piano she'd been given by her mother as a child. She installed customized shelves in the living room and bedroom to accommodate her collection of books and phonograph records. She divided the third room into a wardrobe closet and office with an exercise corner that contained weights and a yoga mat. There was a television set and a seven-foot sofa in the living room where Joe spent much of his time, smoking cigarettes and watching his favorite shows. He helped her move in. He and Joey were her first dinner guests in the new apartment. As Joey recalled, "Marilyn insisted on making lasagna using a recipe and step-by-step instructions provided by Aunt Marie, my father's sister. Evidently something went terribly wrong. The finished dish looked like an afterbirth, all red and gory. I don't think my father cared. He smiled and took us all out to a restaurant for dinner. Marilyn later learned how to prepare spaghetti and spaghetti sauce, and on weekends she'd sometimes make breakfast for my father. She also learned a few words and phrases in Italian. But that was about it."

Hardly disturbed by Marilyn's lack of culinary skill, DiMaggio's main concern had to do with the disorder in the apartment and Marilyn's unwillingness to clean up after herself. He telephoned George Solotaire in New York and complained that the place had begun to resemble the backseat of Marilyn's car. Every stick of furniture in the apartment was covered with discarded items of clothing. Old newspapers and magazines sat in a heap on the kitchen table. The kitchen counters were coated with old coffee and food stains. Dirty dishes were stacked high in the sink. Empty bottles and cans littered the bedroom floor, along with clumps of used tissue paper and an assortment of forks, knives, and spoons. The bathroom was no better. In San Francisco, Marie tidied up after Marilyn, but there was nobody around to clean up after her in Beverly Hills. Joe DiMaggio, fastidious to an almost annoying degree, began buying paper plates and cups to counter the dirty dish situation. When that solution failed, he fled to the Knickerbocker Hotel and spent his nights there.

George Solotaire suggested that Joe hire a housekeeper twice a week to deal with Marilyn's apartment. Joe hesitated. He didn't think she'd give a stranger access to her residence. "The truth of the matter," said Robert Solotaire, "is that Joe happened to be one of the most impecunious fellows you'd ever want to meet. He made up all sorts of excuses why he couldn't spring for a maid, which, by the way, would've been a lot less expensive than staying at the Knickerbocker. But that's Joe DiMaggio for you. He was cheap, probably the result of growing up during the Depression in a household with little money to spare for extras. Just how cheap was he? If you went to a restaurant with him and there were leftovers on the plate, he'd take them home in a doggy bag — not only his leftovers but yours as well. Now, that's cheap. And don't forget, this is a guy who was getting paid a hundred thousand bucks a year to hit a baseball when the average player made far less. He had plenty of cash, and he almost never picked up his own tab; somebody was always treating him to dinner and drinks. As for Marilyn's apartment, he temporarily solved the problem by buying a vacuum cleaner and employing a college coed to go over there once a week and tidy up. The coed lasted less than a month, because after she put everything away, Marilyn couldn't find anything. One item that disappeared was a photograph she had of her half sister Berniece with Mona Rae, Berniece's young daughter. Marilyn blamed the student for the photo's disappearance and fired her. Joe finally hired a commercial cleaning outfit to do their thing. He then called a domestic employment service and found a housekeeper who kept the place reasonably clean."

Whereas Joe DiMaggio could be criticized for having been thrifty, one of Marilyn Monroe's most prevalent traits had to be her unceasing generosity. She perpetually doled out more money than she managed to bring in, and, as a result, constantly found herself in the red. Besides her usual array of expenses, she now had to pay for her mother's maintenance and upkeep at Rockhaven, the posh private facility where she would remain for years to come. A more recently acquired expense was Grace Goddard, who had left Doc Goddard and returned to Los Angeles. By now an unemployed (and unemployable) alcoholic with an addiction to pain medication and sleeping pills, Grace turned to Marilyn for help. Feeling sorry for her former guardian, Marilyn hired her to perform minor secretarial chores. Before the end of the year, learning that she had uterine cancer and only a few months to live, Grace killed herself by overdosing on barbiturates. It was Marilyn who made and paid for the funeral arrangements. Grace was buried at Westwood Memorial Park, a spot in the middle of Los Angeles chosen by Marilyn because of its "beauty and serenity." The ashes of Ana Lower had been interred in the same cemetery in 1948. Marilyn told Joe DiMaggio that when she died, she, too, wanted to be buried there. It comforted her to think of Westwood Memorial as her final resting place. In Joe DiMaggio Jr.'s presence, his father said to Marilyn, "You're much too young to be so preoccupied with death. You've got a whole life ahead of you."

Joe DiMaggio's aggressive attitude toward Natasha Lytess, Marilyn's drama coach, grew in intensity after Twentieth Century–Fox dropped Lytess from its payroll, placing the responsibility for her salary entirely in Monroe's hands. "That's why you never have any money to spend on yourself," DiMaggio berated the actress. Joe wasn't the only Lytess detractor. Allan "Whitey" Snyder, in charge of Marilyn's makeup at Twentieth Century–Fox, thought little of MM's drama coach and said as much. Monroe soon reduced Natasha's salary. Without notifying Lytess, she'd begun studying with Michael Chekhov, the Russian-born nephew of the famous playwright Anton Chekhov. Although

Marilyn frustrated Chekhov with her habitual lateness, he acknowledged her talent and suggested she'd make a good Grushenka in a film version of Dostoyevsky's *The Brothers Karamazov,* a role that continued to fascinate Marilyn for the rest of her life. She told Chekhov, who'd been a student of Stanislavski, the father of Method acting, that she "wanted to be an artist, not an erotic freak." She didn't "want to be sold to the public as a celluloid aphrodisiac. It was all right for the first few years, but now I'm different."

If Marilyn hoped to change her image, it wasn't evident from the *Photoplay* magazine awards ceremony in 1953. Wedged into a skintight, tissue-thin gold lamé gown originally designed for Marilyn to wear in a scene that was ultimately cut from *Gentlemen Prefer Blondes,* Marilyn stole the spotlight from every other reigning Hollywood star in attendance that night. The "scandalous" gown, coupled with the patented Monroe walk, created a backlash of public condemnation. Joan Crawford, for one, announced in the press that Marilyn "must have mistaken the award ceremony for a burlesque show." One of Marilyn's few defenders was Betty Grable, a former Twentieth Century–Fox glamour queen well known for her World War II derrière pinup shot. Interviewed by a reporter, Grable accurately assessed Marilyn's key contribution to the world of cinema: "Why, Marilyn's the biggest thing that's happened in Hollywood in years. The movies were just sort of moving along, and all of a sudden, zowie, there was Marilyn. She's a shot in the arm for Hollywood."

Betty Grable had been cast opposite Marilyn — and Lauren Bacall — in *How to Marry a Millionaire,* which began shooting that April. Based on a bestselling 1951 novel by Doris Lilly, the movie follows the fortunes of three women who rent an expensive New York apartment and scheme to find themselves a trio of millionaire husbands. Doris Lilly met Monroe for the first time just after the *Photoplay* scandal had run its course and a week before shooting got underway on *How to Marry a Millionaire.*

"Famous Artists agent Charles Feldman joined us for lunch at the Café de Paris, Fox's commissary," recalled Doris. "I'd known Charlie for ages. He had a violent crush on Marilyn. They'd had a tryst several years before, but Marilyn had abruptly called it off. Charlie had great intuition. As early as 1950, he told me he knew this young actress named Marilyn Monroe and that she had superstar written all over her. He said she was shrewd, had good instincts, and knew how to create publicity for herself. He eventually became her agent, or at least one of them. At first he assigned her to Hugh French at Famous Artists, but then took her on himself. What I remember about my first meeting with Marilyn is that the commissary was jammed with all sorts of stars — Charlton Heston, Rita Hayworth, Montgomery Clift, Spencer Tracy, among others — and as soon as Marilyn walked in, they stopped eating and started staring, their forks frozen in midair. All motion ceased.

"The next day, I saw her at a Fox cocktail party. The studio bigwigs were all there, including Darryl F. Zanuck and Spyros Skouras, as well as the usual complement of Hollywood lawyers, press agents, talent scouts, publicists, journalists, what have you. And when Marilyn appeared, the place went stone dead. Everyone gaped. The center of the room cleared as she walked through. It was like the parting of the Red Sea, the same reaction she'd inspired the day before in the commissary. Considering her youth, it all seemed rather amazing."

During the making of the film, which was shot in Hollywood and New York, Doris spent a considerable amount of time with Marilyn and came to know her well despite Monroe's forever shifting moods and personality changes. "I'm not the first person to point out that Marilyn was a highly complex individual," noted Doris. "She could tell you a very revealing story about herself in the morning, and in the afternoon she'd relate the same story but with completely altered details. You never got the same story twice. In other words, the earth was forever shifting under her feet — and yours, if you were in her company. There was a mercurial quality to her sensibility that made it impossible to pin Marilyn down."

According to Doris, Joe DiMaggio marched to his own drummer. "He was carved of granite and never changed. He was set in his ways. That's not to say he wasn't an intriguing man. He was intriguing because he revealed so little of himself. Marilyn told you everything, and DiMaggio told you nothing, but ultimately they were both hieroglyphics. It was difficult, if not impossible, to read either one of them."

DiMaggio came and went during the filming of *How to Marry a Millionaire,* leaving Los Angeles on junkets to New York and Chicago, on business trips to San Francisco. Doris Lilly remembered that he visited the set only once. He stood in the back, hidden in the shadows, watching Marilyn like a hawk. Afterward they engaged in a loud argument in her dressing room. He felt her outfits in the film were far too revealing. Marilyn told Doris he'd voiced the same objection on the set of *Gentlemen Prefer Blondes.* It seemed to Doris Lilly as if Joe wanted to put Marilyn in a birdcage, to possess her, and the more he tried to curtail her freedom, the more she rebelled. He resented anyone he perceived as standing in the way of his relationship with her. One name on his enemies list was that of Natasha Lytess. Natasha was at Marilyn's side every night helping her rehearse her lines for the following day's shoot. Doris Lilly happened to be at Marilyn's Doheny Drive residence when DiMaggio confronted Lytess and said to her, "Why don't you find yourself another victim — haven't you stolen enough of Marilyn's money?" On a separate occasion when Lytess called the actress, he picked up the phone and told her, "If you wish to speak to Miss Monroe, contact her agent — don't call here."

Natasha Lytess told Doris Lilly that Marilyn needed her as a coach and that the actress lacked the confidence to "stand up" to DiMaggio. Joe countered Natasha's argument by pointing out that Marilyn didn't have enough faith in her own convictions and depended too heavily on coaches and would-be friends, anyone willing to offer advice of any kind. Doris more or less shared DiMaggio's view, attributing many of Monroe's difficulties on the set to her lack of discipline. She consistently showed up late for shooting, upsetting the director, the producer, and everyone else associated with the film. "They'd start shooting at eight in the morning," said Lilly, "and Marilyn would be at home sitting in her bathtub or getting dressed and applying makeup. And half the time she didn't have her lines memorized. One of the problems was that she couldn't sleep at night. She started taking sedatives, and we all know how that turned out. She became addicted and she began drinking, and the combination of alcohol and pharmaceuticals screwed her up. She never appeared in a film after *How to Marry a Millionaire* that finished shooting on schedule. It wasn't just her tardiness. It was also that she insisted on retake after retake. Each scene had to be shot over and over again. What saved her is that she had that 'certain something' that God gave her — it's what made her a star. Whatever it was, you had to adore her for it."

Above all, Marilyn was a free spirit, unrestrained by the conventions that dictate the behavioral patterns of so many others in her profession, especially those whose careers were inextricably tied to the studio system. "I'd never met anyone like her before," said Whitey Snyder, "and I knew almost all of Fox's leading female players. Long after she became an established star, she'd do things like jog to the Fox studio along Santa Monica Boulevard in a pair of baggy jeans, a scarf tied around her hair, and her face smeared with cold cream to prevent wrinkles. 'I don't know,' she'd joke, 'nobody stops for me. I can't get a ride.' She was quite the character.

Add this to her acting, her beauty, her being, her story, and her legacy, and you have the Hollywood immortal that she eventually became."

In April Joe DiMaggio met in New York with Walter O'Malley, owner of the Brooklyn Dodgers. To Joe's surprise, O'Malley offered him a contract to become manager of the team. O'Malley reasoned that with his super-celebrity status, DiMaggio would help draw fans to the ballpark. Joe declined the offer. He didn't want to be associated with another baseball organization located in the same city as the Yanks. He also wanted to spend more time with Marilyn, and becoming a manager would be more than an all-encompassing commitment. He had signed on to become West Coast vice president in charge of public relations for the Buitoni company, a fancy title that paid well but demanded little of his time. Essentially, he served as a greeter at the company's twice-annual national sales conference, with a few other mundane duties thrown in for good measure.

"While in New York or wherever else he had to be," said Doris Lilly, "DiMaggio called Marilyn ten times a day. He demanded to know what she was doing and whom she was seeing. He didn't trust her, and probably for good cause. There were always men around yearning to get into her panties, which she purportedly didn't wear. And many of them succeeded. I know for a fact that while DiMaggio was courting Marilyn, she was playing the field with men like Mel Tormé, Eddie Robinson Jr., Nico Minardos, Elia Kazan, and Twentieth Century–Fox fashion designer Billy Travilla. There were others as well, especially earlier in her career, pre–Joe DiMaggio, when men were constantly propositioning her, promising to put her in their films in exchange for a roll in the hay. According to Charlie Feldman, Marilyn had been pregnant on more than a few occasions and had undergone a number of abortions and miscarriages. "Over the years, I've read various psychological exposés exploring the reasons behind Marilyn's promiscuity. One book suggested she sought self-respect through the men she was able to attract and that she usually went with men she could look up to. Another book attributed her hypersexuality to her lifelong search for a father figure. A third said she bedded so many men because they afforded her a sense of completion, filling a void that had been with her since childhood. To my mind, all that analytic theorizing is nothing more than a lot of swill. The truth of the matter is that Marilyn just happened to have a healthy appetite for sex, maybe not with everyone, certainly not with the old oxen she slept with in order to advance her career, but in general it seems to have given her great pleasure. She wasn't at all uptight when it came to sex. I mention this because of something she said to me. 'There are times,' she observed, 'when all a girl wants and needs is a nice big stiff cock, no more and no less.' "

This is not to suggest that Marilyn couldn't differentiate between love and lust, desire and fulfillment. Although she claimed to enjoy her intimate encounters with Joe DiMaggio, she told Shelley Winters that she couldn't achieve a climax with him. "That's something very few men can seem to give me," she said. "Porfirio Rubirosa [the swarthy Dominican playboy] went at me all night, but even he didn't succeed. The only climax I usually get is the one I give myself." Marilyn confided in Truman Capote that DiMaggio was able to satisfy her orally. Whatever the extent of her fulfillment with him, it's clear that the sexual attraction between them provided a powerful link. She compared the perfection of his body to Michelangelo's David. He thought hers was, as he once told George Solotaire, "something only God could create."

Nevertheless one of the "few men" able to completely satisfy Marilyn sexually, an unlikely candidate at that, was Wall Street tycoon Paul Shields, whose stepdaughter "Rocky" had married actor Gary Cooper. Shields, born in 1889, had turned sixty-four by the time he met Marilyn in New York in 1953 at a birthday party for columnist Walter

Winchell. He saw her again in Los Angeles during a period when Joe DiMaggio had meetings in his hometown in conjunction with the founding of the Fisherman's National Bank of San Francisco, a project that never quite materialized.

In 1955 Marilyn told Truman Capote about her "two-night stand" with Shields, who had a well-deserved reputation in Hollywood as a bon vivant. A wealthy man (he owned a yacht and a private plane), Shields sat on the boards of a half dozen banks and, as Capote acknowledged, "probably busted up more marriages than Casanova. Marilyn went with him because she knew of his reputation. She wasn't disappointed. She couldn't believe that a man his age could be so energetic and accomplished. She proclaimed him the best lover she'd ever had. Of course, she made the same declaration regarding Joe DiMaggio. So who's to say?"

Joe, meanwhile, indulged in his own abbreviated sexual interlude, probably the only one he had during his courtship of Marilyn. Ironically, it took place at nearly the same time as Marilyn's fling with Frank Shields. Amy Lipps (not her real name), a twenty-two-year-old graduate student from Ocean Grove, New Jersey, had flown to San Francisco to spend a few days with an older brother then residing in Northern California. In the course of her visit, Amy, who, un-coincidentally, bore a striking resemblance to Marilyn Monroe, happened to meet Joe DiMaggio.

Recalling the episode, Lipps said she and her brother had spent the afternoon sightseeing in San Francisco and wound up eating dinner at the DiMaggio-owned family restaurant on Fisherman's Wharf. "Growing up in New Jersey," she remarked, "my brother had always loved the Yankees, so when Joe DiMaggio came over to our table and introduced himself, my brother nearly fell off his chair. I wasn't into baseball, and although I'd heard of Joe DiMaggio, I knew very little about him. He seemed cordial enough. He said the way I looked reminded him of film actress Marilyn Monroe, which is something I'd been told numerous times. One thing led to another, and my brother and I spent the rest of the night barhopping with Joe, listening to him reminisce about his days as a ballplayer. At the end of the evening, he asked if he could see me again the following day and take me to dinner. My brother didn't seem to mind, so I agreed to meet him. The dinner turned out to be at his house near the restaurant. We had a lot to drink, and I ended up spending the night. He was a good lover — very determined, and he took his time. In the morning, he asked if I could stay a day longer, but I'd already booked my return flight. We exchanged a few telephone calls, but then my brother called from California to tell me he'd seen a news item as to how Joe DiMaggio and Marilyn Monroe were considering marriage. I wrote Joe and asked him to explain himself. I never heard back. Until my brother called, I had no idea Joe and Marilyn were involved. He'd mentioned her, but only in passing. I suppose it explains why he was attracted to me."

On May 30, 1953, Memorial Day, an event took place that would play an instrumental role in the DiMaggio-Monroe relationship. While fishing by himself at Bodega Bay, a shallow, rocky inlet of the Pacific Ocean an hour north of San Francisco, Michael Frank DiMaggio drowned. His body was found floating alongside his fishing boat, a hundred yards from shore. He was forty-five, six years older than Joe. Like his father, Michael was short but stocky, with muscular arms and legs. Although no autopsy was performed, a police report filed by local officials indicated that he might have suffered a heart attack before hitting his head against the side of the vessel and plummeting unconscious into the sea.

Joe was vacationing in Mexico when the accident occurred. His sister Marie reached him by telephone, and he made immediate plans to return to San Francisco. He called Marilyn in Los Angeles, where she was about to celebrate her twenty-seventh birthday with Bebe Goddard. Marilyn flew north the following day and joined Joe at his Beach Street home. The house became a virtual funeral parlor, with waves of friends and family drifting in and out, speaking Sicilian Italian and broken English, smoking Italian stogies, and drinking homemade Italian wine. Of the immediate family, nobody took Mike's death harder than Joe. Overnight he seemed to age twenty years. He couldn't sleep, nor could he hold down his food. Marilyn hadn't seen the vulnerable side of Joe before. In her eyes, his weakness became his strength. She consoled him. It was almost a reversal of roles. His family members looked on as she sat in his lap, her arms around his shoulders, her head nestled gently against the side of his face. The certitude and self-assuredness he'd demonstrated since meeting Marilyn had for now been replaced by self-doubt and indecision. When she returned home to North Doheny Drive, Joe went with her. He gave her a belated and unlikely birthday present: a set of golf clubs. He told her that Mike had been a great golfer, and had he wanted to play baseball, he would've been better than the three brothers who did play the game. Marilyn felt touched. For the first time, she began to take seriously his offer, which he'd made more than once, that they get married.

Joe Jr. and his friend George Millman, the

son of Mort Millman, Dorothy Arnold's agent, met Joe and Marilyn at the airport in a limousine when they returned from San Francisco. George, three years older than Joey, observed that the relationship between Marilyn and Joe Jr. seemed "extremely warm and affectionate. They were unusually close. Joey and his father, however, didn't get along. They didn't understand each other." Yet, as Millman recalled, when Joe and Marilyn arrived in Los Angeles from San Francisco following the death of DiMaggio's brother, Joe appeared to have changed. He seemed to have softened. It was as if a wall had come down.

Their reconciliation, if it can be called that, didn't last long. Within a week or two, the wall went back up. DiMaggio returned to his old form, constantly criticizing Joey. Nothing Joe Jr. did measured up to his father's high standards. He wasn't tall enough or strong enough or aggressive enough. He was ten pounds overweight, which in his father's eyes made him "fat." Encouraged by Marilyn, Joey had begun to lift weights. Joe insisted he wasn't lifting enough weight to make a difference. "DiMaggio men are always muscular," Joe chided his son. "So get with the program."

In mid-June Joey went off to summer camp on Catalina Island. As he'd done many times before, he had to shoulder the burden that came with having a family name like DiMaggio. Ned Wynn, grandson of the comedic actor Ed Wynn, attended the same camp and remembered Joey as "a roly-poly kid . . . who was expected to be the best softball player of all the campers, but because he was only average, he was razzed. Even though I was supposed to be his friend, I found myself standing on the sidelines razzing him with the rest of the campers."

"As a teenager," said Joe Jr., "you never become entirely inured to that kind of treatment, though I'd certainly experienced enough of it — having my belongings stolen, being pushed and poked whenever I stood on a line, being heckled and jeered and laughed at. Kids can be very cruel. This is the kind of stuff that went on in camp all the time. It helped that Marilyn wrote to me and sent care packages filled with candy, cookies, cashews, and paperback books. 'I'd send you comic books,' she wrote, 'but I don't want you to read junk. It's bad enough your father's addicted to them.' "

Joe DiMaggio likewise sent his son a care package that summer. It consisted of a deck of cards, a copy of *Lucky to Be a Yankee,* his 1946 "autobiography" (prepared with the help of a ghostwriter), a new baseball mitt, and a published guide to the martial arts that he'd inscribed, "To Joey, Don't let anyone ever pick on you. Love, Dad."

In the summer of 1953, Doris Lilly telephoned Marilyn from New York to find out how things were going with Joe DiMaggio and to say she'd seen a recent cover story on Monroe in *Cosmopolitan* magazine and another by <u>Bennett Cerf</u> in *Esquire*. Marilyn told Doris that Joe "was up to his old tricks." He'd sneered condescendingly at the *Cosmo* and *Esquire* articles because neither magazine had paid Marilyn. "Where's the money?" he'd asked her. He said the same thing every time a periodical ran a profile of her. He even called Harry Brand, publicity director at Fox, and asked him why Marilyn never got paid for these articles, and Brand had patiently explained that it simply didn't work like that. And then, in addition, Joe continued to harp on Marilyn's attire. Her blouses were too tight and her dresses too revealing. Where were all the clothes he'd bought for her? But the biggest bone of contention between them involved the Julius and Ethel Rosenberg case.

The Rosenbergs had been put to death on June 19 because they'd been convicted of slipping the Soviets top-secret documents related to the construction of the atomic bomb. It was that whole Red Scare–Cold War controversy. The Rosenbergs had two small boys. Marilyn didn't believe Ethel Rosenberg had a hand in it or that Julius Rosenberg had access to the kind of information the government claimed he did. "What he gave the Russians," she said, "wasn't enough to build a firecracker, no less an atomic bomb." By contrast, Joe DiMaggio couldn't stop fuming about "those two goddamn commie pinkos. They should've chopped off their arms and legs and put their corpses on display at Yankee Stadium for the whole world to see what we do to spies and traitors."

The Yankee Clipper's bullying tactics and volatile nature came in handy that August when Marilyn found herself on location at Jasper National Park in Banff, Canada, immersed in the shooting of a contrived, cliché-ridden Western, *River of No Return*, costarring Robert Mitchum, whom she'd known casually while involved with Jim Dougherty. From the start, the film was fraught with personality conflicts, particularly between Marilyn Monroe and Otto Preminger, the notoriously controlling and surly director, quoted by Hedda Hopper as saying, "Directing Marilyn Monroe is like directing a dog. You need fourteen takes to get the desired results." When Marilyn read the quote, she cried.

Marilyn intensely disliked both Otto Preminger and her role as a guitar-strumming frontier dance-hall girl. Preminger found little to admire about Monroe and felt the film failed to measure up to his talents. Most annoying for the director was the presence of Natasha Lytess, whom Preminger tried, unsuccessfully, to have banned from the set. Monroe's contract stipulated that Lytess was to have the right of "approval" for every take that involved Marilyn. Unable to rid himself of the drama coach, Preminger took out his hostility on Marilyn, subjecting her to angry tirades and loud outbursts. Talking to Whitey Snyder (who was on the set with his wife, Twentieth Century–Fox wardrobe chief Marjorie Plecher), Marilyn referred to Preminger as an "insufferable ass" and said he belonged in a stable. Preminger called Marilyn "a big-bosomed pain in the butt." As for Natasha Lytess, Preminger dubbed her "an absolute know-nothing. The only thing she's taught Monroe is that lips-apart, eyes-half-shut facial expression, which is supposed to connote sexiness but which to me looks like a half-assed imitation of Greta Garbo."

That was the least of it. Preminger terrorized Marilyn to total immobility. She became convinced that Preminger didn't want her in the picture and would do or say anything to get rid of her. She later told Shelley Winters that he began using obscene language, implying that she lacked talent, and the only reason she'd been suggested for the film was that she'd "sucked and fucked" half the executives at Fox. It reached the point where Marilyn became convinced that Preminger planned to do away with her while she was going over some rapids on a raft. Usually stunt men and women performed these dangerous action shots at the end of the picture, but Preminger decided to do them at the beginning using the actors themselves. Marilyn became suspicious.

One morning Marilyn slipped on a pier and tore a ligament in her left leg. She claimed she couldn't walk. Filming had to be suspended. Marilyn called Joe DiMaggio in New York, and the next day he arrived in Banff, accompanied by George Solotaire. Not knowing Monroe had invited DiMaggio, Whitey Snyder thought he'd come ostensibly to keep an eye on Marilyn and the handsome Robert Mitchum. However, he soon realized that Joe's purpose for being there, aside from spending time with the girl he loved, was to keep Otto Preminger in check and to stop him from continuing his abusive verbal attacks on Marilyn. Indeed, after DiMaggio's arrival, Preminger calmed down and ceased his public remonstrations against the actress.

Doctors placed Marilyn's injured leg in a walking cast, gave her a cane, a pair of crutches, and a wheelchair. DiMaggio became her health attendant, squiring her from their bungalow to medical offices and whisking her by waiting photographers. Marilyn convinced him to pose with her for a camera crew from *Look* magazine. After she recovered sufficiently to go back to work, DiMaggio and Solotaire spent their days fishing for salmon, canoeing, and golfing. Joe steered clear of Natasha Lytess, but he befriended eleven-year-old Tommy Rettig, a child actor in the film. Initially, Rettig, who later found fame playing Timmy on the television series *Lassie,* avoided Marilyn off the set (allegedly warned to keep away from her by his priest), but he couldn't resist the urge to meet DiMaggio, and relations with Marilyn improved gradually. When the entire cast and crew moved from the bungalows they'd inhabited in Jasper National Park to the Mount Royal Hotel in Banff, Joe, George, Marilyn, and Robert Mitchum became permanent fixtures in the card room playing board games and gin rummy. When the picture ended, and Joe and Marilyn got back to Los Angeles, they occasionally socialized with Mitchum and his wife. Mitchum was one of the few Hollywood actors DiMaggio appeared not to resent. Mitchum, in turn, a true baseball fiend, held DiMaggio in high esteem. As for Marilyn, he termed her a "kind of child-woman, but a delightful one at that."

Whitey Snyder admired Joe DiMaggio as well and felt he was good for Marilyn. "My wife and I always had great affection for both Joe and Marilyn," said Whitey. "Marilyn was enormously giving. I recall when somebody at Fox, a worker, needed money for an operation to save his kid's eyesight, she immediately wrote a check for $1,000 and handed it to him. She always supported the underdog. Joe saw past her glittering façade and appreciated her for her fine inner qualities, which wasn't the case with most of the men she knew. He could be difficult at times. He felt people exploited her and that she was gullible enough to let them step all over her, which in a way was true. But in trying to protect her, he went too far. He tried to control her, and of all the people in the world, she was the one person you couldn't control, certainly not by force."

One day Whitey and his wife went on a train ride through the Canadian Rockies with Joe and Marilyn. "It was one of those tourist deals, two railroad cars and a caboose," said Whitey. "The scenery was breathtaking. At a certain point I said to Marilyn, 'Do you see those mountains, darling? If you and Joe went to the other side of those mountains and built a cabin and had some kids, you'd both live happily ever after.' I meant it because I felt Marilyn truly loved Joe, and I didn't think she felt all that fulfilled by the film business. She didn't say anything right away. She didn't want Joe to hear her. But then she leaned over and whispered in my ear. 'I wish I could, Whitey,' she said. 'But I can't do that. I just can't.' "

Although Monroe and Otto Preminger never resolved their differences, they managed to coexist long enough to complete *River of No Return*. Years later, a reporter for the *Los Angeles Times* asked Preminger if he would ever make another film with Monroe. "No," he stated emphatically, "I would not — not for any amount of money." Asked by the same journalist whether she'd ever agree to work with Preminger again, Marilyn responded, "I would, but only if he were the last director left in Hollywood. If he wasn't, I wouldn't."

Joe and Marilyn spent four days in New York in early September before heading back to Los Angeles. Their first night in town, Toots Shor gave a private reception for them in the party room over the tavern. One of the guests was Joe McCarthy, DiMaggio's manager when he first joined the Yanks. McCarthy told Marilyn, "It's a pity you never saw Joe play ball. You missed something. He was the best, the absolute best." The next day the couple attended a ballgame at Yankee Stadium. There they met up with Paul Baer, a friend of Joe's, and Paul's brother, Rudy Baer. Born in Milan, Italy, Paul Baer owned a porcelain factory in Lower Manhattan and played golf with DiMaggio whenever the ballplayer happened to visit New York. He'd known DiMaggio since the days of his marriage to Dorothy Arnold. He also knew Joe Jr., who was the same age as his own son.

"I hadn't met Marilyn Monroe before," said Paul Baer, "but I can vouch for her beauty. We were seated in the boxes directly behind the Yankee dugout. Rudy and I arrived first. Joe and Marilyn didn't get there until the third inning. When they walked in, the stadium erupted like a volcano. The pandemonium didn't cease until Joe and Marilyn both stood and acknowledged the crowd. And then for the duration of the game, many of the Yankee players would stand on the dugout steps facing the crowd for a better view of Marilyn. Not that Joe DiMaggio was exactly a slouch. Here's a guy who floated across the baseball diamond like a butterfly. One season he struck out only seven times. Can you fathom that? That's almost as astounding as his fifty-six-consecutive-game hitting streak. Bob Feller, the great Cleveland Indians Hall of Fame pitcher, used to autograph baseballs by signing his name under the phrase 'I struck out Joe DiMaggio.' Joe and the blonde made some kind of team. Never mind that Marilyn didn't seem to understand the finer points of the game. I think she tried to please Joe, but she just couldn't get into baseball the way he would've wanted her to."

As the game progressed, random kids, mostly young boys, kept drifting over for Joe's autograph. "Joe was very accommodating," said Baer. "He was always nice with kids, always patient, always gave them a smile and a pat on the back. His problem in life was that he couldn't do the same for his own kid. I never understood it. He was wonderful to all his little fans, but on a more personal level, he was the worst father God ever created. And to be honest, Joey Jr.'s mother wasn't much better."

While in New York, Joe met with Bernie Kamber. He told Bernie he loved his son and was concerned because Dorothy Arnold had a new man in tow every other week. He felt Joey would be hurt and confused by her carousel of lovers. "I told him," said Bernie, "Joey would be less confused if he could spend more time with his father. In fact, Joey was in New York at that time visiting with a friend of his from military school. His school didn't start until mid-September. On their last afternoon in the city, Joe and Marilyn took the boy to Rumpelmayer's, a fancy pastry shop on Central Park South. Joe was too cheap to buy Joey an ice cream soda. He wanted to go to a regular coffee shop. So Marilyn slipped the kid a twenty-dollar bill. Joe saw the transaction and told Marilyn off. She didn't know the value of money and so forth. When I heard the story, I took a deep breath. 'What a pisser!' I thought."

Every October Black-Foxe Military Institute sponsored an annual Parents Day, when the parents of students visited the campus and sat in on classes. "Everyone came," said Joe Jr. "I saw Jerry Lewis and Dorothy Lamour, whose sons attended the academy. Neither my father nor mother ever showed up for that particular event. It bothered me."

After Marilyn Monroe entered the picture, Dorothy Arnold, perhaps out of guilt, perhaps out of jealousy, made a bit of an effort to see her son, even if she didn't visit him on Parents Day. She and Lillian Millman, her agent's wife, would occasionally take Joey and George along on overnight trips to Baja California. "My mother had some friends down there," said Joey, "and at night they'd all go out drinking. My mother would come back roaring drunk. She'd get loud. She'd start singing, telling stupid jokes, and begin flirting with any man who passed her way. Back home in LA, she'd continue to drink. She'd show off, do handstands in front of my friends. But she wouldn't be wearing any panties. She'd be naked from the waist down. It was humiliating. I couldn't figure out if my mother was trying in some fashion to compete with Marilyn Monroe. It was ironic. Here was Marilyn, sex symbol of the century, and by comparison to my mother, she seemed demure and innocent. I hate to admit it, but my mother was little more than a tramp."

CHAPTER 7

In the spring of 1953, Michael Chekhov, Marilyn Monroe's most recent drama coach, introduced her to Lotte Goslar, a mime and movement teacher from Dresden, Germany, who conducted private and group classes at the Turnabout Theatre in Hollywood, where she also performed. Chekhov thought Marilyn could benefit from taking Goslar's course. Goslar placed her in a class with ten other students and tutored her individually as well, working with her on *River of No Return* and on many of her subsequent films. In addition to being an instructor, Goslar took on the twin roles of friend and confidante.

"Marilyn seemed to enjoy my class," said Goslar. "She wore no makeup, only a touch of lipstick. She was usually late but always managed to show up. She had considerable ability and was serious about her craft, but she was insecure with regard to her skill and even regarding her beauty. She didn't think she was pretty and needed constant reassurance. She was eager to learn and grateful whenever anyone took the trouble to help her develop her talent. She also had a wonderful little giggle, and when she didn't know what to say, she giggled. Michael Chekhov had recommended that she read *The Thinking Body,* an important book on movement by Mabel Elsworth Todd, and she carried it with her at all times. One evening after class, I went for coffee with her. She revealed to me what she'd previously told Michael, that she hoped to become a bona fide actress, not a dilettante or even a so-called Hollywood star. 'Blond hair and breasts,' she said, 'that's how I started. I couldn't act.' Now she wanted to learn how to express her inner feelings through gestures and body movement. I assured her I would do my utmost to teach her how to use her body as an instrument of expression as well as a thing of beauty."

Goslar recalled being introduced to Joe DiMaggio following one of the group sessions, which met twice weekly. "He would sometimes collect Marilyn after class," said Goslar. "On one occasion, my car had broken down so Marilyn offered to have DiMaggio drive me home when he picked her up. She told me he'd just returned from Washington, DC, having been a guest at a White House dinner party given by President Dwight Eisenhower. Joe struck me as soft spoken and polite, not what I expected of a former baseball player, though Marilyn let me know he wasn't always that gentle. She later told me he was prone to insane bouts of jealousy, such as the time they bumped into her one-time lover at a party, and DiMaggio 'accidentally on purpose' spilled a drink on him and then, an hour later, 'accidentally' stepped on his foot. Still, there was a certain mystique about the ballplayer, a quality Marilyn shared. It set them apart as a couple. They were both extremely good-looking. He didn't have traditional movie star good looks, but he had a certain masculine quality that stood out, a kind of craggy Gary Cooper–like appearance that can only be described as sexy. They had much in common, but there were also major differences. For one thing, DiMaggio was always punctual, and Marilyn was never on time. Except for his fits of jealousy, he appeared to be very sure of himself, Marilyn much less so. He was interested in Marilyn but not in her career, other than to insist that everyone in Hollywood was corrupt and out to use her. He completely underestimated the degree to which Marilyn valued her career. She defined herself as an actress. She and Joe had different priorities and interests. He'd had his fill of public adoration, and she pursued it with a passion. He didn't like books, and she was a compulsive reader. He seemed set in his ways, whereas Marilyn constantly altered her persona in an effort to expand her vistas. All in all, I wouldn't say it was a match made in heaven, though they appeared to be bonded in some curious, indefinable fashion."

Following her return to Los Angeles in the fall of 1953, Marilyn resumed classes with Goslar. She and DiMaggio were living together at the apartment on North Doheny. In the early morning, while Marilyn luxuriated in her bathtub, Joe would buy coffee and doughnuts at a local bakery and meet up with Whitey Snyder, who would return home with Joe to share breakfast with the couple.

Whitey remembered that when Joe wasn't around, Marilyn would listen to and sing along with Les Brown's popular recording of a song (written by Ben Homer and Alan Courtney, published in 1941) called "Joltin' Joe DiMaggio," the lyrics of which included the refrain "He'll live in baseball's Hall of Fame / He got there blow by blow / Our kids will tell their kids his name / Joltin' Joe DiMaggio."

Whitey asked Marilyn if she'd ever performed her little number for Joe, and she said she hadn't. She thought it might offend him. "No it won't," responded Snyder. "He'll appreciate it." So after breakfast one morning, with Whitey Snyder present, Marilyn played the record and went into her song-and-dance routine. "Joe got a big bang out of it," said Whitey. "He couldn't stop laughing. It really was cute. Marilyn in one of her half dozen terry cloth robes doing this jig and singing along with the recording. I never forgot that scene of joy."

Whitey Snyder acknowledged Marilyn's comedic skills. "She was a wonderful mimic and very funny, a bit on the risqué side," he said. "Discussing her romance with Joe DiMaggio, she once described herself as 'the ballplayer's ball player.' And I recall Truman Capote telling me about a conversation he had with Marilyn during which he admitted to her he'd gone to bed with actor Errol Flynn. 'Flynn zigzags,' answered Marilyn. 'He's bisexual.' She mentioned a Hollywood party she attended at which Flynn played 'You Are My Sunshine' on the piano with his penis. She then added that had it been Joe DiMaggio's penis, he probably would've played something a lot more substantial."

Lotte Goslar remembered a less humorous moment. Marilyn called one night and asked her to come over. She sounded concerned. Whitey Snyder and Joe DiMaggio were both there with Marilyn when Goslar arrived. So was Sidney Skolsky. They were later joined by DiMaggio's attorney Loyd Wright, currently working for Monroe as well. Riding the success of *Gentlemen Prefer Blondes* and *How to Marry a Millionaire*, Marilyn had expected to be offered a role in *The Egyptian,* scheduled to start shooting in early 1954.

"As Marilyn explained it that evening, not only had Darryl Zanuck bypassed her for that film, the role he offered her was that of a prim, angrily virtuous schoolteacher who becomes a 'hoochy-koochy' saloon dancer in a motion picture called *The Girl in Pink Tights,* costarring Frank Sinatra." The film was a remake of a 1947 Betty Grable picture called *Mother Wore Tights.*

"The script, which the studio at first refused to send her, was full of breathy suggestive lines. Marilyn wrote the word 'trash' across the title page and sent it back. The studio's jocular in-house response was, 'Well, that never stopped her before.' Marilyn notified Twentieth Century–Fox that she had no intention of reporting for the first day of rehearsals on December 15, eliciting a predictable reply from Zanuck reminding her that she was under contract and had no choice in the matter. If she refused the role, she risked being placed on suspension and possibly having her contract terminated.

"The question was what to do? Should Marilyn simply refuse to accept the role and risk everything, or should she agree to appear in the movie and use it as a bargaining chip for a future film of her choice and a more lucrative contract? Joe DiMaggio had no intention of allowing her to appear in yet another film that exploited her sexuality. 'You have to play hardball with those bastards if you want to win,' he remarked. He said he received demeaning endorsement offers all the time, most recently from a men's hair-coloring firm and another from a denture cream manufacturer, and he routinely turned them down. He advised Marilyn to do the same. Sidney Skolsky agreed. 'It's called show business,' he pointed out, 'with the emphasis on business. Tell them to go fuck themselves.'

"The *Pink Tights* offer was a slap in the face, a debasement," said Goslar, "the more so because Marilyn had become one of the highest grossing and most popular actresses in the industry. She was caught in the cruel and relentless treadmill of fame and stardom. She had so much more to offer than her looks. I think it was earlier that year the Italian film industry gave her an award for one of her pictures. I don't recall which one. I happened to be at the ceremony in Hollywood, and when they announced Marilyn's name, Anna Magnani, seated in the audience, shouted *'Putana!'* — whore. Hollywood refused to grant her the respect she deserved. And that more than anything is what she sought."

Lotte Goslar advised Marilyn to turn down the film and hold out for a more challenging role. Loyd Wright felt that while they would probably suspend Marilyn, they would just as quickly reinstate her. Whitey Snyder made it unanimous. "Why don't you and Joe get married," he said, "and see what happens? I guarantee Zanuck will come crawling."

Zanuck came crawling well before Joe and Marilyn became husband and wife. He dispatched members of his staff to Doheny Drive to try to convince Marilyn to sign on for *Pink Tights*. An irate Joe DiMaggio intercepted Zanuck's emissaries at the front door. Under no circumstances, he informed them, would Marilyn do the film. That was her final decision.

Although Twentieth Century–Fox didn't officially suspend Marilyn until early January, both she and DiMaggio realized the letter would arrive and that her weekly payroll checks would stop coming. Joe told her she needn't worry — they would get married, and he would take care of her. They could live in the house on Beach Street in San Francisco, have a boatload of babies, and grow old together. In fact, he was prepared to fly with her to Reno and get married immediately. In September 1953 she agreed to become Joe's wife, but she wasn't ready to set a date.

"As much as she loved him — and she did love him — Marilyn didn't seem overjoyed at the prospect of becoming Mrs. DiMaggio," said Lotte Goslar. "She foresaw problems. She realized he had contempt for Hollywood and everything related to it, and while she herself disliked aspects of her profession, she knew full well she couldn't just walk away from it and become a full-time housewife. As she put it, 'I'm not Dorothy Arnold,' a reference to his first wife, who did just that. And that's what Joe wanted. He wanted her to become his housewife, and it just wasn't going to happen, not the way he wanted it and certainly not without a number of concessions on both sides. And neither of them was very willing to compromise. He convinced himself that it was his responsibility to save her from a lifetime of servitude to the devils that controlled the evil empire called Hollywood. He wanted as little to do with Hollywood as possible.

"In early November, for example, DiMaggio refused to escort Marilyn to the Los Angeles premiere of *How to Marry a Millionaire.* Marilyn reacted by demanding that he remove his clothes from her apartment, but he apologized, and once again, as she'd done so often, she forgave him. As retribution, however, she made him take her to the Hollywood opening of the play *Call Me Madam.* And after the play, he treated her to a late supper at Chasen's. You might say they were kindred spirits with opposing points of view."

On November 25, Joe's thirty-ninth birthday, Marilyn gave him a gold medallion upon which she had ordered a jeweler to inscribe a line from *The Little Prince,* the fable by Antoine de Saint-Exupéry: "True love is visible not to the eye but to the heart for eyes may be deceived." "I like it," said DiMaggio, "but what the hell does it mean?"

Joe and Marilyn traveled to San Francisco together to spend Thanksgiving with his family and friends. They had their holiday meal at Joe's house and were joined by (among others) Frank "Lefty" O'Doul, his former manager with the San Francisco Seals. O'Doul had been a star outfielder during the 1920s and 1930s; his .349 lifetime batting average remains the fourth best in baseball history — and 24 points higher than DiMaggio's. Reno Barsocchini, a former bartender at the DiMaggio family restaurant, was there too. Lefty and Reno were like family to DiMaggio; both had opened North Beach bistros of their own. Reno's establishment, on Post Street next door to the Ambassador Health Club, had become Joe's West Coast version of Toots Shor's.

After carving the turkey, which had been prepared by Marie, Joe announced that he and Marilyn were planning to tie the knot. Reno stood and raised his glass of wine. "Here's to Joe and Marilyn," he said. "At least there'll be one looker in the DiMaggio household." After dinner, "the looker" helped Marie with the dishes. When an Associated Press reporter, having heard of the possible nuptials, asked Marilyn if she intended to get married to the Yankee Clipper, she said, "It could be. I intend to remain in pictures, but I'll eventually become a housewife, too."

Back in Los Angeles, following Thanksgiving, Marilyn and Joe had brunch with Inez Melson, Monroe's new business manager. DiMaggio had given Inez his stamp of approval, largely because Melson shared his negative opinion of Natasha Lytess. In any event, she was undoubtedly preferable to Doc Goddard, who'd fulfilled the same function until Melson took over. Not that Doc had been dishonest, but he was, after all, the man who'd sexually abused Marilyn as a child, although that story too seemed to change with every telling.

Soon after assuming her new position, Inez convinced Marilyn to appoint her as Gladys Baker's guardian. As such, she made frequent trips to visit Marilyn's mother at Rockhaven and made certain her needs were met. One day, the three of them — Monroe, DiMaggio, and Melson — set out on a drive to Rockhaven to spend the afternoon with Gladys. As Joe later reported to George Solotaire, "Mrs. Baker seemed quite pleased to see her daughter and even more pleased when Marilyn told her we were going to be married. On the other hand, she didn't seem to remember that Marilyn had been married once before."

Lotte Goslar remembered visiting Joe and Marilyn at home during this period. "Marilyn seemed unusually triste," she said. "I thought it might be related to their recent trip to Rockhaven." As they sat and chatted, the reason for Monroe's sudden mood shift became evident. Seeing her mother again had reminded the actress of her birth father. "I hadn't heard the name Stanley Gifford before," said Goslar, "and apparently Joe hadn't either."

In bits and pieces Marilyn revealed how, in 1945, while still married to Jim Dougherty, she'd telephoned Gifford and said, "This is Norma Jeane, Gladys's daughter." He hung up on her. Then, in 1951, she learned that he'd gotten married and moved to a farm in the town of Hemet on the outskirts of Palm Springs. She decided to confront him. With Natasha Lytess along for moral support, Marilyn drove from Hollywood in the direction of Palm Springs. When they reached Riverside, she pulled into a gas station and called Gifford from a pay phone to announce that she was on her way. Gifford's wife answered the phone and said, "He refuses to see you. He suggests you contact his lawyer in Los Angeles if you have any questions. Do you want his number?"

Marilyn's revelation startled Lotte Goslar as well as Joe, and in some strange sense explained the actress's attachment to Natasha

Lytess. Even if she wasn't the consummate drama coach, she had been there for her when Marilyn most needed her. It didn't diminish DiMaggio's dispassion for the woman, but he now understood the reason behind Marilyn's excessive loyalty to her.

In late November 1953 Lytess asked Monroe for $5,000 to help pay for surgery she'd undergone to correct a back problem, and this time Marilyn flatly refused to help, suggesting instead that she turn to Twentieth Century–Fox for the money. Although she was no longer on Fox's payroll, the studio had continued to absorb a portion of Natasha's living expenses. DiMaggio used Lytess's request to distance Marilyn even further from the drama coach. When Marilyn stopped just short of firing her, Joe lashed out at her. "Either she goes, or I go!" he yelled. "Don't threaten me, Joe," Marilyn countered.

Natasha would tell Lotte Goslar that if Marilyn married DiMaggio, she would live to regret it. "It can't possibly succeed," she said. "He becomes infuriated if you're a minute late for an appointment, and Marilyn's usually hours behind schedule. And then he's jealous of every man who even looks at Marilyn. She gets five thousand fan letters a week, including mail from Arab sultans and Texas oil barons, and he reads them all to see if anyone's coming on to her. And that's only the tip of the iceberg."

As early as 1950, Hugh Hefner, a native of Chicago and a copywriter at *Esquire,* envisioned the framework — tastefully photographed nudes amid well-written articles and short fiction — for the men's magazine he eventually called *Playboy.* With borrowed funds and whatever savings he could scrape together, Hefner launched his trend-setting magazine in December 1953. For the front cover of *Playboy*'s first issue and as its first centerfold, he chose none other than Marilyn Monroe.

Displayed prominently in the (originally titled) "Sweetheart of the Month" section of the publication was Marilyn's nude calendar shot. Within days of its initial appearance, the magazine sold out. The "Sweetheart of the Month" feature soon became known as the "Playmate of the Month."

"Like every other full-blooded American male," said Hugh Hefner, "I was well aware of the Tom Kelley nude calendar spread of Marilyn Monroe. It had never been published in a magazine, so I contacted John Baumgarth, owner of the calendar company that controlled the rights to the photo, and made an appointment to see him. He lived in Chicago, as did I, so I drove to his office and told him what I wanted and acquired the publication rights for five hundred dollars. I acquired another Monroe shot or two from him as well for an additional thousand dollars. It was the best investment I ever made, because by the end of 1953, when *Playboy* first materialized, Marilyn had become a major star. That nude calendar shot emerged as the most famous pinup of the twentieth century. Marilyn became the woman most women in the world want to resemble in terms of sex appeal."

The irony of Hugh Hefner's connection to Marilyn Monroe is that they never met. His brother studied acting with her in New York in the mid-1950s at the Actors Studio. Joe DiMaggio visited the Playboy Mansion in Los Angeles on several occasions after Monroe's death, indicating that he harbored no resentment against Hefner for his use of her nude image in the magazine. But the Monroe-Hefner connection doesn't end there. When he heard that the burial vault next to Marilyn's at Westwood Memorial Park Cemetery was still available, Hefner purchased it. "It just seems fitting," he observed, "that I should spend an eternity with Marilyn, given her tremendous contribution to the magazine's success."

"Late in 1953," noted Lotte Goslar, "Marilyn reaffirmed her commitment to Joe DiMaggio. She called me at three in the morning — not an unusual time for her — and told me how sweet, kind, and gentlemanly he could be. On the other side, she added, there were moments when he bored her to death, particularly when he talked about baseball and nothing else. Yet when he wasn't around, she missed him. She even missed their arguments. She'd grown accustomed to his paternalistic guidance and the protective side of his personality. She imagined that if she had a father, he'd be protective of her in the same way as Joe. And here was a father figure with whom she could have sex. And the sex was pretty damn good, if she had to say so herself. In essence, Joe DiMaggio filled a dual role in Marilyn's life, that of father and lover, a dangerous combination, especially considering that he seemed to be obsessed with her at times."

When the couple arrived in San Francisco to celebrate Christmas and bring in the New Year with Joe's family, Marilyn seemed nervous and run down. She hadn't shown up on the *Pink Tights* set on December 15, and the shoot had been put on hold. Her suspension would take effect on January 4, 1954, cutting her off from a studio system that seemed almost parental in its all-encompassing sweep. Although material possessions — furs, jewels, and clothes — generally meant little to Marilyn, her mood brightened a bit when, on Christmas Eve, Joe gave her a pair of diamond earrings, similar to a set he'd once bought for Dorothy Arnold.

On New Year's Eve the couple dined at the DiMaggio restaurant with Tom, Dom, and Reno Barsocchini. Later that night, Joe reportedly told Marilyn he wanted to marry her within the next two weeks. They'd talked about it for months now, and nothing had happened. She kept putting it off. If they didn't marry now, they'd never marry. He wanted to establish a definitive date. It should be a discreet, quiet ceremony — just a few friends and family members. No press, no publicity. Coming from DiMaggio, it sounded more like an ultimatum than a marriage proposal, which was just as well. The one thing Marilyn couldn't afford at this delicate juncture was to lose the only person she could depend on to be there for her no matter what. She agreed. They located a 1954 calendar and chose Thursday, January 14, as their wedding date.

Joe returned to Los Angeles with Marilyn to attend a film industry function at the Ambassador Hotel and a day later went back to San Francisco to make wedding arrangements. Marilyn remained in her apartment at North Doheny Drive. Approached by the press, she denied that she and Joe had a wedding date in mind. Marie, Joe's sister, told a San Francisco reporter named Alice Hoffman, "Marilyn Monroe's plain and honest and warm and shy, just like Joe. They were made for each other."

In his autobiography, movie director Elia Kazan remembered calling Marilyn in 1954. He had not spoken with her in several months; the two had carried on an informal but lengthy affair that began soon after their first meeting on the Fox lot in December 1950, within days of Johnny Hyde's death. Glad to hear Kazan's voice, Marilyn said she had some "wonderful news" and wanted to tell him in person. He invited her over. She showed up in his room at the Bel Air Hotel late at night.

"I'm going to get married," she announced. "I wanted to tell you first, because I'm not going to see you again."

"Who is it? Who are you talking about?" asked Kazan.

"Joe DiMaggio," she said. "He wants to marry me, and I really like him. He's not like these movie people. He's dignified." She went on about Joe for well over an hour, and Kazan could see she really did care for DiMaggio. "It was nice to see someone so happy and so hopeful," he wrote. And then, without another word, she took off her dress and climbed into bed with Kazan. "We made love," he remarked. "Congratulations and farewell."

What was probably most significant about Marilyn's liaison with Elia Kazan was that when she met him in late 1950, he was with a friend, a tall, distinguished-looking gentleman named Arthur Miller who, at age thirty-five, had already established himself as one of America's leading playwrights, having won the New York Drama Critics' Circle Award for *All My Sons* (1947) and the Pulitzer Prize for Drama for *Death of a Salesman* (1949).

Kazan and Miller were both staying at agent Charles Feldman's house. Later that week, Feldman gave a party honoring Arthur Miller. Among others, he invited Marilyn Monroe. She wore a dress that, according to Kazan, barely contained her. Describing Marilyn as "the most womanly woman I ever met," Miller spent most of the evening seated next to her on a couch, chatting away while massaging her feet, intermittently holding on to one of her toes. After the party, Marilyn called Natasha Lytess and said, "I met a man tonight . . . It was bam! It was like running into a tree. You know, like a cool drink when you've got a fever."

There were obstacles that stood in the way of a complete relationship in 1950, not the least of which was Miller's ten-year marriage to Mary Slattery, whom he'd met while an undergraduate at the University of Michigan. They had two children, Jane and Robert, who at that time were nine and six years old, respectively. Though Miller's marriage was in trouble — he and his wife were in therapy together — he wasn't ready to walk away from it.

Miller returned to New York, and Marilyn contented herself by sleeping with Kazan and corresponding with Arthur, whose first letter to her began: "Bewitch them with this image they ask for, but I hope and almost pray you won't be hurt in this game." He recommended that she purchase a copy of Carl Sandburg's biography of Abraham Lincoln. She bought both the book and a portrait of the former president and amused Miller by writing him that in junior high school she'd penned a paper on Lincoln that had won her a prize. She bought and read *Death of a Salesman,* and everything else Miller had ever written. She kept Miller's photo on a shelf behind her bed. But though he maintained an intense interest in her career and continued to correspond with her (often sending her wild love letters), it was Joe DiMaggio who came along and swooped her up.

On January 7, 1954, the day after she made love to Elia Kazan for the last time, Marilyn sent Arthur Miller a short note: "As you probably read in the press, I am going to marry Joe DiMaggio next week. Wish us luck. God knows we'll need it."

CHAPTER 8

Joe DiMaggio wanted to have a Roman Catholic priest conduct the marriage ceremony and to have it take place in the Church of Saints Peter and Paul, where fifteen years earlier he had married Dorothy Arnold. Marilyn had no objection to being married by a priest. But John J. Mitty, the archbishop of San Francisco, saw it otherwise. He informed DiMaggio by letter that the church refused to recognize the validity of his divorce from Dorothy, and if he remarried, the archbishop would have no choice but to have DiMaggio excommunicated. DiMaggio reacted to the archbishop's dire warning by telling George Solotaire, "I'd rather head for hell in due course than give up my Garden of Eden. In other words, let them excommunicate me."

Marilyn remained in Los Angeles while Joe, in San Francisco, worked out the final details of a wedding ceremony he hoped would remain as discreet and private as possible, particularly considering that it involved two

of the most watched and talked-about personages in America. He and Marilyn spoke
constantly by phone. She asked him if his
son knew about their plans. He didn't, said
Joe. Eager to tell Joe Jr. that she and his father
were going to be married, Marilyn visited
Black-Foxe Military Institute. She stood on
the sidelines with other parents watching the
Friday afternoon student parade, and when it
ended, she stretched out her arms and started
shouting his name over and over until he ran
to her for a smothering embrace. "She looked
great," said Joey, "her hair golden in the
sunlight, her warm smile, the incredible
figure. The older guys, the ones in high
school, couldn't stop staring at her. But she
ignored them. She was there for me and let
everyone know it."

They went out to dinner that night, the two
of them, and over dinner Marilyn told Joey
about the impending marriage. He slept over
in her apartment. "She gave me the bedroom," he recalled, "and she slept on the
couch in the living room." The next evening
she took Joey to a movie. "It was a World War
II flick," he continued. "Can you imagine sitting there in the dark, sharing a box of
popcorn and a Coke with Marilyn Monroe,
knowing that in a week or so she's going to
be your stepmother? How cool is that?" It
seemed almost implausible that no one in the
press had learned of Joe and Marilyn's wed-

ding plans. The closest anyone came was Hollywood scribe Louella Parsons, who posited, "If marriage is Joe DiMaggio and Marilyn Monroe's ultimate goal, and I hear it's just around the bend, they must resign themselves to the fact that it can't ever be a completely normal union. Marilyn will remain in show business and Joe will not be able to take it."

"Marilyn resented the column," said Lotte Goslar, "while Joe DiMaggio dismissed it as 'a bunch of newspaper talk.' For myself, I believed Marilyn had finally overcome her reluctance to get married. Having made up her mind to go forward, she was determined to have a family and simultaneously continue her acting career. Or as she put it, 'It's not like I'm giving up my career; I'm simply starting a new one.' "

A day after the column appeared, Marilyn received a telephone call from Harry Brand, head of publicity at Fox, wanting to know if the couple had a date in mind. Marilyn trusted Brand and asked him to keep the news under lock and key until after the wedding took place. She divulged the date, and he more or less kept his end of the bargain. He notified the press but waited until the morning of the fourteenth. As a publicist, he must have wondered if being married might damage Marilyn's status as a sex symbol. Such an eventuality would certainly have been problematic for Twentieth Century–Fox.

In the memoir Marilyn wrote with the help of Ben Hecht, she observed: "I had never planned on, or dreamed about, becoming the wife of a great man any more than Joe had thought about marrying a woman who seemed eighty percent publicity. The truth is that we were very much alike. My publicity, like Joe's greatness, was something on the outside. It had nothing to do with what we actually were."

On Tuesday night, January 12, her last evening in Los Angeles before departing for San Francisco, Marilyn called Anne Karger, Fred Karger's mother, with whom she'd remained on close terms long after her early romance with Fred ended. She told Anne and Anne's daughter, Mary Karger, about her plans to marry Joe. She also contacted Whitey Snyder to tell him. "It seemed only fitting," he said. "I'd been pushing for the marriage for months. I wished her all the best and told her to name their first kid after me."

The next day, January 13, Marilyn flew to San Francisco in full disguise and spent the night at the home of Tom and Louise DiMaggio. The civil wedding service took place on Thursday, January 14, 1954, at San Francisco's city hall. It began at 1:48 p.m., in the chamber of Municipal Court Judge Charles Perry, the chief city officer, and lasted all of three minutes. They exchanged rings — Joe gave Marilyn a platinum eternity band set with thirty-five baguette-cut diamonds — and then he took Marilyn in his arms and kissed her. Among the handful of guests were (best man) Reno Barsocchini and his wife, Tom and Louise DiMaggio, George Solotaire, Lefty O'Doul, and his wife, Jean. Marilyn wore a very natty but proper chocolate-brown broadcloth suit with small rhinestone buttons and a white ermine collar. With the help of another former lover, fashion guru Billy Travilla, she'd bought the outfit the week before off the rack at Saks in Beverly Hills. Joe, having presented his bride with a corsage of three white orchids prior to the ceremony, wore a dark blue business suit and the same polka-dotted tie he'd donned when they first met. On the city register, Joe wrote his age (thirty-nine) and provided his signature; Marilyn gave her legal name, Norma Jeane Dougherty, and noted her age as twenty-five, reducing her actual age by two years.

The group remained in the chamber for another quarter hour, chatting and embracing and wishing the newlyweds well. As Joe and Marilyn left the room, they suddenly found themselves surrounded by the press. More than a hundred reporters and photographers had invaded the lobby and corridors of the building. The couple agreed to pose for one picture. As fifty flashbulbs went off,

Joe planted a kiss on Marilyn's lips. Could they do it again, please? They complied.

Before they could push and shove their way to freedom, they were asked to give the briefest of press conferences. One reporter asked Marilyn what she wanted out of the marriage. "I've got what I wanted," she ventured. "I've got Joe." And what did DiMaggio think of his new bride? "Marilyn's a quiet girl," he said. "She likes what I like." Another reporter wanted to know if they planned to have children — and if so, how many? "A half dozen," responded Marilyn. "At least one," said Joe. And finally, somebody asked Marilyn if she felt excited about being married. "You know," she said, "it's much more than that."

With George Solotaire, Lefty O'Doul, and Reno Barsocchini running interference, the newlyweds, trailed by dozens of reporters and a crowd of five hundred spectators, left city hall through a basement exit and headed for Joe's Cadillac, which they'd prepacked with suitcases. Joe had asked Solotaire to be his best man, but not knowing if he could get there on time, George had willingly surrendered the honorary spot to Reno Barsocchini. Lefty held the car door open for DiMaggio, while Reno and George helped Marilyn into the passenger's seat.

As the couple sped off, a journalist for the *San Francisco Chronicle* asked Solotaire

where the newlyweds were planning to honeymoon. "I have no idea where they're headed,"
he said. "I'm not sure they know." This
exchange, as Monroe biographer Fred Lawrence Guiles accurately assessed it, seemed
an "apt description" of a marriage slated to
last little more than nine months.

They headed for Paso Robles (translation:
"Pass of the Oaks"), a hilly village three hours
south of San Francisco. They stopped long
enough to fill a thermos with hot coffee and
exchange wedding presents. Joe gave Marilyn
a full-length black sable coat. She handed
him the twenty nude transparencies taken of
her in 1949 by photographer Tom Kelley,
including the one that had become the
"Golden Dreams" calendar shot. The transparencies were considered too graphic for
calendar use; they showed Marilyn's pubic
hair before she began bleaching the area to
match the bleached blonde hair on her head.
"When Joe told me about the gift," remarked
Whitey Snyder, "I said, 'Well, you can always
airbrush the photos and hang them in your
den.' I was kidding, of course, but he didn't
see it that way. He refused to speak with me
for a good six weeks."

At six in the evening, they pulled into the
Clinton Motel in Paso Robles, where DiMaggio had reserved room number 15 at the rate
of $6.50 per night. They ate dinner by candle-
light at a steakhouse across the street from

the motel. After their meal, they checked into their room with two bottles of champagne, a box of imported French crackers, and two tins of caviar. Ernie Sharpe, the motel proprietor, later told the *Los Angeles Times* that the couple spent fifteen hours in the room, which came equipped with a double bed, a small refrigerator, and a TV. They checked out at noon the next day. Marilyn looked "radiant." Joe appeared "solemn and tired." "We've got to put a lot of miles behind us," he said as they climbed into the car.

They pushed on in a southeasterly direction and continued straight through until they reached their destination: a quiet hideaway mountain lodge outside Idyllwild, near Palm Springs. The lodge belonged to Loyd Wright, DiMaggio's and Marilyn's attorney. For their convenience he'd filled the refrigerator with food and stocked the liquor cabinet. Tired from the drive, DiMaggio went to bed. Marilyn stayed up and made several telephone calls, one to reporter Kendis Roehlen. "I finally did it," she told Roehlen. "Except for Joe, I've sucked my last cock."

The next morning, Marilyn received a call from Loyd Wright. He informed her that news of her marriage to DiMaggio had made headlines all over the world and that they were being heralded as the ideal couple. One newspaper dubbed them "the Legend and the Goddess." Wright also wanted Marilyn to know that in recognition of her marriage and as a gesture of good faith, Twentieth Century-Fox had lifted her suspension, placing her back on payroll and even agreeing to pick up Natasha Lytess's salary. The only condition was that Marilyn had to return to work — rehearsals for *Pink Tights* were scheduled to begin on January 20. DiMaggio was outraged. He informed Wright he had no intention of allowing his wife to appear in *that* movie or in any movie that called for her to run around half naked, playing a woman of easy virtue.

Monroe's attorney advised Fox of the couple's decision. The studio renewed her suspension. Unwilling to ruin her honeymoon, Marilyn deferred to her husband. She and Joe had struck a bargain whereby she could continue her career so long as he had an active voice in choosing her roles. They didn't argue about it. For once they didn't argue at all. They played a lot of billiards at a nearby bar. They took long early-morning walks in the mountain snow, Marilyn in boots, jeans, and her new sable coat. They built a snowman and had playful snowball fights. They occasionally drove into Palm Springs for dinner, always at small, out-of-the-way restaurants so as to avoid being recognized. Except for Wright's periodic updates, they spoke to no one. The press reported that they'd "dropped off the face of the earth." Marilyn later said the best part of it was that Joe never once turned on the TV set.

Their honeymoon didn't end at Loyd Wright's mountain lodge. The couple returned to San Francisco at the end of January after stopping off in Monterey. With Lefty and Jean O'Doul in tow, Joe and Marilyn boarded a Pan American airliner headed for Tokyo, Japan. The Japanese newspaper *Yomiuri Shimbun* had invited the Yankee Clipper to help launch the Japanese baseball season, and DiMaggio had seized the opportunity to extend his honeymoon by taking along his bride as well as the O'Douls. Jean and Marilyn could shop and go sightseeing together while Joe and Lefty, both of whom had visited Japan in 1951, occupied themselves with baseball-related matters.

As Marilyn depicted it in her personal memoir, the Japanese leg of her honeymoon began on a questionable note. They were still airborne when General Charles Christenberry, a high-ranking US Army officer, came over to introduce himself. After ascertaining that the couple would be staying in Japan for the rest of the month, he asked, "How would you like to visit Korea for a few days and entertain the American troops currently stationed in Seoul as part of the UN occupation force?"

"I'd like to," Joe DiMaggio answered, "but I don't think I'll have time this trip."

"I don't mean you, Mr. DiMaggio," the general replied. "My inquiry was directed at your wife."

"She can do anything she wants," said Joe. "It's her honeymoon."

"I'd love to do it," said Marilyn. "What do you think, Joe?"

Joe shrugged. "Go ahead if you want. As I told the gentleman, it's your honeymoon."

General Christenberry took down the name of their hotel in Tokyo and promised Marilyn he'd be in touch. DiMaggio, forever conscious of his public image, had consented but only because to do otherwise would have seemed unpatriotic.

Thousands of fans greeted the plane when it landed at Tokyo's Haneda International Airport. It soon became apparent that they had come to see Marilyn Monroe rather than Joe DiMaggio. As much as the Japanese loved baseball, they absolutely revered Hollywood movie stars. So eager were they to catch a glimpse of Marilyn that the police, fearing a riot, insisted that the honeymooners depart the plane through the cargo hatch and hide out in the customs office until the crowd dispersed. In Tokyo, the DiMaggios and the O'Douls were given adjoining suites at the five-star Imperial Hotel. The day after their arrival, Joe and Marilyn agreed to a hastily arranged press conference in the hotel lobby. The questions ranged from the risqué to the ridiculous. A reporter for the paper that had invited DiMaggio to Japan asked the actress how and when she'd developed her famous wiggle walk.

"I started when I was six months old, and I haven't stopped yet," she answered. The same journalist wanted to know what Marilyn hoped to do while in Japan.

"I'd like to find a good Japanese restaurant. Any suggestions?"

Another reporter noticed that Monroe had a small splint on her right thumb and asked how she'd injured it.

"I fell out of bed," she quipped. "How else?"

Commenting on Marilyn's arrival in Tokyo, an observant Japanese film critic wrote, "Marilyn Monroe's greatest artistic achievement is the creation of Marilyn Monroe. She is the reincarnation of herself. She is truly an original."

Besides Tokyo, the DiMaggios and O'Douls visited the Japanese cities of Kobe, Osaka, and Yokohama. While at the Imperial Hotel, Joe and Marilyn drew vast crowds whenever they came or went. Hundreds of curious locals gathered on the street in front of the hotel each morning and chanted Marilyn's name until she emerged on the balcony of her suite, like a monarch greeting her subjects. She and Joe were followed around Tokyo by dozens of reporters and news photographers. Although Marilyn assured journalists she was there only in a supporting role and that "marriage is now my main career," the press described her as "Joe DiMaggio's greatest catch" and "America's most famous actress." They labeled her "the Honorable Buttocks-Swinging Madam" and irreverently referred to Joe DiMaggio as "Mr. Marilyn Monroe" and "the Forgotten Man." If Joe hadn't previously understood just how big a star he'd married, he realized it now, and it didn't altogether please him. At times he became surly. And silent. At other times he became pushy. "We're not going shopping today — the crowds will kill us," he told his wife. She obeyed.

At a cocktail party thrown in their honor by the international set of Tokyo, which included several high-ranking US Army officials, they once again encountered General Christenberry. He told the couple he'd completed arrangements for Marilyn's Korean visit with the troops. DiMaggio informed the general that Jean O'Doul would accompany Marilyn on the trip. "That's fine," said Christenberry. "We're all extremely grateful for your wife's service to the country." Cholera and yellow fever shots were administered to both women, and they were issued visas for the trip.

On February 16, Marilyn and Jean O'Doul were flown by helicopter from Tokyo to the

First Marine Division base in Seoul. They were received by a USO representative and several military officials, among them George H. Waple, who'd been assigned the enviable task of looking after Marilyn for the duration of her Korean tour. Their first stop was a US Army medical facility in Seoul, where Marilyn hobnobbed with American soldiers, many of them wounded in the Korean War, which had ended in July 1953. Following the hospital visit, Marilyn and Jean were issued combat boots, long johns, and GI trousers and taken by helicopter to an advance base outside the capital city.

Their living quarters consisted of a couple of cots in a small room in a makeshift barracks. "Marilyn never complained," Waple noted in his report on her stay. "She seemed to like the basic living arrangement. Her only quibble was with the weather. She hadn't expected it to be so cold and snowy. I told her I could give her an electric blanket for her cot, but she declined. She also turned down a small electric space heater for the room, saying she didn't want to be the cause of any concern I might have had for her welfare. She was unspoiled to the nth degree."

Once they reached their room, Marilyn asked Waple to help her out of her combat boots and baggy trousers. He followed orders, relieved (he wrote) that she didn't force him to take off her long johns.

In a period of four days, Marilyn gave ten performances for legions of American troops, representing every branch of the military. Wearing a low-cut, plum-colored, sequined gown (with nothing underneath), she sang and danced, creating "a frenzy of excitement," Waple wrote, "an outpouring of adulation." The lyrics to one of her songs, George Gershwin's "Do It Again," were deemed "too suggestive" by the commanding officer of the base. Acting as her own editor, Marilyn altered Gershwin's original to "Kiss Me Again." Between performances, Waple drove her around to meet the troops personally. Following her last show in front of the Forty-Fifth Division, the actress blew kisses to an audience that cheered and applauded her for half an hour. "This is the best thing that ever happened to me," she told them. "Come see me in San Francisco."

Before she left, the military brass gave her a farewell party, presenting her with an olive green GI shirt that could be worn as a jacket. She told them she was sorry she hadn't seen more of the country, but if they ever needed her services again, she would be there for them.

Marilyn was glowing when she and Jean O'Doul returned to Japan. "It was so wonderful, Joe," she told her husband. "You never heard such cheering." Her brief, throwaway remark hit a nerve, reminding DiMaggio that his bride had surpassed him in popularity and renown. His response, though understated, came across with a resounding thud. "Yes, I have," he said. "I've heard it."

She subsequently came down with a fever and a hacking cough. A doctor in Tokyo diagnosed her illness as a mild form of bronchial pneumonia. She lay in her hotel room at the Imperial for three days, taking antibiotics, arguing with Joe. It seemed to her that he looked on women in one of two ways — they were either housewives or whores, nothing in between. Any time a man looked at her with anything other than casual disinterest, he bristled, accusing her of acting in a provocative manner. At the same time she knew he loved her and would do anything to protect her. He'd been the first man who cared enough to point out that the roles they offered her at Fox were always those of "the dumb blonde." He stood with Marilyn in her battle to attain dignity and acclaim in a business that all too often seemed cruel and indifferent.

Before flying back to the States, Joe and Marilyn received a number of gifts from local government officials, including matching handmade fishing rods. The Emperor of Japan presented Marilyn with a vintage pearl necklace with a diamond clasp, valued in excess of $100,000, which she gave eventually to Paula Strasberg, her then acting coach.

She would give Joe Jr. the GI shirt she'd received in Korea. While still in Tokyo she bought silk kimonos for friends, one of which she presented to Lotte Goslar, who happened to be in San Francisco when the couple arrived there in late February.

"Shortly after they got back," recalled Goslar, "Joe DiMaggio had to leave for New York on business, so Marilyn and I went out for lunch in downtown San Francisco. Marilyn spoke about her tour of Korea. 'Before I went over there,' she said, 'I never really felt like a star. Not really, not in my heart. I felt like one in Korea. It was so great to look down from the stage and see all those young fellows smiling up at me. It made me feel wanted.' "

On March 1 Marilyn sent Joe an incredibly loving two-page, handwritten letter, mailing it to him at the Madison Hotel in New York. In it, she addressed him as "Dad," one of her nicknames for Joe. "I want to be near you," she wrote, "and I feel so sad tonight. Darling, please don't leave me anymore." She signed it simply, "Love, Marilyn."

Joe DiMaggio couldn't have hoped for a more endearing letter had he written it himself.

In a true sense, Joe and Marilyn's honeymoon had been both a beginning and an end. While DiMaggio tried to come to grips with the realization that his newlywed wife had no intention of giving up her career, Marilyn grappled with the notion that her husband would never be satisfied unless she gave it up, or at least reduced it to such an extent that it practically didn't exist. Somehow DiMaggio couldn't comprehend just how much Marilyn, in her difficult journey through life, had come to rely on her acting as a means of self-identification. Their differences (and similarities) also became more pronounced. He craved privacy and hoped to simplify his existence. She couldn't get enough publicity and saw life as an endless labyrinth. He was as neurotically neat and organized as she was scattered and messy. He was introverted, practically repressed. She was hyper and at times manic. They were both stubborn and proud. Both were quick to anger. And they were both stars, but her stardom was here and now; his was a remembrance of days gone by.

Before meeting Joe in San Francisco, Marilyn arrived in Los Angeles for an appointment with Charles Feldman and Loyd Wright to discuss her career options. While in town, she saw Joe Jr. and took him to dinner at Romanoff's, in Beverly Hills. She also saw Sidney Skolsky and told him, rather matter-of-factly — and her recent love letter to Joe notwithstanding — that she had every intention of marrying Arthur Miller. Taken aback by her proclamation, Skolsky reminded her that she'd just returned from her honeymoon with DiMaggio. How, he asked, had she come up with this latest bombshell? She explained that before marrying Joe, she'd obtained a post office box so she and Miller could correspond.

During her trip to Japan, Miller had sent her a note suggesting that in the near future he anticipated leaving his wife. Marilyn assured Skolsky she had far more in common with the playwright than she did with the ballplayer. Joe didn't want her to be a movie star. He wanted her with him at all times. He didn't approve of the women she portrayed on film. He didn't like it when she had to perform a romantic scene and kiss the leading man. He didn't like anything about Hollywood or the studio system. "Show business isn't any business for a girl like you," he'd maintained. How could she possibly stay with Joe? Skolsky listened in semidisbelief. Hadn't Marilyn known all this when she married DiMaggio?

Although at this point Joe knew nothing of Arthur Miller, he couldn't help but sense Marilyn's urgent desire to resume her film career. He took it as a personal rejection. When she rejoined him in San Francisco, he accorded her the same "silent treatment" he'd so often bestowed upon Dorothy Arnold. He'd done it before with Marilyn, but on this occasion, he carried it a step further. He began sleeping in a separate bedroom at the Beach Street house. Marilyn rebelled, telling her husband she knew it was chic for a husband and wife to maintain separate sleeping quarters, but she was an "old-fashioned" girl — she believed a married couple should share the same bedroom and bed. When DiMaggio offered the lame excuse that his present bed was too confining and that he had trouble sleeping, she hired a carpenter to construct a bed seven feet wide and eight feet in length. He resumed sleeping by her side.

In fact, it was Marilyn, much more than Joe, who had trouble sleeping. When she'd torn a ligament in her leg during the production of *River of No Return,* a Canadian physician placed her on Demerol to help relieve the pain. The pain had long subsided, but she'd become addicted to the drug. To combat her insomnia, she procured a prescription for Nembutal. She was currently addicted to both medications, giving DiMaggio something new to vent about. If her profession caused her such pain and anxiety, perhaps she ought to consider doing something else. After all, he reasoned, he'd quit baseball when his injuries became too acute to continue. Marilyn's solution was simply to get hold of more pills. Sidney Skolsky visited from Los Angeles and brought along a satchel of pharmaceuticals. Marilyn dubbed Sidney her "pill pal."

Possibly to appease Joe, if for no other reason, Marilyn told him she'd been thinking of going to school in New York to study history and literature. "I'd love to learn how things get to be the way they are," she said. They could move to Manhattan and start a family while she pursued adult extension courses at Columbia University or NYU. But later that month, *Modern Screen* magazine named her one of Hollywood's five most popular actresses — along with Elizabeth Taylor and Grace Kelly — and *Photoplay* presented her with a Best Actress award for work she'd done in 1953. She and DiMaggio turned up in Los Angeles in March to collect the latter prize, and while there, they sat down with Charles Feldman to discuss further the ongoing negotiations with Fox.

DiMaggio advised Feldman to insist on a partial "creative control" clause in Marilyn's next contract. Such a clause, not uncommon in the case of leading box office names, would at least entitle her to exercise a certain degree of control in the selection and scripting of future films. Although Marilyn's existing seven-year contract could not be completely overturned, it could at least be altered to include raises in salary and a modification of certain individual clauses.

True to his word, Joe supported his wife financially during the period she remained out of work, deciding what to do next. One of the obstacles he encountered, as he told George Solotaire, was that Marilyn was a "bog of contradictions." It was nearly impossible to make concrete plans with her because she constantly shifted directions. She was prepared to go back to school one minute, and the next she had an entirely different idea, one of which entailed starting her own film production company. She and Joe explored the possibility.

From DiMaggio's perspective, it wasn't an ideal solution, but it seemed preferable to being an indentured slave at Fox and having to comply with the whims and fancies of various studio bosses. The main problem with such an undertaking was that it demanded far more knowledge of the film industry than either DiMaggio or Monroe possessed. It might also call for the investment of large sums of private capital, an eventuality that almost certainly didn't appeal to DiMaggio. Moreover, if Marilyn attempted to start her own film production company, she would no doubt face legal action on the part of Fox, which would attempt to invoke the seven-year contract she'd signed with them long before she emerged as a full-blown star.

The couple spent much of the spring in San Francisco, Marilyn seated in a back booth of the DiMaggio restaurant while Joe stood in front greeting customers, many of whom came in with the hope of spotting Marilyn. "She used to sit back there and read, waiting for Joe to finish up," said Dom DiMaggio. "She was reading James Joyce's *Ulysses*. She told me she'd started it months earlier but couldn't get a handle on it. She always had a notebook with her as well, which she filled with lists. She had a list of actors, a list of foods, a list of cities around the world she planned on visiting, and a list of movies and plays she wanted to see. I recall her making a list of composers and their best-known pieces of music: Bach, Bartok, Vivaldi, Beethoven, Mozart, Ravel, Stravinsky. She asked me to name my favorite composer. I told her I wasn't up on composers. 'I thought all Italians loved music,' she said. 'You know — wine, women and song. Or is that a myth? I'm beginning to think Italian men are all cranky and overpossessive, like Joe, and the rest is just a lot of self-promotion.' I'm not sure what I said in response. I didn't tell Joe what she'd said. I didn't want to upset him any more than he already was."

Over spring break, Joe Jr. visited Marilyn and his father in San Francisco. As usual, Joe DiMaggio had little to do with his son, leaving him in Marilyn's care. "Marilyn and I went on long walks together," recalled Joey. "She wore dark glasses that fooled no one. On a few occasions we were followed. One evening we walked to Coit Tower, a well-known tourist site shrouded in fog and mist, and some weird-looking homeless character trailed after us. We visited the San Francisco Zoo, and this creepy guy shadowed us until we managed to lose him in the House of Reptiles. Another day we drove to San Mateo and walked to Seal Point, which is in a park with miles of hiking and biking trails. She took me to the Cliff House for lunch, a landmark eatery in an old chateau, and made me promise not to tell my father because he'd be insulted we hadn't dined in the family restaurant."

At least one harrowing episode took place during Joey's stay in San Francisco. Late one night he heard a loud argument coming from the top floor of the house. "I was asleep downstairs," he said, "and I woke up to the sound of my father and Marilyn screaming at each other. I couldn't make out the words, but it had all the makings of a violent argument. After a few minutes I heard Marilyn race down the stairs and out the front door and my father running after her. I looked out the window, and I could see Marilyn, in a bathrobe, heading away from the house. My father caught up to her and grabbed her by the hair and sort of half-dragged her back to the house. She was trying to fight him off but couldn't. The next morning Marilyn looked ragged. Her eyes were all red and her face swollen. My father wasn't around. I don't think Marilyn realized I'd witnessed the episode. I asked her what happened. 'Nothing happened, Joey,' she said. 'Everything's fine, just fine.' "

On April 14 Twentieth Century–Fox notified Loyd Wright and Charles Feldman that they were once again lifting Marilyn Monroe's suspension. They indicated they would be sending a new version of the contract for Marilyn to sign, with a sizable increase in salary. The studio had canceled plans to go forward with *The Girl in Pink Tights,* and instead would dispatch a script for a musical, *There's No Business Like Show Business.* Feldman passed on the news to Marilyn in San Francisco. She considered the offer a concession on the part of Fox's executives, a victory of sorts, for which she had Joe DiMaggio to thank.

Resigned to the fact that Marilyn could not and would not give up her career, Joe returned to Los Angeles with her in late April. In search of a more spacious residence than the apartment on North Doheny, they rented an Elizabethan cottage for $700 a month at 508 North Palm Drive in Beverly Hills, several blocks from the house she'd shared with Johnny Hyde in 1950. Soon after moving in, Joe and Marilyn drove an hour to visit Vic Masi and his wife at their vacation home in the San Fernando Valley. Vic, a radio sports broadcaster, had known Joe since the late 1940s. The two couples went to a dinner club near Toluca Lake, and, to Joe's amazement, the performer at the club that evening was Dorothy Arnold. Following her set, Dorothy stopped by Joe and Marilyn's table and had a drink with them. It marked the first and only time she and Monroe ever came face-to-face.

On April 30 Joe squired Marilyn to the Hollywood opening of *River of No Return.* Confronted by reporters on leaving the theater, Marilyn sputtered, "Joe and I want many little DiMaggios." DiMaggio turned away. He'd become little more than an appendage to his wife's fame. As one of his biographers saw it, "She'd broken through his wall of invincibility, that aloofness of the Yankee Clipper." She'd bewitched him. She'd obliterated his spirit. The Great DiMaggio had become subservient to his wife's overbearing psychological needs. He must have known by this point in time that there would be no "little DiMaggios," at least not with Marilyn. He must also have realized, without wanting to admit it, that though he maintained a brave front, his future with Marilyn was very much in doubt.

The new contract and the script for *There's No Business Like Show Business,* by husband-and-wife screenwriting team Henry and Phoebe Ephron, arrived by messenger at Famous Artists, Charles Feldman's agency.

He sent them over to North Palm Drive. Marilyn grabbed the packet and started reading the contract. The increase in salary guarantee was clearly notated, but as Marilyn rifled through the document, she noticed that there was no creative-control provision. Not a word. Nothing. Once again the studio had stiffed her, reduced her to what she'd always been to them: a sexy body and a beautiful head of sugar-candy blond hair.

Marilyn turned her attention to the *Show Business* script. It reeked of the same exploitive vapidity as *Pink Tights.* Taking advantage of her status as "the hottest property in Hollywood," Fox had fashioned an all-glitter, no-substance production that called for Marilyn to do little more than torch the screen with a song or two and otherwise wriggle around in a selection of all-too revealing show costumes.

Outraged by both script and contract, Marilyn informed Charles Feldman that she had no intention of going back to work, not under these paltry circumstances. *Show Business* had fewer production values than *Pink Tights;* the script was beyond insipid. And the contract constituted an affront, a slap in the face — it was an attack on her very being. Marilyn had no interest in abstract, impersonal concepts. For her, everything was either completely meaningless or completely personal. This was personal.

In her memoir, Marilyn wrote: "I wanted to be treated as a human being who had earned a few rights since my orphanage days . . . When the rest of the world was looking at someone called Marilyn Monroe, Mr. Zanuck, in whose hands my future rested, was able to see only Norma Jeane — and treat me as Norma Jeane had always been treated."

Feldman called Zanuck and conveyed some of his star client's grievances. The following day, he contacted Monroe. Zanuck, he said, had sweetened the pot. If she agreed to do *Show Business,* he promised to give her the hit Broadway comedy, *The Seven Year Itch,* as her next picture. As for the contract — according to Zanuck, it wasn't negotiable. Take it or leave it. They'd bent over backward to appease her, but they weren't going to bend any further. Marilyn must sign, or the studio would place her back on suspension — and if she went back on suspension, the studio would have to consider taking legal action against her. The cost of a legal defense team could be prohibitive, and there was no guarantee that in the end she would prevail.

Feldman felt she should sign. And Joe? Joe surprised everyone. He, too, recommended she append her signature. They'd allotted her a substantial raise. That counted for something. To continue to hold out would only result in a hardening of positions. What was the point of that? DiMaggio told George Solotaire he couldn't take it any longer. Not now, at any rate. He'd lost the battle but not necessarily the war. He still felt he could one day convince Marilyn to stop making films and start making babies.

CHAPTER 9

"What Joe is to me is a man whose looks, and character, I love with all my heart." Marilyn Monroe's words, as recorded in the pages of her personal memoir, were countered by a more cautionary reflection in the same document. "We knew," she wrote, "it wouldn't be an easy marriage." It wasn't.

The first public rumblings of trouble in the DiMaggio-Monroe union coincided with the start of rehearsals for *There's No Business Like Show Business* in mid-May 1954. Earl Wilson ran an item in his newspaper column suggesting that all was not what it should be at 508 North Palm Drive. Louella Parsons followed with a similarly ominous item.

Jimmy Cannon, Joe's sportswriter pal in New York, called the ballplayer to get his side of the story. DiMaggio denied that he and Marilyn were having marital problems, yet he described his life in Hollywood as "dull." He claimed he tried not to interfere with his wife's work. "I don't resent her fame," he insisted. "Marilyn was working long before she met me — and for what? What has she got after all these years? She works like a dog. She's up at five or six in the morning and doesn't get through until seven at night. We have a bite to eat, watch a little television, and go to bed." Their meals, he hastened to add, consisted primarily of frozen dinners or take-out Italian.

Whatever domestic fantasies DiMaggio might have entertained when he first married Marilyn had long been dashed. When he complained to her that they no longer spent a lot of time together, she reminded him that he'd been the one who pressured her to sign on for the film. She'd been willing to hold out and return with him to San Francisco, but he'd advised her to get on with it. It wasn't her fault she had to spend the entire day in rehearsals. She also reminded him that Natasha Lytess was still coaching her, and since he detested Lytess, she felt compelled to work with her at the studio rather than to invite her back to their house.

Technically speaking, Marilyn wasn't incorrect. It wasn't so much that DiMaggio wanted her to do the film, rather that he had simply given up hope of convincing his wife to walk away from the entire Hollywood scene. He felt lost, trapped by his own jealousy and insecurity. Marilyn had invaded his bloodstream like a virus. She wasn't Dorothy

Arnold, a woman willing to trade in her identity and personal aspirations to be supported and bolstered by her celebrity spouse. And then, too, DiMaggio could no longer claim title to be what he'd once been, the star center fielder for the New York Yankees. He could proclaim himself "the greatest living ballplayer," but he no longer played ball. While Marilyn, for her part, had been unofficially crowned Hollywood's reigning queen. Even if she had married "a commoner," she had no intention of abdicating the throne.

For the most part, DiMaggio passed his days at home, glued to the TV set, nervously smoking his way through one pack of cigarettes after another, waiting for Marilyn to come home. When she arrived after work, she and Joe invariably argued. He demanded a minute-by-minute account of how she'd spent the day. What had she done? With whom had she spoken? DiMaggio wouldn't stop. Weary as she was, he kept at her. When she didn't respond the way he wanted her to, he became physical; on one occasion he ripped an earring from her lobe and scratched her face. The tension between them made Marilyn increasingly resort to sedatives. Yet despite the sedatives, she couldn't sleep at night. The insomnia that had previously dogged her grew worse. To augment her sleeping pill regimen, she began drinking more heavily than usual — and not just champagne but straight, hard shots of vodka and gin. Still unable to sleep and in somewhat of a drunken stupor, she and DiMaggio kept at each other long into the night.

Whitey Snyder recalled that once they started shooting *Show Business,* Marilyn would arrive at the studio half asleep because she hadn't slept in days, and he would walk her around the dressing room for an hour or two to get her blood circulating and work the cobwebs out of her brain.

"They assigned her Betty Grable's old dressing room, and she'd come in all groggy and disoriented," recalled Whitey. "She couldn't remember her lines, or if she did she'd slur them. And because it took me time to get her going in the morning, she'd invariably be late on the set. She apologized, but it didn't do much good. Walter Lang, the film's director, wasn't sympathetic. The worst criticisms came from some of the other cast members. Veterans like Ethel Merman and Mitzi Gaynor began picking on her. Merman, who could belt a song in her sleep, criticized her singing ability. And this made matters even worse. Marilyn collapsed on the set and then developed bronchitis and had to be hospitalized. The delays cost the studio a small fortune."

Whitey suspected that Marilyn's marriage to DiMaggio had begun to unravel, but he didn't know to what extent. "Marilyn realized my wife and I were fond of Joe, so when talking about him to either of us, she chose her words carefully. Then one day in June, Joe called and asked me to meet him for lunch and not to say anything to Marilyn about it. So we met, and Joe seemed upset. And this was a man who very rarely revealed his inner feelings. After going through his usual harangue about the horrors of the studio system and a recitation of his expectations as to a proper wife's domestic role, he started complaining that he saw less and less of Marilyn, that she spent far too much time away from home and on the set. And then out of the blue he asked if I knew Hal Schaefer, Marilyn's voice coach on the film. I told him I did and that Hal had previously coached her on both *Gentlemen Prefer Blondes* and *River of No Return.* And I knew he'd taken it upon himself to help her with an album of songs she planned to record for RCA. DiMaggio evidently hadn't met him on the set of *River of No Return.* 'What does he look like?' he asked. 'Does he have a wife? Is he a ladies' man?' And so on. At the time, I had no idea what he was getting at. Why all the questions? I soon found out."

What Whitey Snyder "soon found out" was that Marilyn and Hal Schaefer were having an affair. Schaefer was twenty-nine, a year and a half older than Marilyn. He had dark

228

hair and eyes and a soft, melodic voice. Though he felt Marilyn never reached her potential as a singer, he worked hard to improve her voice. He was gentle, patient, and encouraging. She told friends he reminded her of an earlier voice coach, Fred Karger, with whom she'd also fallen in love.

"She claimed she loved me," said Hal Schaefer, "but I'm not sure she knew what that meant. In a sense, I think our relationship represented an escape for her from a marriage that had gone bad. I believe she'd simply outgrown DiMaggio. He wanted a homemaker, and she hoped to become a serious actress. She cultivated certain tastes, which he didn't share. After he found out about us, he called me up and said he knew I was in love with Marilyn and she was in love with me. He said I should be a man and come face him and discuss it with him at the house. Like an idiot, I said I would. I could hear Marilyn in the background. 'Don't come here,' she pleaded, 'he'll kill you. He'll beat you up. Don't be foolish.' I absolutely believed her, because she'd mentioned how crude and controlling he was. She'd said he was very severe and had a short fuse. He had a violent streak. He physically abused her at times, slapped her around. I think she put up with it because she lacked self-esteem. She wasn't grounded, the result of her terrible childhood, constantly being shifted around from here to there."

Hal Schaefer acknowledged that despite the menacing presence of Joe DiMaggio, his affair with Marilyn became serious. "We discussed marriage," he said. "Marilyn would have converted to Judaism, which is what she eventually did when she married Arthur Miller. After he learned of the affair, or maybe before, I'm not sure which, DiMaggio hired a private detective to follow us around. He bugged my car, my phone, and my apartment. He bugged Marilyn's car as well. I guess the work was done by the detectives he hired."

Harry Hall and Sugar Brown, a pair of former "mob-connected fixers," often did favors for Joe, as did Abner "Longie" Zwillman, Frank Costello, and Paul "Skinny" D'Amato of Las Vegas and Atlantic City. Over the years, DiMaggio often turned up at Mafia-controlled nightspots and restaurants. They picked up his tabs, gave him expensive presents — even set up a trust account for him at the Bowery Savings Bank into which they made regular deposits. He was their man, the Italian Stallion, the dago with the bat of steel. If DiMaggio needed something done, they did it for him. If he wanted a wire planted in somebody's car, they were only too happy to oblige. If he wished to have some "Jew-boy punk of a voice coach" at Twentieth Century–Fox rubbed out — well, that could no doubt also be arranged.

Hal Schaefer began to conjure the most extreme possibilities. By early July, he'd reached his breaking point. As rumors of his romantic involvement with Marilyn Monroe spread, he tried to kill himself by swallowing sleeping pills and a lethal concoction of rum and typewriter-cleaning fluid. Marilyn rushed to his bedside at Santa Monica Hospital. The press followed.

In an effort to downplay the affair, Schaefer offered reporters the following explanation: "It's ridiculous Mr. DiMaggio should be any more jealous of me than he is of other people working with his wife. Marilyn's one of my voice pupils. As a homework assignment, I gave her Ella Fitzgerald's latest record albums and asked her to study them. She fell in love with Ella's voice and has gotten to know her personally. Marilyn and I are no more than friends."

An embittered Joe DiMaggio appeared unannounced and uninvited on the *Show Business* movie set. When he saw Marilyn, he scoffed at her scanty costume. As she approached him, he walked away and spoke to Ethel Merman, whom he knew from New York. He agreed to pose for a photograph with Merman but declined to do likewise with his wife. Marilyn became so perturbed that she tripped over an electrical cable and sprawled to the ground. The next day she contacted Darryl Zanuck and asked him to ban her husband from the set. A week later, when Joe drove to the studio, a security guard at the front gate turned him away. That evening, Joe and Marilyn had words. He asked her why she'd had him banished from the set. She evidently let loose with a tirade of pent-up emotions, calling him a has-been and accusing him of attempting to damage her career. For the first time in many months, DiMaggio spent the night at the Knicker-bocker Hotel.

The following day when Joe returned home, he found a note waiting for him. Written on the back of a dry-cleaning receipt, it read: "Dear Joe, I know I was wrong! I acted the way I did and said the things I did because I was hurt — not because I meant them — and it was stupid of me to be hurt because actually there wasn't enough reason — in fact no reason at all. Please accept my apology and don't, don't, don't be angry with your baby — she loves you. Lovingly, your wife (for life), Mrs. J. P. DiMaggio."

For what it was worth, DiMaggio folded the letter and placed it in his wallet for safekeeping. It remained there for the rest of his life.

"To some degree, I felt sorry for Joe," said Whitey Snyder. "Marilyn had betrayed and humiliated him. The press exploited the scandal and ran daily stories on Marilyn's affair. I invited Joe over for dinner one night. He looked like a beaten dog. At first he didn't want to discuss Marilyn, but once he began he couldn't stop. He described the note she'd written him and everything that had preceded it but said he didn't see how he could ever trust her again. Yet he still loved her. Maybe he loved her too much. Maybe that was the problem. I said I felt sure Marilyn still loved him as well and that a marriage could succeed even if one or the other partner had cheated. 'This is Hollywood,' I said, 'land of the unfaithful.' Joe winced."

Marilyn continued her affair with Hal Schaefer. "We used a friend's apartment," he remarked. "But I hasten to add that sex wasn't the focus of our relationship. We found solace and comfort in each other's company. It isn't that Marilyn wasn't a wonderful lover, but essentially she regarded sex as her function. She almost felt it was expected of her to have sex with a man, because that's something she could do, something she could give to make a man feel good. I'm afraid she was less successful in terms of her own fulfillment."

Marilyn had barely completed work on *There's No Business Like Show Business* when, on August 10, shooting began in Los Angeles on *The Seven Year Itch*. A comedy/spoof directed by Billy Wilder and co-

233

produced by Wilder and Charles Feldman (Marilyn's agent), the film succeeded commercially and at the same time won wide critical acclaim. Not quite as impressed as the film critics, Marilyn insisted she'd once again been cast as a "dopey blonde" in a "crummy movie."

A month after filming began, the cast and crew flew to New York to shoot the exterior street scenes. As Marilyn disembarked, she found herself surrounded by reporters. "No Joe?" one of them asked. "Isn't that a shame?" said Marilyn. He joined her a day later in an eleventh-floor hotel suite at the St. Regis Hotel on Central Park South. From all outward appearances their relationship seemed to be back on track.

Jim Haspiel, a teenaged fan of Marilyn's who'd been writing to her for several years, learned the location of the actress's suite and decided to pay her a surprise visit. "I was with a friend," he said, "and the two of us entered the lobby of the hotel and climbed the stairs to the eleventh floor. We knocked on the door of her suite and a man opened it. I asked if we could meet Miss Monroe. He said she wasn't available and shut the door. Well, we weren't about to use the stairs again so I rang for the elevator and it came up and Joe DiMaggio stepped out. He looked at us, and we looked at him. I told him we were there because we wanted to meet Marilyn

Monroe. He couldn't have been more gracious. 'Wait here,' he said. He disappeared into the suite and two minutes later came back out with Marilyn. He left her with us. We'd brought a camera, and she posed for pictures with us and chatted and was perfectly delightful. And then she kissed me, and I was in seventh heaven."

Given the events that unfolded a week later, Haspiel (who went on to write a book on Marilyn) detected none of the apparent tensions that had beset the couple in Los Angeles. Yet Haspiel, for all his youthful exuberance, was nothing more at the time than a casual observer. Evelyn Keyes, a cast member of *The Seven Year Itch,* became friendly with Marilyn and witnessed the relationship at close range.

"They were civil in public," she said, "but behind closed doors they were at each other's throats. DiMaggio couldn't accept it that she wasn't totally domesticated and devoted to him. She wasn't a housewife. She was Marilyn Monroe. Marilyn told me DiMaggio had certain expectations for people, such as herself and his son, and if they didn't live up to his expectations, he became disappointed and took it out on them."

In addition to the problems that already existed, there was the question of Marilyn's affair with Hal Schaefer. His ego all but shattered, DiMaggio went on a siege against

Marilyn consisting of daily outbursts of anger and rage. Perpetually late on the set — so much so that the film ran behind schedule and over budget — Monroe told Evelyn Keyes that Joe kept her up all night, every night, yelling and screaming at her. He'd become an erupting volcano, spewing out lava and ash on a nightly basis.

"Marilyn described one particularly nasty fight," said Keyes. "It seems she'd bought a new dress, and she put it on to go out, and DiMaggio accused her of going off to meet a man, and he tore the dress to shreds with her in it. She ran into the bedroom and locked the door. He pounded on the door. 'I'm sorry,' he said. 'I'll buy you another dress. Ten dresses.' He continued pounding until Marilyn, wearing a negligee, finally relented and let him in. He apologized. Then he sat next to her on the bed and attempted to slip her negligee down off one shoulder. She pulled it back into place. He tried to kiss her and she pulled away. He attempted to push her down on the bed, and she stood up. 'Let me get this straight,' he said. 'I'm your husband, but you won't sleep with me?' 'You've got it,' she answered. He rose and left the room. Marilyn relocked the door and tried to sleep.

"The next day she arrived on the set three hours late. Billy Wilder had a fit. He told me privately Marilyn lit up the screen like nobody's business, but he couldn't take all the bullshit that went with it. He contended that Marilyn thought the way she looked entitled her to certain privileges. 'But it doesn't work with me,' he added, 'because I look at her not as a man but as a director.' "

Joe and Marilyn made peace long enough to go out to dinner one evening with George and Robert Solotaire. Joe Nacchio, a Panamanian friend of DiMaggio's, joined them in the middle of the meal. "We went to the Palm restaurant," reminisced Robert Solotaire. "Marilyn and I discussed art most of the evening, while the two Joes talked baseball. What I remember best is that when Joe went to the men's room, Marilyn started complaining about him. And then when Marilyn got up to go to the ladies' room, Joe returned the favor. It wasn't like him to disparage Marilyn. I took it as a sign of his unhappiness. He called her a narcissist and said she tried to please everyone but him."

If Marilyn and Joe's marriage could be considered to have been a theater piece, the curtains were about to part for the final act. On September 15, at two in the morning, a mob of two thousand men, including dozens of photographers, gathered at Lexington Avenue and Fifty-Second Street to watch the famous skirt-blowing scene involving Marilyn Monroe and her *Seven Year Itch* costar Tom Ewell. As word spread that La Monroe was

237

standing over a subway grating, her skirts whirling round her neck, her creamy thighs and peek-a-boo knickers in full view, the crowd grew in size and volume. Walter Winchell located Joe DiMaggio at the St. Regis's King Cole Bar nursing a drink and insisted he come watch his wife perform the climactic scene of the film. There were numerous takes (and camera flashes) as the wind machine underneath the grating lifted Marilyn's low-cut white dress, recreating the effect of a passing train. Marilyn's gushy line as "the train" passed and the wind blew was a whimsical "Isn't it delicious?"

Joe DiMaggio watched in horror as again and again his wife's panties were exposed. He had "the look of death on his face," Billy Wilder would later claim. Cries of "Take it off!" and "Let's see more!" — intermingled with a chorus of shrill wolf whistles — pierced the hot night air. Wilder suddenly stopped the shoot and ordered Marilyn to don a less transparent pair of panties. The diaphanous pair she had on revealed far more than any movie censor would allow to be seen. Marilyn retreated to her trailer to change. By the time she returned to the set, DiMaggio had stormed off. Forlorn and embittered, he headed for Toots Shor's to drown his sorrow in drink. His wife, he told Toots, had just performed a striptease act on Lexington Avenue.

It's unclear exactly what transpired later that night in Marilyn's suite at the St. Regis. The following afternoon when she arrived on the set, both of her eyes were red and swollen.

She told Evelyn Keyes that Joe had repeatedly struck her, inadvertently confirming a press story alleging that guests on the eleventh floor at the St. Regis had heard loud noises coming from Marilyn's suite. She'd told Joe she couldn't help it, that she did what the director told her to do. It was good for the picture. "Bullshit!" he'd yelled by way of response. "It's good for Darryl Zanuck. Good for his fucking wallet, that's all."

That afternoon Joe DiMaggio flew back home to San Francisco — alone. Marilyn and the rest of the cast headed for Los Angeles the following day to put the finishing touches on the film, a process that ran on until early November. According to Lotte Goslar, Marilyn called Joe after she returned home. "Why are you calling me?" he asked. She answered, "Because I'm unhappy when you're hurt, Joe." She wanted to give it one last shot. He resisted, said Goslar, "perhaps because he needed to end up on top somehow. But she persisted until he agreed to fly down to see her. He took her to dinner at the Villa Nova, 'for old time's sake.' He wanted to save the marriage, though he'd lost face because of the way Marilyn had treated him and because

of her affair with Hal Schaefer, which, by the
way, she'd resumed. Joe and Marilyn spent
several days together and never stopped hag-
gling. Marilyn moved out of her house and
into Building 86, called the Stars' Building,
on the Fox lot. DiMaggio followed her
around, spying on her. She'd be in a restaurant eating dinner with a friend, and he'd
burst in and sit down with them. He hired
detectives, which Marilyn told me he'd done
with his first wife when he served in the
armed forces during World War II. This
gentleman of grace and dignity had become
something of a psychopath. Somehow he
didn't frighten Marilyn.

"She knew how to sidestep him, knew his
limitations, and, I think, knew he loved her
too deeply to do her real bodily harm. Still,
he hit her, and no woman should have to
endure such treatment. It made her nervous,
though in some strange way, she didn't mind
it as much as she should have. It kind of
validated her and confirmed for her just how
much he cared about her. Her insomnia never
abated. But it certainly didn't help her
insomnia. Dr. Lee Siegel, Fox's resident
physician, gave her a new prescription for
sleeping pills. When she finally decided to
end the marriage, it was Harry Brand, the
head of Fox publicity, who introduced her to
attorney Jerry Giesler."

A prominent criminal attorney, Jerry

Giesler had nevertheless represented such public figures as Shelley Winters and Ingrid Bergman in divorce proceedings. Marilyn retained Giesler and signed a two-page complaint against Joe DiMaggio, citing "mental cruelty" as the cause of her divorce action. The press located DiMaggio in New York, where he'd gone to take in the 1954 World Series classic between the New York Giants and Cleveland Indians. Refusing to comment on the status of his marriage, he chose instead to talk about the spectacular catch at the Polo Grounds by Giants center fielder Willie Mays of a towering drive by Vic Wertz in game one of the Series. Mays had caught the ball while racing full speed with his back to home plate. "I'd have made the catch, too," claimed DiMaggio with deadpan candor, "but unlike Willie, I wouldn't have lost my baseball cap."

Joe and Marilyn were legally separated on October 5. The following day, a hundred reporters and photographers jammed onto the lawn in front of 508 North Palm Drive. At ten o'clock in the morning, Joe DiMaggio and Reno Barsocchini emerged from the house carrying Joe's luggage. They loaded it into the trunk and backseat of DiMaggio's Cadillac. Climbing into the passenger side of the car, the former slugger couldn't hide his disappointment. "He looked as grim and gray as if he'd just made the third out in the bottom of the ninth with the bases loaded and the Yanks down by a run," wrote Sheilah Graham in a subsequent column. Asked what he planned on doing, Joe said, "I'm going to San Francisco. It's my home and always has been. I'm never coming back here."

According to Marilyn Monroe biographer Donald Spoto, DiMaggio didn't return to San Francisco at once but instead remained in seclusion in the Los Angeles home of Dr. Leon Krohn, Marilyn's gynecologist. The couple had consulted with Krohn on a number of occasions because of Marilyn's seeming difficulties in becoming pregnant.

Dressed in black as if for a funeral, Marilyn appeared on the lawn an hour later. With her were Jerry Giesler and Sidney Skolsky. Supporting herself on Giesler's arm, Marilyn slowly approached a bank of press microphones. But it was Giesler who spoke: "Miss Monroe will have nothing to say to you this morning. As her attorney, I am speaking for her and can only say that the conflict of careers has brought about this regrettable necessity." In response to a barrage of questions, Marilyn, in a quiet voice, hardly more than a whisper, remarked, "I can't say anything today. I'm sorry. I'm so sorry." Resting her head on Giesler's shoulder, she began to cry. As she dabbed her tears with a white handkerchief, she turned away, and with Giesler's help, walked back to her house.

Three weeks later, on October 27, 1954, Marilyn Monroe, America's pinup girl, marched into Santa Monica Superior Court and won an uncontested divorce from Joe DiMaggio. Again wearing black, the tearful twenty-eight-year-old star was accompanied into court by Jerry Giesler, Sidney Skolsky, Mary Karger (Fred Karger's sister), and her business manager Inez Melson. Her voice breaking with emotion, her makeup running, Marilyn told Superior Court Judge Orlando Rhodes (and a packed courtroom) that DiMaggio had often been testy and even refused to allow her to have friends in their home.

"I voluntarily gave up my work in hopes that it would solve our problems," she said, "but it didn't change his attitude. I hoped to have out of my marriage love, warmth, affection, and understanding, but the relationship was one of coldness and indifference. My husband would get into moods when he wouldn't speak to me for periods of sometimes ten days. If I would try to reproach him, usually he wouldn't answer me at all. When he would, he would say, 'Leave me alone.' If I would say, 'What's the matter?' he would say, 'Stop nagging me.' "

Inez Melson, Marilyn's corroborating witness, confirmed her employer's testimony, pointing out that DiMaggio "would push Marilyn away when she tried to show affection for him and would say, 'Don't bother me.' " Because she'd been on excellent terms with Joe, Melson informed him prior to the hearing that she'd been asked to testify against him, a gesture the ballplayer appreciated. They remained friendly long after the divorce.

Some of Marilyn's recitations of her husband's shortcomings sounded startlingly similar to Dorothy Arnold's condemnations of DiMaggio during their divorce trial. To her credit, Marilyn never mentioned the episodes of physical abuse she'd suffered at Joe's hands. Such testimony would have been redundant. Twenty minutes into the proceedings, Judge Rhodes brought his gavel down, terminating the 286-day Joe DiMaggio–Marilyn Monroe marriage, granting an interlocutory decree that would become final one year after issuance.

An intriguing footnote to the hearing is the disappearance of the entire courtroom record pertaining to the divorce. It disappeared for good after being transferred several years later to the trial records archive in Los Angeles. Following the hearing, DiMaggio wrote to Judge Rhodes requesting that the file be sealed. Rhodes denied the request. According to a clerk of the court, "The trial record, including Marilyn Monroe's complete testimony, was available to anyone who wanted to see it. My guess is that one of

DiMaggio's friends, acting on his behalf, came in, requested the file, and then walked out with it. No doubt embarrassed by Monroe's testimony, DiMaggio wanted to make the file disappear. That's only a guess, but in light of everything that transpired following their divorce, it's probably pretty close to the truth."

The first Saturday following the divorce hearing, Marilyn went to see Joe DiMaggio Jr. "She picked me up at Black-Foxe and took me to lunch at Chasen's," said Joey. "We sat way in the back so nobody could see us. I'd heard all these news reports as to how she'd given an Oscar-winning performance at the hearing, but I could tell the divorce saddened her. She didn't look well. She told me how sorry she was it hadn't worked out with my father, that he'd called her the night before the hearing and asked her to reconsider. 'I adore your father,' she said, 'but we just can't seem to live together.' Then she told me that even though she and my father had gotten divorced, she hadn't divorced me, and she planned on staying in touch and would that be all right? And of course I said 'Yes.' After that we took a long drive. We headed south and wound up in San Diego, more than two hours from Beverly Hills. Marilyn didn't say much. I guess it was a kind of therapeutic exercise for her. We ate dinner at some lobster shack on the beach in San Diego, and then we drove back. And when we reached Black-Foxe that night, Marilyn told me to open the glove compartment. Inside, on top of a bunch of road maps, I found a small gift-wrapped package. 'It's for you,' she said. 'I missed your thirteenth birthday. Open it.' It was a leather billfold with my initials engraved on it. Inside was a crisp hundred-dollar bill and a wallet-sized photo of Marilyn with an inscription that read, 'For Joey — Love, your forever step-mom.' "

Joe DiMaggio had moved out of Dr. Krohn's house and into a room at the Knickerbocker Hotel. A week after the divorce, he called Sidney Skolsky and asked him to come over. He wanted to talk with him. As Isabella, Sidney's wife, drove him to the hotel, the journalist said, "If I get hit over the head with a bat, you know where you delivered me."

Skolsky needn't have worried. By the time he saw the ballplayer, DiMaggio's rage had melted away.

"It was about noon when I entered Joe's room," Skolsky wrote in his autobiography. "He pointed toward the bed and asked me to sit down. I sat on the edge of the bed. He drew his chair up close to me.

" 'There's one thing I must know,' he said as softly as a torch singer squeezing the pathos out of every note. 'Is there another man? Why did Marilyn divorce me?'

"I felt awful. No man should be confronted by an idol on his knees, begging to have his clay feet examined. And I had no balm for them.

"How could I tell him he'd bored her? How could I tell a man his ex-wife became ex because she found him dull?

"I spoke all around it, saying that Marilyn wasn't mature enough to be a wife, that she had failed before, that Marilyn's ever bigger ambition didn't call for a husband, and that she didn't want to cater to Joe's likes and dislikes.

"Joe thanked me. I honestly don't believe he had the slightest inkling of what I had avoided saying."

Whatever Sidney Skolsky did or didn't think of Joe DiMaggio, he wasn't the ballplayer's only source of information regarding Marilyn. Joe went to see Inez Melson at her home in the Hollywood Hills, where, as a hobby, she raised and trained parakeets. Inez had helped Joe pack his belongings the day before he left North Palm Drive and had agreed to store a number of cartons in her own home. When he visited her after the divorce, they sat on her porch at dusk and watched the deer dart in and out of the woods surrounding her property. Joe, usually the picture of poise and dignity, had to be consoled and soothed while he spoke about his "baby" and all that had gone amiss in the marriage.

Among other things, he concluded that he'd never been able to relax with Marilyn. In her company, he'd come to expect the unexpected. He never knew what might happen next, who might come along and try to whisk her out of his grasp. If he was too controlled and controlling, she was uncontrollable. She could be cold, calculating, and manipulative. Yet she could also be warm, loving, zany, offbeat, and comical. These were the traits — combined with her physical beauty and an underlying sadness of soul — that had so completely bound him to her.

And then there was Frank Sinatra. Winner of that year's Academy Award for his work in *From Here to Eternity,* Frankie suddenly reemerged in DiMaggio's life. Sinatra and DiMaggio shared one important credential: they'd both lost women they loved. DiMaggio had lost Monroe; Sinatra and his wife since 1951, actress Ava Gardner, had recently separated. Sinatra hired private investigator Barney Ruditsky to keep an eye on Ava. Ruditsky had spotted Ava with a young Mexican beach boy on one occasion and a female dance instructor on another. Frank and Joe commiserated with each other over drinks, usually at the Sunset Club on Sunset Boulevard, at other times at the Villa Capri, an Italian restaurant owned by Pasquale "Patsy" D'Amore, a pal of Frank's.

As a favor to Joe, Sinatra instructed Ruditsky to keep tabs on Monroe as well as Gardner. Even though Marilyn and the Yankee Clipper were legally divorced, Joe wanted to catch Marilyn with Hal Schaefer, whom he suspected she was still dating. He had convinced himself that if he did catch Marilyn "in the act," the interlocutory decree would be voided and the divorce action reversed.

"In those days, in California," said Hal Schaefer, "to finalize a divorce, you had to go through a one-year waiting period before it became absolutely final. If you could prove that your partner was having an affair, you could have the proceedings made null and void, and you would have to start over again. It was a ridiculous, antiquated, uncivilized law, which was almost never invoked. But DiMaggio knew about it and kept trying to find Marilyn in some compromising situation so he could halt the inevitable."

On the night of November 5, DiMaggio, Sinatra, and a couple of Sinatra's cronies, Hank Sanicola and Billy Karen, were drinking and eating a late dinner at the Villa Capri when Barney Ruditsky called and said that Marilyn and a man who looked like Hal Schaefer had entered an apartment building at 8112 Waring Avenue in West Hollywood. He believed he knew which apartment they were using. Minutes later a car screeched to a halt in front of the building. DiMaggio, Sinatra, Karen, and three other people jumped out and were met by Barney Ruditsky and Phil Irwin, a private investigator with whom Ruditsky often worked.

On the drive over, Sinatra had tried to quell DiMaggio's rage, but by the time they arrived, the ballplayer was "ready to kill." Fearing what DiMaggio might do if he caught Schaefer with Monroe, Sinatra and Ruditsky tried to convince him to wait in front of the building while the rest of the crew went inside. Joe refused.

The squadron of seven entered the building and, with Rudisky leading the way, located the suspected apartment. At approximately eleven thirty, the tenants of the building heard a thunderous crash as DiMaggio and his gang broke down the front door and invaded the apartment.

Hearing movement coming from the bedroom, they rushed in, breaking furniture along the way, turning on lights, and taking snapshots as photographic evidence to document their findings. The only problem was, they'd entered the wrong apartment. The bedroom was occupied all right, but not by Hal Schaefer and Marilyn Monroe. Instead they came upon Mrs. Florence Kotz, a fifty-year-old woman who'd been asleep and was now cowering in her bed, her eyes wide as saucers, her mouth agape as she let loose a bloodcurdling shriek. Marilyn and Hal Schaefer happened to be in the same building but on a floor above Mrs. Kotz's flat.

"Now and again Marilyn and I used an apartment that belonged to actress Sheila Stuart, one of my voice students," said Hal Schaefer. "We were in her apartment the night of November 5, when I heard a commotion in front of the building. I peeked out the slats of the window and saw Joe DiMaggio and Frank Sinatra standing across the street with a bunch of tough-looking characters. I knew they'd come looking for us, and I also knew if DiMaggio ever got his hands on me I'd be in trouble. He blamed me for the divorce, though Marilyn would've left him with or without me. DiMaggio lived in a bubble. He was a man who'd had everything he ever wanted in life with one exception — and that exception was Marilyn Monroe. He needed to blame somebody other than himself. At any rate, we managed to sneak out of the apartment and down a back stairwell. I never saw Marilyn again after that night. It just became too scary. You can just imagine. We were both torn up about it."

The building's landlady called the police. The police report cited the episode as an "attempted burglary," without mentioning the names of any of the key players. In May 1957 Florence Kotz filed suit against DiMaggio, Sinatra, et al., for $200,000, but Mickey Rudin, Sinatra's attorney, managed to settle the suit out of court for $7,500. And then matters became complicated.

Confidential magazine got wind of the story, called it the "Wrong Door Raid," and ran a lengthy exposé. The California State Senate launched its own investigation into the raid, calling Sinatra and friends to the witness stand. They attempted to subpoena DiMaggio as well but couldn't locate him. Sinatra brought in a battery of lawyers and testified he'd been nothing more than an innocent bystander. Billy Karen said he didn't remember any details of the event. Hank Sanicola claimed he'd remained behind at the Villa Capri. Barney Ruditsky was excused from testifying due to a heart ailment. When the press finally found DiMaggio and asked him about the Wrong Door Raid, he insisted he hadn't been part of it and had nothing to say.

The day after the raid, Charles Feldman and Billy Wilder gave a party for Marilyn at Romanoff's, attended by Hollywood's Royal Guard. Among the guests were Clark Gable, Darryl Zanuck, Jack Warner, Sam Goldwyn, Humphrey Bogart, Lauren Bacall, Gary Cooper, Doris Day, Jimmy Stewart, William Holden, Claudette Colbert, Susan Hayward, and Irving "Swifty" Lazar. *Life* featured the gala in its next issue.

Charles Feldman toasted Marilyn, calling her "the eighth wonder of the world." She drank champagne and danced with Gable, Zanuck, and Bogart. She sang a duet with Mrs. Billy Wilder and apologized to Billy for her constant tardiness during the filming of *The Seven Year Itch.* Photographer Sam Shaw saw her home at the end of the evening. A new acquaintance, Shaw had been hired by Fox to shoot a set of publicity stills of Marilyn. In his spare time he'd been teaching her how to use a camera that Joe DiMaggio had given her as a present.

Two days after the Wrong Door Raid and a day after her "coming out" party, Marilyn entered Cedars of Lebanon to undergo corrective surgery for her ongoing gynecological condition. She hoped the procedure would enable her to have children. Joe DiMaggio drove her to the hospital. Dr. Leon Krohn performed the operation on November 8. Marilyn remained at Cedars for five days, DiMaggio by her bedside. He stayed with her after she returned to North Palm Drive. On November 25, still recuperating from her surgery, she celebrated Joe's fortieth birthday by taking him to the Villa Capri for dinner. Joe used the occasion to ask her to come back and start again. It was the one birthday present she wasn't able to give him.

Joe DiMaggio returned to San Francisco the next morning. Reached at his Beach Street home by a local reporter, he offered a brief comment blaming the film industry and

Twentieth Century–Fox for their sexploitation of Marilyn Monroe, ruining her reputation and in turn their marriage.

When Roy Craft, a leading member of Fox's publicity department, read DiMaggio's unflattering characterization of the studio, he decided to issue his own statement to the press: "Marilyn Monroe had a flamboyant reputation when Joe DiMaggio married her. The point is, if you build a home behind a slaughterhouse, you don't complain when you hear the pigs squealing."

CHAPTER 10

Marilyn Monroe had become the world's
number one female box office attraction. That
fact notwithstanding, she remained, as Joe
DiMaggio had constantly reminded her, a
hapless victim of the pernicious Hollywood
system. Twentieth Century–Fox continued to
dictate her selection of films, roles, costars,
producers, and directors. Moreover, although
she'd recently received an increase in salary,
it didn't come close to the pay base com-
manded by other high-visibility stars. While
she and DiMaggio had discussed the possibility of her breaking away from Fox and
starting her own independent film production company, nothing had come of the idea.
Ultimately, it was Milton H. Greene, a young,
opportunistic magazine photographer, who
persuaded Monroe to take matters into her
own hands.

Marilyn first met Greene in September
1949 at a Beverly Hills house party. He'd
come to town to put together a photo essay

for *Life* magazine on promising Hollywood starlets. Johnny Hyde, with whom Monroe was then living, had gone to Palm Springs for the week on a business-related matter.

Attracted to the vibrant, darkly handsome, twenty-seven-year-old photographer — and hoping to be included in his photo essay — Marilyn spent two nights with him at what he referred to as "my West Coast house," the Chateau Marmont, overlooking Sunset Boulevard. After his return to New York later that month, he received a playful telegram from Marilyn addressed to Milton "Hot Shutter" Greene:

. . . .
It's that I think you are superb –
And that, my dear, is not just a blurb. . . .

Marilyn and Milton didn't meet again until October 1953, when he returned to Hollywood with Amy Greene, his newlywed bride, a former New York fashion model. In the interim, Greene had moved from *Life* to *Look* magazine. Monroe again spent time with the couple in September 1954, during the New York location filming of *The Seven Year Itch*.

Like Joe DiMaggio, Milton felt strongly that Twentieth Century–Fox had exploited Monroe and that she possessed far more promise and talent than the studio seemed willing to admit. Frank Delaney, Greene's lawyer, read

Marilyn's contract with Fox and contended that it was basically a "slave labor agreement" and therefore invalid. By December 1954, encouraged by Milton Greene, whose judgment she'd come to trust, the "not-so-dumb blonde" had made up her mind to sever her connections with Fox and to leave Hollywood altogether and relocate to New York.

In the back of her mind lurked the enticing figure of Arthur Miller, who worked and lived in New York. But there were other considerations as well. Her old flame Elia Kazan had often spoken to her of the Actors Studio, located in Manhattan, which he had co-founded and which acting guru Lee Strasberg ran.

The school taught the Method approach to acting, and it had earned a reputation as the country's leading training ground for both novice and experienced performers. The school would be an ideal place for Marilyn, insisted Kazan, since it represented an extension of the acting style she'd previously studied with Michael Chekhov. While still in Los Angeles, Marilyn Monroe met with Paula Strasberg, Lee's wife, and she, too, offered encouragement, suggesting Monroe could refine her acting skills by taking courses at the Actors Studio at the same time as she launched her film production company.

To expedite Marilyn's move to New York, Milton Greene flew to Los Angeles and helped her pack. On her last night in Hollywood, she and Greene went nightclubbing with Sammy Davis Jr., Mel Tormé, and Shelley Winters, who'd studied at the Actors Studio and gave it high marks. The entire group, including Greene, assured Marilyn she'd made the right decision. The next day, escorted by Milton Greene, she flew to New York.

In early January 1955, having checked into a sixth-floor suite at the Gladstone, an apartment-hotel on Fifty-Second Street, off Park Avenue, Marilyn held a press conference announcing the establishment of Marilyn Monroe Productions, Incorporated (MMP). Not surprisingly, she named Milton Greene as the other major partner in the corporation. Marilyn, as president, controlled fifty-one percent of MMP's 1,012 shares, which went public that spring. Greene quit his $50,000-a-year job at *Look* in order to devote more time to the new project.

Fox executives were outraged by what they regarded as Marilyn Monroe's blatant refusal to live up to her existing contractual obligations. They threatened to sue and vowed that she would never again appear in a Hollywood film, depicting her in the press as a talentless floozy who dared to make preposterous artistic demands on the greatest and noblest of Hollywood's film studios. "It was as though," wrote one film critic, "Cinderella had betrayed her fairy godmother."

Marilyn's bold step pleased Joe DiMaggio. He congratulated his former wife and complimented Milton Greene for having liberated Marilyn from the Fox "salt-mine," a feat even he had not been able to accomplish. He did, however, take some satisfaction in the knowledge that his constant badgering had evidently played some role in Marilyn's decision to part company with the studio. It must also have occurred to him that if Marilyn were to remain in New York, he might stand a reasonable chance of getting her back. Lest one forget, New York belonged to Joe DiMaggio.

Retaining her suite at the Gladstone, Marilyn began spending time at the Greene residence on Fanton Hill Road in Weston, Connecticut, an hour from Midtown. For her part, Amy Greene seemed blithely unaware — or unwilling to concede — that her husband and Marilyn had been sexually involved. Even harder for her to believe was the possibility that they were still lovers, though years later she would describe Marilyn to author Donald Spoto as a "home wrecker" and her husband as a cagey, elusive man, "given to excesses and indulgences he seemed unable to control," one of which was evidently a long-term addiction to pharmaceuticals. In fact, he soon replaced Sidney Skolsky as Marilyn's "candy man," regularly supplying her with pain pills and barbiturates. He had no problem getting prescriptions, as several members of his family were physicians.

Despite her ongoing affair with Milton, which ended only that spring, Marilyn managed to establish a close friendship with Amy. They often drove into New York together to shop for clothes at Saks and Bonwit Teller, Marilyn hidden under her usual disguise of sunglasses and a black wig. With her background in fashion, Amy helped Marilyn put together a "proper" New York wardrobe, a collection of outfits of which even Joe DiMaggio would have approved.

Marilyn became very much a member of the Greene household, claimed Amy. The Greenes had an infant son, Joshua, for whom Marilyn often babysat. She enjoyed bathing and feeding the young child, and she frequently bought him presents, including a large stuffed bear named Socko. She told Amy that more than anything she wanted to have children of her own but feared that she couldn't, having undergone a number of early "two-dollar" abortions.

As Marilyn's latest confidante, Amy heard stories about the failed marriage to Joe DiMaggio, a marriage that might have succeeded had he permitted her to get on with her career. "I don't know whom he thought he was marrying when he married me," she told Amy.

Marilyn characterized her marriage to DiMaggio as "a sort of crazy, difficult friendship with sexual privileges." Later in life, it occurred to her that that's what marriages often turn out to be. At another point, she maintained that she never should have married Joe — she never could have been the Italian housewife he wanted her to be. She'd married him, she said, because she'd felt sorry for him; he seemed so lonely and sad. A number of years later, she would describe her marriage to Arthur Miller in much the same way.

As Amy Greene saw the marriage to DiMaggio, "Joe never fit into her life, and she never fit into his. They were in love, but unmatched, except sexually. They fucked like bunny rabbits."

Joe and Marilyn's friendship had not ended. In late January, Milton Greene and Marilyn traveled to Boston to meet with Henry Rosenfeld, the wealthy dress manufacturer who'd once had a brief interlude with the actress. Presently in Boston to open an apparel factory, he'd contacted Marilyn and invited her to join him to discuss the possibility of his investing a large sum in MMP. He hadn't counted on her bringing along her business partner. Nor did he realize that Marilyn was still involved with Joe DiMaggio.

The ballplayer happened to be visiting his

brother Dom and Dom's wife at their home in Wellesley, Massachusetts. Marilyn called DiMaggio at his brother's and said she wanted to see him. He picked her up at her hotel, and they spent the next five days together at Dom's house.

"The instant the press got wind that Joe and Marilyn were staying together, they were on top of us," recalled Dom DiMaggio. "We couldn't go anywhere or do anything without the press coming along. One evening we drove to Boston and went out to dinner. As we were finishing our meal, a journalist came over to the table. He wanted to know if Joe and Marilyn were reconciling. Joe looked at Marilyn. 'Are we, darling?' he asked. Marilyn paused, then said, 'Let's just call it a visit.' "

Several days later, a half dozen press cars sat across the street from Dom DiMaggio's house. They'd been there for hours waiting for Joe and Marilyn to emerge. One by one they began to leave. Ed Corsetti, a reporter for the *Boston Herald American,* sat behind the wheel of a brand-new, black-and-white Ford with photographer Carroll Myett. They, too, were about to leave when the door to Dom's house opened, and out walked the celebrated couple. Marilyn wore a big floppy hat and sunglasses. Without a word, they climbed into a Cadillac convertible and drove off. Corsetti and Myett followed them.

"DiMaggio must have driven five miles

before he realized we were behind him," said Corsetti. "We were on Route 9, headed west. I didn't know where he was going. Maybe he was going back to New York. Carroll had his camera, one of those big old cameras, up by the windshield. I didn't know for sure if DiMaggio, looking through the rearview mirror, saw this car following him with this guy with a camera. But he put on the gas. And I mean, he took off. We were following him and he had to be doing eighty miles per hour! Carroll kept saying, 'You're going to get us killed!' I was hoping like hell the state troopers would show up and stop him. As I was trying to pull alongside him so Carroll could get his shot, he pulled his car to the left. I had to brake and back down. We must have chased him for fifteen or twenty miles. He put it in overdrive. He had to be going a hundred miles per hour. I said, 'This is crazy. We're driving a Ford, and he's driving a Cadillac.' We let him go. I'll give him credit — he was a hell of a driver. And the two of them were as big as anything in the country at the time."

Ed Corsetti had been correct. Joe and Marilyn were indeed en route to New York. He dropped her at the Gladstone Hotel and headed straight to Toots Shor's, where he bumped into Red Smith and Lou Effrat, a sportswriter for the *New York Times*. Elated by the five days he'd just spent with his former wife, Joe intimated that he and Marilyn might soon embark on a second honeymoon.

That DiMaggio remained hopeful regarding a possible second marriage is evidenced by entries he made at this juncture in an ongoing series of notebooks he had begun keeping in the late 1940s, a kind of chronological journal of his comings and goings. A second set of notebooks — twenty-nine of them — covering the years 1962 to 1999, were even more impersonal than the first set and made no mention at all of Marilyn. Both sets served primarily as a daily reminder of appointments as well as a detailed record of DiMaggio's expenditures — how much he'd spent and where. Yet buried within his first set of jottings are two pages devoted to Marilyn.

The first page presents a list of guidelines for what to do and what not to do in Marilyn's presence: reminders to himself to avoid being critical, to be humbler and to share his true feelings and show affection, to practice patience, and to refrain from jealousy.

The other journal page devoted to Monroe recounts details of a conversation between Joe and Marilyn, where, in making a date to see each other, Marilyn requested time to apply makeup because, she averred, "You like me in makeup." He says he told her, "You look good anytime, made up or not. You have natural beauty."

Their late-evening date took place on February 9. Joe stayed overnight with Marilyn at the Gladstone, where their room service breakfast consisted of champagne and caviar. They met again a few weeks later, when he invited her to accompany him to a private birthday party for Jackie Gleason at Toots Shor's.

Jane Duffy, a guest at the Gleason party with her husband, remembered being introduced to Marilyn. "Mike Duffy, my husband, was a good friend of George Solotaire," said Jane. "Joe DiMaggio and George were staying in a two-bedroom suite at the Hotel Madison. Later they moved into the Mayflower. At any rate, the four of us went to dinner quite often, usually at '21.' You couldn't get through a meal without a dozen strangers approaching the table to ask DiMaggio for an autograph, including the waiters and busboys. He wasn't a rocket scientist, and he didn't strike me as terribly deep, but there was definitely something special about him. Let's face it: he was as renowned as they come. I mean, here's a guy who partied with the likes of Ernest Hemingway, Margaret Truman, Fred Astaire, Judy Garland, Dietrich, Sinatra, Orson Welles, and the Rockefellers. Yet, for all his fame, he exuded a real shyness. He wasn't aloof or stuck up, but he was exceedingly private. He almost never mentioned Marilyn.

"So anyway, we were at Jackie Gleason's birthday party and Joe introduced me to Marilyn. She had a voluptuous figure, naturally, but she was small boned, which added to her beauty. She was smaller in person than she looked on-screen, which I suppose is true of most movie stars. I could understand what DiMaggio saw in her. She had what Billy Wilder once called a kind of 'elegant vulgarity.' On a personal level, she seemed polite but distant. She didn't say much. I asked if I could bring her a glass of Piper-Heidsieck, which is the champagne they were serving, and she said, 'No thanks, I don't drink.' An hour later she had a glass of champagne in her hand and looked half-crocked. The next time my husband and I dined with George and Joe, I asked DiMaggio whether Marilyn drank alcohol. 'Does a bear shit in the woods?' he answered. Coming from Joe DiMaggio, that made for quite a statement."

For reasons that Joe DiMaggio could never understand, Marilyn suddenly disappeared from his life. She took his phone calls and continued to seek his advice, but she was always too busy to see him in person. For one thing, she found herself enmeshed in legal discussions with Twentieth Century–Fox.

To avoid a costly legal battle with the studio, Marilyn Monroe and Milton Greene agreed to let her attorney Loyd Wright work out a compromise with Fox. The renegotiated agreement called for Marilyn to star in four Fox films over the next seven years. However, she would have director approval and the right to veto "substandard" screenplays. She would receive $100,000 per film and a percentage of the profits. Most important, she retained the right to make one film each year for a studio other than Fox, which cleared the way for the operation of Marilyn Monroe Productions. Milton Greene estimated that, with any degree of luck, MMP stood to make a minimum of $1 million a year for the next seven years and far more thereafter. With this figure in mind, he agreed that the production company would underwrite all of Marilyn's living expenses.

In addition to her involvement with MMP, Marilyn had begun taking acting lessons with Lee Strasberg, director of the Actors Studio. Born in Budaniv, in the former Austro-Hungarian Empire in 1901, Strasberg rapidly emerged as one more in her never-ending list of surrogate fathers. "He became my coach, friend, advisor, mentor, hero, champion, and savior," said Marilyn. Strasberg compared Marilyn's talents favorably to those of Marlon Brando, the most esteemed of his acting students. "I saw that what Marilyn looked

like was not what she really was," noted Strasberg. "And what was going on inside was not
what was going on outside, and that always
means there may be something there to work
with. It was almost as if she had been waiting
for a button to be pushed, and when it was
pushed, a door opened, and you saw a residue
of gold and jewels."

One of Lee Strasberg's standard suggestions — practically a requirement — was that
students enhance their reservoir of primal
memories and emotions (what he called
"sense memory") by entering psychoanalysis.
He and Paula were undergoing analysis, and
both felt, among its other advantages, that it
had strengthened their marriage. Turning to
Milton Greene for advice on the subject,
Marilyn was soon given a referral. Greene
himself had been in therapy for several years
with Dr. Margaret Herz Hohenberg, who,
like Lee Strasberg, had come to the United
States from Hungary to escape the concentra-
tion camps of the Third Reich.

A follower of the Viennese school of psychoanalysis founded by Sigmund Freud, Hohenberg, at fifty-seven, was a tall, heavy woman
with white hair that was often braided and
wrapped around her head. She lived at 11
Riverside Drive and worked out of an office
located at 155 East Ninety-Third Street, off
Lexington.

On Milton Greene's recommendation,

Marilyn met with the analyst. By March 1955, she was seeing Hohenberg five times a week. Monroe's presence on the block did not go unnoticed; Hohenerg's neighbors would frequently stop her on the street and inquire, "How is Miss Monroe doing today?"

During their sessions, for which Marilyn invariably arrived late, they dealt with the traumas of Monroe's chaotic childhood, her lack of self-esteem, her lust for approval, her dread of rejection, her obsessive search for a father figure, her need to satisfy "everybody," and her fear of abandonment.

To facilitate the analytic process, the actress recorded her thoughts and dreams in a series of binders that, in 2010, were posthumously published as a single volume called *Fragments,* which seemed an appropriate title considering Hohenberg's pronouncement, made soon after she met Marilyn, that the actress possessed "a fragmented mind."

Typical of Marilyn's nightmarish notations in *Fragments* is one that reads: "For Dr. H— Tell her about that dream of the horrible, repulsive man — who is trying to lean too close to me in the elevator — and my panic and then my thought despising him — does that mean I'm attached to him? He even looks like he has a venereal disease."

After six months of treatment, Hohenberg diagnosed Monroe as suffering from border-line personality disorder, a psychological condition characterized by intense turmoil and instability in relationships and behavior. Marilyn demonstrated two of the conditions commonly associated with BPD: dissociation and depersonalization. Under stress, her mind and body would literally shut down, which helped explain (at least to Hohenberg) why Marilyn was always late for appointments and had difficulty remembering her lines when appearing in films.

Strangely enough, Hohenberg also determined that Marilyn had a hearing dysfunction in her right ear. She sent her to Dr. Eugen Grabscheid, an audiologist, who confirmed that she had a mild case of Ménière's disease, a permanent buildup of fluids in the inner ear, a potentially dangerous, difficult-to-treat ailment that led to hearing loss and bouts of dizziness.

"Marilyn took it as a sign of aging," Hohenberg told Iselin Simon, a bridge partner and sometime companion, one of the few people the therapist spoke to about her famous patient. "She was panicky about growing old. She took two bubble baths a day and lathered herself with all sorts of lotions. My office was located a few doors down from a Whelan's Drug Store, and she spent hours walking the aisles searching for beauty ointments and creams, anything and everything to help stave off the inevitable aging process. She could never have grown old. Never!"

Confirming Dr. Hohenberg's summation, Amy Greene remembered Marilyn's telling her, "I'm going to die young like Jean Harlow." Marilyn, said Greene, yearned to be Harlow. "All of Marilyn's men were disasters — like Harlow's. She based her life on Jean Harlow and often spoke of playing Harlow in a biographical film. In later years, I believe she even went to visit Jean Harlow's mother." Amy went on to say that though Marilyn claimed she needed to master her craft and become a serious actress, "I never bought it." Marilyn, she asserted, "loved being all tits and ass. She invented tits and ass. She wanted to be a movie star, not an actress. Tits and ass were at her very core."

Amy Greene grossly underestimated Marilyn's resolve to improve her acting skills and perform in films she deemed worthy of those skills. "I'm tired of being a symbol," she told Dr. Hohenberg.

Under Lee and Paula Strasberg's influence, she became an earnest devotee not just of Method acting but also of Freudian analysis. She took an interest in all things Freud. She delighted in learning that Dr. Grabscheid, the audiologist, had once been Sigmund Freud's physician. Through Grabscheid, she became acquainted with Harry Freud, a New York cousin of Anna Freud, Sigmund's

271

daughter, at the time living and practicing psychiatry in England. After meeting with Monroe, Harry Freud wrote to Anna: "I was surprised that today's most glamorous and sexy film star has the intellectual capacity to be interested in Freud." Harry's evaluation of Monroe stood in stark contrast to the tongue-in-cheek self-appraisal put forth in Marilyn's personal memoir: "I try to hide it, but I'm quite dumb."

"Marilyn was anything but dumb," said Whitey Snyder, "but I never agreed with her decision to move to New York. Milton Greene lured her there by making all sorts of promises. He was a wily, manipulative, conniving man who saw Marilyn as little more than a commodity on whose shoulders he could ride in his bid to become a successful and wealthy film producer. However, I have to add that to some extent he put his own ass on the line. To raise initial capital for the venture, he mortgaged his house and took out loans. Of course, in the back of his mind, he was convinced he'd make a fortune off Marilyn. But at least he made an effort to aid the cause, which is more than I can say for the Strasbergs. If you ask me, Marilyn put the Actors Studio on the map rather than the other way 'round. The majority of Lee's pre-Monroe students, with the notable exception of Montgomery Clift and Brando, were in the theater; the big film names, like De Niro and Pacino, became involved long after Marilyn made the place famous."

The worst of it, from Whitey's perspective, concerned Paula Strasberg. "Lee's wife was an absolute disaster," said Snyder. "Marilyn hired her to replace Natasha Lytess as her 'on-location' acting coach. She was known in the trade as the 'black witch.' Obese and obnoxious, she perpetually wore black and knew absolutely nothing about acting. She robbed Marilyn blind. And so, for that matter, did Lee. They charged her immense sums of money for their so-called services, and Marilyn, in her naïveté, and with her insecurities, paid. Lee Strasberg took credit for creating Marlon Brando. I knew Brando, and I once asked him what he thought of Lee Strasberg. Marlon said, 'Lee Strasberg popularized, bastardized, and misused Method acting. He's an ambitious, selfish, untalented man who used and exploited his students. I have no respect for him. The only reason I attended the Actors Studio is that it was a good place to pick up women.' "

The Strasbergs had two teenaged children, Susan and John, both of whom in time turned to acting as a profession. Describing Marilyn's dealings with his parents, John Strasberg told author Anthony Summers, "People took advantage of Marilyn . . . even my father, in a way. They glommed on to her special sort of life — her special characteristics — when what she needed was love. My parents did give her some love, but it was inextricably linked with the acting."

Susan Strasberg provided an equally blunt explanation when she said, "My dad fell in love with Marilyn, while she in turn regarded him as a father figure. Despite his amorous feeling toward her, he did want to improve her acting skills. He used to tell her she lacked discipline and technique, and while he could impart the latter, she had to develop the strength to discipline herself. Regarding my mother, when she looked at Marilyn, she saw dollar signs, a means to an end. I'm certain she liked Marilyn, but it was more a question of what Marilyn could do for her. And I'm also sure she considered Marilyn a threat to her marriage, which is one reason she kept such a close eye on her. As for me, I suppose I represented a kind of kid sister to Marilyn. When I turned eighteen, she sent me to a gynecologist and paid for a diaphragm. She gave me a birthday card, which said, 'I want you to be free, but I don't want you to get pregnant.' "

Joe DiMaggio Jr., still in Los Angeles attending Black-Foxe Military Institute, heard from Marilyn on a regular basis even after she moved to New York. "She'd promised to keep in touch with me, and she did," he said. "She used to write all the time. I recall her sending me a photograph of a beautiful female cat somebody had given her. The cat became pregnant, and she had to give away the kittens. She named one of them 'Joey,' after yours truly. Then she had to give the mother cat away because Sydney Guilaroff, the Hollywood hairdresser, gave her a couple of parakeets, Butch and Bobo. She sent me a snapshot of the birds. She sent me another photo of herself atop a pink elephant that she rode in Madison Square Garden at the 1955 opening of the Ringling Brothers and Barnum & Bailey Circus. She was scantily attired in sequins and spangles, and I remember hearing that when the press ran the picture, my father called her up and excoriated her for appearing in public 'practically in the nude.' She shut him up by explaining that the day's proceeds were being donated by Ringling Brothers to a charity [the Arthritis and Rheumatism Foundation]. She also reminded him that they were no longer married, and she didn't have to account to him for her actions."

Later that year, Marilyn was approached by Gardner Cowles, the publisher of *Look,* who told her that Greek shipping magnate Aristotle Onassis wanted to meet with her to discuss the possibility of her getting together with Prince Rainier of Monaco. It seemed that the fabled prince wanted to find a wife in order to produce an heir to his Mediterranean fiefdom. "Marilyn thought it highly amusing that Rainier would consider her," said Joe DiMaggio Jr. "She began signing her letters 'Princess Marilyn.' In the end, he married Grace Kelly, and Marilyn's next letter to me read, 'One more competitor bites the dust.'" Marilyn sent Grace Kelly a telegram that read "I'm so happy you found a way out of this business."

On April 8, 1955, Edward R. Murrow interviewed Marilyn on *Person to Person,* the popular television program. Joe Jr. watched the show with classmates in his dormitory's recreation room. The interview took place at the Greene residence in Connecticut. "The Greenes did far more talking than Marilyn," said Joey, "and you could see that Edward Murrow wasn't the least bit interested in anything they had to say. He wanted to hear what Marilyn had to say. You came away from the program with the distinct impression that the Greenes were using her to satisfy their own particular needs. Of course, my classmates were up to their usual antics, yelling and yelping whenever Marilyn appeared on camera. 'What a pair!' one of them shrieked. And then they all went off like a bunch of jackals."

Establishing herself in her new setting, Monroe received help from *New York Post* syndicated columnist Leonard Lyons and photographer Sam Shaw (along with his wife

Anne) as well as from Milton Greene. She lunched with Pulitzer Prize–winning playwright Sidney Kingsley, actor David Wayne, and Broadway producer and lyricist Richard Adler. She met photographers Philippe Halsman, Richard Avedon, and Bert Stern. She befriended poet Norman Rosten, his wife, Hedda, and their young daughter, Patricia. Tennessee Williams visited the Greenes one evening and offered Marilyn the female lead in the film version of his latest play *Cat on a Hot Tin Roof,* which she considered but ultimately declined. At a New York dinner party, she was introduced to Mary Leatherbee, *Life* magazine movie editor, and Tom Prideaux, *Life* entertainment chief. The prevailing feminine style when Marilyn arrived on the New York scene was tall, slim, and elegant. The top models of the day were Suzy Parker, Dorian Leigh, and Anne St. Marie. But Marilyn, as the magazine editors and photographers soon discerned, had her own style. "Curves and sex are suddenly in vogue," said Truman Capote.

Capote saw a good deal of Marilyn following her arrival in New York. They went dancing together at El Morocco. Marilyn would kick off her shoes to reduce their height difference. She told him she liked to dance naked in front of a mirror and watch her breasts "jump around." They window-shopped on Madison Avenue, attended the theater, and watched movies together on television. Capote introduced her to the Southern novelist Carson McCullers, who was also staying at the Gladstone Hotel, and the three of them went to a jazz club and then to a party at the St. Regis.

One evening, Truman and Marilyn ate dinner with a disoriented Montgomery Clift, after which Marilyn told Capote, "Monty's the only person I know who's worse off in life than me." Capote concurred. Monty Clift was hopelessly addicted to amphetamines, whereas Marilyn, according to Capote, had become dependent on "downers" — sleeping pills and tranquilizers — which she washed down with booze. Capote took Marilyn to a party hosted by Hearst newspaper society columnist Igor Cassini at Le Club, the exclusive Manhattan nightspot, and by evening's end, she had passed out. She gave an encore performance a few days later at the Stork Club. Capote referred Marilyn to a Park Avenue internist, who recommended that she cut back on her therapy sessions and attendance at the Actors Studio. Marilyn had no intention of following the doctor's advice.

On April 28, 1955, Truman and Marilyn met at the Universal Funeral Home, down the block from the Gladstone Hotel, to attend the funeral of British Shakespearean actress Constance Collier. Marilyn had once taken a breathing class taught by Collier in

Hollywood, and Collier had spoken to Capote about her pupil, referring to her as "a big beautiful child," giving rise to a Capote profile of Monroe that he entitled, "A Beautiful Child."

In his profile, Capote recalled that Marilyn had arrived late for the Collier funeral, so they'd sat in the back row of the funeral home. After the service they went to a nearby bistro and shared a bottle of "bubbly." As they sat and drank, Marilyn said, "I hate funerals. I'm glad I won't have to go to my own. Only, I don't want a funeral — just my ashes cast on the waves by one of my kids, if I ever have any." Marilyn spoke about how much she loved New York and loathed Los Angeles. "Even though I was born there, I can't think of one good thing to say about it," she remarked. "If I close my eyes and picture LA, all I see is one big varicose vein." They discussed actors and acting. Marilyn wanted to know what Elizabeth Taylor was *really* like. "Well," responded Capote, "she's a little like you. She wears her heart on her sleeve and talks salty." To which Marilyn said, "Fuck you, Truman."

They finished their bottle of champagne and wandered down Third Avenue, past P. J. Clarke's saloon. Capote wanted to drop in, but Monroe didn't. "It's full of those advertising creeps," she said. "And that bitch Dorothy Kilgallen — she's always in there getting bombed. Capote, an acquaintance of the columnist's, defended her. Marilyn disagreed. "Kilgallen has written some bitch stuff about me," she said. "All those cunts hate me. Hedda. Louella. I know you're supposed to get used to it, but I just can't. It hurts. What did I ever do to those hags?"

They continued down Third and looked in shop windows, one of which displayed a handsome grandfather clock. "I've never had a home," said Marilyn. "Not a real one with all my own furniture. But if I ever get married again, and make a lot of money, I'm going to hire a couple of trucks and ride down Third Avenue buying every damn kind of crazy thing. I'm going to get a dozen grandfather clocks and line them all up in one room and have them all ticking away at the same time."

They went to a second bistro, and over a second bottle of champagne, Marilyn talked about Prince Philip ("He looks like he might have a nice prick"), Babe Paley ("She makes me look like pig slop"), and Joe DiMaggio ("I still love him — he's genuine"). Capote brought up Arthur Miller. He'd heard that Marilyn and Miller were lovers. Marilyn admitted only that they were in communication and had been for quite some time.

They ended the day by taking a taxi to the South Street Pier, past the Bowery with its pawnshops, blood-donor stations, bars, and fleabag hotels advertising 50-cent cots and $1 beds. Looking out the cab window at the ancient bums squatted curbside amidst broken glass and heaps of debris, Marilyn became upset. She began to cry when a purple-nosed "scarecrow" leaped out of the shadows and started swabbing the taxi windshield with a wet rag clutched in a shaking hand. The cab took off and finally reached South Street, where they were greeted by the sight of the Brooklyn skyline across the water and cavorting seagulls white against a marine horizon streaked with thin fleecy clouds. They stepped out of the cab and saw a man with a chow on a leash. Marilyn paused to pat the dog's head. As she reached out, the chow's owner said, "You should never touch strange dogs. They might bite." "Dogs never bite me," responded Marilyn. "Just humans." The man recognized Marilyn and asked for her autograph. She gave it to him, and then she and Capote walked to the end of the pier. Leaning against a mooring stanchion, the breeze fluffing her hair, Marilyn looked soothed and at peace. In the course of his profile, Capote wrote of Marilyn, "I hope, I really pray, that she survives long enough to free the strange lovely talent that's wandering through her like a jailed spirit."

In April Milton Greene decided Marilyn needed a more prestigious address than the

Gladstone Hotel and signed a sublet lease in her behalf for actress Leonora Corbett's twenty-seventh-floor, three-room suite at the Waldorf-Astoria Towers on Park Avenue — the same hotel where Dorothy Arnold had stayed following her divorce from Joe DiMaggio. The cost of the sublet was $1,000 per week. Other tenants at the Waldorf included General Douglas MacArthur, performer Tallulah Bankhead, and former president of the United States Herbert Hoover.

Although he hadn't seen Marilyn since just after Jackie Gleason's birthday party, Joe DiMaggio helped her move in. Their reunion was short lived. Marilyn's twenty-ninth birthday on June 1 coincided with the New York premiere of *The Seven Year Itch* at Loew's State Theater, in Times Square.

Monroe invited DiMaggio to the film, and he accepted. He then took the opportunity to arrange a late-night surprise birthday celebration for her at Toots Shor's. As he subsequently told George Solotaire, he'd expected to return to her Waldorf suite with her after the party. It turned out that she'd arranged a postparty rendezvous with Marlon Brando, whom she'd been dating on and off for several months.

Robert Solotaire attended the surprise birthday party with his father and recalled the argument: "Joe was already in a miserable mood because of *The Seven Year Itch* premiere. To gain entrance to the theater, he'd been forced to walk under a fifty-foot sign of Marilyn on the subway grating, her private parts practically exposed. It brought back painful memories. So, when Marilyn informed him she wouldn't be spending the night with him, it was like pouring gasoline on a hot fire. Joe loved Marilyn beyond anybody's imagination."

In his 1994 autobiography, Marlon Brando revealed that he'd first met Monroe on the Twentieth Century–Fox lot and then again at the Actors Studio. He saw her next at a New York cocktail party, where she sat alone, unnoticed in a corner, softly playing the piano. While holding a drink, Marlon spun around and hit her head. "I'm so sorry, it was an accident," he said. "There are no accidents," she replied.

He joined her at the piano, and they spent the evening talking and laughing. He called her several nights later, but she was busy. Then one night she called him. "I want to come over and see you right now," she said. Their love affair began that evening. The morning after going to bed with Brando, Marilyn reportedly said to Milton Greene, "I don't know if I do it the right way."

Referring to Marlon by the code name "Carlo," she described him to Amy Greene as "sweet and tender." On another occasion, she was quoted as saying, "Personally I react to Marlon Brando. He's a favorite of mine. He's one of the most attractive men I've ever known."

In his autobiography, Brando reflects on Marilyn, finding her extremely sensitive and misunderstood, much more perceptive than most people assumed. She'd been "beaten down in her life," but she had survived "because of her strong emotional intelligence." She had, he wrote, "a keen intuition for others' feelings and a most refined intelligence."

By midsummer 1955, Brando and Monroe's affair had evolved into an intimate friendship. "Despite their very different backgrounds," said Susan Strasberg, "they were like brother and sister. They both loved pranks and practical jokes. Marilyn once placed a life-size cutout of herself from *The Seven Year Itch* on the front lawn of actress Jane Wyman's Los Angeles residence. She resented Wyman because Fred Karger had married her instead of Marilyn, and she wanted to taunt Wyman, who was older and not as beautiful as Marilyn. Not to be outdone, Brando played a trick of his own on Marilyn. She'd told him she had a strong attraction to Albert Einstein, that she'd even sent him a fan letter requesting his autograph. So Brando went out and bought a glossy photograph of the mathematician and mailed it to Marilyn. He inscribed on it, "To Marilyn, with respect and love and thanks. Albert Einstein." Marilyn was thrilled at first, until she realized that Einstein had been dead for about six months. It didn't take her long to figure out who'd sent it.

CHAPTER 11

In June 1955, several weeks after their public spat at Toots Shor's, Joe DiMaggio wrote Marilyn Monroe a letter inviting her to join him at Cooperstown, New York, in July for his induction into the National Baseball Hall of Fame. His letter went on to say, "There's no reason that two people who love each other can't live together in marital bliss. It happens all the time." Joe's timing was unfortunate. Not only was Marilyn still dating Marlon Brando, she had also at long last reunited with Arthur Miller. It seemed as if, having been wed to one of America's greatest athletes, she now wanted to experience one of its most renowned intellectuals. The switch from DiMaggio to Miller could be viewed as symbolic of her desire to transform herself from a glamourous Hollywood star into a respected artist endowed with integrity and earnest commitment.

Still married and living with his wife and children on Willow Street in Brooklyn

Heights, Miller succumbed to temptation by indulging in an affair he felt he should probably have initiated when he first encountered Marilyn in Hollywood four years earlier. Making up for lost time, Arthur and Marilyn quickly became involved. Miller followed her wherever she went: the Greene residence in Connecticut, Norman Rosten's summer cottage in Port Jefferson, Long Island, the Strasberg vacation retreat on Fire Island, and Marilyn's posh suite at the Waldorf.

He rehearsed scenes with her that she then performed at the Actors Studio. Often accompanied by Sam Shaw (acting as beard), they took Arthur's basset hound Hugo for long walks in Prospect Park, sat at coffee houses in Greenwich Village, strode across the Brooklyn Bridge, fished for striped bass in Montauk, went boating at City Island, attended a Goya exhibit at the Metropolitan Museum of Art, and cruised around in Marilyn's black convertible Thunderbird, bought for her by Milton Greene with MMP funds. With Eli Wallach and his wife, Anne Jackson, fellow members of the Actors Studio, they drove to Far Rockaway Beach where they picnicked and played badminton. At other times they met in small, obscure Manhattan restaurants.

They lunched at Childs in Times Square with Robert Whitehead, the producer of Miller's plays. They rode their bikes through

Central Park and along the bike path that ran parallel to the Ocean Parkway in Brooklyn. Miller accompanied Marilyn to a photo shoot in connection with an advertising campaign she undertook for a lipstick manufacturer. He joined her, the Strasbergs, and the Rostens at dinner in the Sheraton-Astor Hotel following a fund-raiser for the Actors Studio. The couple visited friends of his in New Jersey and smoked pot. A two-minute color film of Marilyn dragging on a joint that afternoon was auctioned in 2009 for $275,000.

Monroe told Truman Capote that she and Arthur did weed together "quite often." And when they did, she said, he delighted in watching her perform her wink-wink, come-hither rendition of "Diamonds Are a Girl's Best Friend," from *Gentlemen Prefer Blondes*. It turned him on. And no wonder.

In *Timebends,* the playwright's 1987 autobiography, Miller wrote: "I no longer knew what I wanted — certainly not the end of my marriage, but the thought of putting Marilyn out of my life was unbearable. My world seemed to be colliding with itself, the past exploding under my feet."

Marilyn's nicknames for Miller, eleven years her senior, were "Popsie-Wopsie," "Poppy," and "Pa." She described him to Lotte Goslar as a serious man, but one with a wonderful sense of humor. "We laugh and joke all the time," she told Goslar. "I've always been alone," she continued. "I felt alone when I arrived in New York. Now, finally, I have Arthur. He's going to make my life better, a lot better."

Lotte Goslar had come to New York that summer to visit relatives and found Marilyn in an exuberant frame of mind. "I don't think I'd ever seen her happier," said Goslar. "She was so radiant she practically glowed. For starters, she'd taken steps to advance her career. She'd replaced her talent agency, Famous Artists, with MCA and had hired Arthur P. Jacobs and his New York public relations firm to handle her publicity. She'd also replaced Joe DiMaggio — to whom she now referred as 'Mr. D.' or 'My ex ex' — with Arthur Miller. She felt absolutely taken with him, and he felt the same about her. The only problem was that Miller still had a wife, but that fact didn't seem to deter Marilyn.

"Arthur and Marilyn had more in common than Marilyn and Joe. As a playwright, Miller understood the exigencies and extremes of an actor's mind. He comprehended the subtle nuances of Marilyn's complex nature. And since she was intellectually driven, she and Miller seemed well suited. I'm not sure how they matched up in the bedroom. Sexuality had obviously been the most important factor in her relationship with DiMaggio. I'm not certain that was the case with Miller. I imagine that what attracted her to him was his intellect and his creative spirit. One might even say that Arthur Miller did with a pen what Joe DiMaggio accomplished with his bat and baseball mitt."

The "secret" romance soon began hitting the press. "Joe must have read about Miller and Marilyn in the columns," said his golfing pal Paul Baer. "I saw him in late June, and he looked like shit. He'd lost about twenty pounds. He claimed his ulcers were acting up, and he couldn't eat. He said he was having trouble sleeping at night, and this is a guy who could literally fall asleep standing up. In addition, he was drinking heavily, but he refused to blame his troubles on Marilyn. He didn't want to talk about her, but you knew that her liaison with the playwright must have dimmed any hope he might have retained of getting back with her. The only negative comment I heard him utter — and it was an indirect comment at that — occurred when I told him I'd read a magazine article entitled 'Never Marry an Actress.' 'Tell me about it,' he responded. But in general, you couldn't bring up her name, because if you did, you were dead meat. I recall one fellow at Toots, a sportswriter, telling him he didn't think Marilyn could act, and he shot back, 'What the fuck do you know about acting — or about Marilyn, for that matter?' He never spoke to the guy again."

Like others in Joe's inner circle, Paul Baer recognized that Joe "carried a torch brighter and heavier than the one held by the Statue of Liberty. Marilyn Monroe was the one person in the world who seemed able to make Joe come alive. One evening my brother and I went to a Midtown Manhattan movie theater to catch a John Wayne flick. We each bought a bag of popcorn and climbed the stairs to the balcony. And I'll be damned if Joe DiMaggio wasn't seated up there by himself in the last row looking lost and unhappy. I invited him to join us. 'Thanks,' he said, 'but nobody will bother me back here and I'd rather be alone tonight.' By the time the movie ended, he'd vanished into thin air."

For the most part, Joe stopped going out at night, choosing instead to hibernate in his hotel suite, watching television, smoking cigarettes, and ordering his meals from room service. It was his usual means of escape. Very occasionally, when the mood struck, he'd drop into Toots Shor's, where he'd drink to excess and catch up on the news. Jackie Gleason saw him there one night and asked him, "Where the hell have you been?" "To hell and back," he answered. On another occasion he had dinner at Toots Shor's with Earl Wilson and his wife. In uncharacteristic fashion, Joe poured out his grief to the couple, asking where he'd gone wrong with

Marilyn, and what could he do to get her back.

"He seemed rather desperate," recalled the columnist, "and looking back, I probably offered him bad advice. I told him I didn't think it was hopeless, that Arthur Miller didn't offer much in the way of competition, that he represented a passing infatuation on Marilyn's part, nothing more. Besides, there was talk Miller was being investigated by HUAC — the House Un-American Activities Committee — and would probably wind up either in Mexico or prison. I wanted to ease his pain, but essentially I think I infused him with a false sense of optimism. The next thing I heard was that he was stalking Marilyn, convinced that he could rekindle her interest and win her back."

Jim Haspiel, still exultant over his previous year's brief encounter with Marilyn outside her hotel suite at the St. Regis, passed his days that summer camped in front of the Waldorf. "I used to sit on the stoop of a building opposite the front entrance of the hotel," he said. "I was there with a friend one afternoon, and my friend suddenly spotted this fellow lurking in the shadows, and, upon closer examination, it turned out to be Joe DiMaggio. He couldn't have been more than ten yards from us. And like us, he was focused on the hotel, hoping to catch a glimpse of Marilyn."

Fueled by his enduring jealousy, DiMaggio employed a variety of methods in his efforts to ascertain the actress's whereabouts. Wearing a fake beard, he'd spend hours seated in the Waldorf lobby, pretending to read a copy of the *New York Times*. He bribed a doorman to keep tabs on Marilyn's visitors. In time he became more aggressive, tipping the elevator operator to take him to Marilyn's floor, so he could confront her in person.

"Marilyn would phone my father at three in the morning to complain that Joe DiMaggio was harassing her, following her around, pounding at her door at all hours," said Susan Strasberg. "She wouldn't let him in, but she also refused to call the police because she didn't want him to be arrested. In early July he hired a private detective, and the man broke into her Waldorf suite and took one of her address books. Initially, I couldn't understand what Marilyn saw in him. They were compatible in bed, but you don't marry someone just because the sex is good. She told me he was very rigid in his beliefs. He wanted her for all the reasons any man would want her — she was gorgeous. He found her beautiful and sexy, but he didn't want any other man to see in her what he saw."

Susan Strasberg eventually figured out why Marilyn tolerated Joe's odd behavior and why she never completely severed their connection. According to Strasberg, Marilyn always knew where she stood with Joe. She knew she could count on him. She knew he was always there for her. No matter what the circumstance, she could always call on him. He was the one person — the only person — she could depend on. She could always lean on him, and he asked for little in return other than to be with her. For a woman whose existence was so unsettled, there was great relief and comfort in that notion. In a life marked by so much turmoil, he was her one constant: a lover, a father figure, and a friend.

The main problem for DiMaggio was that when he wasn't with Marilyn, he was visited by demons. In late July he drove up to Cooperstown by himself to be inducted into the Baseball Hall of Fame. The annual three-day event always drew thousands of rabid baseball fans and other Hall of Famers who'd already been inducted. The ballplayers were housed gratis at the Otesaga, a majestic five-star hotel bedecked by sprawling verandas overlooking a large, pristine lake and the rolling countryside of upstate New York. An eighteen-hole golf course was located a half mile away. When the old-timers weren't attending banquets and the official induction ceremony, which included a motorcade through the streets of Cooperstown, they would fish, golf, hobnob, and drink.

The owner of a baseball memorabilia shop in town remembered the '55 induction ceremony. "DiMaggio came up with his fishing rod and set of golf clubs," she said. "It was the first of many visits. He'd come up every year for the ceremony, and because he was the Great DiMaggio, he'd be given the best suite at the hotel and shown every courtesy. I can tell you from personal experience that he was a miserable character, a real jerk."

The shop owner went on to say she knew a bellhop at the Otesaga who could attest that DiMaggio never tipped. "My friend would carry his luggage up to the suite and be dismissed with a mere nod of the head," she said. "He didn't tip the hotel waiters, the hotel bartender, the golf course caddies, or the restaurant personnel who served him in town. In '55, he was particularly annoying. He refused to give autographs and even snubbed the kids that came up with their parents to watch him get inducted. He had a bug up his ass, and I suspect the bug's name was Marilyn Monroe."

In early August, following his return from Cooperstown, DiMaggio received a telephone call from Horace Stoneham, owner of the New York Giants. As reported by Leonard Lyons in the *New York Post,* Stoneham made Joe an incredible offer for that time: $40,000 for just one time at bat for the Giants in an upcoming game against their archrival, the Brooklyn Dodgers. DiMaggio turned down the offer on grounds that he still considered himself a New York Yankee. To don another team's uniform, even once, constituted high treason.

When George Solotaire asked him why he'd refused Stoneham's offer, DiMaggio responded, "Aside from the fact that I'm a Yankee, there comes a time in every ballplayer's life when his brain tells him to do one thing and his body says, 'You must be shitting me.' The last thing in the world I want to do is go down on strikes in front of sixty thousand screaming spectators. And that's exactly what would happen."

In the spring of 1951, Joe DiMaggio's final season with the Yanks, *Look* ran a profile of the Clipper, portraying him as nothing less than the Don Juan of the baseball diamond. "Joe is a heart-throb," read the piece, "a lady-killer, and the ideal male from a feminine point of view. Just bashful enough to be effective . . . Joltin' Joe is so attractive to women he has to wait in the clubhouse after each game to avoid being mobbed."

Joe's amorous adventures, so prolific in the past, all but ended during his years with Marilyn Monroe. With Marilyn by his side, there had been little need (or desire) on his part for outside stimulation. Yet without her — and concomitantly without baseball — his life lacked purpose.

In the first weeks following Marilyn's disappearing act, hidden away in his Mayflower Hotel suite, DiMaggio had attempted to escape the tedium of his pain and isolation by turning to New York's girl services for entertainment and relief. "It's like being back in the majors," he later told Robert Solotaire, his roommate's son. "Most of [the girls] were groupies, others you paid for . . . After a while, the girls all looked alike."

After weeks of sampling his share of high-priced escorts, DiMaggio received a telephone call from Frank Sinatra. The crooner wanted to introduce him to "a friend," a Las Vegas showgirl and burlesque queen named Liz Renay. Blond, boisterous, and buxom, Liz bore a distinct resemblance to Marilyn Monroe, so much so that in 1952 one gossip magazine declared her "the girl who looks more like Marilyn Monroe than Marilyn Monroe." But Liz had more in common with Marilyn than mere good looks.

Born in 1926, the same year as Monroe, Liz, like Marilyn, had endured a traumatic adolescence. By the age of eighteen, she had run away from home, married twice, and had two children. By twenty-nine, her list of lovers ran the gamut from film impresario Cecil B. DeMille to gangster Mickey Cohen. Judging from the title of one of her autobiographies — *My First 2,000 Men* — Renay wasn't shy about displaying an all but insatiable appetite for sex.

"I could never understand what Marilyn had that I didn't have," said Liz, "but she obviously had something. In any case, Frank Sinatra called me one evening and asked if I wanted to meet Joe DiMaggio. He said, 'Joe's very lonely.' I told him to give Joe my phone number. A few days later, I heard from him. We went out to dinner, got drunk, and stumbled back to his suite at the Mayflower. I figured if he turned on Marilyn, he must be pretty good in the sack. I decided to try and make him forget Marilyn. I must have done something right, because he came back for more."

Liz Renay found Joe "a bit aloof but still a nice guy, a good man, sweet and refined. He was a romantic. He used to send me bouquets of red roses. And yes, he was wonderful in bed. He acknowledged I looked like Marilyn, but that's all he said about her. I had a feeling the memories were still too raw. Mostly, he spoke about his childhood and how his father had been a fisherman. And of course he talked about baseball. He told me his brother Dom held the Boston Red Sox record for hitting safely in consecutive games, whereas Joe held the major-league record. In 1949 Dom DiMaggio hit safely in thirty-four straight games. When the thirty-fifth game rolled around, it was Joe who ended his brother's streak by catching a sinking line drive in the eighth inning in a game between the Yanks and Red Sox. 'He never forgave me,' said Joe. 'Talk about sibling rivalry,' I remarked. He laughed."

Liz noted that publishers and producers constantly besieged DiMaggio with book and film offers. "They could've given him ten million dollars, and he wouldn't have given in," she noted. "His privacy meant too much to him. He was the American hero that nobody knew. Some people claimed he didn't say much because he had nothing to say. That wasn't the case. He wasn't a chatterbox, but he had his moments. He talked about what it meant to be famous and the pressures that came with fame. He discussed his baseball career, the overbearing need he felt to get a hit even in an insignificant game before a few thousand spectators — after all, there might've been one fan that had never seen him play before. Another topic that enthused him was money. He advised me to invest in real estate. The next time we met he brought along a dozen brochures and spent hours going over them with me. On his recommendation, I put funds into a Florida motel chain and over the next five years made more than three times my original investment."

Surprisingly, as Liz learned, Joe liked to gossip. "He wanted to know all about my previous lovers, especially the well-known ones. I told him Alfred Hitchcock liked to be hog-tied and flogged with a dog leash. Cecil

DeMille had a foot fetish and loved sucking women's toes. Joe knew I'd been with Frank Sinatra and wanted to know if he was good in bed. 'He's okay,' I said. 'Is he better than me?' Joe wondered. I said, 'Sinatra can't carry your jock strap, and he certainly can't fill it.' Of course, Frankie asked me the same question about Joe. And I gave him more or less the same response — 'You're the best, Frankie.' That's what all men want to hear, even if it's total bullshit."

Liz Renay's relationship with DiMaggio encompassed a dozen dates spread over a ten-week period. "I realized mine wasn't the only name in his little black book," she said. "A drugstore delivery boy told me every time he brought an order to the suite, Joe would have a different woman with him. That didn't bother me because I saw a good deal of him in August, and I thought we might one day get married."

In late August, accompanied by George Solotaire, Joe took a break from Liz and flew to Italy to visit Isola delle Femmine, the Sicilian fishing village where both his parents were born and where he still had several distant cousins. According to Solotaire, they were treated like a couple of visiting potentates. Everywhere they went the crowds applauded the Clipper. DiMaggio thought the Italian fishing village looked and felt like Martinez, his birthplace, and began to understand why his parents had felt at home in California. A local teenager handed Joe a bat and softball, and the villagers watched in awe as DiMaggio belted the ball out of sight and into the sea.

After touring the rest of Sicily, Joe and George set out for Venice and that city's annual film festival. While in Venice, DiMaggio met French actress Anne-Marie Mersen, and their photo appeared prominently in the press. Joe and George then traveled to Rome and took a tour of the Vatican. Joe met Swedish actress Anita Ekberg at a Roman nightclub, and the two danced the night away. Joe and George spent a day in Paris and ended their European sojourn in London. Sir Cedric Hardwicke, the venerable British actor, drove them around the city. He offered to take them to a cricket match, but only if they had "six months or more to spare."

Back in the States, Joe appeared as the "mystery guest" on *What's My Line?*, the television game show hosted by John Daly, an occasional drinking partner of Joe's at Toots Shor's. Liz Renay accompanied DiMaggio to the TV studio and sat in the green room while four blindfolded panelists tried to guess the name of the guest. "When he stepped out on stage," said Liz, "the live audience went nuts. I mean, here was Joe DiMaggio on a television game show. It was so unlike him. And when it was Arlene

Francis's turn to guess, she said, 'My good-ness, only President Eisenhower and Marilyn Monroe would get that kind of reception.' The panel quickly established Joe's identity. But the mention of Marilyn's name jolted Joe. It was a painful reminder of just how savagely she'd injured him. I think it also pointed to the vast ego problem that had always existed between Joe and Marilyn. Before meeting her he was looked up to by millions. But after marrying her, a whole new generation of journalists arrived on the scene, some of whom thought of Joe as 'Marilyn's man.' He couldn't stand that. I mean, this is the guy they had to sneak out of Yankee Stadium after ballgames, so he wouldn't be mobbed and trampled by his army of fans."

After DiMaggio's return from Europe, he continued to date Liz Renay, creating the expectation in her mind that he might even propose to her. "I convinced myself that he would ask me to marry him," she said. "But one day the phone stopped ringing. I waited and waited, and nothing happened. Not a word. Tired of waiting, I dialed Joe's private number. An operator came on and said the number had been disconnected and the new number was unlisted. That ended that! I'd been unceremoniously dumped. I was heart-broken, primarily because Joe hadn't had the balls to break up with me in person."

Joe DiMaggio sought refuge in other Monroe look-alikes, not always with positive results. When told by a burlesque house proprietor that she looked like Marilyn, exotic dancer Dixie Evans retorted, "Everybody in Hollywood looks like Marilyn Monroe." She nevertheless tailored her act in imitation of Marilyn, walking, talking, and gyrating like the original. Joe DiMaggio checked out her act at Place Pigalle, an upscale burlesque house in Miami. He'd gone to Florida to visit Sid Luckman, the onetime quarterback for the Chicago Bears. Dixie joined Joe at his table at closing time. He walked her home and made a date to see her the following day. She'd forgotten she had scheduled a court appearance that day and, unable to reach Joe at the Fontainebleau Hotel, where he was staying, inadvertently stood him up. She never heard from him again.

More successful was his relationship with Gregg Sherwood Dodge, a former New York chorus girl at the Latin Quarter and a girlfriend of Dean Martin. Born Dora Fjelshad in Beloit, Wisconsin, Gregg had changed her name after competing in the Miss America Pageant. Joe first met her while playing for the Yankees. Her then husband, Walter Sherwin, held the position of box office treasurer for the team. After Sherwin and Gregg divorced, she later married aging motorcar scion Horace Dodge II.

"I knew Joe via our mutual connection to the Yankees," said Gregg, "but I didn't know him in the biblical sense until after his divorce from Marilyn. Our affair began in the back seat of a limousine in Palm Beach, Florida. He told me I looked like Marilyn, and I suppose that's what did it for him. As for me, I'd always liked him. He was regarded as the greatest ballplayer since Babe Ruth. I found him sexy. Having once been married to Marilyn Monroe made him seem even sexier.

"Regarding Monroe, I soon learned you never spoke of her to him, not even if he brought her up first. In that case, you merely listened. It was clear from the way he spoke that he'd been profoundly hurt by her. He was obsessed with her to the extent that for several years he couldn't work. All he did was play golf, drink, and move around from place to place, attempting to find solace in the arms of other women, a number of whom looked like Marilyn Monroe. For a while, he did the nightclub circuit. His photo would pop up in the papers with a different girl every few days. He had no difficulty meeting women. One young lady I knew went to bed with him and then divorced her husband with the expectation Joe would marry her, which of course he didn't.

"Another woman, about to be married, was so taken with Joe she went to bed with him and then informed him he was her 'last fling.'

The only good that came of his divorce from Marilyn is that it softened him somewhat. He'd always been a bit of a hard-ass, but after Marilyn he became more human, more understanding. All in all, Joe and I dated on a sporadic basis for a period of approximately three years. And after that, we remained friends, occasionally talking on the phone or meeting for dinner. Although he never said it directly, I concluded that he was smart enough to have ultimately figured out that Marilyn Monroe simply wasn't good wife material. She was what she was: a delightful companion and bed partner, but not a wife."

And then there was Francie (a pseudonym), an airline stewardess he encountered in the late summer of 1955 while visiting his pal Joe Nacchio in Panama City, Florida. "We met at a nightclub," she recalled. "I happened to be there with a girlfriend, and he came over and asked me to dance. I knew of him because I grew up in Boston, and my father, an avid Red Sox fan, used to take me with him to the ballpark. I'd met Ted Williams on one occasion, and when I told Joe about it that evening, he became quite animated. Williams batted .406 the same year [1941] that Joe hit in fifty-six consecutive games. Joe told me there had been talk between the owners of the Yanks and Red Sox to set up a trade: Williams would go to the Yanks, and Joe would play for the Red Sox. And his brother Dom

DiMaggio, Boston's center fielder, would be moved to right to make room for Joe."

From the beginning, Francie, a raven-haired version of Monroe, realized that any romance with DiMaggio had its limitations. "I'd been engaged and had broken it off shortly before I met Joe," she said. "I needed to recuperate and sort things out. Joe's marriage to Marilyn had ended badly. Neither of us wanted a serious relationship. We were happy to see each other only now and again. We'd meet in different cities, depending on my flight schedule. Joe had a friend in Philadelphia named Eddie Liberatore, a scout for the Dodgers, and he'd put us up. And there was a man in Chicago, Sam Brody, a clothing manufacturer, and he'd do the same. And when I had a layover in New York, I'd sometimes stay with him at the Hotel Lexington."

Meanwhile, Marilyn's liaison with Arthur Miller had become a matter of public record. At the end of September 1955, she accompanied him to the opening night of his latest play, *A View from the Bridge,* at New York's Coronet Theater. The play, which in part depicts a vile and violent Sicilian family engaged in the business of commercial fishing, may well have been fueled by Marilyn's representations to Miller concerning the physical abuse visited upon her by Joe DiMaggio. In any case, Arthur's wife, Mary, had learned of the affair and had ordered her husband out of their Brooklyn Heights apartment.

Soon after October 17 — his fortieth birthday — Arthur Miller (following a telephone session with his onetime psychiatrist, Dr. Rudolph Loewenstein) moved into the Chelsea Hotel on West Twenty-Third Street and then into an elegant West Side brownstone. Marilyn moved as well. Her six-month sublet at the Waldorf having ended, she took over a sublet on an apartment at 2 Sutton Place, with views of the East River and the Queensboro Bridge. Then, on October 31, 1955, she appended her signature to the final decree of divorce, legally and irrevocably terminating her marriage to Joe DiMaggio.

Joe was with his flight attendant Francie in New York a month after the filing in the California court system by Monroe's lawyer of the final set of divorce papers. "It was only a technicality," Francie noted. "The actual divorce proceeding had taken place the year before. Still, Joe seemed rather despondent over the phone. I didn't realize how despondent until I reached his hotel suite. There, atop his bed, he'd placed a life-sized porcelain-and-rubber doll made up to look exactly like Marilyn Monroe. The platinum hair looked real. It had lifelike arms and legs. The coloring, including makeup, was hers. The finger- and toenails of the doll were coated with red polish. The figure had obviously been constructed with great attention to detail and at considerable expense. There was an almost indecent authenticity to the breasts and other erogenous zones."

Francie's first reaction was disbelief, followed by confusion. Her plane, a night flight from Los Angeles, had arrived at eleven o'clock, and she'd taken a cab straight to Joe's hotel only to be confronted by the macabre mannequin.

"How do you like her?" asked DiMaggio.

"I don't," she said.

"I like her," remarked DiMaggio. "She's Marilyn the Magnificent. She can do anything Marilyn can do except talk."

"Can she make love to you?" asked Francie.

"Absolutely," answered DiMaggio. "Would you like a demonstration?"

As the onetime Yankee Clipper began to unbuckle his belt, Francie the flight attendant, still clutching her overnight bag, made her exit.

"It had to be one of the weirdest experiences I ever had," she said. "It absolutely and totally creeped me out. It goes without saying I never again spoke to Mr. DiMaggio."

Matters grew worse for Joe long before they got better. There seemed no way he could escape Marilyn. She was perpetually in the news. She'd agreed to return to Hollywood to begin shooting *Bus Stop.* She and Arthur Miller planned to get married. She wanted to convert to Judaism and have his babies. Miller was the first man she ever loved. Joe heard the latter declaration while watching television with Edward Bennett Williams, the prominent attorney he'd known since 1951 and at whose Washington, DC, home he stayed from time to time. (Williams was also TV game show moderator John Daly's father-in-law.) Marilyn's photo appeared on the covers of *Life* and *Time,* to say nothing of a dozen lesser publications. Joe couldn't avoid her image or erase the memory of the humiliating headlines they'd run when she left him, how the Great DiMaggio had "Struck Out" with the actress — headlines all too reminiscent of those published in Japan during their honeymoon, when they'd referred to him as "Mr. Marilyn Monroe." The indignity and shame he suffered from the most recent onslaught of news items dogged his every waking hour. His face would darken at the mere mention of her name. How could he begin to get over her if her image and words appeared everywhere all the time? And how dare "they" treat an American idol, one of history's greatest ballplayers, as if he were nothing more than a minor leaguer?

In early 1956 Paul Baer convinced Joe to "get away from it all" by accompanying him on a Florida golfing junket. "Joe wasn't a bad golfer," said Baer. "As one might expect, he had a beautiful swing. He just couldn't putt. On a good day he'd shoot in the midseventies. I recall one round we played in Tampa. I believe his pal Charlie Rubaleave, a commercial photographer, was with us that day. This was about the time the press was crowing about Marilyn Monroe's affair with Arthur Miller. One of our caddies had a copy of the local newspaper with Marilyn's photo in a swimsuit on the front page. We were on the fifth or sixth hole, a par three, and we had to wait at the tee for the foursome ahead of us to finish up and get off the green. So while we stood there, the caddie with the paper starts to glance at the front page, and the other caddie sees the photo of Marilyn, and he emits a loud wolf whistle. And Joe peers over between practice swings and figures out what it's all about. The poor caddie didn't mean anything by it, but Joe took it the wrong way. He grabbed the paper out of the first caddie's hands, rolled it up, and swatted the second caddie over the head with it. He then tore up the paper and stalked off the course. So much for our round of golf."

Paul Baer never saw the notorious Marilyn Monroe look-alike mannequin but heard about it from George Solotaire. "Evidently Joe paid some toy manufacturer ten thousand dollars to custom-produce this life-size, one-of-a-kind doll," said Baer. "It could fold up to fit into a leather carrying case that came with it. Supposedly he took it along when he traveled. George Solotaire told me that at some point in 1957, Joe destroyed it, which I took to be a promising sign."

DiMaggio may have longed for Marilyn, but in reality there was never a shortage of women to choose from. Aside from the more obvious Monroe imitators, Joe dated a number of starlets and actresses such as Gloria DeHaven, Diana Dors, Gina Lollobrigida, and Jayne Mansfield (often billed as "the poor man's Marilyn Monroe"). Francie was only one of several airline hostesses in his post-Marilyn life. The gossip columns played up his romances with TWA stewardesses in addition to "glamour girls" Myra Dell and Philadelphia Main Liner Peggy Deegan. Elsa Maxwell, the celebrated society hostess, took Joe under her wing and began inviting him to her many well-publicized parties. Through Elsa, DiMaggio met and dated a whole new crop of performers, including Cleo Moore, Shirley Jones, and Linda Darnell. Another actress, nineteen-year-old Italian sensation Georgia Moll, purportedly received a chinchilla bikini and a diamond pin from DiMaggio, a publicist's claim that he vehemently denied.

Publicists, press agents, and gossip scribes tended to make more of DiMaggio's social pursuits than they were worth. Lee Meriwether was a case in point. A former Miss California from San Francisco, Meriwether was crowned Miss America in 1955. In 1956 she returned to Atlantic City to crown her successor. With the twenty-year-old "former" beauty queen were her mother and brother. As Richard Ben Cramer relates the story in his DiMaggio biography, Joe chanced upon the trio in the lobby of an Atlantic City hotel. Lee's mother approached Joe and said to him, "I don't know if you remember my husband, but he used to come into your family's restaurant." The Clipper couldn't have been more polite. "It's possible," he responded, "I'm not sure." Taking stock of Mrs. Meriwether's daughter, he invited the whole family to dinner that night. Lee's mother and brother couldn't make it, so Lee went alone. Joe took her to Skinny D'Amato's 500 Club, the Mob's favorite Atlantic City hangout. Joe was more than a little familiar with the place; whenever he came to town, he stayed in a small, private apartment that D'Amato let him use on the second floor of the building. Not only did Skinny regularly play host to DiMaggio, but he also often slipped him a couple grand to appear at his club. The Clipper's presence in any drinking establishment created more publicity and thus more foot traffic. On this particular night, Joe had agreed to be interviewed on the weekly radio show that broadcast each

Sunday from the club, a "favor" D'Amato repaid by giving the Daig twice the usual handout.

Dinner with Lee went well, as did Joe's radio interview. He reminisced about his days as a Yankee. The second radio guest that evening was Walter Winchell. The columnist spent several minutes at the microphone telling the listening audience that he'd always been a "huge" admirer of Joe DiMaggio. "And do you know who he's with tonight?" Winchell added. "He's with the former Miss America, Lee Meriwether. I hear they're quite a team. Are there wedding bells in their future? Stay tuned."

After the radio show, Winchell insisted Joe and Lee accompany him to the Cotton Club, where there was a dance act that "couldn't be missed." In the cab on the way to the Cotton Club, the columnist turned to the couple and said, "Thanks for the scoop."

"Ah, Walter, come on," DiMaggio said. "You realize how long I know this girl? Maybe three hours."

Winchell remarked, "Are you saying you deny it?"

"Stop it, Walter. You're beginning to bug me."

Winchell knew enough to let it drop. But two days later, in the *New York Mirror,* he ran a full-page picture of DiMaggio and Meriwether taken at the 500 Club — the photo ran under a boldfaced headline: "TO WED?"

Meriwether, at the time the women's editor for NBC-TV's *Today* show, hosted by Dave Garroway, was asked by the program's producer if she wanted to deny the story on air. The next morning, Miss America 1955 informed ten million viewers that she barely knew Joe DiMaggio and had no intention of marrying him, now or ever.

Lee Meriwether didn't hear from DiMaggio until roughly six months later when, at two in the morning, the telephone rang in her bedroom, rousing her out of sleep. "It's Joe DiMaggio," said a voice at the other end. "I need to see you."

As her mind began to clear, she could hear that DiMaggio had been drinking. "Where are you?" she asked.

"Please, I need to talk to you. Can I come over?"

"What time is it?"

"What's the difference?" he said. "I'm coming over."

Lee felt uncomfortable. "How do you know where I live?" she inquired.

The caller hung up.

Despite the awkward content of their telephone conversation, Lee Meriwether occasionally dated Joe DiMaggio, accompanying him to New York nightspots, but only as a platonic friend and nothing more. There were other Miss Americas who found themselves in the same position. Marian Mc-Knight, Miss America 1957, didn't look very much like Marilyn Monroe but nevertheless did an impersonation of the Hollywood star during the talent phase of the pageant competition. Attired in a tight satin gown, long silk scarf, and a Yankees baseball cap with the number 5 on it, McKnight, a South Carolinian, warbled a cute new song she'd written about DiMaggio and Monroe in which, while making love, the ballplayer looks up and asks, "What's the score?" The Clipper caught the act while attending a dress rehearsal and was quoted in the press as saying, "That's my wife, all right. Miss McKnight does a good imitation." He and Marian had dinner together. Some time later she told the press, "Joe DiMaggio's a very sweet, down-to-earth man. We're friends, not very close friends, but we manage to keep in touch."

Yolande Betbeze, Miss America 1951, was likewise nothing more than Joe's friend, whose occasional dates were well covered by the press. The Stork Club would pay them to drop in and lend the place a bit of glamour. One reason the pair never connected on a deeper level had to do with Yolande's awareness that Joe, in the months following the dissolution of his marriage to Monroe, was emotionally incapable of sustaining anything approximating a real relationship.

Yolande had seen quite enough of DiMaggio stumbling from one Manhattan nightclub to another, wanting to touch the bright lights of the city without getting burned, a feat he could seemingly accomplish only when semi-polluted. She witnessed DiMaggio at his worst while both were visiting Paris, France. As Yolande related the story, she had brought along a female friend to help the friend get over a romantic involvement. In Paris, at the Hotel George V, where all three were staying, they ran into Joe.

One evening the trio went drinking, first at the Club Lido on the Champs Elysées, then at Au Lapin Agile in Montmartre. When they arrived back at the George V, DiMaggio, "totally shit-faced," put the make on Yolande's friend. Yolande was treated, as she put it, to the sight of DiMaggio sitting on an upper-floor staircase of the hotel very late at night, trying to talk Yolande's girlfriend into bed. The problem was that Joe had put away so much booze he could barely get out a coherent word. He was so smashed, in fact, he wasn't aware that his pants were wide open and his member was fully exposed. "And that," Yolande recalled, "was the biggest thing you ever saw."

CHAPTER 12

<u>Joshua Logan</u>, the director of *Bus Stop,*
Marilyn Monroe's next film, couldn't say
enough on behalf of his star's acting abilities.
"When I tell people Marilyn Monroe may be
one of the very finest dramatic talents of our
age," he ventured in an article for the *New
York Times,* "they laugh in my face. But I
believe it. I believe it to such an extent that I
would like to direct her in every picture she
wants me for, every story she can dig up."

Based on a hit Broadway play by William
Inge, *Bus Stop* marked the first collaborative
film effort between Twentieth Century–Fox
and Marilyn Monroe Productions. In ac-
cordance with her latest contract with Fox,
Monroe sanctioned the project, the director,
the screenwriter, and the cinematographer.
She'd had approval on Fox's selection of cast
members. She likewise had the last say on
the choice of costumes, though her *Bus Stop*
outfits turned out to be as low-cut and risqué
as every other film wardrobe she'd ever

slithered into. She replaced Natasha Lytess with Paula Strasberg, an action which so infuriated Lytess that she threatened to write a "tell-all" exposing her former pupil for what she was: "an ungrateful monster."

MM hired Hedda Rosten, Norman's wife, as her personal secretary at $250 per week. The Rostens attended the University of Michigan at the same time as Arthur Miller; Hedda and Mary, Miller's first wife, had been college roommates. Marilyn hired Hedda primarily because she'd heard that the Rostens were having money problems but also because, as a former social worker, Hedda had the capacity to be nurturing and supportive. And in February 1956 Marilyn leased a house at 595 North Beverly Glen Boulevard in the Westwood section of Los Angeles to serve as home base during the filming of *Bus Stop*. Marilyn shared the residence with Milton, Amy, and Joshua Greene, their two retainers, and Florence Thomas, her own housemaid.

Although Josh Logan's glowing assessment of Marilyn's performance in *Bus Stop* seems accurate enough, the movie itself, at least by contemporary standards, ranks with the most mediocre of Marilyn's previous films. In *Bus Stop* a naïve and simple-minded young rodeo cowboy named Bo (played by Don Murray) falls in love with Cherie (Marilyn Monroe), a hillbilly café singer whom he meets on a bus. His intentions are honorable — he wants to marry her — but his temper and jealous side are too much for her. When she tries to run away, he finds her and forces her to board a bus bound for his Montana ranch. When the bus stops at a diner, the passengers learn that the road ahead has been closed by a snowstorm and that poor Cherie is a kidnap victim. After spending a night in the diner, waiting for the storm to abate, the passengers prepare to reboard the bus. Our rodeo cowpoke is suddenly contrite and sorrowful enough for Cherie to reconsider her options. At the end of this rather unremarkable "boy-gets-girl" melodrama, the Monroe and Murray characters clamber aboard the bus and ride off into a glorious sunrise.

So much for plot! One wonders just what Marilyn (and Milton Greene) saw in this tiresome film script and what compelled them to make it MMP's virginal coproduction, though in fact it did well at the box office. Perhaps Monroe detected flashes of Joe DiMaggio in Bo's demanding and controlling manner. Or maybe she simply welcomed the opportunity to be her own boss, regardless of the property.

Before filming began, she noticed that actress Hope Lange, making her film debut, had a head of hair the same color as hers. She demanded that Hope's tresses be darkened so as not to compete with her own shade of platinum. Although Marilyn complied with Josh Logan's request that Paula Strasberg be kept off the set, she sulked whenever the director made her reshoot a scene. And when he dared cut a scene she liked, her fangs came out. A year after the release of *Bus Stop,* when Logan tried to visit her in her dressing room on the London set of *The Prince and the Showgirl,* she lambasted him: "Why the hell did you cut out that scene in the bus? I'll never forgive you as long as I live." Logan told her he didn't have final cut on the picture. Marilyn didn't believe him. She slammed the dressing room door in his face. What Marilyn should have known was that few directors have final cut on a studio picture. It was Twentieth Century–Fox she should have blamed.

Paula Strasberg did her coaching in Marilyn's dressing room or at the actress's rented home. Like Natasha Lytess before her, she made herself indispensable. She knew how. She created a need and then filled it. She became Marilyn's alter ego, patiently listening to all her laments and regrets, assuaging her anger, soothing her ruffled emotions. She talked Marilyn through her insecurities: Could she play the role? Would Arthur Miller stop loving her? She combated Marilyn's fears and the resentments of producers, directors, and costars. When Marilyn flubbed or forgot a line, Paula shouldered the blame. In short, she held Monroe's hand. She became Lee Strasberg's surrogate, doing what he would have done had he been present instead of his wife. "Operation Marilyn," as the Strasbergs called it, brought in more money than they made with the Actors Studio and conferred upon Paula a newly discovered status. Her critics called her an opportunist and a starfucker, a designation they similarly bestowed upon Lee Strasberg.

During one of her days off from the *Bus Stop* shoot, Marilyn and Inez Melson, her business manager, drove to Verdugo to visit her mother at the Rockhaven Sanitarium. Milton Greene had allocated $300 per month of MMP funds to pay for Gladys Baker's health care. Melson took care of the finances. She frequently sent cards to Gladys, often signing Marilyn's name. When Monroe returned from her visit with her mother, she felt so thoroughly deflated she called her analyst, Dr. Margaret Hohenberg, and asked her to fly from New York to Los Angeles for a personal consultation. Hohenberg complied and evidently succeeded in helping Marilyn to recover.

Monroe also saw Joe DiMaggio Jr. during this period, inviting him to visit her on the set at the Hollywood studio. She took a taxi to Black-Foxe and brought along enough food to feed half his dorm.

The actress spent most of her spare hours running through her lines. And late at night, unable to sleep, she would talk by phone with Arthur Miller, particularly when cast and crew found themselves on location, first in Phoenix, Arizona, and then at Sun Valley, Idaho.

To avoid the red tape of a New York divorce (and probably to be nearer to Monroe), Arthur Miller temporarily moved to the Pyramid Lake Guest Ranch, forty miles north of Reno, Nevada. Since the cottage he'd leased lacked telephone service, he resorted to a pay telephone booth a quarter mile away, on the edge of the property. When using a long-distance operator to connect them, Miller answered to the name Mr. Leslie, and Marilyn to Mrs. Leslie. Having been tipped off to the true identity of the Leslies, a television camera crew soon showed up at the ranch and started asking questions. The first person they queried was fiction writer Saul Bellow, Miller's neighbor at the ranch; like Miller, Bellow had come to Nevada to seek a divorce. Bellow and Miller frequently ate dinner together, each vocalizing the strains and tensions of his last marriage. After cornering Bellow, the television crew asked if he'd seen Arthur Miller.

"Can't say I have," responded Bellow.

What about Marilyn Monroe — had he run into her?

"I'd certainly know if I *ran* into Miss Monroe, and I can assure you I haven't."

It wasn't until 1959 that Saul Bellow met Monroe. They had dinner together in Chicago, after which Bellow observed that to be close to Marilyn "is like holding on to an electric wire and not being able to let go."

Arthur Miller couldn't let go. Besides the phone calls, he wrote to Marilyn every day, sending her long, confessional letters that she kept in a stack by the side of her bed. Disregarding Nevada's six-week residential requirement, he drove to Los Angeles and checked into an apartment that she'd rented for them at the Chateau Marmont, again using the pseudonym Mr. Leslie. Mrs. Leslie — Marilyn — soon joined him, and the couple spent the night together.

Over the next month, they had two additional clandestine meetings at the same hotel. One evening they ventured to the Mocambo club on Sunset Boulevard to hear Ella Fitzgerald. It had been Marilyn, in 1955, who'd convinced the owner of the legendary Los Angeles nightclub to break the color code by offering Ella a singing engagement. Ella later told an interviewer, "The owner said yes, and Marilyn was there, front table, every night. I never had to play a small jazz club again." In fact, every year for the next five years, Fitzgerald appeared at the Mocambo, and often credited Marilyn for having helped to advance her career. "Marilyn Monroe was an unusual woman, a little ahead of her time. And she didn't know it."

In 1956, after attending a Beverly Hills party at which she'd met (and charmed) Achmed Sukarno, president of Indonesia, Marilyn came down with bronchitis and had to be hospitalized, interrupting production on *Bus Stop* for nearly a week. Having learned of her illness, Joe DiMaggio flew from New York to Los Angeles and dropped in on her at Cedars of Lebanon. He'd sent her a large bouquet of roses the day before. But it wasn't a good visit. Arthur Miller phoned Marilyn from Nevada while DiMaggio was still in the room. Joe, who later related some of the details of his visit to George Solotaire and Paul Baer, excused himself and waited in the hospital's sitting room for Marilyn to finish her call. When he returned, she told him outright what he'd expected to hear: that she and Arthur Miller were going to be married.

"Joe responded by telling Marilyn he'd read as much in the press but had wanted to hear it from her," said Paul Baer. Paul accompanied George Solotaire to Los Angeles to meet up with DiMaggio. The three men then drove to Las Vegas, where Edward Bennett Williams awaited them.

"Joe wasn't a happy warrior," said Baer. "Of course, there wasn't anything he could do to alter the situation. He said to us, 'Let's go find Arthur Miller and take care of him.' He wasn't serious. He had contempt for the intelligentsia, but it didn't compare to his hatred of Hollywood bigwigs. He had nothing against Arthur Miller. He figured Miller was in the picture primarily because he — Joe — had screwed up. If he hadn't screwed up, he'd still have been married to Marilyn Monroe. That's not to say he wasn't upset. That first day or so, he drank himself sick. He drank in his Vegas hotel room because he didn't want to tarnish his public image. I had the feeling, though, that he'd already mourned the end of his marriage. A day or two later, he came downstairs and joined us in the casino. He didn't gamble much — he never did — but he chatted it up with the gangsters, the high rollers, the hookers, and the bookmakers, swapping stories about baseball and the underworld. And then he started jawing away with some showgirls. And as luck would have it, he wound up in bed with one of them."

Kurt Lamprecht, a German-born writer living in New York, contacted Marilyn Monroe through Arthur Jacobs, her new PR agent, requesting an interview for the German press. Back in her Sutton Place apartment in early June, having completed work on *Bus Stop,* Marilyn agreed to the interview.

"She was enormously popular all over Europe, arguably the best known and most popular American actress," said Lamprecht. "I found her to be an utter delight. Full of vitality and wonder, she also had an unquenchable desire to learn, to pick up knowledge and process it. She asked all sorts of questions about what my life had been like in Germany before I came to the States. Somehow we began talking about poetry. She showed me a letter she'd received from T. S. Eliot. 'We're pen pals,' she giggled. She had an intense interest in politics and regularly wrote to the national affairs editor at the *New York Times.* We discussed the Actors Studio. She said she had grave doubts concerning her acting skills but felt the Strasbergs were helping her. In her eyes, Lee Strasberg could do no wrong. She called him 'the Great White Father.' She revealed that before performing a scene for the Actors Studio with Maureen Stapleton from Eugene O'Neill's *Anna Christie,* she became so nervous she peed in her panties. 'And I don't usually wear panties,' she added."

Lamprecht, an acquaintance of Arthur Miller's, felt that Marilyn wanted to marry the playwright in order to validate her intellect. Not that there wasn't also a sexual component to their relationship. Several days after his first interview with Monroe, Lamprecht accompanied the couple to lunch at Sardi's. "They both looked suffused with a glow," he remarked, "that could only come from a highly charged sexual relationship. To me it seemed obvious that sexuality represented an important factor for both. But evidently not everyone realized they were involved. Joan Copeland, Arthur's younger sister, joined us for coffee and dessert that day, and it was clear she didn't have the faintest idea they were anything other than good buddies. Joan, like Marilyn, took courses at the Actors Studio. But she seemed unaware that Marilyn would soon become her sister-in-law. I'd spoken to Truman Capote concerning Arthur and Marilyn, and he suggested that Miller was all but addicted to her — he was not merely besotted with her, he was smitten. Like Joe DiMaggio, Miller was in love, seriously, completely, with the full force of a man trapped in quicksand. Capote said to me, 'If you ever write a book about the two of them, you ought to call it *Death of a Playwright*.' "

After lunch, Lamprecht returned to Marilyn's apartment to complete the interview he'd begun with her a few days before. "She suddenly became very serious and at the same time sarcastic," said Lamprecht. "She began talking about Arthur Miller's problems with the government, how they'd unconstitutionally canceled his passport because maybe he'd once read a book by Karl Marx. She talked about his pending June 21 appointment to appear before the House Un-American Activities Committee, which she referred to as 'an agency dedicated to the destruction of morality, creativity, and intelligence as we know it in this country.' She was on her soapbox. She said that in August 1955 she, herself, wrote to the Soviet embassy, requesting an application for a visa to visit the USSR. It had nothing to do with politics. She'd hoped to see Russia because she wanted to look into the possibility of producing (and appearing in) a film version of *The Brothers Karamazov*. After she contacted the Russian embassy, all hell broke loose. The *Daily Worker,* an American Communist Party newspaper, ran an article reporting on her request to visit Russia. The FBI began tracking her every move, as if she were selling state secrets to the KGB. She surmised that by now her FBI file bulged with reports documenting all her 'subversive' activities, including her romantic involvement with, as she called him, 'Comrade Miller.' Marilyn insisted it was all part of the same whole-cloth plot: Congress wanted to implicate anyone and everyone they considered even remotely controversial. An amusing side note to all this is that whenever Marilyn got angry at Arthur, she called him 'that Communist.' "

As scheduled, on June 21, ten days after Arthur Miller secured his divorce from Mary Slattery, he traveled to Washington, DC, to testify before the House Un-American Activities Committee. Having been implicated by his relationship to Elia Kazan, who infamously named names for the HUAC, Miller was adamant that he was innocent and that he would provide no names for its witchhunt.

Marilyn Monroe remained in her New York apartment and watched the proceedings on television. Before the hearing began, ABC-TV aired a brief interview conducted several days earlier with Monroe, in which she vigorously defended Miller, proclaiming him "the only man I ever loved." During the hearing, Miller, who purportedly attended a half dozen meetings of the Communist Party in the late 1940s, stated he was not and never had been a party member, and to the best of his knowledge had never attended a Communist Party meeting. He requested that his passport be returned to him. He wanted to go to England because for one thing, *A View from the Bridge* was opening in London in October, and for another, because "I want to be with the woman who will be my wife." He went on to say that he and Marilyn Monroe planned to be married, and she, too, had to be in England to begin work on a new movie.

Edward Bennett Williams told sportswriter Maury Allen that the hearing broadcast, including the opening interview with Monroe, had "hit Joe DiMaggio like a brick wall. I figured he would cancel a dinner date we'd made for later that evening. He didn't. He went straight ahead with it and never said a word about Marilyn all night. Joe has a way of blocking unpleasant things out of his mind like that. If he doesn't want to discuss something that would hurt him, he just forgets about it."

Once the HUAC hearing was over and had gone reasonably well, Miller and Monroe held an impromptu press conference at Marilyn's apartment, the purpose of which was to formally announce their forthcoming nuptials. "Because of Miller's HUAC hearing, half the country already knew of their plan, so I suppose the announcement was directed at the other half," said Kurt Lamprecht, who attended the event. "One of the more notable incidents that afternoon took place when Marilyn hugged Miller. She embraced him with such force that he told her to stop, 'or I'll fall over.' I didn't know him personally, but I had difficulty imagining Joe DiMaggio making such a comment."

Just as notable were the remarks Marilyn offered concerning the institution of marriage, a portion of which seemed directed specifically at DiMaggio as well as at the foster families the actress had experienced during her formative years: "I guess I was soured on marriage because all I knew were men who swore at their wives and others who never played with their kids. The husbands I remember from my childhood got drunk regularly, and the wives were always drab women who never had a chance to dress or make up or be taken anywhere to have fun. I grew up thinking, 'If this is marriage, who needs it?' "

Regarding her feelings for Arthur Miller, she said: "For the first time I have the feeling I'm going to be with somebody who'll shelter me. It's as if I've come in out of the cold. There's a feeling of being together — a warmth and tenderness. I don't mean a display of affection or anything like that. I mean just being together."

On June 29, the day of their planned civil marriage ceremony, Arthur and Marilyn were being driven along a winding country road by Morton Miller, Arthur's cousin, when it became evident that they were being closely followed by another car. Morton sped up, as did the other vehicle. They were in Roxbury, Connecticut, where the playwright owned a small house he would soon sell, reinvesting the money in another Roxbury property, a 1783 two-story colonial farmhouse on 325 acres. Just as Morton rounded a bend, the driver of the second car lost control and careened off the road, crashing into a row of trees. Morton stepped on the brake. Marilyn jumped out and started running in the direction of the wrecked car. The driver looked dazed and badly injured. His passenger had been thrown through the windshield and lay unconscious by the side of the road in an ever-widening pool of blood. The driver eventually recovered. The less fortunate passenger died later that day. Her name was Mara Scherbatoff. She was a forty-eight-year-old New York bureau chief for the French magazine *Paris Match*. By chance, she'd attended the Sutton Place press conference and since then had been following Monroe and Miller for additional news on their imminent marriage. Marilyn took the tragic accident to heart. When asked by the Associated Press for a comment, she remarked: "It's more than sad that Miss Scherbatoff should have perished in pursuit of a news story as trivial as my third marriage. It once again demonstrates the very arbitrary and futile nature of existence."

The civil wedding ceremony uniting Arthur Miller and Marilyn Monroe took place on Friday, June 29, 1956, at the Westchester County Court House in White Plains, New York. Conducted by Judge Seymour Rabinowitz and organized by Sam Slavitt, a lawyer friend of Arthur's, the ceremony started at 7:21 p.m. and ended ten minutes later. Marilyn wore a casual sweater-and-skirt combination. Present for the occasion were Morton Miller and his wife, Florence; Lee and Paula Strasberg; Milton Greene; and Marilyn's new friend, interior decorator/fashion designer John Moore.

To satisfy Arthur Miller's Orthodox parents and because she "yearned to belong," Marilyn eagerly agreed to convert to Judaism and to participate in a religious wedding ceremony. Her conversion consisted of little more than a sixty-minute chat with a rabbi friend of the playwright, in the course of which they discussed the current political plight of Israel rather than anything to do with religion. The official double-ring, Jewish wedding took place on Sunday, July 3, two days after the civil ceremony. Rabbi Robert Goldburg of Congregation Mishkan Israel, in Hamden, Connecticut, conducted the wedding in the Waccabuc, New York, home of Kay Brown, Miller's literary agent. Marilyn wore a beige satin and chiffon wedding dress and a matching veil. Miller wore one of the two suits he owned. (His total lack of sartorial splendor represented a radical departure for Marilyn from the always fashionably attired Joe DiMaggio.) Thirty friends and relatives attended the Miller-Monroe nuptials. Lee Strasberg gave away the bride, and Morton Miller served as Arthur's best man.

The matrons of honor were Amy Greene, Hedda Rosten, and Judy Kantor (a friend of the Rostens'). Reporting on the event, the *New York Herald-Tribune* noted that Marilyn "was said to look fabulously beautiful and completely content." Conspicuously absent from the ceremony were all of Marilyn's

Hollywood friends and the usual array of photographers and reporters one would expect to find at a celebrity wedding. Because the wedding band he'd ordered wasn't ready, Miller had to borrow his mother's ring. The wedding band he finally gave Marilyn bore an inscription: "A to M. June 1956. Now is forever." On the back of a wedding picture taken by Paula Strasberg, Marilyn wrote: "Hope, Hope, Hope." In one of her notebooks, she penned the thought "A good marriage is a very delicate balance of many forces, but there is much more to it than that."

A week after the wedding, the US State Department notified Joseph Rauh, Arthur Miller's lawyer (whose legal fees nearly bankrupted his client), that they were going to renew Miller's previously suspended passport. Marilyn applauded the action by jovially offering it as final proof of what she had always contended: "Arthur Miller is more American than un-American." As to her religious conversion, she would henceforth describe herself as a "Jewish atheist." The term said it all. Following her marriage to Miller, Marilyn rarely discussed Judaism and never attended services. For that matter, she had little use for any form of organized or traditional religion.

In Marilyn Monroe's eternal quest to be part

of a family, she did her utmost to demonstrate to Arthur Miller's parents that she could be a dutiful and loving spouse. Once in a while when she and Arthur were in the New York area, they would drive to Brooklyn to eat dinner at Isidore and Augusta Miller's home. Except for a Knabe grand piano (which Arthur had played as a child), the small house had seen better days. The most inviting room was the kitchen. Just as the DiMaggio clan had tried to instill in Marilyn a desire to cook Italian food, Augusta Miller, Arthur's mother, taught her new daughter-in-law how to prepare borscht, chicken soup, matzoh balls, and other Jewish delicacies. To better communicate with the elderly but proud Brooklyn hausfrau, Marilyn attempted to speak Yiddish and even managed a phrase or two. In truth, the two most important women in the dramatist's life had nothing in common other than the dramatist himself. Interviewed by the press, Augusta said, "Marilyn is very sweet and obviously very beautiful. She opened her heart to me." Marilyn offered the press a similarly perfunctory comment regarding Augusta, calling her "a wonderful cook and a caring person."

Marilyn's relationship with Isidore, Arthur's father, was far different. Formerly a manufacturer of ladies' coats and a successful store owner until the Depression, Isidore had intense feelings for the actress, and she for him. "He simply lit up at the sight of her," his son would write. She called him Dad, wrote him letters, sent him poems and sketches, and frequently spoke with him by phone. She also flirted with him, on one occasion placing his hand on her hip, which didn't exactly please his wife. Marilyn told Lotte Goslar that where previously she had only Joe DiMaggio, she presently had no less than three "father figures" on whom to rely: Lee Strasberg, Arthur, and Arthur's dad.

Lotte Goslar visited the newlyweds at Marilyn's Sutton Place apartment. "I gave them a lace tablecloth as a wedding present," she said. "A year later Marilyn told me Arthur's dog had chewed it to shreds. 'Hugo likes lace,' she said, 'what can I tell you?' But she didn't say it in a nasty way. I think she felt lousy about it but didn't know quite how to phrase it. She sort of made light of it."

Goslar's sense of Arthur Miller at this stage was that he appeared to be conflicted. He seemed to retain a degree of guilt over his recent divorce on the one hand, but on the other he obviously took a great deal of satisfaction in "knowing he possessed a woman whom millions of men longed for. Joe DiMaggio had given off the same vibe when they were together. And like DiMaggio, Miller evidently felt he needed to protect and even save Marilyn, though from what I'm not sure — maybe from herself. Miller and

DiMaggio were both a good deal older than Marilyn, and both were famous, though not as famous as Marilyn. They represented both sides of the Greek ideal: body and mind. Marilyn told me Arthur Miller had a brilliant mind, and one of the reasons she married him was that through him she hoped to get out of being Marilyn Monroe, by which she meant she could begin playing legitimate roles. Presumably people would start taking her seriously. Other than that, Arthur and Marilyn were totally preoccupied. They were preparing to go to England so Marilyn could begin working with Sir Laurence Olivier and a predominantly British cast on *The Prince and the Showgirl.* She'd met Olivier earlier that year when he came to New York to discuss the project. I didn't communicate my feelings to Marilyn, but in all honesty I couldn't fathom the two of them appearing side by side in a film. I knew Olivier somewhat. In terms of temperament and personality, he and Marilyn were like oil and water. I couldn't see it."

Before departing for London, Marilyn called Joe DiMaggio Jr. in Los Angeles. "I knew she and Arthur Miller were dating, and then I read about their marriage, and I thought perhaps I wouldn't hear from her for a while," he said. "So I was pleasantly surprised when I did. She called me at my mother's house because I was on summer break from school. I only attended camp for a month that summer, having fallen off a horse and broken my arm. She sounded pretty much as she always did. She didn't say much about her marriage, only that she'd be in England for several months making a new movie. She asked me how things were going. I told her about my arm, and she said, 'Well, now you can relax and read a few good books.' Then she asked whether I'd heard from my father. I said, 'He calls me all the time these days because he knows you and I speak. I'm suddenly very popular with him. I have clout. I'm no longer in the shadows.' She laughed, told me she loved me — as she always did when we spoke — and that she'd write from England as soon as she could. She only wrote to me once during her stay in Britain. She evidently had problems. But one thing she did was to send me a whole slew of magazine subscriptions. When I got back to school that fall, I started receiving *National Geographic, Time, Life,* and so forth. She even took out a subscription for me to the *New York Times.* I guess she figured I should be more up on current events. I remember her saying once that the California papers, including the *Los Angeles Times,* were full of it. I don't know why she thought the *New York Times* was any better. I guess given her liberal Democratic political point of view, she had more faith in the *New York Times.*"

Milton Greene and Irving Stein, an attorney involved with Marilyn Monroe Productions, left for England on July 9. Marilyn had several last sessions with Dr. Hohenberg and arranged to continue her therapy by long-distance telephone two or three times a week. She and Miller departed for London on July 13. Paula Strasberg, Hedda Rosten, and Amy Greene (with little Joshua) followed ten days later.

Matters began to go awry almost from the start. The newlyweds were given the run of Parkside House, a luxurious Georgian mansion that belonged to the owner and publisher of the *Financial Times.* Situated on ten lush acres in Egham, an hour from London and even less from Pinewood Studios, where *The Prince and the Showgirl* was to be shot, the residence came with a full staff of household retainers. The moment the British press learned of the couple's arrival, they camped out on the periphery of the estate and never left. Despite their presence and that of the household help, a pair of burglars gained access to the mansion and made off with a cache of Monroe's jewelry, including several items that Joe DiMaggio had given her.

Another early problem was the enmity that existed between Monroe and Vivien Leigh, Laurence Olivier's British-born wife. A two-time Oscar winner, Leigh had played Marilyn's role in the original stage version of the film. Titled *The Sleeping Prince,* the play, written by Terence Rattigan, had won wide critical acclaim. Milton Greene had purchased the film rights for Marilyn and MMP/ United Artists. Laurence Olivier (wearing a monocle and adopting an austere Eastern European accent) would not only perform opposite Marilyn in this supposedly comedic film but also produce and direct. Vivien Leigh clearly resented Monroe for having taken over her role. She treated the American actress with such utter disdain that Marilyn soon stopped talking to her. One of Leigh's statements to the press represented nothing short of a personal attack on Monroe. "That girl," she said, "has the audacity to give herself top billing in the film, even over my husband, Lord Olivier. What hubris! What a laugh! I mean, what does that little tart think? She's popular for two reasons, and it's pretty obvious what they are."

Marilyn responded to the criticism by reminding the press that having purchased the project she was, after all, "Olivier's boss." The comment served only to further anger Olivier's wife.

As production on *The Prince and the Show-girl* began, Leigh announced publicly that, after years of marriage and at age forty-two, she was pregnant with Laurence Olivier's child. The news placed Leigh on the front pages of England's Fleet Street tabloids, knocking Monroe off. "She replaced me in the film, and I replaced her in the press," said Leigh, whose fragile nature and ego-related uncertainties were as well documented as Monroe's. In mid-August Leigh supposedly suffered a miscarriage, though rumors persisted that she'd never been pregnant and had confabulated the entire story only to annoy Monroe and perhaps to demonstrate that her marriage, long said to be troubled, had magically repaired itself.

On the whole, Lotte Goslar had accurately surmised that the chemistry between Laurence Olivier and Marilyn would be lethal. Not long into the production, Monroe began showing up on the set hours late or not at all. When she did appear, she looked and sounded hung over from alcohol and sleeping pills. Her insomnia hadn't ended with her marriage to Arthur Miller. If anything, it had intensified, though she insisted on hanging yards of black fabric over her bedroom windows to block out even the slightest hint of light. Moreover, she insisted on bringing Paula Strasberg along to the set, overruling Olivier, who didn't want her anywhere near the set. Olivier couldn't abide Paula, particularly since she repeatedly usurped Olivier's directorial authority. As director, he felt if he cracked the whip, the actors were expected to jump. Furthermore, he totally rejected the

Method style of acting. When Lee Strasberg arrived on the set during a three-day visit to England, Olivier asked him to leave. Laurence Olivier wasn't Lee Strasberg's sole detractor. Arthur Miller had nothing against him personally but criticized his professorial demeanor. He ridiculed Lee for his "endless lectures completely devoid of content," and Marilyn's quiet devotion to him — how awestruck she was when she whispered his name.

Joshua Logan, who'd directed Marilyn in *Bus Stop,* also showed up on the *Prince* set. "Why didn't you tell me it was going to be like this, what with that beast Paula Strasberg?" a chagrined Olivier asked him. "What did you do when you were explaining how the line should be read, and Monroe walked away from you before you were finished because Strasberg had told her otherwise?"

To add to the professional differences that existed between Olivier and Monroe, there was a growing rift between Arthur Miller and Milton Greene. Miller accused Greene of "looting MMP," buying English antique furniture for his home with corporate funds, whereas Greene accused Miller of essentially the same "crime," namely "living off" Marilyn and basking in her fame and glamour. Miller and Greene argued incessantly. And just as Joe DiMaggio had lamented the existence of Natasha Lytess, Miller felt the same way when it came to Paula Strasberg. He told Marilyn that between "Larry Olivier and Paula Strasberg, there's no question which one knows better how to deliver a line." Paula, he ventured, "knows nothing about acting — you're paying her all that money, and for what?" As to Hedda Rosten, her sole function aside from opening the five thousand fan letters MM received each week was simply that of a drinking companion. Although he generally liked the Rostens, he didn't know why his wife should have to support them financially.

Then, in the midst of the tumult, a potentially disastrous situation developed. Marilyn spotted her husband's journal on top of the kitchen table. It had been opened to a passage relating to Marilyn. In a moment of doubt, with tension and strife engulfing the production of the film, the playwright expressed his dismay with Marilyn, asking himself how he could have made the same marital mistake twice, further pointing out that he could think of no "legitimate response" to Laurence Olivier's burgeoning "anger and resentment" toward the actress. The passage went on to say that he found Marilyn difficult to deal with, unpredictable, at times "out of control," a forlorn "child-woman" whose endless emotional demands were more than he could handle. He feared his own creative efforts would be thwarted in the process of looking after her. He brought up one particularly painful incident: a recent suicidal threat Marilyn had made one night while inebriated and high on drugs — drugs that Milton Greene made available to her by the bucket-load. And when Greene couldn't produce the desired pharmaceuticals, she could always count on Paula Strasberg, to whom Miller referred as "a walking apothecary."

Arthur's journal entry came as a shock to Marilyn. She felt betrayed, stabbed in the back by one of the few people she thought she could trust. Lee Strasberg recalled a sobbing Marilyn calling him at three in the morning to report what she'd read. "It was something about how disappointed he was with me, how he thought I was some kind of angel but now he guessed he was wrong — that his first wife had let him down, but I had done something wrong. Olivier was beginning to think I was a troublesome bitch, and Arthur no longer had a decent answer to that one."

The following day, after Laurence Olivier viewed rushes of the film to date, he told Marilyn her teeth looked yellow and advised her to brighten them by brushing with lemon and baking soda. Marilyn fumed and walked off the set. Olivier called her "a professional amateur." She mockingly referred to him as "Mr. Sir" and told Paula Strasberg she wouldn't continue filming until he offered her an apology. She told Hedda Rosten she wouldn't continue her marriage unless Arthur Miller gave her a suitable explanation for the comments he'd written about her. When Marilyn left Parkside House, she checked into the London Hilton, where she proceeded to wash down half a bottle of tranquilizers with a half dozen glasses of champagne. She returned to the Georgian mansion the following day and confronted her husband. Unable to respond, he withdrew. Marilyn asked Milton Greene to call Dr. Hohenberg. Greene not only phoned Hohenberg, he coaxed her into boarding the next flight for London. It marked the second time in as many films that Marilyn's psychoanalyst had been summoned to restore Monroe's equilibrium. The difference on this occasion was that Hohenberg had to return to London a second time. Two round-trip cross-Atlantic journeys — Arthur Miller termed it "mail-order psychoanalysis"; he might just as well have called it "checkbook psychoanalysis" — the two visits combined cost MMP in excess of $20,000.

On her first visit, Hohenberg found Marilyn in a state of deep depression. As she told Iselin Simon, Marilyn hadn't slept in days. She'd been threatening to walk out on the film as well as on her husband. She'd removed Arthur Miller's photo from her dressing room and replaced it with a snapshot of Joe DiMaggio. Hohenberg managed to calm the patient, but after the therapist returned to New York, she again heard from Milton Greene. Arthur and Marilyn had argued, and Marilyn had suffered a setback. Could the good doctor kindly return?

On her second visit, Dr. Hohenberg listened as Marilyn read excerpts from her notebooks. Monroe's written musings reflected the depth of her despair. Arthur Miller's "betrayal," she noted, what she'd "always been deeply terrified of, to really be someone's wife, since I know from life one cannot love another, ever, really." From another page, she read: "And I in merciless pain . . . but we must endure, I more sadly because I can feel no joy." She read Hohenberg a letter she'd written to Lee Strasberg in which she said: "I'm embarrassed to start this, but thank you for understanding and having changed my life — even though you changed it I still am lost. I mean I can't get myself together."

Before leaving London following her second visit, Hohenberg contacted Anna Freud, whom she'd known in Vienna, and asked the eminent psychiatrist to meet with Marilyn during her absence. An appointment was arranged. High on the sedative Dexamyl, Marilyn drove to Dr. Freud's home office at 20 Maresfield Gardens. Paula Fichtl, Anna Freud's housekeeper, recalled Monroe "arriving in a black Rolls-Royce, wearing white slacks and a plain blue gabardine jacket with its collar up. No makeup. A soft white hat covered her platinum blonde hair, and her large, dark sunglasses rendered her almost unrecognizable.

"Before their session, Dr. Freud took Miss Monroe next door to the nursery school she helped run and where she conducted much of her research, children being a key [according to Sigmund Freud] to an understanding of the development of the adult psyche. Marilyn played with the children for nearly an hour. She then returned with Dr. Freud to her office. She came every day for more than a week."

Anna Freud's diagnosis, as recorded in her clinical files, indicated a far more serious condition than that which Hohenberg had previously rendered. Freud described Monroe as "emotionally unstable, highly impulsive, and needing continuous approval from the outside world. She cannot bear solitude and gets profoundly depressed when faced with rejection. She is paranoid with schizophrenic undertones, in other words a paranoid schizophrenic."

Schizophrenia: the term terrified Marilyn. Her mother suffered from schizophrenia. Other forebears on her mother's side of the family had been similarly afflicted. Thankfully, Freud didn't disclose her diagnosis to

Marilyn, though she sent a copy of her report to Dr. Hohenberg in New York. After receiving the report, Hohenberg phoned Milton Greene, her other "celebrity" patient, and advised him that he'd made a mistake to go into business with Monroe. Hohenberg said she didn't know how long the arrangement could continue under the present circumstances. Eventually learning of the conversation, Marilyn used it to terminate her treatment with Hohenberg, citing it as an example of unprofessional conduct, a violation of her right to privacy. Hohenberg's harsh words following the breakup with Monroe turned out to be prophetic. "When she left me," she said, "I knew sooner or later she would kill herself."

For the moment, matters grew worse before they got better. In mid-August, after she'd returned to work on the film, Marilyn learned from a British gynecologist that she was pregnant. Above all, Milton Greene thought it necessary to keep the pregnancy from Laurence Olivier. Greene needn't have concerned himself. On Saturday, September 8, Marilyn miscarried, enduring the same fate purportedly suffered by Vivien Leigh. Monroe later told Lotte Goslar she was extremely disappointed because she'd hoped, despite her earlier sense of betrayal, to show Arthur she could be a devoted wife and a good mother. Starting a family, having a baby, would rectify everything that wasn't right in their marriage.

Somehow *The Prince and the Showgirl* neared completion but not before Hedda Rosten and Paula Strasberg returned to New York, and Marilyn spent additional time with Anna Freud. When filming finally ended, Monroe distributed a letter of apology to the entire cast and crew, including Laurence Olivier: "I hope you will all forgive me. It wasn't my fault. I've been very sick all through the picture. Please, please don't hold it against me."

There was a light moment, one of the few, when Marilyn Monroe met Queen Elizabeth. In October the Queen walked down a reception line of twenty international actors at the Empire Theatre in London, greeting each in turn as they performed the usual bow or curtsy. Included in the group were Brigitte Bardot, Victor Mature, and Joan Crawford. Arriving late, Marilyn stood at the end of the line. When the Queen reached Marilyn, she stopped and stared. Wearing an off-the-shoulder gown that left little to the imagination, Monroe once again became the talk of the town.

That same month, Monroe accompanied her husband to the London premiere of *A View from the Bridge.* Following the performance, Miller proudly wrote Norman Rosten that Marilyn had worn "a garnet-colored velvet gown, halting traffic as far north as

Liverpool, and had conquered everyone."

Five weeks later, the Millers were back in the United States. Browsing through a stack of back-issue magazines, Marilyn came across a Newsmaker item in a three-month-old issue of *Time* that caught her attention. Joe had been spotted playing in the annual Old Timers' Day game at Yankee Stadium, which amused Marilyn. She sent a handwritten note to George Solotaire: "George, sweetie — Please tell Joe congratulations on his gargantuan homer this past August at Yankee Stadium. Also please tell him that as far as I'm concerned, he's no Old Timer! Love, Marilyn."

Solotaire gave DiMaggio the letter and advised him to contact Marilyn. DiMaggio decided against it. "She's impulsive," he told Solotaire, "and often does things she later regrets. I'll wait."

Gladys Baker with her infant daughter, Norma Jeane, 1926.

Joe DiMaggio at a DiMaggio family gathering in 1936.

Joe DiMaggio and Dorothy Arnold wedding, 1939.

Norma Jeane Baker with her first husband, James Dougherty, on Catalina Island, ca. 1943.

Joe DiMaggio with Frank Sinatra in 1949, before Marilyn Monroe entered either of their lives.

Alfred Eisenstaedt's portrait of an American actress, 1953.

Monroe and DiMaggio wedding, January 1954.

In Ch'unch'on, South Korea, Monroe entertains U.S. military personnel.

Marilyn Monroe's *Seven Year Itch* (1954) subway dress, pictured here, reportedly fetched $5.52 million at auction. The photo was the catalyst that brought the DiMaggio-Monroe marriage to an end.

The Monroe-DiMaggio marriage makes front page news on Oct. 5, 1954.

Emily and Dom DiMaggio join Marilyn and Joe for dinner in Boston, 1955.

Marilyn Monroe with Milton Berle and J. Edgar Hoover at a luncheon in the Grand Ballroom of the Waldorf-Astoria Hotel, NYC, 1955. In his story "A Beautiful Child," Truman Capote quoted Marilyn as saying, "Everybody says that Milton Berle has the biggest schlong in Hollywood. But who cares?"

Truman Capote dancing with his "Beautiful Child," Marilyn Monroe, 1955.

Mr. and Mrs. Arthur Miller, New York City, 1957.

Marilyn Monroe at a cocktail party with her lover Yves Montand shortly before the end of her marriage to Arthur Miller.

Marilyn Monroe engages both JFK and RFK.

Actress Marilyn Monroe on the set of the unfinished film "Something's Got to Give."

Frank Sinatra and Sam Giancana owned the Cal-Neva Lodge, Lake Tahoe, where Peter Lawford took Marilyn for some "peace and quiet" and a respite from the Kennedy men, 1962.

Psychiatrist Ralph Greenson (*center*), to whom Marilyn confided the details of her Kennedy affairs, is shown here at her funeral.

Joe DiMaggio and Joe Jr. joined in grief at the Monroe funeral.

The 48-year-old Yankee Clipper Joe DiMaggio at bat during Oldtimers' Day, Yankee Stadium, 1963.

Despite his legendary baseball career, many people remember Joe DiMaggio as "Mr. Coffee."

Chapter 13

England with Marilyn Monroe had been an eye-opening experience for Arthur Miller. The couple had departed from the States only two weeks after their marriage. The trip constituted their first extended period together, the first time Miller had been exposed to the "real" Monroe as opposed to the fantasy figure he'd concocted for himself based on more than four years of letter writing and a year of informal dating. The journal entry that Marilyn had seen in London reflected Miller's awakening; his having to deal firsthand with many of the same forces that had driven Joe DiMaggio half mad: her sleep deprivation, insecurities, anxieties, fears, paranoia, and increasing dependence on drugs and alcohol.

Looking back on his own growing addiction to Marilyn, Miller would assert that he hadn't been "sophisticated enough" to have recognized the multitude of issues that would ultimately destroy his marriage and then

Marilyn herself.

Calling Marilyn "an extraordinary child of nature," Arthur Miller would say, "I began to dream that with Marilyn I could do what seemed to me would be the most wonderful thing of all — have my work and all that this implied, and someone I just simply adored. I thought I could solve it all with this marriage. She was simply overwhelming, as I guess I was to her, for a while. It was wonderful to be around her. Until she got ill."

What seemed most disconcerting for the playwright — what the marriage to Monroe came to represent to him — was his inability to get any meaningful work done during that period. There was always something on his plate to distract him from his desk and typewriter. The distractions weren't always related to Monroe.

When the couple returned from England, Joseph Rauh, Miller's attorney, notified them that the FBI had launched a new investigation, partially aimed at Monroe but mainly directed at Miller. Identified in FBI files as the "darling of the left-wing intelligentsia," Marilyn (and Miller) had been accused of diverting funds through Marilyn Monroe Productions into the coffers of several pro-Communist organizations, none of which were specified. In February 1957, after Arthur and Marilyn returned to New York from a vacation in Half Moon Point, Jamaica, the playwright was indicted by a federal grand jury for two counts of contempt of Congress. At a first hearing in March, Miller pled not guilty. In May, accompanied by Marilyn, he attended another hearing and this time was found guilty of contempt. The conviction carried with it a $500 fine, a thirty-day prison sentence, and the mandatory revocation (for a second time) of his US passport. A year later, his conviction was overturned by a court of appeals, which ruled that the chairman of HUAC had provided Miller's attorney with misleading information. Marilyn helped pay her husband's legal costs.

While all this went on, Miller and Monroe became embroiled in a legal skirmish with Milton Greene, who, they claimed, had "swindled" Marilyn out of thousands of dollars by his intentional mismanagement of Marilyn Monroe Productions. In addition, Miller questioned Greene's artistic sensibility and credentials. "He may be a good photographer, but he knows nothing about filmmaking," claimed Miller, citing as an example of Greene's incompetence his selection of *The Prince and the Showgirl* as a vehicle for Monroe to demonstrate her acting skills.

After months of vituperative legal threats, conferences, and strategies, Milton Greene settled for a single lump-sum payment of $100,000 in exchange for his stock holdings in MMP. Eager to break her contract with

Greene and thereby mollify her husband, Marilyn thoroughly embarrassed her former business partner by announcing publicly that he'd taken advantage of her. She told the press: "My company wasn't organized to parcel out nearly half of my earnings to Mr. Greene for seven years." Arthur Miller, also quoted in the press, said, "Milton Greene . . . lived off my wife's work. She prevented him from gaining majority control and then had to pay a hundred thousand dollars to rid herself of him. The company was doomed from the start. The contract my wife made with Mr. Greene was completely disadvantageous to her. Milton Greene thought she was working for him, instead of the other way around. He never separated his personal expenditures from company expenses. The finances were a mess. As for Mr. Greene's work ethic, he was all talk and no action."

The termination of Marilyn Monroe's agreement with Milton Greene ended his brief film career. He went back into magazine photography. For all intents and purposes, it likewise marked the end of Marilyn Monroe Productions. According to Amy Greene, Marilyn told her that Milton had been "the only man she ever trusted, and she regretted that she hadn't had the strength to stand up to her husband." Indeed, Marilyn's main impetus at this stage may well have been directed at trying to save her shaky marriage.

Prior to the dissolution of MMP, Marilyn and Milton Greene had been exploring the possibility of doing a production either of *The Brothers Karamazov* or *The Jean Harlow Story,* neither of which came to pass.

In subsequent years, Joshua Greene, Milton and Amy's son, offered a similarly slanted comment defending his father's honor: "Arthur Miller wanted my father out of the picture so he could have all the money. My father was the only man in Marilyn's life that never took her for granted and never took things from her." Apparently Milton Greene's son never heard of Joe DiMaggio.

The only residual connection between the Greenes and Joe DiMaggio involved the $225 outfit Marilyn wore in January 1954, when she and Joe married in San Francisco. While staying with the Greenes at their Connecticut home in early 1955, Marilyn let Amy Greene's mother borrow the outfit for a special occasion. Forgetting to return it, Amy's mother stowed it away in her wardrobe closet, where it remained until 1999, thirty-seven years after Monroe's death. In September of that year, Amy Greene found it and sold it at auction at Sotheby's for the considerable sum of $33,350. Although Milton Greene and his family no doubt benefited financially from their association with Monroe, it can be argued that not only did he recognize Monroe's undeniable talent but he also put his own career on the line in order to help the actress further her own cause. "Milton Greene may have been a charlatan," said Truman Capote, "but at least he was an honest charlatan."

In mid-1957 Marilyn gave up her sublet at 2 Sutton Place and purchased a much larger thirteenth-floor cooperative apartment at 444 East Fifty-Seventh Street, not far from her previous apartment building. Her new apartment consisted of a master bedroom, guest bedroom, living room (with a working fireplace and floor-to-ceiling bookcases), a small study, dining alcove, three bathrooms, and a modern kitchen. Over time Marilyn fashioned the apartment according to her own taste. She carpeted the residence in white, brought in the white-lacquered baby grand piano her mother had given her as a child, acquired a mirrored table for the dining area, a pair of off-white love seats, a white tub chair, a large white sofa, a rare oriental vase painted with white flowers, white draperies, and other select pieces of furniture for the living room. She owned a small bust of the ancient Egyptian Queen Nefertiti and soon bought a painting by Toulouse-Lautrec and a black metal female nude sculpted by William Zorach. She tore down several walls and built several new ones. On one of the living room walls she mounted an enlarged photograph

Cecil Beaton had taken of her the year before. She placed Marlon Brando's jocularly inscribed photo of Albert Einstein atop her baby grand. On the nightstand next to her queen-sized bed sat two photographs: Abraham Lincoln and Marilyn's mother. Also perched on the nightstand was a first edition of Carl Sandburg's 1926 biography of the sixteenth president. Despite her work on the apartment, she was never satisfied with the results, and for the rest of her life she constantly changed furniture, furnishings, ornaments, and accessories. Although she'd insisted on sharing a bed and bedroom while married to DiMaggio, she gave Arthur Miller the guest bedroom, which later doubled as a laundry and sewing room. Arthur also had full run of the study, though by his own admission he got little work done in it.

Patricia Rosten, the then eleven-year-old daughter of Norman and Hedda Rosten, had vivid memories of Marilyn and the apartment. "The guest bedroom and bath had lovely white porcelain doorknobs with flowers painted on them," she noted. Marilyn's bedroom, on the other hand, "was kept dark, slightly mysterious," and everything in shades of beige: "rugs, curtains, bedspread. She had a champagne-colored quilt on the bed, which I used to flop on when I visited." Patricia remembered diving into Marilyn's makeup box. "She used to act like it was the most natural thing in the world to find me there. She plunked me down at her vanity table, and since I was intrigued by the art of makeup, she would show me how to do the job right. For the next twenty minutes, I was in a dream as I watched her skillful hands transform my kid's face into something glamourous. She made my eyelids glimmer, my cheekbones appear accentuated, and my mouth rosy. She also arranged my hair into an elegant French twist."

Patricia Rosten went on to say that she adored Marilyn because the actress "had real empathy" for children and thought nothing of "breaking the rules," and she also believed that young people love adults who aren't afraid to break the rules.

She recalled her visits to Arthur Miller's Roxbury, Connecticut, farmhouse, which Marilyn had decorated and where the couple often spent their weekends. In an article Patricia Rosten wrote concerning her childhood experiences with Marilyn, she observes that the star "would not hesitate to allow Hugo," Arthur's dog, to come into the house "rain-soaked and muddy" from the garden. "She would let the front part of him in and carefully wipe off his front paws, then, coaxing in the rest of him, she would carefully wipe off the back ones." When Hugo needed a soft bed, Marilyn gave him the best, most expensive wool blanket she owned.

Marilyn once rescued a "small half-starved beagle-type puppy that staggered in out of the woods." She "nursed it back to health, brought it to New York," and gave it to Patricia.

Reiterating her point about Marilyn's natural love for children, Patricia Rosten ventured the opinion that Marilyn might have been happier with a child or children of her own. "When Marilyn touched me or held me," she wrote, "I felt a warmth and softness (dare I use the word maternal in relation to her?) that was very reassuring. It was not unlike falling into that champagne-colored quilt that graced her bed. She, who was so much like a child herself, always had a sympathetic word or touch for 'another' child, and it was this that endeared her to me."

So far as children were concerned, Jane and Robert Miller, Arthur's offspring by his first wife, visited their father and glamourous stepmother on alternate weekends, usually in Connecticut, and sometimes in Amagansett, Long Island, where the couple rented a cottage from early 1957 to July 1958. There Marilyn enjoyed nothing more than to take long walks along the beach or to play tennis at a nearby court.

Rupert Allan, originally a West Coast editor of *Look* and later a publicist with the Arthur Jacobs firm, reflected on Monroe's relationship with the two children, acknowledging that while she felt close to both, she felt closer to Robert. "In 1957 the boy was about ten, and his sister was three years older. So the girl, being around thirteen and very sensitive, felt a trace of resentment toward Marilyn. She liked Marilyn, but I imagine she regarded her as the person most responsible for breaking up her parents' marriage."

Monroe told Allan that one day in Amagansett, she found Robert wearing his sister's clothes, while Jane was dressed in clothing that belonged to her father. "Marilyn, a most understanding woman when it came to such matters, nevertheless found the cross-dressing a wee bit unusual," said Allan. "The kids told her they didn't like their own clothes, so she took them shopping and bought each a new wardrobe. A few weeks later, she told Robert, 'Your birthday's coming up — I'm going to throw you a party.' He said he'd never had a birthday party before. So Marilyn went all out. She gave it at her Manhattan apartment, inviting all his friends, hiring a caterer, buying him all sorts of great presents. His father popped his head out for a minute or two, then locked himself in his study and stayed there for the rest of the afternoon. Marilyn ran the whole show herself. She could be very nurturing. When Jane and Robert weren't around, she'd write letters to them pretending to be Hugo, the basset hound. She most definitely had a way with young people. And

I recall even after she and Arthur divorced, she kept pictures of his children on display with photographs of all the other children she'd known. Of all the children, the one she most cherished, I believe, was Joe DiMaggio's son. She spoke about him all the time, wrote to him, called him, sent him gifts, did all the little things his father evidently didn't do."

Tired of Monroe's perpetual lateness, though she'd often promised to be more punctual, Lee Strasberg gave one of his students, actor Delos Smith Jr., the job of seeing to it that Marilyn got to class on time. Delos soon learned from Marilyn that the main reason she indulged herself with long baths before going anywhere was that at the orphanage as a child, she could only shower; when she lived with foster families, she was forced to bathe in water they'd already used on themselves. But what Smith also observed is that when she finished bathing, she'd come out and get into bed to lie down, and after that it became impossible to get her moving. So when she was in the bath, Delos would climb into her bed and be lying there when she came out. The maneuver worked. Marilyn would immediately dress, and the two would head out for class. The problem is that when Delos wasn't present, the actress would revert to her old habit and once again be late.

"You never quite knew what to expect from Marilyn," said Delos Smith Jr. "She had wild, pendulum-like mood swings, and her moods determined her behavior. At her best, she was fantastic: sweet, funny, sexy, effervescent, creative, generous, and clever. At her worst, she was a total mental case: depressed, manic, tense, angry, insecure, worried about growing old, heavily addicted to pills and booze. The Strasbergs tried to be there for her when she wasn't well and couldn't cope. They coached her, shopped for her, counseled her, and stayed up with her when she couldn't sleep. They would let her stay in their apartment overnight, and Lee would coddle her like a baby. There were times when she needed a twenty-four-hours-a-day nursemaid, and he would attempt to fulfill that function. Yet there were those who insisted that the Method the Strasbergs imparted had sinister and dangerous underpinnings when it came to Marilyn; that it was all geared to their own selfish needs, that they took advantage of her, lined their pockets at her expense. Arthur Miller came to feel that way, and nothing Marilyn said or did could ever change his mind."

Nowhere were Marilyn's mood fluctuations more apparent than in her own writings. Two diary entries related to Arthur Miller were excerpted in *Vanity Fair* in November 2010. In the first, she writes: "I am so concerned about protecting Arthur. I love him, and he is the only person — human being — I have ever known that I could love not only as a man . . . But he [is] the only person . . . that I trust as much as myself."

A second entry, written at the Roxbury farmhouse a short while later, demonstrates a complete change of heart: "Starting tomorrow I will take care of myself for that's all I really have and as I see it now have ever had. Roxbury — I've tried to imagine spring all winter — it's here and I still feel hopeless. I think I hate it here because there is no love here anymore."

Further along in the same entry, she provides a painful self-image: "I see myself in the mirror now, brow furrowed — if I lean close I'll see — what I don't want to know — tension, sadness, disappointment, my blue eyes dulled, cheeks flushed with capillaries that look like rivers on maps — hair lying like snakes. The mouth makes me the saddest, next to my dead eyes."

In a continuing effort to contain her many personal problems and issues — and encouraged to remain in therapy by Lee Strasberg — Marilyn telephoned Anna Freud in England for the name of a psychoanalyst. She'd convinced herself that Dr. Hohenberg had betrayed her confidences and could no longer be trusted, particularly because Milton Greene remained her patient. Anna Freud recommended Dr. Marianne Kris, a childhood friend from Vienna who'd practiced psychiatry in New York since 1940. Oskar Rie, Marianne's father, had been the Freud family's pediatrician. By coincidence, Dr. Rudolph Loewenstein, Arthur Miller's former psychiatrist, who'd met Marilyn on one occasion, also recommended Marianne Kris, the widow of his former colleague, Ernst. There existed one other notable coincidence. Dr. Marianne Kris lived and worked at the Langham, 135 Central Park West, the same prewar luxury apartment building into which the Strasbergs had moved the year before from their former residence at the Belnord, a fortlike structure at Broadway and Eighty-Sixth Street.

Most mornings after her psychoanalytic session with Dr. Kris, Marilyn took the elevator to the seventh-floor, nine-room Strasberg apartment for a one-on-one acting lesson with Lee. Or if she had an afternoon appointment with Dr. Kris, whom she saw five times a week, she would merely reverse the order. Arthur Miller had mixed feelings about Marilyn's insistence on being in analysis. In his own case, he'd stopped, claiming it had inhibited his creativity. In Marilyn's case, he initially supported the idea but subsequently changed his mind, asserting that Dr. Kris and Lee Strasberg both took advantage of Marilyn's childlike dependence on anyone who showed her the slightest kindness, even if she had to pay for it.

Like Dr. Hohenberg, Kris was a recently widowed Jewish immigrant with a strong background in Freudian analysis. Unlike Hohenberg, she had two children of her own. Also unlike Hohenberg, a large percentage of her patients were children, though she saw adult patients as well. In the mid-1960s, following the assassination of President John F. Kennedy, she treated Jacqueline Kennedy. Here was yet another coincidence in the making. It is reasonable to assume that when Jackie began therapy with Dr. Kris, one subject she probably delved into had to do with her late husband's frequent infidelities. No doubt Marilyn Monroe's name came into play.

In the summer of 1957, Joe DiMaggio made his annual pilgrimage to Cooperstown, New York, to attend the Baseball Hall of Fame's induction ceremony. The event that year held more significance than usual for Joe, considering that Joe McCarthy, his first manager with the Yanks, was being inducted. Directly after the ceremony, Joe flew to San Francisco. While in the Bay Area, when he wasn't at the DiMaggio family eatery, Joe could be found at Liverpool Lil's, devouring honey-roasted peanuts and ice-cold bottles of Pabst Blue Ribbon beer.

The patrons at Liverpool Lil's regarded him as visiting royalty, always attired in a crisp white dress shirt, well-cut blue blazer, burgundy tie, sharply cut slacks, and spit-shined shoes. He could be pleasant enough, but he usually chose to be gruff and cranky. If anyone mentioned Marilyn Monroe to him, he rose and left. Later that summer, he accompanied Ernest Hemingway to a middleweight boxing championship at Madison Square Garden. A fan came over and asked Joe for his autograph. The fan stared at the bearded gentleman seated next to DiMaggio. "Hey, aren't you somebody too?" he asked. "You bet," replied Hemingway. "I'm Mr. DiMaggio's personal physician."

The Hemingway story found its way into the *New York Post,* and Marilyn showed it to Arthur Miller. "He became annoyed," said Kurt Lamprecht, who maintained his friendship with Marilyn. "What the hell was the baseball player doing with the world's leading writer of fiction? I think Miller always had a kind of vague resentment toward his predecessor. Strangely enough, the two men weren't all that different. Naturally they excelled in completely different fields, but Arthur Miller, like Joe DiMaggio, could be very jealous when it came to Marilyn. The difference was that Miller tended to internalize his feelings, and DiMaggio didn't. If somebody danced with Marilyn at a nightclub or party and held her a little too close or whispered into her ear, Miller got nervous. He tried not to show it, but you couldn't miss it. Of course, Joe DiMaggio, under similar circumstances, would've probably gone over and sent Marilyn's dance partner on his way. From what Marilyn told me about him, he could be pretty intimidating."

DiMaggio brought along a date the night he and Ernest Hemingway attended the fights. Her name was Lola Mason, and she was all of nineteen. A future television starlet, she worked at that time in publicity and took acting lessons on the side. She had soft blond hair and a voice to match. She and Joe met one night at El Morocco. He was there with Lee Meriwether. Lola was with a male friend. The friend asked Lola why she didn't have a steady man in her life. "Because," she said, "the only man I *really* want is Joe DiMaggio. I've never met him, but he seems ideal." Lola's friend said, "Well, now's your chance. He's sitting behind you a few tables away." Lola mustered her courage, walked the short distance to Joe's table, and introduced herself. DiMaggio took her phone number and two days later asked her out. Sure enough, he was just as she'd imagined him: handsome, debonair, quiet, refined, and earnest. The problem was, there were dozens of other women in Joe's life now that Marilyn wasn't in it. Joe and Lola dated on and off for several years. What DiMaggio appreciated about their affair was that it didn't make the papers. She wasn't well enough known and wasn't in it for her own publicity. There was something refreshing about it. "If only I were ten years younger," Joe told Paul Baer, "I'd probably marry the girl."

In mid-June 1957 Marilyn Monroe said, "A man and a woman need something of their own. A baby makes a marriage. It makes a marriage perfect." She'd just learned she was pregnant again. Coming as it did at the same time as Arthur Miller's ongoing problems with the Washington contempt hearings, the pregnancy struck a positive note. "The very idea of her as a mother," observed the playwright, "ultimately swept me along . . . There were moments of a new kind of confidence, a quietness of spirit around her, or so it seemed. If a child might intensify anxieties, it would also give her, and hence myself, a new hope for the future."

With three new homes (one of them leased) and a baby on the way, the Millers appeared to have overcome a number of their previous obstacles and seemed headed along a promising path. Then, on the morning of August 1, while staying at their Amagansett cottage, Marilyn awoke with a violent pain in her belly. Arthur called an ambulance. They arrived at Doctors Hospital in Manhattan at noon. Doctors Bernard Berglass and Hilliard Dubrow examined her. They informed Arthur Miller, nervously pacing in an adjacent waiting room, that Marilyn had an ectopic (tubular) pregnancy, which would have to be surgically terminated as soon as possible.

Initially elated over the prospect of having a child of her own, the loss of the baby — her second failed pregnancy with Miller — sent Marilyn into a tailspin. She remained at Doctors Hospital for ten days following the surgery, and when she left on August 10, she found herself surrounded by a brigade of reporters. "If there's all this clamor because I lost my baby, I hate to think how much publicity I would have generated had I given birth," she commented bitterly.

The Millers returned to Monroe's East Fifty-Seventh Street apartment. Paula and Susan Strasberg were among her first visitors. "Arthur Miller, no great fan of my parents, turned to them following the loss of the baby," said Susan Strasberg. "He didn't know what to do with Marilyn. She was utterly miserable. She stuffed herself with Nembutals. She took pills to sleep, pills to wake up, pills for constipation, pain pills, diet pills, pills to clear her skin, and a dozen other medications all washed down with scotch or Dom Pérignon, followed by Binaca mouth spray in a failed effort to mask the odor of alcohol. She was full of guilt, self-loathing, resentment, and anger. After we left, my mother said, 'Susan, she had abortions. I'm not sure how many. God forgives her, but I'm not sure she forgives herself.' "

The next day Marilyn collapsed on the sofa from an apparent overdose of barbiturates. Arthur Miller succeeded in rousing her. But later that week he found her unconscious in bed, an empty bottle of Nembutal on the nightstand. Describing the scene to Lee Strasberg, Miller revealed how he tried to revive her by lifting her into a sitting position and massaging her shoulders. When that failed he half carried, half dragged her into the bathroom, placed his leg on a stool, and bent her over his knee with her face directly over the toilet bowl. He then tried to jam his fingers down her throat, but he couldn't pry her mouth open, so he pinched her nose shut and her mouth opened. He could hear her gagging as he stuck two fingers deep into her mouth. She began to vomit, disgorging scotch, pills, bile, and putrid-smelling particles of half-digested food. He led her back to bed and called emergency services. The following day, speaking from a hospital bed, Marilyn told Lee Strasberg, "I didn't try to commit suicide. I just took too many pills."

Despite her denial, a posthumously published diary entry, written by Marilyn just after the loss of her baby, provided a true indication of her mind-set at the time. "I wish that I were dead," she wrote, "absolutely non-existent — gone away from here — from everywhere . . ."

John Strasberg, then still in his teens, recalled being "too shy" to approach Marilyn but acknowledged freely that his parents, Lee and Paula, always "hovered protectively" around her, presumably making it more difficult for him (or anyone, for that matter) to get close to her. "I remember feeling," he writes in *Accidentally on Purpose,* his somewhat disjointed but compelling memoir, "that everybody used Marilyn; they said that they only wanted to help, but they devoured her energy. Damaged and desperate as she was, she mistook this attention for love. As a needy child grasps for affection, Marilyn . . . tried to reach out for help."

John Strasberg points out that "as part of the family," Marilyn would occasionally stay with the Strasbergs, particularly "when she was suffering through some emotional crisis." Such was the case not long after the surgical termination of her pregnancy and her would-be suicide attempt.

Although Arthur Miller had very likely saved her life, he seemed (to Marilyn, at least) incapable of providing her with the warmth and understanding she so drastically craved. In defending his seeming lack of support at such critical moments, Miller would proclaim that he was "only human — Marilyn required some kind of Superman-like creature to look after her needs." In Marilyn's mind, Lee Strasberg represented not a Superman figure but something more akin to Clara Barton, Sigmund Freud, and Florence Nightingale all rolled into one.

When Marilyn stayed with the Strasbergs, as she did on this occasion, she slept in sixteen-year-old John's bedroom while he took over the living room couch. Late one night, according to his written account, "she came half-crawling into the living room where I was asleep . . . She groped along the wall in an effort to stand up. She wore a wrinkled white slip of a nightgown . . . 'Johnny, I can't sleep,' she whispered in her unique woman-child voice. She floated over to where I was now sitting up and slumped down next to me. Her body odor was heavy with the drugs that she was taking . . . 'Do you mind if I just sit here awhile?' she asked. We looked at each other. I didn't know what to do. The situation that millions of men fantasized about terrified me . . . At that moment, she was so doped up that I wasn't sure she knew where she was. She was semilucid, but she faded in and out without even moving."

Though he may have imagined otherwise, Marilyn wasn't on the teenager's couch for anything other than conversation and solace. She didn't want to awaken his parents. "We talked," he writes, "or rather she rambled on senselessly while I half-listened, wondering when she would calm down or tire out. She finally did go back to sleep." John's encounter with the sparsely clad actress evidently continued to haunt him: "I often pondered, later on in life, what might have happened if either one of us had reached out in that thick, smoky air. Would we have held one another in the embrace of a man and a woman, or would it have been the desperate embrace of longing to love and be loved that is known to children of all ages who cannot bear to be alone?"

At a somewhat later date, confiding in Susan Strasberg, John's sister, Marilyn admitted adding amphetamines to her already toxic mixture of drugs and pharmaceuticals. "The slightest upset brought on new forms of terror," said Susan. "I used to see Marilyn crawling half-naked on all fours along the hallways of our apartment. She would crawl to my parents' bedroom and scratch at the door. To help her fall asleep, my father would cradle her in his arms and sing, 'Go to sleep, little baby . . . and dream of angels.' It was the same lullaby he used to sing to me when I was a little girl. My father paid more attention to Marilyn than he did to either of his own children, and we began to resent her for it."

After starting with the amphetamines,

Marilyn began hallucinating and having phantasmagoric dreams. She dreamt of monsters, sometimes friendly but usually not. In another dream, reported to Susan Strasberg, Marilyn encountered her long-lost birth father at a cocktail party. He didn't recognize her, so she seduced him, and after doing the dirty deed, she said to him: "You just fucked your own daughter, you miserable son of a bitch."

Marilyn also told Susan about the day she went shopping for a new dress at Bonwit Teller, having swallowed a handful of pills for breakfast. "Marilyn walked into the department store and looked around," said Susan. "And that's when she began to hallucinate. She suddenly found herself surrounded by all sorts of wild animals: lions, tigers, elephants, water buffalo, apes, giraffes, rhinos, and hippos. There were clusters of tall, dark trees and hanging foliage. Knee-high yellow grass filled the aisles. A huge king cobra dangled from an overhead tree branch. Small yattering monkeys rode the vines, swinging from tree to tree. Exotic birds sang menacing songs. Thorny black spiders and giant red ants scurried across varnished countertops. A swarm of blood-thirsty mosquitoes enveloped Marilyn's head. She turned and ran. Once outside on Fifth Avenue, she felt safe. But as far as I know, she never returned to Bonwit Teller. I can only imagine how real that impenetrable jungle must have seemed to her."

To handle the hundreds of film scripts that arrived regularly at her Manhattan apartment, Marilyn hired May Reis, and soon asked her to replace Hedda Rosten as her private secretary. Lena Pepitone, another new household employee, was hired in 1957 to serve as Marilyn's New York maid and wardrobe mistress.

"I think the reason Marilyn hired me," said Pepitone, "was because of my Italian heritage. The first time we met, she told me, 'I love Italians. My second husband was Italian.' 'I know,' I responded. 'You were married to Joe DiMaggio.' 'Hey,' Marilyn laughed, 'you know about him?' 'Of course,' I answered. 'Everybody knows about Joe DiMaggio.' "

Marilyn asked Pepitone if she knew how to cook Italian food. "I'm an Italian food fanatic," she said. "Joe used to take me for the greatest Italian dinners."

Monroe paid Pepitone $150 a week. "Aside from my salary," she recalled, "Marilyn constantly gave me little presents and large Christmas bonuses. She did that with all the household employees. She gave Florence Thomas, her housekeeper, a small fortune. She was enormously generous. That Christmas she gave a Chagall drawing to Susan Strasberg. She gave Paula Strasberg the string of pearls she'd received from the emperor of Japan during her 1954 honeymoon with Joe DiMaggio. She gifted Lee Strasberg with hundreds of dollars' worth of books, records, clothes, and cases of champagne. She turned over her black Thunderbird to John Strasberg on his eighteenth birthday. She gave Joe DiMaggio Jr. his first car as well. Arthur Miller received a leather-bound edition of the *Encyclopædia Britannica* for Christmas. I had the feeling her generosity stemmed in part from a desire to be loved, like the little girl that thrusts a bunch of daisies into her mother's hand."

Instead of daisies, Marilyn presented her mother with a new Christmas wardrobe. She sent Inez Melson (whom she'd named her mother's conservator) money with which to buy Gladys Baker an assortment of slips, vests, pants, gowns, hose, sweaters, shoes, boots, and a raincoat. In return, Melson sent Marilyn a packet of four dinner place mats that Gladys had made in occupational therapy. In an accompanying letter, Melson wrote that when she last visited Gladys at Rockhaven, refreshments had been served in the garden, and Gladys "presided over the coffee urn. She also arranged all the cookies and sandwiches on the trays." The letter, Lena Pepitone attested, reduced Marilyn to tears. She said to Lena, "My mother lost her memory, and I can't forget anything except for my lines. It's all there, all the time, buzzing around in my brain. That's why I'm afraid I'll end up going as crazy as my mother and her mother."

It didn't take Lena Pepitone long to discover that Marilyn had mounted a full-length poster of Joe DiMaggio in one of her bedroom closets and would often stand in front of it and stare at it while listening to "The Man I Love," as sung by Billie Holiday. "It was a baseball poster," Pepitone noted, "the kind you'd find in a sports memorabilia shop. He had on his Yankee uniform and it showed him swinging a bat. Considering that she and Arthur Miller were married at the time, I wondered how she got away with it, until it dawned on me that he never bothered looking in her closet. He usually slept in the guest bedroom and spent most of his time locked away in the study. I didn't say anything to Marilyn about the poster — or about her little song ritual — until the day she brought it up. 'What do you think of the poster?' she asked. Not knowing what to say, I blurted out something like, 'Well, I've heard he had the perfect swing.' 'He also has a perfect physique,' she responded, 'and he knows it. He used to boast about it all the time. That is, until I gave him two gift-wrapped presents: a mirror and a ruler. That shut him down, at least for a while.' "

Lena Pepitone had a friend named Judy

who'd dated Joe DiMaggio on a few occasions since his breakup with Marilyn. "They were only buddies," said Lena. "I got to know Joe somewhat in later years, but Judy told me something about him I found interesting. He felt awkward with adults but not around children. He came alive with children. After Marilyn, he began visiting orphanages in and around New York. He became active in the Little Leagues. Judy said his personality changed with children. He related to them. In this respect, he was like Marilyn. When I asked her about Joe's affinity for kids, she said, 'It's true, as long as they're not his own. He doesn't get along at all with Joey Jr., his son.'"

CHAPTER 14

In September 1957 Joe DiMaggio Jr. transferred from Black-Foxe Military Institute in Los Angeles to Lawrenceville Prep School in Lawrenceville, New Jersey. At the time a boys' boarding school, Lawrenceville was fifty miles southwest of New York, five minutes south of Princeton, New Jersey, and forty miles north of Philadelphia. Sixteen-year-old Joey thrived in his new environment. At five foot eight and 165 pounds, he was still filling out, though he would never be as tall and as muscular as his father. Yet he became a shot-putter on the school's winter track team and a javelin thrower on the spring team. Not big enough to play a position on the football team, he practiced for hours and became the team kicker. When asked by a member of the press why he hadn't tried out for the varsity baseball squad, he said he wanted to concentrate on track. It was the old story. He knew he couldn't compete with his father's feats on the baseball diamond, so why try?

"I tried like hell to make the junior varsity football team," Joey recalled. "The coach told me if I got good at it, he'd give me a spot as a placekicker. That's all I needed to hear. Every afternoon after class I'd be out there with a dozen footballs, practicing field goals, extra points, and kickoffs. I'd practice kicking until the rest of the team went off for dinner. I'd be out there booting footballs half the night. I suppose I wanted to prove to my father that I was good at something."

Joey developed a number of interests at Lawrenceville. He joined the staff of the school newspaper (the *Lawrence*), the science club, and the chess team. He became a chapel usher and appeared in a school play. He eventually became president of the Open Door Society, which arranged for prospective underprivileged students to visit the campus. He continued his childhood interest in aviation, taking flying lessons at a small airport outside Philadelphia. His father paid for the flight lessons as well as for the fees associated with school. And until his son turned twenty-one, DiMaggio had to keep up his child support payments to Joey's mother.

Although Marilyn Monroe had endured more than her share of recent difficulties, she continued to remain in close contact with Joey, especially now that they were both on the East Coast. His connection to Monroe also ensured Joey a direct line to his father, who called regularly to find out about Marilyn.

"At first he made no effort to visit me at school," said Joey, "but he did call. I'd hoped he'd come to our first football game. When we lost seven to six because I missed the extra point, I felt relieved he wasn't there. When I told him the final score, he surprised me with his answer. 'You'll make it next time,' he said."

Joined by a classmate from Lawrenceville, Joe Jr. spent Thanksgiving break of 1957 with his father in New York. George Solotaire provided the boys a pair of theater tickets to *My Fair Lady,* followed by a late-night dinner at Dinty Moore's. The following day, Thursday, Toots Shor hosted Joe and the two boys for Thanksgiving dinner at his home. Joey and Chuck Heller then went to a new Broadway musical called *Rumple,* after which they returned to Toots's apartment, where Joe Sr. introduced them to Frank Gifford, Kyle Rote, and Charlie Conerly of the New York Giants football team. On Friday DiMaggio took George Solotaire, Joey, Chuck Heller, and a third Lawrenceville student to dinner at the Colony. On Saturday the group (including jockey Eddie Arcaro's daughter, Toots Shor and his daughter, and John Daly) went to Philadelphia for the annual Army-Navy football game. On Sunday they were at the Polo Grounds to watch the football Giants take on the San Francisco 49ers. Late that afternoon, Joey and his friend left New York and returned to school.

All in all, though his father hadn't spent much time alone with his son, it had been a good visit, probably the best in years. Joey's letter home to his mother, while on the whole enthusiastic, nonetheless reflected a degree of doubt, as if Joey couldn't quite accept Big Joe's sudden transformation: "JD has tried to be charming in his miserable sort of way, but then I guess he's doing better than I expected, and he knows no different so we bless him and give him our love."

While he regularly spoke to Marilyn by phone, Joe DiMaggio Jr. didn't see her until early in February 1958. "She'd bounced back from the problems she'd been going through and wanted to visit me at Lawrenceville," said Joey. "I told her I'd come to New York to see her. I didn't want a repetition of the troubles I'd had with my classmates at Black-Foxe every time she appeared on campus. She told me to come in on a Sunday, because Arthur Miller wouldn't be around. I said I'd come by train, but she insisted on sending a limousine service to pick me up and then drive me back at night. It had snowed pretty heavily earlier in the week, so we went to Central Park and built a snowman. We ate lunch at a small restaurant near her house. Then she had me up to her apartment, and we just chatted. I told her about my Thanksgiving visit with Dad. I told her about a falling-out I'd had during the summer while visiting with relatives on my mother's side of the family and how I had no intention of ever seeing them again. 'Isn't that a bit harsh?' she asked, and then she inquired after my mother. I told her my mother had been going out with a restaurant owner in California named Ralph Peck. His real name was Pickovitch, but he'd shortened it for professional reasons. My mother, I said, had been given a few small film roles but, as usual, was frustrated by her overall lack of success. 'Maybe she's lucky,' said Marilyn. 'Fame isn't all it's cracked up to be. There are times when I wish I were still Norma Jeane. There's comfort in anonymity.'

"She didn't say much about my father, although I had the sense she wasn't altogether happy in her current marriage. My suspicions were confirmed two weeks later when I heard from her at school. She called to report she'd just seen my father. They'd spent an afternoon together. They planned on being together now and then, when it was mutually convenient — nothing formal, just the two of them. She still loved him — always had and always would. Nobody knew about them. Marilyn swore me to secrecy. What's amazing, I suppose, is that despite all the journalists and biographers that wrote about

Marilyn Monroe, not one seemed aware of her relationship with my father during her marriage to Arthur Miller. They all realized that Dad and Marilyn began seeing each other again in the spring of 1961, following her divorce from Miller. But the truth is that their affair, if you want to call it that, began much sooner and always remained a secret."

Other than Joe Jr., the one person who did know of the affair was Paul Baer. It was in Baer's apartment that Joe and Marilyn carried on their tryst.

"One evening in early 1958," said Baer, "I went to dinner with Joe, and he did something almost unheard of for him: he began talking about Marilyn. He'd read about her troubles and wondered whether he could be of help. After all, he knew her as well as anyone. She'd always considered him a kind of paternal figure as well as a lover. But there were several problems, not the least of which was Arthur Miller. What if Miller found out Joe had tried to contact Marilyn? Maybe he'd go public with the news, possibly contact the press — and wouldn't that prove embarrassing? And then, too, Marilyn had recently changed her home phone number, and Joe didn't know how to reach her. Finally, if he did reach her, and she consented to see him, where the hell could they meet? He couldn't very well have her up to his hotel suite. The hotel personnel all knew him and would almost certainly recognize Marilyn, even in her usual disguise."

Paul Baer immediately understood that Joe ached to see Marilyn again but couldn't risk the possibility of getting caught. He also understood why DiMaggio had brought him into the equation. Paul currently resided on Fifth Avenue, but he maintained a second apartment, a small rental on the Upper West Side, which would make an ideal hideaway for Joe and Marilyn.

As Baer put it, "I had a petite one-bedroom flat on Central Park West in the midnineties, which I held on to after I moved because the rent was moderate, and I could use it to put up friends from out of town. I also used it for weekly poker parties. Joe came on several occasions. I'd prepare lots of spaghetti and lasagna, and we'd feast before the games. Joe used to say I made the best lasagna in New York."

Located on the fifteenth floor of an imposing building, Paul Baer's apartment consisted of a bedroom, living room, and small kitchen alcove. All rooms looked out on the Central Park reservoir. The living room contained a rubber tree that practically filled the entire room. It left space only for a couch, a bar, and a card table. A king-sized platform bed dominated the bedroom, which contained a desk and dresser.

Inez Melson provided DiMaggio with

Marilyn's new telephone number at her East Fifty-Seventh Street apartment. He called, and she immediately agreed to meet him at his friend's Central Park West apartment.

"They arranged to get together on a Wednesday afternoon," said Baer. "It had to be a well-orchestrated operation because the press was always around. In addition, there was this devoted New York fan club — they called themselves the Marilyn Monroe Seven — and they followed her everywhere. She encouraged them. She'd invite them over for dinner now and then. So, anyway, I gave Joe a key to the apartment. He told me he'd be wearing a fake beard and a low-slung hat when he arrived at the building. He'd use the name Mr. Morse, as in Morse code, and he'd get to the building ten minutes before Marilyn. She'd use the name Mamie, as in Mamie Eisenhower, the then First Lady. The next order of business involved taking care of Bob, the building's hardworking, cross-eyed, not so bright, daytime doorman. I took Bob aside, gave him twenty bucks, and explained that a friend, Mr. Morse, would come by on Wednesday to use my apartment for a few hours. And then I added that a friend of his, a woman named Mamie, would be joining him. I instructed Bob to let them both go upstairs to my apartment. Bob gave me a cross-eyed wink. 'Don't worry, boss,' he said. 'I'll let them in.' "

Paul Baer tidied the apartment, put fresh sheets on the bed, stocked the refrigerator with champagne, bought a bouquet of flowers for the bedroom, and left Joe and Marilyn a business card that read simply, "Have fun, kids! Yours, Paul Baer."

"With one notable hitch, the plot worked to perfection," recalled Baer. "Joe called the following day to thank me. He said they'd disposed of a bottle and a half of champagne and made good use of the bedroom. It had been like old times with Marilyn — everything had gone as planned. He just wanted to make sure nobody else found out about it, not even his great buddy George Solotaire. I told him not to worry — nobody would know. The next time I went to the building, I happened to see Bob, the doorman. I handed him another ten dollars in addition to the twenty I'd already given him. 'Bob,' I said, 'thanks for taking care of my friends.' For someone who rarely demonstrated any emotion, Bob suddenly became very animated. 'Boss,' he yelped, 'I kept my cool, but you won't believe who went up to your place the other day.' Without waiting for a response, he said, 'Joe DiMaggio and Marilyn Monroe! They had on these ridiculous disguises, but you couldn't mistake them. Can you dig it, boss? DiMaggio and Monroe. Joe and Marilyn. Did you know they were using your apartment? And by the way, what the hell

ever happened to Mr. Morse and Mamie?
They never showed.' "

CHAPTER 15

Although Joe DiMaggio met with Marilyn Monroe only periodically in the years between 1958 and 1960, it appeared they met often enough to assuage his damaged soul. So eager was he to continue seeing Marilyn that he agreed to seek professional counseling in order to overcome his jealousy and anger issues. Dr. Kris, Marilyn's psychoanalyst, provided her patient with the name of a psychiatrist for DiMaggio. Marilyn passed it on.

Joe went for a while, and the sessions seemed to help. Although he remained critical of those he deemed a threat to Marilyn's happiness, he learned to temper his condemnations. He appeared better able to deal with Marilyn on her terms as opposed to his own. For her part, she appeared better able to deal with DiMaggio now than when she'd been his spouse.

Marilyn still had the Big Fellow very much on her mind. To Lena Pepitone, she mused,

"I guess everybody I've ever loved, I still love a little." Or maybe more than a little — who was to say? In addition to the poster of Joe Marilyn had mounted in her closet, she now carried a small snapshot of Joe in her wallet. She changed the combination on her jewelry box to 5-5-5, honoring Joe's retired Yankee number. When she informed DiMaggio of the change, he said, "You should've made it 36-24-36."

Joe's psychiatrist, whose name has never been divulged, advised him to rejoin the workforce and to do something not directly related to baseball. In mid-1958, through retired quarterback Sid Luckman, he connected with the V. H. Monette Company, based in Smithfield, Virginia. The company was the leading supplier of merchandise and goods to military exchange stores and outlets in the United States and Europe. He signed on as corporate vice president and was paid a salary of $100,000 a year plus expenses. Among other benefits, the company paid for DiMaggio's executive suite at the Lexington Hotel in New York.

In his new position, DiMaggio served as a kind of public relations figure, often traveling to military bases with the boss, Val Monette. He dined with generals and admirals, visited local officers' clubs, and played an occasional round of golf with the company's clients. He smiled, shook hands, and doled out his autograph. He met with the kids on the base and sometimes tossed a baseball around with them. Besides France, Germany, Italy, and Denmark, Joe accompanied Val to Poland and Russia, simply because Monette wanted to visit those countries. Joe remained with his employer through July, 1962.

"It was a good job for him," said Joe DiMaggio Jr. "It kept him busy but not all that busy. He had plenty of downtime. He even visited me at school. Marilyn shamed him into it. When she learned that he hadn't come out to see me at Lawrenceville, she said to him, 'If you don't visit your son, I will.' So he and George Solotaire drove out one day. And my dorm mates went gaga. The head of the athletic department and the baseball coach heard he was visiting and came around to meet him. They couldn't get over being in the same room as the great Joseph Paul DiMaggio. They kept asking question after question about his days as a Yankee. I felt almost embarrassed for these two guys. George Solotaire just kept rolling his eyes."

Although unaware of Marilyn's clandestine meetings with DiMaggio, Lena Pepitone acknowledged that Joe called Marilyn from time to time. "Marilyn enjoyed hearing from him," said Pepitone. "She knew how much he loved her — and she always loved him. I remember the afternoon she went to Gallagher's steak house with press agent John

Springer. She came home afterward and said she'd seen Joe's picture in the restaurant and how much that pleased her. I recall the day Lew Wasserman, her agent at MCA, called her to inquire whether she thought DiMaggio might agree to be the subject of a feature film. 'You must be kidding,' she told him. 'That's the last thing in the world he'd want.' "

According to Pepitone, one of the basic problems in Marilyn's marriage to Arthur Miller was that he never wanted to do anything other than sit in his study with the door closed. "One evening," said Pepitone, "Marilyn suggested they go to a movie that had just opened. He agreed. She bathed and dressed and sat in the living room waiting for him. After a while, when he failed to materialize, she went to his study and timidly knocked at the door. 'I'm working,' he said. Marilyn was crushed. She went to her bedroom, tore off her blouse, and began to sob. The one function she succeeded in getting him to attend in 1958 was Elsa Maxwell's April in Paris Ball at the Waldorf. She knew Joe DiMaggio sometimes attended Elsa's parties, and I think she hoped he might be there. He wasn't. But her presence at the function caused absolute pandemonium. The place went wild. DiMaggio also showed up at the Actors Studio the day she and John Strasberg performed a scene out of *A Streetcar Named*

Desire. It was standing room only."

On weekends when Miller and Monroe happened to be in Roxbury, they sometimes visited Elia Kazan, whose country estate wasn't far from theirs. Miller had reconciled with Kazan, at least professionally. The playwright still felt emotionally distanced from the director, but, as he wrote in *Time-bends,* "the whole Communist issue had gone cold." Miller chose Kazan to direct a production of *A View From the Bridge* because, wrote the playwright, "I was not at all sure that he should be excluded from a position for which he was superbly qualified by his talent and his invaluable experience with The Group."

"Seeing his old crony wasn't a social commitment that particularly bothered Miller," said Pepitone. "Kazan's house was usually overridden with members of the Actors Studio: Ben Gazzara, Eli Wallach, Anne Bancroft, Walter Matthau, Paul Newman, and others, including Marlon Brando on occasion. They played softball in the afternoon, and as I heard the story, the first time Marilyn came to bat she belted the ball a country mile. None of them had hit it that far before. As she rounded the bases and touched home plate, Ben Gazzara said, 'My God, Marilyn! Where the hell did you learn to do that?' And she responded, 'I had a good teacher. Remember? I was married to Joltin' Joe.' Needless to say, Arthur Miller didn't exactly appreciate her response."

If Marilyn felt emotionally cut off from Miller, he, too, felt frustrated in the marriage. "One subject Marilyn refused to discuss was money," noted Pepitone. "Whenever the topic arose, she put her hands over her ears. 'I don't know a thing about money,' she'd say. 'I just want to act. I want respect. I don't want to be laughed at. I want to be happy.' She was totally impractical when it came to finances. I remember, for example, that for a while she used Kenneth as her hairdresser. He later became famous for styling Jacqueline Kennedy's hair. He used to come to the apartment to do work on Marilyn, and she'd keep him waiting for hours. She paid him by the hour so she didn't think it mattered to him if he had to wait. The trouble is that the final cost of a visit became exorbitant."

For all her difficulties with her husband, Marilyn remained infatuated with the thought of having a baby. "Whenever she saw a baby carriage with an infant in it, she would get excited," remarked Pepitone. "A couple one floor below us at 444 East Fifty-Seventh Street had a newborn, and the baby nurse would take the infant for a carriage ride every morning. On weekends, the baby's mother would push the carriage. Marilyn became friendly with her and began asking her all sorts of questions. What was it like giving birth? What did she feed the baby? Did the baby sleep at night? After they became friendly, the mother let Marilyn hold and play with the baby. Marilyn confided in the woman that she wanted a baby of her own but was having difficulties. 'Why not adopt?' the woman asked. 'I know all about adoption,' said Marilyn. 'I want to give birth and then raise the child. More than anything, that's what I'd like.' "

The actress told Norman Rosten that she felt torn between becoming pregnant again and making another film. "I'd love my child to death," she remarked. "I want to have one, yet I'm afraid. Arthur says he wants it, but he's losing his enthusiasm. He thinks I should do the picture. After all, I'm a movie star, right?"

The "picture," as Marilyn referred to it when talking to Norman Rosten, was *Some Like It Hot,* a United Artists production costarring Marilyn, Tony Curtis, and Jack Lemmon. Produced and directed by Billy Wilder, who'd last worked with Marilyn on *The Seven Year Itch,* the new film began shooting in Los Angeles at the beginning of August 1958. A spoof about a pair of musicians (Curtis and Lemmon) who witness a gangland massacre and then, to avoid being bumped off themselves, dress up as women and join an all-girls orchestra, *Some Like It Hot* became a film classic. It is one of the funniest American comedies of its time — or of any time, for that matter. Monroe's performance netted her a Golden Globe Award for Best Actress in a Comedy or Musical. She told Earl Wilson that she thought she deserved an Oscar. In reality, although Marilyn had hoped to succeed as a serious actress performing serious roles, her greatest successes came in comedies such as this one.

The quality of her *Some Like It Hot* performance aside, Marilyn's personal behavior had never been worse. "Her lack of professionalism during the making of *Seven Year Itch* was bad enough," complained Billy Wilder, "but it reached new heights in the present film." With her endless lateness and pathological block against remembering even the most mundane bits of dialogue, she managed to antagonize almost everyone connected to the film. A scene in which Marilyn uttered a three-word line ("Where's the bourbon?") had to be reshot more than sixty times. Weakened by drugs, MM missed entire days on the set, remaining fast asleep in her bungalow at the Beverly Hills Hotel. When on the set, she complained nonstop about numerous aspects of the film, starting with the fact that she'd once again been cast as "the dumb blonde." She criticized the studio for shooting the film in black and white. She wasn't getting along with Billy Wilder. She couldn't stand Tony Curtis. Although she was top-billed, she thought it all wrong that the film's plot line should revolve around her two male costars.

Rumor had it that the only reason she'd signed on to do the film was because she and Arthur Miller had run out of money. Angry that she'd agreed to star in *Some Like It Hot,* Marilyn took out her wrath on the film's director, embarrassing Wilder in front of the other actors by telling him he was incompetent and refusing to follow his instructions. "Don't tell me what to do," she berated him. "I'll play the scene my way."

Marilyn's delicate emotional state was nowhere more evident than in her diary entries, one of which read: "Help, help, help. I feel life coming closer when all I want is to die."

A letter she wrote to Norman Rosten while on location at the Hotel del Coronado in San Diego was only slightly more uplifting: "Don't give up the ship while we're sinking. I have a feeling this boat is never going to dock. We are going through the Straits of Dire. It's rough and choppy."

Sensing that Arthur Miller could neither control nor help his wife, Paula Strasberg telephoned Dr. Kris in New York and asked her to come to California and see Marilyn in person. Monroe had bombarded Kris all summer with letters, telegrams, and phone calls. Kris had contacted Anna Freud in London to discuss Marilyn, and Anna had advised her to see Marilyn on the set. Her presence did little good. In addition to her massive drug abuse, MM was drinking more than ever. After each take, she insisted she be brought a thermos of coffee, but as Billy Wilder soon discerned, the thermos was filled with vermouth and not coffee. At the completion of the film, Wilder sent Arthur Miller a letter of complaint: "Had you, dear Arthur, been not her husband but her . . . director, and been subjected to all the indignities I was, you would have thrown her out on her can, thermos bottle and all, to avoid a nervous breakdown. I did the braver thing. I had a nervous breakdown."

It had been Miller who apprised Wilder that his wife had again become pregnant. Dr. Leon Krohn, Monroe's gynecologist, had confirmed the pregnancy. At the same time, he cautioned the actress that the effects of accumulated barbiturates — and other drugs — could cause her to lose the fetus. He advised her to cease her use of sleeping pills and to reduce her hours on the set. Arthur Miller asked Wilder if Marilyn could leave every day no later than four in the afternoon, to which the director responded, "That's the time she usually gets here. If you bring her at nine in the morning, ready to shoot, I'll let her go at noon."

The possibility of giving birth, an eventuality Marilyn anticipated with both hope and dread, encouraged her to follow her physician's recommendations. She stopped drinking and cut back on her consumption of drugs, limiting herself to the use of Amytal, a milder barbiturate than Nembutal. She began turning up early for work, as Wilder had suggested. He, in turn, kept his end of the bargain and most days allowed her to leave the set just before lunch. The damage, after all, had already been done: the film was more than two months behind schedule.

Marilyn contacted Lena Pepitone in New York and asked her to buy a cradle for the baby. "She told me she sensed it would be a girl," recalled Pepitone, "so she wanted the cradle to be pink. 'And if it's a boy?' I asked. 'What's the difference?' said Marilyn. 'No baby ever cared about the color of its cradle. That's an adult perversion.' So I went to an antique store and purchased a pink handmade wooden cradle, with a pink-checkered baby girl in a bonnet carved into the tiny headboard. A pink baby lamb had been etched into the side of the cradle."

Shooting on *Some Like It Hot* came to an end on November 6. Billy Wilder threw a cast party but didn't invite Marilyn, though in the end, it was largely her comic brilliance that made the film such a success.

On November 8 the Millers were back in New York. Marilyn placed the tiny cradle next to her bed and spent most of the next five weeks at home, resting. She wrote poems, sending one or two of them to Norman Rosten with a letter that she signed "e. e. cummings," in imitation of the famous American poet who rarely used capital letters. She took one night off to accompany her husband to the opening of Yves Montand's one-man Broadway show in which the Italian-born (but French-speaking) actor demonstrated his skill as a singer.

Montand and his wife, actress Simone Signoret, had starred in the French film version of Arthur Miller's play *The Crucible,* and the two men had become friends. Following the show that evening, Miller, Montand, and Monroe ate a late-night dinner and discussed the possibility of Yves and Marilyn working together on a film. When the Millers returned home, Marilyn admitted that she liked Montand and found him attractive.

Sadly, in mid-December, despite her precautions, Marilyn suffered yet another miscarriage. She was taken by ambulance to Manhattan Polyclinic Hospital. News of the miscarriage received wide media coverage. When he heard, Joe DiMaggio called her at home. They spoke briefly. DiMaggio told Paul Baer that Marilyn couldn't stop crying.

Lena Pepitone had forgotten to remove the

newly bought pink cradle from Marilyn's bedroom. "I tried to take it out after she returned from the hospital," said Pepitone, "but she insisted I leave it. That night, she hurled it against the wall, and it broke into pieces. 'This was my last chance,' she wept. 'My last chance.'"

Late at night on December 26, a highly distraught Arthur Miller called Norman Rosten and asked him to come over as soon as possible. The Rostens arrived at three in the morning. Marilyn had taken Amytal plus Nembutal with wine. Unable to rouse his wife and seeking to avoid unwanted publicity, Miller had called a physician friend of his, who'd come over and pumped her stomach. She made a rapid recovery. On New Year's Eve, the Millers attended an Actors Studio party given by Lee and Paula Strasberg.

Some Like It Hot premiered to rave reviews and record box office revenue on March 29, 1959, at Loew's State Theater on Broadway. Plugging the film in Los Angeles, Tony Curtis was asked what it was like to have kissed Monroe in the film. "It was like kissing Hitler," he said. Marilyn's response to her costar's hurtful remark was offered in a *Life* magazine interview conducted in the summer of 1962. Asked how she felt about Curtis's earlier remark, she said, "That's his problem."

Tony Curtis perpetrated one further indignity against Marilyn, claiming in his book *The Making of* Some Like It Hot, published in 2009, and in a number of interviews publicizing the book, that he'd had a fleeting affair with Monroe during the production of the film. Yet in his autobiography, published sixteen years earlier, Curtis makes no such claim, stating only that he and Marilyn had dated informally when both were new to Hollywood. When asked about the discrepancy by a British journalist, Curtis — who died in September 2010 — responded, "I'm not the only Hollywood actor who fantasized about sleeping with Marilyn Monroe. To put it another way, I so frequently dreamed of sleeping with her that it seemed almost as if I had. But I do stick to my earlier statement: kissing Marilyn was like kissing Hitler. Of course, that's also a debatable statement, since I never had the pleasure of kissing Herr Hitler — I never even met the man."

In mid-April 1959 Truman Capote met with an editor friend to discuss his novella *Breakfast at Tiffany's,* which was soon to be made into a feature film. Having just seen Marilyn Monroe in *Some Like It Hot,* Capote felt she would make a wonderful Holly Golightly, the book's main character, a kind of wholesome harlot, a girl-woman with her own set of values and a singular vision of the world. "Marilyn's perfect for the role," Capote told the editor. He'd discussed the possibility with her, and she'd expressed interest.

"Have you seen her lately?" asked Capote's companion. "I heard from Delos Smith that her psychiatrist put her on Tuinal, a barbiturate composed of Seconal and Nembutal. She takes five Tuinal pills at night to try to sleep. Seven Tuinal can kill you. She's two pills away from oblivion. I have the feeling that girl's not going to be around much longer. Delos agrees. He says in class at the Actors Studio she sits next to him and keeps whispering to him, 'Let's kill ourselves.' "

"She should be monitored," remarked Capote. "Blood tests and all that. Her shrink's got to monitor her."

Capote went on to say that there were two Marilyns. There was the frenetic, fast-talking, street-savvy, tough, sometimes mean and spiteful Marilyn, often so drugged and drunk that she didn't know who or where she was. But when she felt relaxed, she changed into the other Marilyn. She became a soft, lovely person with a wonderfully sweet smile and a full, hearty laugh, a bit shy, a keen listener, with wide, inquisitive eyes, nice but always naughty.

"The two Marilyns in combination," said Capote, "are what make her the perfect Holly Golightly."

Lee and Paula Strasberg were against Marilyn's accepting the role. The last thing she needed was to play the part of a hooker, even a sophisticated one. Paula called the producers to remove Monroe's name from the list of actresses being considered. Audrey Hepburn came away with the part. When the film came out in 1961, Marilyn sent Hepburn a telegram congratulating her on a fine performance. She graciously told Truman Capote, "Audrey probably did a better job of it than I would have."

"Joe DiMaggio finally confided in my father about seeing Marilyn again," said Robert Solotaire. "I believe she considered him a great friend, somebody she could always count on. She obviously didn't want to lose him. She enjoyed sleeping with him, so that feature became part and parcel of their new arrangement. Being on intimate terms with Marilyn Monroe, sex goddess, idol of millions, probably meant more to Joe than it did to Marilyn. He believed no other man could love her as much as he did. And he was probably right."

DiMaggio sent Marilyn flowers when, on June 23, 1959, she underwent surgery at Lenox Hill Hospital in New York to try again to correct her chronic endometriosis, an ailment that would continue to flare now and then until the end of her life.

Marilyn saw Joe at Paul Baer's house in early September. Then, later in the month, she flew to Los Angeles to attend a Twentieth Century–Fox luncheon for the Russian premier, Nikita Khrushchev. Spyros Skouras, organizer of the event, had called Marilyn in New York to tell her that Khrushchev had personally requested her presence at the function. Perhaps because he wanted to avoid further problems with the government, Arthur Miller had refused to attend.

Zsa Zsa Gabor, one of the four hundred invited guests, recalled that the guest list featured some of Hollywood's most recognizable names, including Gregory Peck, Cary Grant, Frank Sinatra, Judy Garland, Charlton Heston, Jimmy Stewart, Yul Brynner, David Niven, Shelley Winters, Bob Hope, Bing Crosby, Gary Cooper, Rita Hayworth, and Kim Novak. Elizabeth Taylor was there with her then husband Eddie Fisher, and they were seated opposite Debbie Reynolds, of all people, the woman Fisher had dumped to marry Liz. Nina Khrushchev, wife of the Russian premier, sat between Bob Hope and Sinatra, and showed them snapshots of her grandchildren. Sinatra looked bored. Marilyn Monroe entered via a side door on the arms of a pair of Fox security guards and was placed at a table near the dais, between Josh Logan and producer David Brown. Khrushchev gave a very long and angry speech, in Russian, which was then translated into English by an interpreter. "It contained all the usual and expected attacks on the sins of capitalism," said Gabor, "and was followed by a few lighthearted comments by Darryl Zanuck."

When the luncheon ended, Khrushchev headed straight for Monroe. He spoke to no one else. "To everyone's amazement," said Gabor, "Marilyn addressed him in Russian, having worked out a little welcoming speech with Natalie Wood, who spoke fluent Russian. Khrushchev seemed impressed, all the more so because Marilyn smiled sexily and wiggled her hips. In broken English, Khrushchev told her how popular she happened to be in Russia. If his wife hadn't been there, I don't doubt for an instant he would've enjoyed going off with her someplace."

Returning to Twentieth Century–Fox for her next film, Marilyn Monroe decided on *Let's Make Love,* a romantic comedy directed by George Cukor and produced by Jerry Wald. Shooting had been scheduled to begin in the fall of 1959, but as was commonplace on most Monroe films, there were problems. In the first place, Marilyn was unhappy with Norman Krasna's film script; she insisted that Arthur Miller be brought in to "doctor" the script, though he'd already begun working on a script for Marilyn's next film, *The Misfits,* based on a short story he'd written.

In need of money, Miller was only too glad to turn his attention to *Let's Make Love.*

And then there was the question of whom to cast in the romantic male lead opposite Monroe. Initially cast in the role, Gregory Peck withdrew when he read Miller's rewrite. Cary Grant and Charlton Heston turned it down as well. Arthur Miller suggested his old pal Yves Montand, and Marilyn may well have recalled the discussion they'd had about working together on a film. Familiar to French film audiences, Montand remained a relative unknown in the States. Monroe convinced Darryl Zanuck and George Cukor to offer him a contract, assuring them that he was a first-rate actor.

"I could tell Marilyn felt something for Montand, at least physically," said Lena Pepitone. "After Twentieth Century–Fox offered him a contract, and before she left for Hollywood, she said, 'He's great looking. He looks just like Joltin' Joe. If Joe could act and sing, he'd be Yves Montand.' "

Arthur and Marilyn departed for California in early November, nearly a year to the day after shooting ended on *Some Like It Hot.* They checked into the same bungalow at the Beverly Hills Hotel they'd occupied during *Some Like It Hot.* "Marilyn arrived armed to the teeth with every drug imaginable," said Whitey Snyder, who was again working with her. "Her psychiatrist, Dr. Kris, prescribed drugs, and Paula Strasberg's doctor also prescribed medication for her. And if she wanted additional drugs, she'd go see some local quack. In those days, they were only too happy to oblige.

"Her dressing room for *Let's Make Love* looked like a pharmacy. I remember seeing bottles of Amytal, Tuinal, Nembutal, Doriden, Luminal, and Seconal. I thought she probably had more of the same back at the hotel. I made a list of the drugs to show to my own doctor. I also noticed she'd arrive on the lot in the morning and swallow a handful of pills with a glass of ice tea laced with gin. And then she'd continue, another additional effect on her mood swings. The large quantities of medication caused chronic constipation, so that by the end of 1959, she'd subject herself to occasional enemas. I regret I didn't say anything to her about her drug and alcohol use. Neither did Arthur Miller. He seemed content to let her consume whatever it took to get through the day."

Although Whitey failed to address Marilyn's drug issues, he did mention Joe DiMaggio: "I asked if she'd heard from him recently, and she looked at me as if I knew something I shouldn't know. In truth, I hadn't spoken to Joe in nearly a year. I learned later they were having a secret affair, but at the time, I knew nothing. Marilyn smiled and said, 'Joe's my personal lifeguard. He's always there to look out for me. And when he sees I'm drowning, he swims out and pulls me to safety.' "

Toward the end of 1959, Marilyn learned that Carl Sandburg was in Hollywood writing the film script for *The Greatest Story Ever Told*. Owning a copy of his biography of Abraham Lincoln, she sought him out and the two met. One evening Arthur Miller and Marilyn took Sandburg out to dinner at Chasen's. They were eating when the door to the restaurant opened, and in walked Joe and Dom DiMaggio. Joe was in Los Angeles on behalf of the Monette Company, and Dom had flown in to get together with his brother. The restaurant meeting with Marilyn was purely a chance encounter.

"Marilyn saw us from across the room and waved," said Dom DiMaggio. "We went to her table. She stood. Joe took her hand and pressed it. I kissed her on the cheek. She introduced us to Arthur Miller and Carl Sandburg. Strange as it may seem, Sandburg knew my brother from some charity event they'd both attended years before. Marilyn seemed impressed. 'You know everyone, Joe,' she said. We remained standing while Miller and Sandburg half stood and shook our hands. This marked the one and only time Joe came face to face with the playwright. I can't say Miller was all smiles, but he certainly wasn't unfriendly. On the whole, he seemed almost pleased to have finally met Marilyn's previous husband. Perhaps he felt sorry for Joe because he knew firsthand how difficult it sometimes was to be with Marilyn — it was like living with a hurricane, only you never knew in which direction the wind might blow."

In early 1960 Yves Montand and Simone Signoret arrived from France. They were placed first at the Chateau Marmont and were then moved into bungalow 22 at the Beverly Hills Hotel; the Millers occupied bungalow 21. As work progressed on *Let's Make Love,* Marilyn became friendly with Signoret, who the year before had won an Oscar for her performance in *Room at the Top.* Every evening after filming ended, Monroe would appear in the Montand bungalow to talk and sip champagne with the French actress. Signoret soon noticed what everyone else had sensed for weeks: Marilyn's mood shifts were becoming increasingly erratic — so erratic she began to feel that Marilyn might be suicidal.

Whitey Snyder noticed as well. "Marilyn seemed deeply depressed one minute," he said, "and almost giddy the next. She'd slip in and out of these moods very rapidly. One moment she'd be talking normally, and the next she'd become extremely agitated and upset. She thought, for example, that Fox had bugged her dressing room and that they were transmitting the tapes to the FBI. She insisted on hiring a private detective to sweep the room and ascertain whether there were any hidden recording devices. The investigator found nothing."

While Agnes Flanagan styled Marilyn's hair for the movie, the film studio hired hairdresser George Masters to work with her on publicity appearances. Masters was astounded to find the actress in such an utter state of disarray. "My first meeting with Marilyn Monroe is etched in my memory," he said. "She was a mess. She was waiting for me in her bungalow at the Beverly Hills Hotel . . . in a terry cloth robe, one shoulder torn, her yellow hair hanging down around her neck, no makeup, champagne and caviar everywhere. Thus began my adventures with the world's greatest sex symbol."

Rob Saduski, a Hollywood costume designer and faithful friend of Masters's, recalled the hairstylist talking about his initial reaction to Marilyn and how he took her in hand and tried to restore the glamour that drugs and her damaged self-image were slowly eroding. "She didn't want people to know she had a hairdresser," said Saduski. "She wanted people to think she just looked that good. She was as calculating and vain as she was innocent and confused. Whenever Marilyn had to make a personal appearance during the making of the film, George would have to duck down in the car so nobody knew he was there. He'd work on her hair, and when they reached their destination, she'd emerge from the backseat looking resplendent, and the press photographers would start blazing away with their cameras. He remained her private hairstylist on and off until the end of her life. She gave him a brand-new white Lincoln Continental as a gift. Suffice it to say, she was enormously generous and thankful to anyone who reached out to her."

In an ironic twist of fate, the title of the picture — *Let's Make Love* — soon became a moniker for a personal escapade that, in the end, created more interest among the press and public than the humdrum film that eventually emerged. Despite Marilyn's apparent alliance with Simone Signoret, the distinguished French actress soon became a victim of Monroe's promiscuous nature. Called back to Paris to discuss a new film project, Signoret found herself out of town at the same time that Arthur Miller happened to be in New York. Left alone, Montand and Monroe began an affair. Montand, naturally, blamed Marilyn for initiating the relationship, claiming she seduced him in her bungalow over vodka and caviar, his favorite repast. "After we ate and drank," he reportedly told friends, "she laid her head in my lap. What was I supposed to do?"

For roughly six weeks, Montand and Monroe were a couple. They were seen together at several Hollywood house parties, such as the poolside bash given by studio executive David Selznick. Gregson E. Bautzer, an entertainment lawyer and California socialite, spotted the pair at the party and walked over to them. Confronting Marilyn, he accused her of being ungrateful to Joe Schenck, her early benefactor. If she cared about him, spouted Bautzer, she would visit him in the hospital. He was seriously ill and quite possibly wouldn't make it. Marilyn burst into tears and pleaded ignorance — nobody had told her about Joe. She went to see him the following day and spent two hours by his bedside.

Not long after the affair ended and while production on the film wound down, Montand told Hedda Hopper about his fling with Monroe. Montand's "confession" resulted in a slag heap of predictable headlines. When Rupert Allan, Marilyn's publicist, asked Montand why he'd gone public with the story, Montand responded, "Because too many people have speculated about it. Boo-hoo, I'm sorry."

In a follow-up interview with Hopper several months later, Montand offered further commentary on the scandal: "Marilyn is a simple girl without any guile. I was too tender and thought she was as sophisticated as some of the other ladies I have known. Had Marilyn been more sophisticated, none of this would have happened. Perhaps she had a schoolgirl crush. If she did, I'm sorry. But nothing will break up my marriage."

Rupert Allan pointed out that when Yves Montand accepted the role to play opposite Monroe in the film, he was ecstatic: "A well-known actor in Europe, he'd been searching for a vehicle to establish himself in the States. The Montands and Millers became close friends. Then Arthur found out his 'friend' was fucking his wife. It goes without saying Arthur was deeply hurt. When I spoke with him, he said, 'You know, Marilyn and I are breaking up.' "

When the movie finally wrapped, Montand called Rupert Allan and asked him to become his publicist. "Once again," said Allan, "he began chatting about his affair with Marilyn, as if this was his strongest selling point. He was a real prick — ungallant and indiscreet. He said when Marilyn came on to him, it was her time of the month, and it was awful. She smelled awful. She was dirty and unkempt. 'That's more information than I need,' I told him. 'Besides, I thought you Frenchmen were so liberated. Frankly, I'd take Marilyn Monroe with or without her period if I could have her.' 'First of all, I'm an Italian,' said Montand. 'But, anyway, hygiene is important to me.' I told him to fuck off and find himself another publicist. I don't know who ended up representing him, but I can safely and happily say that instead of *Let's Make Love* enhancing his career, the film and the scandal attached to it all but buried him, at least in this country."

Prior to Marilyn's affair with Montand, Lotte Goslar went to dinner with Marilyn and Arthur Miller. "They'd just started the picture," said Goslar. "That evening I saw a side of Marilyn I'd never noticed before. She acted very bitchy toward Arthur. First of all, she began talking about Joe DiMaggio and what a great dresser he was. 'Arthur only owns two suits,' she said. As we were leaving, she started ordering him around: 'Get my purse, Arthur, I checked it.' When he got back with the purse, she said, 'Where's my mink coat? They were on the same claim check. Get me my mink.' She practically called him an idiot. She began yelling at him as he went back to the cloakroom to retrieve her mink. She treated him like a slave. She absolutely degraded him. It was terrible. And a little later, she conducted that very flagrant infidelity with Montand. I knew how audacious and bold she could be if she wanted something. Arthur Miller, by comparison, seemed an innocent, completely out of his depth. I felt for him. Everyone did. It was almost as if Marilyn had wanted to hurt him. I think she felt he hadn't supported her emotionally. When we were alone, she said he was a great writer but a lousy husband. She remarked that the only reason he stayed on with her was to collect a paycheck for writing the screenplay to *The Misfits,* Marilyn's next film."

Monroe's treatment of her third husband grew even harsher when she learned that he'd telephoned Simone Signoret in Paris to discuss the romance. "What does his wife have to do with it?" Marilyn asked him. "Instead of Simone Signoret, why didn't you call Yves Montand? Why didn't you belt him in the mouth? That's what Joe DiMaggio would've done. Or why didn't you slap me around? You should've slapped me."

Simone Signoret's only public comment regarding Yves Montand's liaison with Monroe came after the filming of *Let's Make Love* ended: "If Marilyn fell in love with my husband," she said, "then she has good taste."

"Can you believe this?" Joe DiMaggio asked George Solotaire one evening over drinks at Toots Shor's. Joe had a copy of Hedda Hopper's newspaper column in hand and was waving it in George's face. "Why would Marilyn sleep with this guy?" Joe asked, not expecting an answer. "I don't get it. Is she that insecure?"

Bernie Kamber, DiMaggio's PR buddy, also present on this occasion, recalled Joe's somewhat dramatic outburst — dramatic, that is, for Joe. "The first thing I did every morning," said Kamber, "was read the New York, LA, and Washington, DC, papers. In my business, you had to know what was going on. So I'd already read about Marilyn and Yves Montand. But I hadn't expected it to upset Joe to such an extent. Of course, I didn't realize at the time that they were in touch again. I knew about some of his other ladies, including Phyllis McGuire, the youngest and prettiest of the McGuire Sisters, the popular singing trio. Phyllis had several other boyfriends, among them Sam Giancana, the Chicago Mob boss, a guy you wouldn't want to meet in a dark alley — or anywhere else, for that matter. So she and Joe were bosom buddies, if you know what I mean. The truth is that half the eligible women in New York were after Joe, and a large number of the ineligible ones were as well. But Joe was obsessed with Marilyn. He was in love with her, plain and simple. In any case, I said to him, 'Well, Joe, at least Yves Montand looks like you. That should give you some satisfaction.' I was kidding, but Joe wasn't. Within five minutes or so, he knocked off about a half dozen shots of scotch. George Solotaire and I had to practically carry him home that night."

DiMaggio evidently made no mention of Montand to Marilyn. They continued as

417

before with telephone calls and infrequent meetings at Paul Baer's Central Park West apartment. Art Buchwald remembered seeing "quite a bit of DiMaggio in 1960. That's the year Edward Bennett Williams made arrangements to purchase the Washington Redskins. He paid around four million dollars for the franchise. A bunch of his buddies, including DiMaggio, bought shares in the team. I think Joe anted up a hundred thousand dollars. He'd come to Washington on weekends to take in the home games. He's the only guy I ever knew who insisted on wearing a business suit to a football game. Besides myself and DiMaggio, the regulars in the group included *Washington Post* editor Ben Bradlee, Senator Edmund Muskie, John Daly, Chief Justice Earl Warren, Williams's law partner Colman Stein, and Ethel Kennedy, Bobby Kennedy's wife. This was the year John F. Kennedy ran for president, and it was before JFK became involved with Marilyn Monroe. But even though nothing had happened as yet, Joe couldn't stand the Kennedys. Ethel didn't realize this, and she kept trying to sit next to DiMaggio at the games. 'You sit next to her,' he'd say to me under his breath. It turned out to be kind of prophetic, I thought, given Marilyn's death a few years later. Among those DiMaggio held responsible for her death were the Kennedys. He accused Jack and Bobby Kennedy of having 'killed' the woman he treasured and loved. 'They might as well have put a loaded gun to her head,' he told me, 'and pulled the trigger.' "

CHAPTER 16

During the filming of *Let's Make Love,* following the termination of her affair with Yves Montand, her marriage to Arthur Miller all but over, Marilyn Monroe called Milton A. (Mickey) Rudin, her new West Coast attorney, and asked if he could provide the name of a Los Angeles psychiatrist. Deeply depressed and sedated to the point where she could barely speak coherently, Marilyn somehow managed to explain that Dr. Marianne Kris, her New York therapist, had gone to a medical conference in France and couldn't be reached. Rudin felt he could help. His brother-in-law, Dr. Ralph Greenson, lived in the area and happened to be one of the nation's foremost practitioners of classic Freudian psychoanalysis. The lawyer offered to arrange an appointment for Marilyn, setting in motion a doctor-patient relationship that would ultimately become a contributing factor in the patient's untimely death.

Born Romeo Samuel Greenschpoon on

September 20, 1911, in Brooklyn, the psychoanalyst's family was Russian in origin. He and Juliet, his twin sister — the pair was known by name as "Romeo and Juliet" — were the eldest of the family's four children. Elizabeth, his younger sister, a talented cellist, had married Mickey Rudin. Ralph Greenson (Romy to his friends after he legally changed his name) had completed his undergraduate studies at Columbia University and attended medical school at the University of Bern in Switzerland, where he met his future wife, Hildegard (Hildi). The Greensons were married in 1935 and had two children, Daniel and Joan.

After completing an internship in psychiatry at Cedars of Lebanon Hospital in Los Angeles, Greenson established his practice and simultaneously held the position of professor of clinical psychiatry at the UCLA School of Medicine. He would later become the subject of a feature film, *Captain Newman, M.D.,* starring Gregory Peck as Greenson. The film was largely based on Greenson's work with American soldiers during and after World War II.

In late 1959 Greenson visited London and there met Anna Freud and Anna's good friend Marianne Kris. One of the topics they discussed was the case of Marilyn Monroe. Hence, Greenson knew about Marilyn before he even met her.

The initial encounter between Greenson and Monroe took place in her bungalow at the Beverly Hills Hotel shortly after he'd been contacted by Mickey Rudin. He quickly noticed her slurred speech and unfocused gaze, both of which he attributed to her drug habit, particularly her dependence on medication to combat her insomnia. She was taking enough medication, he told her, to sedate a basketball team and put all five players to sleep. She confessed to her drug regimen, placing the blame on compliant doctors who plied her with whatever pharmaceuticals she requested.

According to Greenson's patient notes, Monroe claimed that when she did sleep, she had nightmares. She would see the shapes of monsters gyrating against a pitch-black screen. She complained about Arthur Miller's "failure to respond" to her, his domination by "a Jewish mother," and his contempt for commercial filmmaking, as opposed to the intellectual rigors of "serious theater work." Greenson insisted that despite Marilyn's problems and complaints — real or imagined — she would have to cut back on her use of barbiturates and other drugs.

Impressed by Greenson's directness, Marilyn telephoned Lena Pepitone in New York and reported that she'd found her "Jesus" — a man who would save her from herself. Seven years earlier, he'd done the same for

Frank Sinatra, who'd also been a patient. Not surprisingly, Sinatra's attorney was Mickey Rudin. Besides Sinatra, Greenson's celebrity-dominated patient roster included such familiar names as Peter Lorre, Tony Curtis, Vivien Leigh, Celeste Holm, Mario Lanza, Vincente Minnelli, Kim Stanley, and Oscar Levant.

By June 1960, Marilyn had begun psychoanalysis with Greenson, undergoing daily sessions at $50 per hour, usually at his five-bedroom, Spanish-style house on Franklin Street in Santa Monica, less often at the Beverly Hills offices he shared with fellow psychiatrist Dr. Milton Wexler, who on occasion, when Greenson wasn't available, substituted for him. At times Marilyn's sessions with Dr. Greenson lasted far longer than an hour, not infrequently running an entire morning or afternoon.

Like Anna Freud, Greenson diagnosed Marilyn as a paranoid schizophrenic. In a letter to Dr. Kris, he wrote that as "Marilyn becomes more anxious, she begins to act like an orphan, a waif, and she masochistically provokes people to mistreat her and to take advantage of her." Although Dr. Milton Wexler saw Marilyn only now and again, he perceived a similar pattern. "As fragments of her past history tumbled out," he said, "she started talking increasingly about the traumatic extremes of growing up an orphan. She saw herself as a victim, destined to die at an early age."

When he first met Arthur Miller, Greenson found the playwright quite different from the person Marilyn had described. He appeared to be deeply concerned with his wife's well-being and profoundly disappointed that the marriage seemed to be failing. On the other hand, Miller appeared to have reached an end point, telling Greenson that he and Marilyn had spent a long weekend together in New York that summer, and she had again attempted to harm herself. This time she opened a window at the East Fifty-Seventh Street apartment and tried to climb out onto the ledge. He'd pulled her back into the room.

Lena Pepitone and the Strasbergs were present and had witnessed the latest suicide attempt and, like Miller, heard Marilyn scream, "Let me go, I deserve to die! What have I got to live for?" Lena Pepitone ran around removing every sharp object she could find in the apartment. As for Miller, he felt he had given Marilyn all he had to give, but his strength and patience had finally begun to run out. Marilyn's growing dependence on drugs and doctors took precedence over everything. Miller told Greenson that she'd never so much as acknowledged his help, never once thanked him. All his energy had gone into trying to sustain Marilyn's career, while his own had gone into hibernation. He'd accomplished little during their years together.

While they were still on their brief visit to New York, Miller overheard a conversation between his wife and Lena Pepitone in which the actress asked Pepitone to call the Monette Company and find out how she could reach Joe DiMaggio. Lena complied and learned that Joe was visiting army bases in the South as well as going to minor-league ballparks, where he'd talk to the young players and take batting practice as a way to draw attention to the games and fill the stands. He was in transit and couldn't be reached.

Marilyn departed New York for Los Angeles in July 1960 to "prepare" for her role in *The Misfits,* the film for which Arthur Miller had written the script. To be directed by John Huston (who'd directed her in *Ladies of the Chorus,* one of her first ventures) and produced by Frank Taylor, the film was scheduled to begin shooting on July 18; also in the cast were Clark Gable, Monroe's longtime (father figure) idol, and her Actors Studio friends Montgomery Clift and Eli Wallach.

Marilyn arrived in California without Arthur Miller and checked into a suite at the Beverly Hills Hotel, not into the bungalow she'd occupied while involved with Yves Montand. A footnote to the assignation with

Montand was that she did see him one last time in New York in November, after completing work on *The Misfits*. They rendezvoused at Idlewild Airport in the backseat of a Cadillac limousine and said their farewells over a bottle of champagne. Montand was on his way back to Paris and the open arms of his wife.

Besides prepping for her role in *The Misfits*, Marilyn had other reasons to be in town: she had arrived in Los Angeles in early July in order to attend the Democratic National Convention, which was being held that summer in LA. The actress had already contributed $3,000 to John F. Kennedy's campaign fund.

She'd first crossed paths with the Massachusetts senator three years earlier at a party given by British-born actor Peter Lawford and his wife, Patricia Kennedy, Jack Kennedy's sister, at their Santa Monica beach house, where they entertained Jack whenever he found himself marooned on the West Coast. Nothing happened at the first meeting between Kennedy and Monroe. They met and took a long walk along the beach. They talked politics, and Jack asked a lot of questions about the film business.

They met again in 1959, this time for what amounted to a furtive sixty-minute tryst in the Kennedy-leased penthouse suite atop the Hotel Carlyle in New York. It was a delicate point in both their lives. Marilyn's marriage to Arthur Miller was in deep trouble. And Jack's marriage to Jackie had never really been good, or at least had never prevented him from seeking extramarital romance.

No stranger to Hollywood or Hollywood starlets, JFK had always been captivated by Monroe. In October 1954, while undergoing spinal surgery in a New York hospital, visitors to his room were treated to a poster of Marilyn hung over his bed. The poster featured Marilyn in a tight white blouse and blue shorts, her legs spread wide apart. Senator George Smathers of Florida, a close associate of Kennedy's, recalled that Jack had turned the poster upside down "so it looked as if her legs were in the air." The scene in JFK's hospital room reminded Smathers of "a college boy's frat house bedroom, the college kid working away on himself as he peered over his shoulder at the golden goddess with the voluptuous, slam-bang bod."

Smathers was more than a little familiar with JFK's extramarital antics. Following the 1956 Democratic Convention, he'd been aboard a yacht in the Mediterranean with JFK, his brother Teddy Kennedy, and a "boatload of broads," while Jackie Kennedy, waiting for her husband in the States, suffered a miscarriage. "If you ever want to be president," Smathers warned JFK, "you'd better haul ass back to your wife."

In the fifty years since JFK's 1963 assassination, a multitude of articles, films, and books have attested to Kennedy's numerous affairs both before and during his marriage and presidency. "The Kennedy boys — Jack, Bobby, and Ted — were like dogs," said Truman Capote. "There wasn't a fire hydrant in the city at which they wouldn't stop to take a piss." John White, a companion of Jackie's prior to her marriage, recalled that Jack Kennedy "had a little black book full of names, and he plowed through them like a wartime tank." Nancy Dickerson, an attractive Washington journalist who dated JFK when he first served in Congress, said, "You couldn't help but be swept over by Jack. I was, but I somehow managed to avoid giving in to his charms. I realized that sex for Jack Kennedy was like another cup of coffee, or maybe dessert. For Jack, sex wasn't to be confused with love, and I'm not certain he was capable of the latter."

Peter Lawford, a pal of Monroe's since the late 1940s when he started out as an MGM contract player, had been aware from the beginning of the possible dangers, as well as the potential benefits, that a relationship between JFK and Monroe might bring for both of them. Since products are (and were often) sold by star endorsements, Marilyn's closeness could be a boon to Jack's presidential aspirations. Similarly, his friendship could bring Marilyn a degree of happiness presently lacking in her life. The other possibility, of course, was the peril of exposure. Nobody would elect for president a man known to be cheating on his wife. There was concern among the candidate's aides, particularly when they learned that Marilyn Monroe planned on being with Kennedy during part of the Democratic Convention, while Jackie, pregnant with John Jr., remained behind at the Kennedy compound in Hyannis Port, Massachusetts.

During the convention, oblivious to the possibility of public exposure, the future president asked Peter Lawford to invite Marilyn to a small dinner party at Puccini's, a local restaurant owned by Frank Sinatra and a handful of silent partners. "There were only four of us," recalled JFK's brother-in-law. "It was Jack, Marilyn, Ken O'Donnell [a top Kennedy aide] and myself. We had a private room off the main dining salon. I soon realized that Marilyn had probably spent the previous night with Jack because, before he arrived, she described him as 'a most democratic and penetrating man.'

"That evening was very likely the only time in her life that Marilyn arrived anywhere on time. After Jack showed up, they became very cozy. I noticed he liked to pat and squeeze her. He was touching her here and there under the table when a bemused expression suddenly crossed his face. Marilyn told me later he'd put his hand up under her dress only to discover she wore no panties."

Monroe was part of the crowd of one hundred thousand that jammed the Los Angeles Coliseum on July 15 to hear Kennedy, who'd won a first-ballot victory as the Democratic Party's presidential candidate, give a rousing acceptance speech. Hildi Greenson, Dr. Greenson's wife, a loyal JFK supporter, sat next to her. Marilyn attended a skinny-dipping party at the Lawfords that night, and a day later turned up at the victory bash that Joe Kennedy, JFK's father, gave for his son at Romanoff's. At some point in the evening, Marilyn asked Peter Lawford why Jack had selected Lyndon Johnson as his running mate, and Lawford responded, "Because he wants to be president and knows that LBJ can deliver the vote. On a personal level, they can't stand each other."

John F. Kennedy remained in Los Angeles for a day after the convention and spent it with Marilyn. He then flew back to Boston. Monroe made a second contribution to his campaign fund, this one for $5,000. She rallied friends and asked them to donate to JFK's war chest as well.

"As usual," said Kurt Lamprecht, "Marilyn telephoned about two in the morning. If it had been anyone else, I'd have hung up. She said, 'Kurt, you've got to send a donation to

John Kennedy. For the good of the nation, we've got to defeat Richard Nixon.' I told her I normally voted Republican, but if she thought Kennedy a better bet, I'd vote for him — and of course I'd contribute. Naturally, I didn't know that Marilyn and Kennedy had shared the same bed."

"I thought Marilyn was by far the most interesting 'other' woman in Jack Kennedy's life," said Peter Lawford. "They were a fascinating couple. They were both charismatic and complex. Marilyn was particularly complicated. I never understood how such a creature could be filled with so much warmth and joy and at the same time such misery and pain. Someone once said that Marilyn spent her entire life looking for a missing person: herself. The thing about her relationship with JFK is that at some point — I don't exactly know when — she convinced herself she could marry him, replace Jackie Kennedy, and move into the White House as First Lady. It was pure fantasy, but unfortunately she believed it, though I repeatedly cautioned her that her friendship with JFK would have to remain very much under the radar."

News of JFK and Marilyn Monroe eventually filtered back to Jackie Kennedy. She brooded about her husband's latest affair and reportedly told close friends that she hadn't been certain if Jack's nomination at the Democratic National Convention "signaled a beginning or an end."

Ralph Roberts was Marilyn Monroe's masseur, friend, and confidant. He'd met her at the Actors Studio in New York. During the production of *The Misfits,* Roberts served as the company masseur, though he'd been hired primarily because Marilyn insisted on it. He'd likewise been offered a small role in the film, that of an ambulance attendant.

Roberts had first started giving Marilyn therapeutic massage treatments when she stayed over at the Strasbergs' in their Central Park West apartment, the theory being that the treatments would help her relax before bedtime. Too often, however, they seemed to stimulate Marilyn, making it more difficult for her to fall asleep. Yet she grew dependent on the treatments and on Roberts as well. She considered him a brother. They were psychic siblings.

"I like to think she was as candid with me as she was with anyone," he said. "From the moment I met her, she appeared to be down on Arthur Miller. The reason she stayed with him was that she wanted to have a baby, and when that didn't happen, she withdrew. I met him on several occasions, mostly on the set of *The Misfits.* He struck me as coldhearted, dispassionate, intellectually pretentious, cheap, and afraid to give of himself. He had no sense of humor. Marilyn told me that early in their marriage they were at a party, and someone said, 'I hope your children have Arthur's looks and Marilyn's brains.' Well, she laughed, and he became infuriated. Moreover, Miller couldn't handle Marilyn psychologically. He claimed her addictions and mood swings kept him away from his sacred typewriter, but the sad fact is he was incapable of dealing with anyone who showed emotion of any kind. The most constant male figure in Marilyn's life had always been Joe DiMaggio. Because he possessed a strong center and because he loved her, DiMaggio could better cope with Marilyn's frailties. He just couldn't cope with the movie racket or the Hollywood celebrity scene, which meant that while they could be friends and lovers, they couldn't be husband and wife."

Ralph Roberts joined Marilyn on location in Reno, Nevada, on July 18, the day production began on *The Misfits,* another aptly titled cinematic endeavor, considering the chaotic events that would shortly ensue. The title, in fact, actually alluded to the film's plot: a plan on the part of several modern-day Nevada cowboys to rope mustangs — known as misfits, because they're too small to ride — and sell them to a company that would process them into dog food.

Arthur Miller had arrived on location a few days before, while Marilyn was still at the Democratic National Convention in LA, spending time with Jack Kennedy. Miller and Monroe shared a two-bedroom suite at the Mapes Hotel and Casino in Reno; their marriage in tatters, they occupied separate rooms and were rarely seen together. When they were seen together, the spectacle wasn't always pretty. Monroe delighted in humiliating and embarrassing her husband before cast and crew alike, as when she climbed into a car and then slammed the door in his face before he could climb in behind her. Marilyn spent the majority of her spare time with her entourage, of which Ralph Roberts was the newest member; others in the group included Paula Strasberg, May Reis, Agnes Flanagan, and Whitey Snyder.

Whitey remembered the tension between Monroe and Miller. "She felt," he said, "that Arthur had written dialogue for her that was totally insignificant and extraneous to the film. She complained that the movie had to do with cowboys and their horses, and had nothing to do with her character in the film. 'I don't believe he ever wanted me in it,' she said. She remarked that Arthur often complained about her to John Huston, and that's why Huston treated her like a jerk. One day in her dressing room, she exploded at Arthur, accusing him of having forced her to get rid of Milton Greene. 'You're an evil bastard!' she yelled. 'I should've stayed with Joe.' "

The same problems existed that had undermined all of Marilyn's other recent films. John Huston became as frustrated as had the other directors with whom she had worked. "You've got to get your wife off those pills," the director told Arthur Miller. "They're going to kill her." Contrary to Dr. Ralph Greenson's suggestion that she limit her consumption of drugs, Marilyn did just the opposite.

Arthur Miller and Paula Strasberg walked into Marilyn's bedroom one night in time to see a local doctor searching for a vein in her arm so he could inject her with Amytal. Monroe ordered her husband to get out. Feeling that he should do something, Miller called the head of the UCLA Medical School; the doctor advised the playwright to place his wife in a drug rehab program.

Finally, taking matters into his own hands, Miller threw away all the drugs he could locate in their suite, and for a day or two, the tactic worked. However, within forty-eight hours, Monroe managed to replenish her supply of prescription medication by turning to the same physician who'd injected her with Amytal and who, it turned out, had been recommended to her by Montgomery Clift, her *Misfits* costar. Between takes on the set, Clift and Monroe would frequently huddle and compare notes on drugs and pharmaceuticals. Monty, like Marilyn, was the consummate insomniac.

Miller's confiscation of Marilyn's cache of drugs so annoyed her that she moved out of their two-bedroom suite and into a similar suite with Paula Strasberg. In 1967, five years after Monroe's death, Miller informed a *New York Times* reporter that while he'd known of Monroe's addictions, he hadn't realized the severity of her habit. "Marilyn's addiction to pills and drugs ultimately defeated me," he admitted. "If there was any key to her despair, I never found it. I didn't realize her addiction was at the center of her problem. The psychiatrists thought it was a symptom. Regardless of their intentions, in the end they actually prescribed more pills."

Well into production, John Huston suspended work on the film. He'd reached the same conclusion as the head of the University of California Medical School: Marilyn needed to enter a drug rehabilitation facility. She seemed to be walking around in an utter daze, a trance. Her words were garbled; her eyes didn't focus. She'd stopped functioning. Once again she'd tried to end it all by swallowing too many pills.

Flown to Los Angeles, MM was admitted to Westside Hospital, a private, high-priced clinic that catered primarily to victims of drug and alcohol abuse. Dr. Kris arrived from New York to oversee Marilyn's treatment program. To avoid unwanted publicity, Frank Taylor announced that Monroe had been hospitalized for nervous exhaustion. Aside from Dr. Kris, Dr. Greenson, and Paula Strasberg, Marilyn's only visitor during her ten days in the unit was Joe DiMaggio, who'd read about her hospitalization and marital problems.

"When Marilyn returned to Reno," said Ralph Roberts, "she told me Joe DiMaggio had paid her a surprise visit at the hospital. 'How did it go?' I asked. With a big smile, she said, 'Not bad — he spent the night. But when he wanted to leave in the morning, all the nurses and hospital aides started bothering him for his autograph.' 'What did he do?' I asked. 'He sighed and signed,' she answered."

After her brief abstention from pharmaceuticals, and despite DiMaggio's unannounced visit, it didn't take Marilyn long to revert to her former drug obsession and her narcotics-crazed behavior. One evening the phone rang in Marilyn and Paula Strasberg's suite. Paula answered. It was Arthur Miller, whose waking hours were now spent working on endless script rewrites for the next day's shoot.

"Believe it or not," Paula said into the phone, "Marilyn's asleep."

"It's you I wanted to speak to," said Miller. "Have you been keeping an eye on Marilyn?"

"As much as possible. Why do you ask, Arthur?"

"Because I heard she's been running

around the hotel in the nude."

"I'm afraid it's true," admitted Paula. "She was in the hotel elevator, traveling up and down, completely naked. She wandered into the casino. She was high as a kite."

"I'm not surprised," said Miller. "Last year the wife of the owner of the Algonquin Hotel in New York bumped into Marilyn on Fifth Avenue. Marilyn had on a new mink coat. The woman asked what Marilyn was wearing with it, and she replied, 'Nothing,' and opened the coat to prove it."

A few days after Miller's phone call and the nude elevator episode, Marilyn left a note for Paula next to the phone: "Oh Paula, I wish I knew why I am so anguished. I think maybe I'm crazy like all the other members of my family."

Once more in the care of Dr. Ralph Greenson, Marilyn's ongoing drug involvement led the psychoanalyst to bring in a colleague, Dr. Hyman Engelberg, an internist and "physician to the stars," whom Greenson had consulted about Monroe during her stay at Westside Hospital. Greenson first met Engelberg while an intern at Cedars of Lebanon. Born in New York in 1913, a graduate of the Cornell University School of Medicine, Engelberg shared with Greenson a profound interest in left-wing politics.

In overseeing Marilyn's drug regimen, Engelberg placed the actress on chloral hydrate, a sedative she'd sampled previously with mixed results. Ralph Roberts recalled a meeting he attended with Doctors Greenson and Engelberg, Marilyn, and Paula Strasberg, at which he was put on a massage schedule related to MM's intake of the sedative. "I gave her four massages a day," he said. "I massaged her in the morning before she left for the set, again during her midday break, then twice at night — once before dinner and then before she tried to fall sleep. I'd massage her in the near dark. Her body seemed to give off light. She'd take the chloral hydrate with the final massage. If she woke up during the night, she'd call me and I'd go to the front desk and pick up a chloral hydrate pill left there earlier in the evening by Dr. Engelberg. Marilyn wasn't permitted to keep any other sedative in her suite or dressing room."

The plan enabled Greenson and Engelberg to monitor what she took and when she took it. Her disposition and demeanor improved, even more so when Engelberg began giving her injections of multivitamins and liver extract. Clark Gable took her aside and told her she was the best-adjusted person connected to the film. In a more positive frame of mind, she told Dr. Greenson that she'd heard about plans to make a movie in Hollywood based on Sigmund Freud's life. She wondered what he thought of her participation in such a project. Greenson communicated Marilyn's inquiry to Anna Freud, who instantly rejected the offer. "We'll find you another role," Greenson assured her.

In early November 1960 the production finally drew to a close, forty days late and millions of dollars in the red. "But at least it's done," said an exhausted John Huston. Marilyn and her entourage celebrated by spending a weekend in San Francisco. "Joe was, I think, in New York," said Ralph Roberts, "so Marilyn went down to the wharf and visited some of his brothers and sisters at the family-owned restaurant. Evidently they were thrilled to see her again. Next she dropped in on Lefty O'Doul at his bar. He didn't recognize her at first. She wore a kerchief over her hair, dark glasses, a loose-fitting blouse, and pants. When he realized it was Marilyn, he went bananas. She said she had a wonderful time with Lefty. He kept saying to her, 'You've got to come home again, Marilyn. You've got to come home.' "

That night the group — Marilyn, Paula, May, Agnes, Agnes's husband, and Ralph Roberts — went to the Blue Fox for dinner. "The hostess threw her arms around Marilyn," said Roberts, "practically crying with joy. She was a cousin of Joe's, and she seemed genuinely touched by Marilyn's presence. Monty Clift joined us for dessert. After dinner, we went to Finocchio's, a famous nightclub featuring female impersonators. We all wore dark glasses, with the agreement that if anyone recognized either Monty or Marilyn, we'd all rush out. We were seated at a big table in the second row and, amid much giggling and merriment, ordered our drinks."

One of the first performers was dressed and made up to look like Marilyn. The performer had captured her mannerisms, movements, and voice to an impressive degree. Marilyn whispered to Roberts that she felt as if she were looking at herself in one of her movies. At the end of the entire show, as the various performers lined up for a company call, Roberts noticed that the Monroe impersonator was staring straight at the real Marilyn. "I'll never forget the electric shock that came into her eyes when she realized that Marilyn was in the audience," said Roberts. "She started frantically whispering to the performer that stood next to her, and the word spread down the line like wildfire. We'd paid and were about to leave. Marilyn blew her impersonator a kiss, and we hit the street. The next day Marilyn and I attended an Ella Fitzgerald concert. After the concert, we went to her dressing room, and Marilyn regaled her with the story of her impersonator from the night before."

By early November 1960, Marilyn had returned from California to her apartment on East Fifty-Seventh Street in New York.

Arthur Miller had flown back by himself and moved into the Hotel Adams on East Eighty-Sixth Street. The newspapers were filled with reports of their impending divorce. One person who read the breakup news with avid interest was Joe DiMaggio Jr., currently a freshman at Yale University in New Haven, Connecticut.

"I hadn't spoken to Marilyn in a while," said Joe Jr. "After I finished up at Lawrenceville, she mailed me a check for a thousand dollars as a graduation present. I used the money to sail to Holland in June 1960 with Barrett Price, the son of Vincent Price. We bought bikes in Rotterdam and spent a couple of months touring Europe. When I got back, I tried out for the position of placekicker on Yale's junior varsity football team, but there was this Hungarian soccer player who regularly booted fifty-yard field goals — and he did it barefoot, no less. So that didn't work out.

"Marilyn called me in late November. Her first concern was my happiness. How did I like Yale? I told her the truth: I didn't, and I liked New Haven even less. What I didn't mention was that I'd basically stopped attending classes. The only reason I'd been admitted to Yale was my family name, not because of my high school grades or college entrance exams. Of course, Marilyn had her own problems. She and Arthur Miller were about to get divorced. In addition, Clark Gable had just suffered a fatal heart attack, and apparently his widow, Kay, who was pregnant at the time, blamed Marilyn's antics during *The Misfits* as the cause of Gable's sudden death. Later they made up, and Kay invited Marilyn to the infant's christening. Marilyn told me that the day Gable died, she called my father, and he arrived at her apartment and spent the night with her, and they talked about death. 'I was amazed your father believes in an afterlife,' said Marilyn. In later years, I thought to myself how odd it seemed that *The Misfits* marked not only Clark Gable's last film but Marilyn's, too."

Not long after Joey's telephone conversation with Marilyn, the dean of students at Yale contacted Joe DiMaggio to report that his son had more or less dropped out of school. They didn't want to expel him, but unless he began attending classes again, they would have little choice. "Treat my son as you would any other student," DiMaggio responded. At the end of the first semester, Joe DiMaggio Jr. received a letter expelling him from the university. "Marilyn seemed more disappointed about it than my father," said Joey. "I figured at least I'm saving him some money!"

Joe DiMaggio spent Christmas of that year in San Francisco but sent Marilyn a huge basket of poinsettia. He flew to New York to celebrate New Year's with Marilyn. Joining them for dinner, Lena Pepitone prepared a meal of spaghetti with sausage followed by a roast chicken. At midnight, Joe gallantly kissed both ladies. Marilyn wouldn't allow Lena to clean up. She sent her home by taxi with a $200 tip. The next morning, Lena served the two lovers breakfast. They held hands across the table and called each other "Darling." Marilyn wore a white terry cloth robe; Joe wore a white dress shirt and tie.

On January 19, 1961, Marilyn Monroe, accompanied by her latest New York attorney, Aaron Frosch, and Pat Newcomb, a publicist who'd taken the place of Rupert Allan, traveled to Juárez, Mexico, to finalize divorce proceedings against Arthur Miller. The divorce was granted a day later by Judge Miguel Gomez Guerra on uncontested charges of "incompatibility of character."

The playwright shed few tears over the woman *Newsweek* proclaimed "the most famous female on the planet." He'd already become involved with Inge Morath, a Magnum Agency photographer he'd met on the set of *The Misfits* and then met again when both were back in New York. Tall, dark haired, and slender, the Austrian-born Morath would become, in February 1962, Miller's third and last wife. Unhappy with the scorn that Monroe had heaped upon him during the final phases of their marriage, the usually discreet Miller told the press, "If I'd known how we would end up, I would never have married her."

Marilyn's only public comment had it that "Mr. Miller is a great writer, but it didn't work out for us as husband and wife." Other than that, she told reporters she was upset and didn't wish to be "bombarded with publicity right now."

Miller reserved the brunt of his bitterness for future consumption. He depicted her as a crazed, tyrannical bitch-goddess in *After the Fall,* a poorly received play he wrote about Marilyn less than a year after her death. In *Timebends,* his somewhat vindictive autobiography, he said of Marilyn: "I could not place her in any world I knew — like a cork bobbing on the ocean, she could have begun her voyage on the other side of the world or a hundred yards down the beach."

CHAPTER 17

Marilyn Monroe's five-year marriage to Arthur Miller may have lasted longer than her union with Joe DiMaggio, but it was no more successful, and in a sense, was actually far less satisfying because it ended on dire terms. There was no residual friendship, nothing further to discuss, whereas the relationship between Joe and Marilyn never really ended. "Marilyn and I are back in business," the Yankee Clipper told Toots Shor.

"In fact, they'd never been out of business," said Paul Baer. "They'd been away from each other for a few years, but they were sleeping together again long before she and Miller were divorced. There was a real, long-lasting, almost unspoken intimacy between Joe and Marilyn, which is something she had with no other man.

"Still, there was the realization on Monroe's part that none of her three marriages had endured. Nor had she been able to have children. And then, too, she had this terrible addiction to drugs and alcohol, which to a greater or lesser extent had never been addressed by any of her psychiatrists, all of whom knew each other. They'd take her off one drug and put her on another, and this lamentable practice went on for years. It was a conspiracy of shrinks. Whenever Joe asked her about the drugs, she'd tell him she knew more about pills than any doctor, so he needn't worry."

After officially reuniting in early January 1961, Joe DiMaggio gave Marilyn a gold necklace from which hung his diamond-encrusted 1951 World Series ring. She wore it at home whenever she and Joe were together. Ironically, DiMaggio's other World Series rings were stolen from his hotel room in 1960. Marilyn's ring was the sole survivor, until years later, when future Yankees owner George Steinbrenner gave him a replica set of the rings that had been stolen.

On February 1, Marilyn — accompanied by Montgomery Clift — attended a New York preview of *The Misfits*. Arthur Miller was there with his children. He couldn't bring himself to acknowledge Marilyn. After the film ended, she passed him on the way out of the theater. "Hello, Arthur," she whispered. He gazed in her direction and gave a vague nod. The only other interaction between them took place some weeks later when Marilyn attended his mother's funeral. She went, she told Paula Strasberg, to console Isidore Miller, Arthur's father, with whom she remained on close terms and continued to call "Dad."

Whether because of her divorce from Miller, the termination of her affair with Yves Montand, the death of Clark Gable, or simply her reimmersion in the culture of barbiturates, the week that followed, much of it spent at the Strasbergs, nearly did Marilyn in. When she wasn't with Lee and Paula, according to Lena Pepitone, she would lie in bed (in her darkened bedroom) in a drug-induced stupor, not eating, not sleeping, and not talking. Her daily therapy sessions with Dr. Marianne Kris provided her only excuse to climb out of bed.

Joe DiMaggio, still with the Monette Company, had agreed to serve as a batting instructor at the New York Yankees' spring training camp in St. Petersburg, Florida. Had he been present, he surely would have prevented Marilyn from agreeing to Dr. Kris's recommendation that she voluntarily check into the Payne Whitney Psychiatric Clinic, a few blocks from her apartment.

Marilyn Monroe signed into Payne Whitney in early February, under the alias "Miss Faye Miller," and was placed in a kind of interrogation room. For the next three hours, a procession of doctors, their arms folded in front of them, entered the room to observe Marilyn and fire off what she considered a volley of meaningless questions. She was then placed in a locked ward for the mentally ill. Once in, as Marilyn quickly learned, there was no way out.

Although Marilyn had entered Payne Whitney of her own volition, it had been Dr. Kris who filled out the admissions papers, characterizing the patient as "potentially self-destructive, even suicidal." Kris later claimed she had no idea the ward was locked and that Monroe couldn't leave whenever she pleased. In any event, everything the actress brought with her, including her pocketbook and clothes, was confiscated. A nurse handed her a towel and washcloth, a baggy brown jumpsuit, and a pair of slippers. Her closet-sized room, also locked, had cement-block walls, a narrow bed with a rubber sheet, a lightweight metal chair, and a wash basin atop a small, round wooden table; a minuscule bathroom in a corner of the room contained a sink and a toilet. A pane of one-way mirror glass, cut into the room's steel door, enabled hospital personnel to peer in on Marilyn without their being seen. The bathroom door had a built-in mirror of its own. The wails, moans, and cries of Marilyn's fellow "inmates" could be clearly heard throughout the ward. The iron bars across the windows lent credence to what had always been Marilyn's worst fear: that of ending up locked away and left to rot in a lunatic asylum. The question had crossed her mind a thousand times: Had she inherited the same schizophrenic blood virus that festered in her mother's delusional brain?

In a seven-page letter that Marilyn addressed to Dr. Ralph Greenson on March 2, 1961, she described the harrowing experience in all too graphic detail, including her failed efforts to get out. For hours she had begged them to release her. She had stripped naked and stood in the middle of the room screaming. They threatened to put her in a straitjacket. She went into the bathroom and turned on the water faucet and let it run until she'd created a flood. They entered her room and locked the bathroom door, at which point Marilyn reportedly picked up a chair and slammed it against the bathroom mirror. As she explained in her letter to Greenson, "If they were going to treat me like a nut, I'll act like a nut." She then threatened to do herself harm, which, she is reported to have said, "is the furthest thing from my mind . . . since you know . . . I'm an actress and would never intentionally mark or mar myself. I'm just that vain."

When an earlier broken-glass suicide attempt failed to elicit the desired reaction, Marilyn went on a hunger strike; she began to eat only after they advised her that if she didn't eat, they would have to give her intravenous nourishment. When she refused to bathe, she was carried face-up into a shower room and was hosed down, after which she was made to sit in a bathtub. She cursed the nurses when they tried to force her to go to occupational therapy. When she again insisted they release her from the hospital, they informed her that only Dr. Kris could sign her out.

Unable to reach Kris by phone (she was permitted one call per day), she decided to write to Lee and Paula Strasberg: "Dr. Kris has had me put into the New York hospital . . . under the care of two *idiot* doctors. They *both should not be my doctors* . . . I'm locked up with all these poor nutty people. I'm *sure* to end up a nut if I stay in this nightmare, please help me, Lee, this is the *last* place I should be . . . I love you both. Marilyn. P.S. . . . I'm on the dangerous floor! It's like a cell."

As with Dr. Kris, Marilyn couldn't reach the Strasbergs by telephone. And probably for good reason: as she eventually learned, it had been Lee who'd first suggested to Dr. Kris that Marilyn, "for her own good," be sent to Payne Whitney for observation. When she finally learned of the Strasbergs' involvement in the "plot" to put her away, Marilyn accused them (in her words) of "treason and treachery."

On her third day at Payne Whitney, Marilyn asked the nurse to place a long-distance call to Joe DiMaggio in Florida. Nearly hysterical, Marilyn implored Joe to help her get out. He promised to be there the following day.

At six in the evening on Friday, February 10, Joe DiMaggio stood in front of the nurses' station on the sixth floor of the hospital and asked to see his wife. A nurse's aide recalled the occasion: "I immediately recognized Mr. DiMaggio," she said. "He was a tall, handsome, imposing figure in a double-breasted dark blue suit, French-cuffed shirt, hand-painted tie, spit-polished shoes, and a designer overcoat on his arm. He was powerful-looking, with streaks of gray in his dark hair. I wondered how he'd gained access to the floor, since it was a locked ward. I soon found out. I went and located the head nurse, and she asked him how he'd gotten in. 'I was let in by the chief of security for the hospital,' he responded. 'We're buddies. He used to work security at Yankee Stadium.' Then he repeated his request regarding Marilyn Monroe. She'd registered under a different name, but we all knew her true identity. The head nurse balked. She stated that the only person who had jurisdiction over Miss Monroe was Dr. Kris, her psychiatrist. In a very low, controlled but threatening voice, DiMaggio said to her, 'I'll give you five minutes to get her out here, or I'll tear this fucking place apart brick by brick.' So the nurse went and brought back Marilyn Monroe. 'Now get me everything she had on when she checked in,' ordered DiMaggio. The nurse said she would, but if he wanted her released, they needed Dr. Kris's signature. He gave her Dr. Kris's phone number. She answered. It seems DiMaggio had already spoken to her, because she said she'd be right over to sign the papers. DiMaggio told the nurse he'd send Dr. Kris upstairs when she arrived but, in the interim, he and Marilyn would wait in the lobby. Marilyn changed into her street clothes, and they left."

Realizing that Dr. Kris's signature would be required, DiMaggio had made prior arrangements with Ralph Roberts to pick up the psychiatrist by car and drive her to the hospital. Roberts remembered how upset Kris seemed on the way over: "She was crying. 'I did a terrible thing,' she said. 'My God, I didn't mean to, but I did. I should never have listened to Lee Strasberg.' She must have repeated this mantra a dozen times. When we arrived at Payne Whitney, she went to sign the papers. Joe told Marilyn he'd head back to his suite at the Hotel Lexington and then join her later that night in her apartment. When Kris returned, she began apologizing to Marilyn, but the damage had been done. Marilyn screamed at her in the car, threatened to sue her for malpractice, and told her she was done. She was like a hurricane. After that night, Marilyn never saw or spoke to Dr. Kris again."

Joe DiMaggio understood that, whatever Marilyn's condition before her hospitalization, she remained extremely upset, all the more so given her treatment at Payne Whitney. She agreed to enter a hospital in a more comfortable and less menacing setting, provided she could leave without having to go through a middleman and provided Joe be listed as her caretaker. In addition, DiMaggio promised to fly in from Florida to visit her whenever he had a day off. At five o'clock on February 11, having made arrangements through the team physician of the New York Yankees, Joe accompanied Marilyn to the Neurological Institute of the Columbia-Presbyterian Medical Center, where she remained without incident for three weeks, until March 5. DiMaggio visited her on a half dozen separate occasions, flying in twice a week.

"Joe DiMaggio remained convinced that Marilyn's career was slowly killing her," said Ralph Roberts. "I tended to agree."

In many respects Joe DiMaggio appeared to be a changed man, perhaps due to his limited exposure to psychotherapy but more likely the result of his realization that if he didn't alter his personality, he and Marilyn could never work out their differences. He seemed more tender, gentle, and patient with her, less prone to fits of jealousy and anger, more understanding. They were closer now — and nicer to each other — than they'd ever been. He apparently told her that if he'd been married to his former self, he too would have sought a divorce. When he visited from St. Petersburg, they sat in her room at Columbia-Presbyterian and had long, heartfelt conversations — mostly the actress talking and the ballplayer listening. Marilyn introduced him to the doctors and nurses at Columbia-Presbyterian as "my hero — the man who rescued me from that utter hellhole."

By middle age, about to turn forty-seven, DiMaggio had changed in other respects as well. Because of his ulcers, which came and went, he cut back on his cigarette habit and indulgence in alcohol, limiting himself to a half pack a day and a couple of glasses of beer at dinner. He'd taken to drinking tea instead of coffee and had given up rich desserts. He was more generous when it came to money. When Marilyn told him she'd overdrawn her checking account at Irving Trust by $7,000, he generously covered it for her. Although never a simple man, he still had simple tastes. As one of his pals put it, "Give Joe a cup of tea and turn on the TV set, and he's a happy man." For this reason, if for no other, the relationship with Marilyn didn't — and probably couldn't — work full-time. It was his growing awareness that this was the case, and his gradual acceptance of that fact, that imbued their current bond with an intimacy it had previously lacked.

The day that Marilyn walked out of Columbia-Presbyterian, Joe invited her to join him at the Yankee spring training camp in Florida. Even among the veteran Yankee players, it became known that Joe had undergone a certain metamorphosis. "I always regarded DiMaggio as a haughty, imperious type of guy," said Mickey Mantle. "He struck me as somebody who just didn't like people, who wanted to be left alone, and who was above it all. That's not to say he wasn't one of the greatest ballplayers of all time, but he certainly wasn't one of the warmest. But in 1961, for whatever reason, he seemed different. He'd stick around and eat dinner with the young guys on the team. He'd give them tips. He'd give the old guys tips as well. He'd tell stories. He'd invite players for breakfast. He began to socialize. Then he disappeared for a while. We heard Marilyn Monroe came to visit him, and he wanted to spend time with her."

Joe and Marilyn occupied separate but adjoining rooftop suites at the oceanfront Tides Hotel and Bath Club, in the quiet and peaceful, predominantly residential town of North Redington Beach, Florida. They rested, swam, fished, walked along the beach at sunset, collected seashells, biked, dined alone, and attended several Yankees spring training games together. It was like a second honeymoon but without the wedding ceremony.

Mercifully, the press didn't know where to find them and the Yankee front office wasn't talking. *Sports Illustrated* ran a photo of Marilyn ogling Joe (wearing his old number 5) as he hit fly balls to prospective outfielders, but that was the extent of the press coverage. One morning as they sat on the beach at North Redington — Marilyn in a loose-fitting white dress, sunglasses and a large floppy hat — they were spotted by a group of tourists, one of whom approached and asked Monroe for her autograph. "Leave the lady alone," snapped Joe, a seeming reversion to his former possessive self, for which he later apologized to Marilyn, explaining that he was merely "trying to preserve her privacy."

They spent several days in Gainesville, where Marilyn visited with her half sister Berniece Miracle and Berniece's daughter, Mona Rae. Marilyn borrowed Joe's car one afternoon and drove to Miami Beach to see Isidore Miller. On April 11, back in New York, she sat next to Joe DiMaggio in the press box on opening day at Yankee Stadium. The pregame ceremony included Jane Morgan singing "The Second Time Around," which Bob Hope introduced by dedicating it to "Joe and Marilyn." At the end of the game, Yankees coowner Dan Topping hugged Marilyn and handed her a baseball signed by the entire team. A few months later, she sent the ball to Joe DiMaggio Jr., who subsequently sold it to a sports memorabilia shop for $400.

"After busting out of Yale," said Joey, "I did the dumbest thing I've probably ever done. I moved to San Francisco and married a girl I barely knew. We eloped. It lasted a month. I then moved to my mother's house in LA, and within a couple of weeks, I racked up a six-hundred-dollar phone bill. So I gave her the money from the sale of the baseball and split. I moved in with a guy named Tom Law, who earned a living of sorts as an extra in the movies. He got me a job working at his uncle's rug factory in Santa Monica, which ended when a crane veered off course and gouged a large hole in my leg. After it healed, I joined the marines. I figured the armed forces were probably more interesting and less dangerous than working in a rug factory."

In 1994 Berniece Miracle (with daughter Mona Rae Miracle) coauthored *My Sister Marilyn,* recalling (among other episodes) a stay with her half sister in New York in late April. The visit had been arranged when Marilyn spent time with Berniece in Gaines-ville, Florida. When Berniece came to New York, Marilyn paid to have her hair styled by Kenneth and bought her a new wardrobe. Joe DiMaggio squired Gladys Baker's two daughters around town, taking them to lunch at Serendipity (he drove them there but didn't go in) and provided them with theater tickets. Berniece, who was modest and down-to-earth, had fond memories of DiMaggio. In her Marilyn memoir, she described him as "unpretentious" and "full of common sense and concern for Marilyn." Joe was equally impressed with Berniece. Before her departure, he gave her an eight-by-ten glossy photograph of himself in a Yankees uniform, which he inscribed: "To Marilyn's lovely sister Berniece — whose pleasant company was appreciated, Joe DiMaggio."

Lena Pepitone recalled that Joe and Marilyn spent a good deal of time together during April and the beginning of May. They would stay either at her apartment or in his suite at the Hotel Lexington, a few blocks away. "Arthur Miller had removed some furniture from the apartment," said Pepitone, "and you could see stains all over the white carpeting where his dog had peed or pooped. Joe hired a carpet cleaner and went furniture shopping with Marilyn to replace what Miller had taken out. I thought they might be preparing to live together again. Then one night they had an argument. Joe found a discarded grocery bill in the trash. He added it up and discovered that the store had charged Marilyn nearly twice what she should have paid. 'Why don't you look the bills over before you pay them?' he scolded her. Marilyn grabbed the bill out of his hand. 'It's none of your business,' she growled. 'It's my money, not yours.' That's how it started. It ended with Joe giving Marilyn a bit of a shove as he rushed past her out the door in a burst of anger."

They soon had words again, this time over the surprise arrival at Marilyn's apartment of a white French poodle puppy, a gift from Frank Sinatra, Joe DiMaggio's onetime pal. Marilyn referred to Sinatra alternately as "Frankie" or "Francis." So why, DiMaggio demanded to know, had Frankie or Francis delivered a puppy to Marilyn's door? He realized that Sinatra and Monroe knew each other, but he didn't know the extent of their friendship. Most of Hollywood's leading actresses, particularly the more attractive ones, had at some point crossed paths with Sinatra. But how many of them were the recipients of small, cuddly puppies? Why the dog? Why now? It made no sense. Joe pressed her for an answer, until she finally offered him one. It sounded all too familiar.

"It's none of your business, Joe," she said. "You and I are no longer married. I don't have to answer to you."

And he said: "You never did answer to me, even when we were married. You did what you wanted to do, and that was probably part of the problem."

Marilyn Monroe once named Frank Sinatra one of the two most fascinating men she'd ever known, the other being Marlon Brando. The legendary entertainer first met the legendary actress before she married Joe DiMaggio. He'd been cast opposite her in the ill-fated *Girl in Pink Tights.* Reportedly, Marilyn had sought refuge in Sinatra's Coldwater Canyon home for a day or two immediately following her divorce from DiMaggio. Although still involved with Hal Schaefer, Monroe had evidently indulged in a brief romp with Sinatra. And then there had been the scandalous Wrong Door Raid in which DiMaggio, aided by Sinatra, attempted to catch Marilyn "in the act" with Schaefer. Neither DiMaggio nor Schaefer had the slightest inkling that the target of the raid was also involved with one of its chief perpetrators. "I had no idea that Marilyn and Frank Sinatra were lovers," said Hal Schaefer.

In the mid-1950s, at the height of Marilyn's New York period, she and Sinatra had continued to see each other occasionally. Once, when Sinatra performed at the Copa in New York, Marilyn arrived unexpectedly with Milton and Amy Greene, only to be told that without reservations they couldn't get in. Sinatra spotted Marilyn and instructed a waiter to set up an extra table at the foot of the stage. To the amazement of the Greenes, he proceeded to sing the entire set directly to Marilyn. Their affair resumed after Monroe's divorce from Arthur Miller. Lena Pepitone admitted that on at least one occasion Sinatra had spent the night with Marilyn in her New York apartment. "I served them dinner at night and breakfast in the morning," she said, "and this was one day after Joe DiMaggio had slept over."

Sinatra's gift to Marilyn of a cute little puppy told Joe DiMaggio everything he needed to know, or almost everything: he wasn't the only Italian American in Marilyn's life, though he may well have been the only one that truly loved her. But there wasn't much he could do or say. After all, as Marilyn had conveniently pointed out, they were no longer husband and wife. The elation Joe experienced after publicly resuming their relationship quickly turned into confusion. In reality, Sinatra was only part of the story. The other part — Marilyn's involvement with John F. Kennedy, the newly elected president of the United States — represented a chapter that seemed almost fictional.

In what must surely be considered an intricate juggling act, Marilyn somehow managed to compartmentalize and yet combine her trio of lovers. DiMaggio, Sinatra, and Kennedy had Marilyn in common. She stayed with JFK at the Carlyle during one of his periodic trips to New York, finding him "strong yet fragile." As for Sinatra's gift, Marilyn named the poodle "Maf" (or "Maaf-

Honey") because of the crooner's purported Mafia connections. To spite Arthur Miller, Marilyn let Maf sleep on an expensive white beaver coat that the playwright had given her as a birthday present.

If Joe DiMaggio resented Marilyn's reluctance to be with him on an exclusive basis, he tried not to show it. He saw her whenever she seemed willing to see him and otherwise busied himself socially with one or another of a long list of standbys, his favorite being Phyllis McGuire, if only because she was already spoken for and therefore couldn't object to his ongoing pursuit of Monroe. In fact, McGuire's beau, Chicago mobster Sam Giancana, coincidentally a friend of Sinatra's, called Joe and invited him for a round of golf. "Giancana soon became a regular golf partner," said Paul Baer. "They made for an odd twosome, particularly because Joe would occasionally spend time with Phyllis, Giancana's girlfriend, and the arrangement didn't seem to bother Sam."

Evidently not the possessive type, Giancana had a second girlfriend, Judith Campbell, a former Las Vegas showgirl whom Frank Sinatra had introduced to Jack Kennedy in 1960. Like Marilyn Monroe, Campbell attended the Democratic National Convention in Los Angeles that summer and continued her relationship with JFK after he entered the White House. Not only did Giancana know about Campbell's affair with the president, but he encouraged it. Campbell became a glorified courier, carrying messages back and forth between Giancana and Kennedy, Kennedy and Giancana. To add to the intrigue and make matters even more complicated, Judith Campbell was likewise sexually involved with Frank Sinatra and now, thanks to Giancana, with Joe DiMaggio. It all made for an unholy alliance, with Joe DiMaggio and Marilyn Monroe at the center of what would become an interlocking circle of tragedy and misfortune. "It's difficult to believe," said Peter Lawford, "that JFK and Marilyn Monroe would soon both be dead."

Having dismissed Marianne Kris as her psychoanalyst and having learned that Lee Strasberg had been instrumental in placing her on a locked ward at Payne Whitney, Marilyn Monroe decided to leave New York, return to Los Angeles, and resume her therapy sessions with Dr. Ralph Greenson. Tired of living out of a suitcase at the Beverly Hills Hotel, Marilyn sought a more permanent address and found it in a ground-floor flat at 882 North Doheny Drive, the same Beverly Hills apartment complex in which she'd resided before marrying Joe DiMaggio. Gloria Lovell, Frank Sinatra's personal secretary, lived on the same floor in the same building. While waiting for workmen to renovate the apartment, Marilyn moved in with Frank Sinatra. Comedian Joey Bishop, a sometime member of Sinatra's Rat Pack, saw her at Sinatra's house in early June 1961.

"I'd gone over there for our weekly poker game," said Bishop. "Dean Martin, Sammy Davis Jr., and two or three other guys were there, and in the middle of the game, this tiny white puffball of a puppy waddled into the room. 'New dog?' Dino asked, and Sinatra said, 'It's Marilyn Monroe's dog. She named it Maf, as in Mafia. Isn't that a dumb name?' And then Marilyn came into the room, evidently looking for the dog. And the thing is, she was completely nude except for a pair of emerald earrings that Sinatra had given her. We froze, and she stopped dead in her tracks. I could tell that Sinatra wasn't too pleased about her not wearing any clothes. I'd heard she'd just recently undergone some minor gynecological surgery at Cedars of Lebanon, but she'd seemingly recuperated because she looked pretty damn good. After saying hello to everyone, she gathered up the mutt and went back into Sinatra's bedroom. Marilyn was thirty-five at the time and perhaps a bit afraid of losing her great sex appeal, and I couldn't help but think that being with Sinatra confirmed for her that she still had it — in spades. I'd seen her with Sinatra at his home in Palm Springs and at the Palm Springs Racquet Club. I once went out with them on a yacht; before we left, Marilyn went wandering around the pier trying to find someone who could provide her with sleeping pills because she'd forgotten to bring hers along. Another place Sinatra brought Marilyn was the Cal-Neva Lodge at Lake Tahoe, which was coowned by both Sinatra and Sam Giancana. Then there were all sorts of crazy rumors involving Marilyn, Sinatra, and John F. Kennedy, the wildest being that on November 6, 1960, they had a threesome in Palm Springs. JFK, on the campaign trail at the time, stayed at Sinatra's home that day. Sinatra even mounted a plaque in the house to the effect that Kennedy 'had slept' there. But that was the extent of it. There was never a threesome. There were two twosomes, both involving Marilyn. But I can also tell you that the most important man in Marilyn's life was Joe DiMaggio. His love for her knew no limits. And though their marriage ended in divorce, she loved him as well. When she needed him, he'd race to her side, like one of those Saint Bernard dogs in the Swiss Alps."

Joey Bishop acknowledged hearing rumors of a possible marriage between Sinatra and Monroe but rejected the notion. "They were lovers and friends," he said, "but essentially they were friends. Marilyn enjoyed Sinatra's company and liked talking to him. He was a great listener and an excellent dispenser of advice. He could also be a bit of a jerk. He'd lose his temper and start yelling at her, particularly when she got drunk. I remember being in Las Vegas at a party Sinatra threw for Dean Martin. Marilyn was drinking out of a flask, and Sinatra started shrieking at her. It was almost comical. 'Shut your fucking filthy mouth, Norma Jeane,' he bellowed. 'Just shut your fucking filthy mouth.' "

Ralph Roberts had caught up with Marilyn in Los Angeles and went with her to the Dean Martin party. "It took place on June 7," he said, "and Marilyn drank a lot, too. But there was good reason for it. That entire spring she had digestion problems and a chronic pain on her right side. I convinced her to have a complete physical."

Marilyn went to see Dr. Hyman Engelberg and told him she had to return to New York to finish packing up her apartment, so Engelberg set up an appointment for her with an associate of his at the French and Polytechnic Medical School Hospital (closed since 1977). Ralph Roberts accompanied her to New York. On June 28 a physician at New York Polyclinic Hospital examined the actress and determined she had an impacted and inflamed gallbladder. A two-hour operation to remove the gallbladder was performed the following day. Joe DiMaggio stayed in the hospital with her the first night and visited her daily for a week, until he flew to San Francisco on family business, thereafter calling Marilyn several times a day until her release from the hospital on July 11. As she left the hospital, she found herself surrounded by hundreds of screaming fans and a hundred reporters and press photographers. "It was frightening," said Ralph Roberts, who picked her up by car and drove her back to her apartment, where she recuperated until the second week of August, adding painkillers and the diet pill Dexedrine to her once again burgeoning amalgam of barbiturates.

Roberts recalled that Joe DiMaggio, currently on a lengthy business trip for the Monette Company, managed to see Marilyn in New York on several occasions in late July and early August. Another time Roberts drove Marilyn to the Waldorf to visit with Frank Sinatra, in town on a singing engagement. "She downed a flask of vodka in the car on the way to his hotel," recalled Roberts. "I wasn't crazy about her affair with Sinatra. I liked Joe DiMaggio. I believe if she'd married him again, she would've been happier and less lonely. She told me Dr. Greenson didn't like Sinatra for her either, though strangely enough he didn't object to John F. Kennedy.

"While still in New York, Marilyn tried to find a New York therapist. She had no intention of resuming with Dr. Kris, but she couldn't find anyone to take her place. Had she found an adequate replacement, she very likely would've remained in New York, a city she loved. But then, also, she'd begun to pull away from the Strasbergs. She credited them for having helped her both professionally and personally, but she couldn't get past the Payne Whitney disaster for which Lee Strasberg was partially to blame."

Before returning to California, Marilyn asked Ralph Roberts to drive her to Roxbury so she could retrieve some personal belongings. She'd made Roberts call Arthur Miller to let him know they were coming. When they arrived, the farmhouse was empty. Marilyn gathered some of her clothes, a few pairs of shoes, some books and records, and her tennis racquet. On the way back to Manhattan, Monroe wondered aloud why her former husband hadn't bothered to show up. "We could've said our good-byes," she mused. Then she added, "Maybe he's right — what's over is over."

Marilyn wanted Ralph Roberts to return with her to Los Angeles. She offered to put him up at the Chateau Marmont, while she shifted back and forth at first between her new apartment on North Doheny and Frank Sinatra's Coldwater Canyon home. After several weeks, she moved back into her apartment. That fall, she leased a Thunderbird for Roberts, and he drove her around, at the same time continuing in his role as her masseur.

"At the end of October," said Roberts, "Joe DiMaggio Jr. paid Marilyn a visit. He wrote to Marilyn all the time, and she wrote to him. He was the closest she ever came to having a child of her own. He was on better terms with her than he was with his father. He'd talk through his problems with Marilyn. She used to give him spending money. In any case, he'd enlisted in the marines and attended boot camp in San Diego. He had a young girlfriend, Pam Reese, to whom he'd become engaged. He brought her along. Marilyn didn't like her, but she nevertheless asked me to let them borrow the car for the weekend. Within a period of two days, Joe Jr. managed to rack up half a dozen traffic violations. That's when Marilyn bought him his own car and told him that henceforth he'd be held responsible for his own summonses. I once talked to Joe DiMaggio about his son. 'Joey's an okay kid,' he said, 'but he makes messes and expects others to bail him out. He imbibes beer the way most people drink water. Hopefully the Marines will help him mature.' There seemed to be an undertone of anger in his voice. I had the feeling he resented the fact that his son had a relationship with Marilyn separate from his own."

Once more on drugs and drink, seeing Dr. Greenson six (and sometimes seven) days a week, Marilyn Monroe appeared to be back on the same roller coaster she'd ridden so many times before. "Dr. Greenson had long given up hope of weaning Marilyn off pharmaceuticals," remarked Ralph Roberts. "He gave her whatever she wanted in the way of medication, because he realized she'd go elsewhere if he didn't. The irony is that Dr. Hyman Engelberg was doing the same. As a result, Marilyn was getting double doses of a number of pharmaceuticals. Greenson didn't seem to know what Engelberg was giving her, and vice versa."

That fall of 1961, according to Roberts, Marilyn appeared to be severely depressed. One reason for her downward turn may have been her relationship, however fleeting and sporadic, with the president of the United States. On November 19 she attended a dinner party at Peter Lawford's beach house; JFK attended, as did Janet Leigh, Kim Novak, and Angie Dickinson (another of Kennedy's girlfriends). Aware of the president's liaison with Monroe, the two Secret Service agents on duty that evening noted in their daily report that Kennedy and Marilyn had spent the night together in Peter and Pat Lawford's bedroom. Marilyn's periodic encounters with JFK surely filled her imagination with visions of a possible future with the president. "I think I'm good for his back," she joked with Peter Lawford, referring to Kennedy's chronic back problems. "I'm a soldier," she added, "and he's my commander in chief." Despite the frivolity and heightened drama of the moment, even Monroe must have realized the futility of the affair, adding the element of uncertainty to her already delicate state of mind.

"By this point in time, I knew all about Marilyn and the president," said Ralph Roberts. "In a way, I guess I knew all along. She didn't discuss the matter in detail with me, but she left little doubt. For example, the morning after the Lawford party I picked her up with the car. 'How did it go with President Kennedy?' I asked her. 'If I told you,' she responded, 'I'd have to kill you.' "

Normally Roberts would arrive at Marilyn's North Doheny apartment at nine in the morning and drive her to Dr. Greenson's house for her therapy session. Some days she'd have a double session. Other times she'd stay the entire day, taking her meals with the psychiatrist's family and relaxing in the guest bedroom. Greenson adopted her in a manner not unlike the Greenes or the Strasbergs, incorporating her into his private life, creating an illusion of dependence on Marilyn's part not particularly useful to the therapeutic process and completely at odds with the classic methodology described in his own textbook, *The Technique and Practice of Psychoanalysis*. Greenson's methodology with respect to Monroe struck her friends and acquaintances as highly unorthodox and unprofessional, if not potentially dangerous to her mental well-being. And there was no denying, as Ralph Roberts was quick to notice, that the more Marilyn saw of her psychiatrist, the worse her condition became.

One morning in early October, Roberts went by Marilyn's apartment to pick her up. He rang the doorbell, but there was no answer. "I began getting vibrations that something was wrong," he ventured. "I had a set of keys to Marilyn's apartment, and I tried to open the door, but it was double-locked from within. Gloria Lovell, Frank Sinatra's secretary, lived in the next apartment. I had the keys to her place as well. I rang her bell. There was no answer, so I went in and called Marilyn on the phone. She finally answered. She sounded totally incoherent, as if she'd had a stroke or something, so I went outside, jumped a fence, and started banging at Marilyn's window with a garden hose. After a while she came to the window and said, 'I'm a little tired this morning, Ralph. I'll see you tomorrow.' "

Roberts arrived the next day at nine in the morning, and the scene repeated itself. The front door was double-locked from inside, and there was no response. Roberts called Dr. Greenson, and the psychiatrist ordered him to break into Marilyn's apartment, so Roberts jimmied open the bathroom window and went in. "Marilyn heard the commotion and came to the bathroom door," said Roberts. "She was very, very drowsy — completely out of it. She mumbled something about a wild party in the building the night before, and the revelers found out she lived there and kept ringing her doorbell until she finally called the police. Anyway, she got dressed, and I drove her to Greenson's house. She seemed upset when she went in but much more so when she came out after her session. In fact, I'd never seen her so upset before. She said Greenson wanted her to come back in and have a double session. I told her I'd wait. When she came out again, she seemed extremely withdrawn. On the way home, the only thing she said was that everyone was swindling her. She didn't sound totally rational. I called her early the next morning and asked if I should come over. 'Ralph,' she said, 'Dr. Greenson thinks you should go back to New York, and he's sent over a woman to take care of me and drive me around. He doesn't want me to speak to a lot of people, including the Strasbergs.' "

Ralph Roberts flew back to New York later that day. He called Gloria Lovell a few mornings later to tell her he'd returned to New York. He also told her about the woman Dr. Greenson had sent over to look after Marilyn.

"I bumped into the woman in the corridor,"

474

said Gloria. "She introduced herself to me. Her name's Eunice Murray. She claims she's Marilyn's new housekeeper."

"Housekeeper, my ass!" scoffed Roberts. "She's Marilyn's watchdog. Greenson wants to control her by severing her ties to the outside world."

Born in Chicago in 1902, Mrs. Eunice Murray first met Ralph Greenson in 1948 when she sold him her Santa Monica house. Through her connection to Greenson, Mrs. Murray had worked as a psychiatric nurse both in mental hospitals and on a private baisis. Paid $200 per week, Eunice, who had a married daughter named Marilyn, fulfilled multiple roles in Monroe's life, one of which, as Roberts asserted, was that of watchdog. She regularly reported back to Greenson, keeping him fully apprised of his prize patient's comings and goings, including the names of any and all visitors.

There is no question that Greenson attempted to separate Monroe from those he considered a negative influence or counterproductive to her mental health. There is likewise little evidence to indicate that Greenson possessed great insight into Marilyn's particular set of problems.

At this stage in the psychoanalytic process, Marilyn remained steadfastly loyal to Greenson, oblivious to his questionable approach to her condition and happy to be included in his family's activities. She began attending the chamber music recitals he organized at his home on Sunday afternoons. She befriended his wife as well as his two grown children. She treated Joan Greenson, his twenty-year-old daughter, like a younger sister, teaching her how to dress, dance the Twist, and walk in a sensuous manner. She engaged in political discussions with Dan Greenson, four years older than his sister Joan, a medical student at Cal Berkeley.

Dr. Greenson gradually lured Marilyn into his lair by making himself available to her whenever she needed to talk. She had his permission to call at all hours, day or night. Because he had so many sessions with her, he granted her a preferential fee of $50 an hour. He gave her a tape recorder and encouraged her to make free-association tapes, recording her daily thoughts, a process she seemed to enjoy. Yet for all his seeming generosity and openness, behind her back in a never-ending cascade of indiscreet notes and letters, the psychiatrist continued to describe his patient in terms that most assuredly would have wounded her.

Ralph Roberts, Pat Newcomb, Susan Strasberg, Lee Strasberg, and Whitey Snyder would all point out that Marilyn was "lonely and had so few friends" principally because Greenson had cut her off from the world. They further agreed that her psychotherapy didn't help her much, and the more time and money she invested in it, the more depressed she became. As for the "day" and "night" nurse, they were one and the same, and her name was Eunice Murray.

"Marilyn and I kept in touch by telephone," said Ralph Roberts. "Late in 1961, she called and said she'd be coming to New York for a few days. She missed Joe DiMaggio and wanted to see him. She said he was going to lend her some money. She'd borrowed from him in the past. She surprised me by stating she was having a miserable time of it in therapy but figured her best option for the moment was to remain with Greenson. She said she missed her New York friends and asked me to return with her to California when she flew back. 'What about Dr. Greenson? He won't approve,' I said. 'To hell with him,' she responded."

The plane Marilyn boarded for New York encountered engine trouble and had to return to Los Angeles. Waiting for the airline to arrange a second flight, she sent DiMaggio a telegram: "Dear Dad Darling, . . . Leaving again on another plane at 5 p.m. . . . I thought about two things, you and changing my will. Love you, I think, more than ever." Marilyn signed the telegram "Mrs. Norman," one of her many pseudonyms.

DiMaggio gave Marilyn a check for $15,000

and arranged to visit her in Los Angeles over Christmas and New Year's. She flew back to California with Ralph Roberts. "She felt happy she and Joe were going to share the holidays together," Roberts recalled. "She called him her 'best friend ever.' 'I love him and always will,' she went on. 'The problem with our marriage was that Joe formulated an image in his stubborn Italian mind of a traditional wife — one who would be faithful, do what he told her to do, and devote all her time to him. There was no way I could stop being Marilyn Monroe and suddenly become someone else, even if I'd wanted to. It didn't take either of us very long to realize the situation and end our marriage. But it didn't end our love for each other.' "

Marilyn told Roberts that they'd both changed. Joe was calmer, less pushy, more concerned with protecting her. And she was less ambitious, more concerned with finding happiness outside the motion picture business. She was even contemplating going to college and getting a degree. "Joe and I are both high school dropouts," she remarked. "That's a rather sad commentary, I must say."

Eunice Murray encountered Joe DiMaggio for the first time in Marilyn's apartment several days before Christmas. He was drinking tea that Marilyn had brewed for him. He struck Murray as cordial but quiet. That evening, the couple ate dinner at La Scala.

The next day they visited Olvera Street, the block of Mexican shops in downtown Los Angeles, where they bought Christmas tree ornaments to decorate a small evergreen in Monroe's living room. They did some quick gift shopping and then met with Whitey Snyder and his wife for drinks. They spent one day and one night at a rental cottage not far from the Racquet Club in Palm Springs, and were back in Marilyn's apartment for Christmas Eve. On Christmas Day they joined a half dozen couples at the Greensons'. The other male guests clustered around DiMaggio and asked him question after question about his playing days with the Bronx Bombers. Marilyn sat next to Joe and listened quietly. Joan Greenson later remarked that Joe and Marilyn reminded her "of an old married couple still very much in love." On New Year's Eve Joe and Marilyn entertained Joan Greenson and her boyfriend with champagne and caviar. They roasted chestnuts in Marilyn's fireplace and danced. The next morning — January 1, 1962 — Joe took off for San Francisco and the family restaurant. Marilyn sent him a telegram, which read, "I love you, Joe. Happy New Year!"

Having heard that Joe and Marilyn had spent the holidays together, columnist Earl Wilson called Monroe and put it to her squarely.

"Are you and Joe going to get married?"

"I like my freedom," Marilyn answered. "I like to play the field."

"Particularly the outfield," quipped Wilson.

"Frankly, I'd rather be the catcher," laughed Marilyn. She spoke fondly of Joe, reiterating what she'd said many times before:

"We tried marriage once. Right now we're the best of friends, and that's not a bad place to be after so many years."

CHAPTER 18

"Thank God for Joe, thank God," Marilyn had proclaimed after he'd secured her release from the psychiatric ward at Payne Whitney. Joe DiMaggio had become Monroe's voice of reason, her lifeline to the world of the living and sane. "Joe gives me hope for the future," she told Lotte Goslar. "We're closer now than we've ever been."

Despite their apparent closeness, Joe and Marilyn were not — and never had been — totally candid with one another. DiMaggio did not, for example, reveal that Marilyn's psychoanalyst, Dr. Greenson, had long been in communication with him, almost to the point where Joe had become a kind of junior colleague. In an incredible breach of medical ethics, Greenson not only divulged details of his diagnosis of Marilyn's condition — he also shared with DiMaggio his views regarding many of Marilyn's "friends," including Frank Sinatra and Ralph Roberts, both of whom Greenson deemed detrimental to the cause. He also discussed the contents of some of the free-association tapes Marilyn had been preparing — her admission that she'd become multi-orgasmic as well as her confessional fantasy of wanting to be debauched by her father, a father she didn't know and had never met.

For her part, Marilyn kept secret from Joe news of a meeting she'd had in November 1961 with Twentieth Century–Fox to discuss her next film, the prophetically titled *Something's Got to Give,* to be directed by George Cukor (who'd previously directed her in *Let's Make Love*), and to feature Monroe, Dean Martin, Cyd Charisse, Wally Cox, and Phil Silvers. Scheduled for preproduction in late April 1962, the script called for Marilyn to perform a lengthy nude scene. Looking ahead, she couldn't imagine that Joe would be particularly receptive to the idea of her appearing in the buff for all to see.

Nudity per se meant little to Monroe. She had few inhibitions so far as her body was concerned. Kurt Lamprecht visited her while on a junket to Los Angeles. "I had a writer friend named Will Fowler, and he'd met Marilyn several times, so I invited him along when I went to see her. The apartment itself seemed sparsely decorated. We were in the living room. She had photos of her three stepchildren — Joe Jr. and the two Arthur

Miller offspring — and she still communicated with all three, sending them gifts and loving notes. 'Like me, they're from broken homes,' she remarked. There was a photograph of Marilyn on the wall that had been taken by famed cinematographer Jack Cardiff, and Marilyn said it had been Arthur Miller's favorite portrait of her, but he'd simply left it behind in her New York apartment. Pretty sad, I thought. She didn't have many positive things to say about Miller, though she seemed fond of his kids. Miller and Monroe were apparently sexually incompatible, and she constantly referred to him as 'a mama's boy.' In any case, she had on a terry cloth bathrobe, and after a few minutes, she slipped out of it and started walking around in the nude. No explanation, nothing, and we certainly weren't going to complain. The odd thing is there was nothing sexual about it. She might as well have been at a nudist colony. She wasn't trying to entice or seduce anyone. She was simply enjoying the moment, walking around without any clothes on."

Entertaining casual male guests in the nude wasn't an activity Monroe would have likely talked about with DiMaggio. What she did discuss with him was her precarious financial situation, particularly as she'd borrowed money from him several times. He perused her account books, compiled for her by her latest personal secretary, and discovered that, in 1961, Marilyn had spent $22,000 on clothes, $33,000 on doctors, and something over $60,000 on lawyers, accountants, hairstylists, maids, secretaries, and publicists. Joe noticed that Hedda Rosten, who'd stopped working for Marilyn long before, was still on her payroll. Marjorie Stengel, Monroe's New York secretary in 1961, had inadvertently been paid nearly twice her salary. And an assistant to Aaron Frosch, MM's New York attorney, had apparently skimmed funds from Marilyn's account. Because the IRS had audited Monroe on several occasions, DiMaggio recommended that she keep all bills, contracts, bank statements, and other pertinent documents in a filing cabinet. He likewise suggested that if Marilyn wanted greater independence from Eunice Murray, she would do well to hire her own car and driver to get her around town. Marilyn contacted a local limousine service, and they sent over Rudy Kautzky. Rudy became her regular driver, taking her on her daily rounds, from Jurgensen's for groceries to Elizabeth Arden for makeup. Her most repeated stopover was Vicente Pharmacy, which supplied her with her voluminous storehouse of prescription drugs.

It was Dr. Greenson who suggested that she would be more comfortable in her own house in the Los Angeles area as opposed to her small North Doheny Drive apartment. Ralph Roberts saw Greenson's suggestion as "an obvious attempt to nail Marilyn down so she couldn't leave Hollywood and return to New York, which is what she wanted to do and should've probably done. Owning a house entails far more responsibility than renting an apartment. Although she had mixed feelings about it, once she bought the place, she became a virtual prisoner. Joe DiMaggio liked the house but didn't like the underlying idea *behind* the house; Greenson tried to convince him that it would somehow solve all her psychological issues. Greenson apparently felt that owning her own home would be a suitable substitute for the baby and husband she didn't have. A house could provide her with a sense of security. 'It will save her from herself,' said the shrink. As time would tell, he couldn't have been more wrong."

In an interview Alan Levy conducted with Monroe that was published in *Redbook* magazine in August 1962 — the month she died — she was quoted as saying, "I could never imagine buying a new home alone. But I've always been alone, so why couldn't I imagine it?" In the same interview, she spoke about her second go-round with Joe DiMaggio: "I've always been able to count on Joe as a friend after that first bitterness of our parting ended. Believe me, there is no spark to be kindled. I just like being with him, and we have a better understanding than we've ever had."

In addition to DiMaggio's brief exposure to the rites of psychotherapy, he'd more recently attended a series of classes in anger management. Now able to contain his temper, a task made easier by his all but having given up alcohol (he still had an occasional glass of champagne), he was far more capable of harnessing his emotions. He no longer insisted that his present relationship with Marilyn need end at the altar. He happily accepted the role she thrust upon him, that of friend, mentor, and lover. When Marilyn told him — over a game of gin rummy — that Dr. Greenson wanted her to acquire a house in Los Angeles and "settle down," he finally admitted that Greenson had discussed the matter with him. DiMaggio's advice to her was to purchase a simple abode, nothing fancy or elaborate, and certainly not one of those garish movie star monstrosities to be found in Bel Air and sections of Beverly Hills.

It happened to be Eunice Murray who came across the "ideal" house for Marilyn. Located on one acre of sloping lawn at 12305 Fifth Helena Drive in Brentwood, only a mile and a half (how convenient!) from Dr. Greenson's Santa Monica home, the L-shaped 2,300-square-foot Spanish colonial hacienda featured dark beamed ceilings, arched doorways, adobe stucco walls, a wood-paneled dining room, and a sunken living room with fireplace. Built in 1929, the house contained three bedrooms and two baths. Marilyn's bedroom, the largest of the three, had its own bathroom in addition to a fireplace; the room faced the front of the house. A kidney-shaped swimming pool, surrounded by tropical foliage, sat behind the residence. A red brick driveway led to a two-car garage and an attached guest cottage. Fifth Helena Drive was a cul-de-sac, and the hacienda stood at the end of the street, guaranteeing Marilyn at least partial privacy. It was also conveniently located near San Vicente Boulevard, Brentwood's main thoroughfare.

"I never owned a house before," said Marilyn. "It's a cozy place, not at all ostentatious. It was just for me and for a few friends." Putting a positive spin on the purchase, Marilyn added, "It's a fortress where I can feel safe from the world."

Before closing on the deal, Marilyn called Joe DiMaggio in San Francisco and asked him to come look at the house. He flew down, and Eunice Murray drove the couple to the property. 'You'd better duck down so nobody recognizes you,' Murray warned DiMaggio. 'They may get the wrong idea.' 'He can't hide his nose,' remarked Marilyn. DiMaggio laughed. Marilyn led him through the house, room by room. At the end of the tour, Joe admitted the place looked sturdy and had charm. He suggested she build a small apartment over the garage for either a household employee or extra guests. To maintain privacy, he advised her *not* to put her name on the mailbox at the edge of the driveway. Finally, he lent her another $15,000 to help her purchase the residence. She made a down payment of $42,500 and took a fifteen-year mortgage on the remainder, which cost her $320 per month. The total price of the house was $77,500.

Enthusiastic about the purchase, Marilyn busied herself decorating the new acquisition. She bought a Norman Norell–designed red fabric couch for the living room, which arrived only days before her death and remained encased in the guest cottage. From a local collector, she bought a bronze copy of a Rodin statue (*The Kiss*), the original of which she'd seen on exhibit at the Metropolitan Museum of Art in New York. She acquired an oil painting of a bull by Poucette, an acclaimed contemporary French female artist. She transformed the smallest bedroom into a fitting room and began modernizing and refurbishing the kitchen and bathrooms as well as the two remaining bedrooms, the living room, and the guest cottage, selecting mostly dark, rustic wooden furniture and fabric in imitation of Dr. Greenson's Spanish-style house. Like Greenson, she placed a low wooden coffee table in front of her living room fireplace. She installed new lighting fixtures throughout. She created a sleeping nook for Maf in the guest cottage because he tended to bark at night, keeping the actress awake. She ordered a red carpet to be woven for the guest cottage and commissioned an artisan to hand-paint the rafters with flowers and leaves. She made plans to install a potted herb garden and bought a number of flowering plants and citrus trees from Frank's, a nearby nursery. To further her interest in gardening, she subscribed to *Horticulture* magazine and hired a landscaper and a gardener to help develop the grounds. She hired two handymen — Eunice Murray's son-in-law, Norman Jefferies, and his brother, Keith — to make new kitchen cabinets, refinish the floors, and do other odds and ends around the house.

Describing her aspirations and current state of mind for the benefit of photographer George Barris, a recent friend, Marilyn said, "I'm going to live in my new house all alone with my snowball, my little white poodle . . . Oh, sure, I'd rather be married and have children and a man to love — but you can't always have everything in life the way you want it. You have to accept what comes your way."

Of the house itself, she noted, "It's small, but I find it rather comfortable . . . It's quiet and peaceful — just what I need right now . . . There are fourteen red stone squares leading to my front door, where there is a ceramic tile coat of arms with the motto *Cursum Perficio,* meaning 'end of my journey.' I hope it's true."

On February 1, 1962, two weeks before she departed Los Angeles on a furniture shopping expedition to New York and Mexico, Marilyn attended a dinner party at the home of Peter and Pat Lawford. Their guest of honor that evening was Robert F. Kennedy, the attorney general of the United States and President Kennedy's younger brother. Marilyn had attended a party for JFK at the Lawfords only ten weeks earlier. Obviously, the president had mentioned Monroe to his brother because when Lawford asked Bobby if there was anyone in Hollywood he wanted to meet, he immediately named Marilyn Monroe. As JFK's former campaign manager, Bobby had encountered her briefly at the Democratic National Convention in the summer of 1960. No doubt aware of the extent of his brother's relationship with Monroe, Bobby eagerly anticipated the dinner, as did Marilyn.

Peter Lawford sat them next to each other and watched with amusement as Bobby's eyes more than once traveled the distance between Marilyn's visage and her more than ample (yet very firm) bustline. "He wasn't exactly subtle about it, but then the Kennedy men never were very subtle when it came to women and sex. She bombarded him with questions related to civil rights, Cuba, the Soviet Union, and J. Edgar Hoover. She asked him if he and his brother planned on firing Hoover, and he said they wanted to but wouldn't. Marilyn told me later that Dan Greenson, her psychiatrist's son, had helped her frame the queries. However, I don't think her purpose was simply to impress Bobby. Politics truly interested her. Bobby must have been pleasantly surprised because he called the following day and said, 'Jack's got good taste. I didn't realize Marilyn Monroe was as bright as she is. And she also has a terrific sense of humor.'"

Joan Braden, whose husband, Tom Braden, had been a top operative with the CIA, attended the party and noted that Bobby was "enthralled with Marilyn to the point where he ignored everyone else, including Kim Novak, who sat to the attorney general's right while Marilyn sat to his left. We were all but invisible to him. Kim suffered in silence. Ethel, Bobby's wife, was there as well, but the Lawfords had seated her at another table near Gene Kelly and Judy Garland. Ethel seemed oblivious to Bobby's very intense interest in Marilyn."

Marilyn was taken with Bobby. "The General," as she later came to call him, struck her as vibrant and authentic, unusual traits in a profession abundant with egocentric phonies. Then again, Bobby was thirty-six — young for a full-fledged politico, and only a year older than Marilyn. She was still "the president's girl," but she liked Bobby. He was fun, and he wasn't a bad dancer either, as she discovered after dinner. Before the evening ended, Bobby gave her his private line at the Department of Justice and told her to call whenever she wanted. "You might come to regret that offer," Marilyn warned him.

When Marilyn arrived in New York, she invited Norman and Hedda Rosten to spend an evening with her and Frank Sinatra. Rosten described Marilyn, in a simple green print dress, as looking "like a young girl — sixteen or eighteen — going to a school dance." She was "giddy, high spirited, and nervous." Sinatra still excited Marilyn. She saw him several evenings and shopped for furniture (for the Brentwood house) during the day. Another evening she attended a party for President Kennedy at socialite Fifi Fell's Park Avenue penthouse apartment, then (according to FBI and Secret Service files) stayed with JFK at the Carlyle. Following her stopover in New York, she spent a weekend in Miami Beach with Joe DiMaggio, rewarding him for his generous and frequent financial loans by giving him a formal portrait of herself by artist Jon Whitcomb, which Joe later hung in the bedroom of his San Francisco house. DiMaggio gave Marilyn several self-help books, among them a guide to finding happiness in a difficult world. During their weekend together, Marilyn introduced DiMaggio to Isidore Miller, who was again wintering in Florida. Joe and Marilyn ate dinner in a small Italian restaurant on Collins Avenue. DiMaggio evidently made no mention of his competition; by this point, he no doubt knew of Marilyn's romances with both Sinatra and JFK but probably convinced himself that being Monroe's part-time lover represented a happier circumstance than not having access to her at all.

On February 21 Marilyn flew from Miami International Airport to Mexico City on the second leg of her furniture treasure hunt. Eunice Murray had visited Mexico a week earlier and had returned with names of dealers, galleries, collectors, and shops for Monroe to visit in the course of her trip. With Marilyn in Mexico were hairdressers Sydney Guilaroff and George Masters, Pat Newcomb, and Eunice Churchill, the medical secretary to both Ralph Greenson and Hyman Engelberg. Marilyn's therapist and personal physician currently shared office space at a medical facility at 436 North Roxbury Drive in Beverly Hills. Eunice Churchill's function on the Mexican junket was to pose as an interior decorator, enabling Marilyn to gain reductions on the purchase of furniture and furnishings, including ceramic tile for the bathrooms of her Brentwood property.

"Our first stop in Mexico City was a Catholic orphanage," recalled Sydney Guilaroff. "Marilyn had brought along all sorts of gifts for the kids: clothes, toys, candy bars, the works. They loved her for it." These children were among the poorest of the poor. And Marilyn, of course, understood their hopelessness, what it meant to be locked away in an orphanage. She filled out papers to be able to adopt one or more of the orphans.

In Mexico City, the group stayed at the Continental Hotel, where they were greeted each morning by hundreds of fans chanting "Maraleen! Maraleen!" A pair of security guards had been hired to protect the actress. Pat Newcomb arranged a press conference for her in the hotel's grand ballroom. Two days into the trip, Marilyn and her entourage visited the Byrna Gallery, where Monroe bought three paintings by prominent Mexican artists. At a fine-arts shop, she ordered glass and metal sconces for the light fixtures, a silver-framed mirror for the dining room, and two large rectangular mirrors for her bedroom. She acquired a hand-carved chess set and ordered several art deco chairs. "She also bought clothing and jewelry," said Sydney Guilaroff, "but instead of placing the jewelry in her hotel room safe, she wrapped it in tissue paper and kept the packet in a pair of her shoes. There had been several recent robberies in the hotel, and I guess Marilyn figured her jewelry would be more secure in a shoe than in a safe."

Marilyn traveled around Mexico with Fred Vanderbilt Field, a disinherited member of the prominent American family and a long-time associate of the Greensons, whose pro-Marxist and Communist leanings made Field a major FBI target. He and his wife, Nieves, took Marilyn on a tour of Mexico, driving her to Cuernavaca, Taxco, and Borda. The actress's brief association with Field led to a flurry of FBI reports, one of which (sent by an official of the FBI's Domestic Intelligence Division) clearly demonstrated that Eunice Murray had become a bureau informant. "According to Eunice Murray," read an FBI memorandum to J. Edgar Hoover, dated March 2, 1962, "the subject (Marilyn Monroe) still reflects the political views of Arthur Miller. Her views are very positively and concisely leftist. However, if she is being actively used by the Communist Party, it is not general knowledge among those working with the movement in Los Angeles."

And then there was José Bolaños, the thirty-five-year old actor/screenwriter/film producer from Mexico City, who spotted Monroe in a restaurant and sent a dozen roses to her table. Dark, intense, masculine, and moody, Bolaños had once been a matador, a bullfighter. Passionate and romantic, he was, Monroe told Lena Pepitone, "the greatest lover in the world." The only problem was his jealousy. "He's worse than Joe," she said, referring to the DiMaggio of old.

Bolaños and Monroe spent a night in Acapulco. The next day, he took her into the dense forests on the outskirts of the city to the Pancho Villa House, a shrine to the famous Mexican Robin Hood who lived at the turn of the century. A hero to some, a villain to others, Pancho Villa remained a mythic figure whose army of lovers — females of all ages — had purportedly numbered in the thousands. Visitors to the shrine paid $25 each to watch women lie on a bed and make love to the spirit of Pancho Villa. They would go through all the motions of lovemaking. They would writhe, thrash, moan, groan, tremble, and gyrate, while the paying spectators watched in stunned silence. They would call out Pancho's name as they reached climax. It didn't occur to Marilyn until she'd returned to the States that Pancho Villa's "lovers" were nothing more than a bunch of performers being paid to put on an exhibition. And that the so-called Acapulco shrine to Pancho was only one of many scattered around Mexico and run by a band of enterprising operators.

When Marilyn's eleven-day Mexican sojourn ended, she returned to Los Angeles via New York. She told Lena Pepitone that José Bolaños had proposed to her. On March 5 Bolanos joined Marilyn in Hollywood and accompanied her to the annual Golden Globe Awards. Once again the Hollywood Foreign Press Association found a reason to give Marilyn a statuette, this time naming her the World's Favorite Female Star. It wasn't an Oscar, but it would have to do. *The Hollywood Reporter* noted that her acceptance speech was slurred, suggesting she'd downed too many pills or too much booze — or both. Joe DiMaggio, in New York, read about José Bolaños and hopped the next plane for Los Angeles. By the time he arrived, Bolaños was on his way back to Mexico. Marilyn had checked him into the Beverly Hills Hotel, and then, in his words, "she never came back." Without funds to pay for his lodging, Bolaños had no choice but to check out.

With Joe DiMaggio's newfound acceptance of psychotherapy, he'd taken steps to forge a peaceful relationship with Dr. Ralph Greenson. But when Joe arrived in Los Angeles in early March, an event transpired that affected both his attitude and his budding friendship with the therapist. Opposed to Marilyn's fleeting romance with José Bolaños, Greenson suggested that she stay at his house until the screenwriter left town. Having brought over a toothbrush and little else, she was still there when DiMaggio showed up to drive her home. Greenson told DiMaggio that he'd sedated Monroe and that she was asleep in one of the upstairs bedrooms. He said it would be best if she remained in his home until further notice. Evidently awake, Marilyn heard DiMaggio's voice and began yelling his name. The ballplayer bolted past Greenson, ran up the stairs, found Marilyn, and brought her back downstairs. She complained that Greenson had forced her to stay against her will, that she'd planned on spending a single night but that he hadn't permitted her to leave. Joe ushered her out of the house and into his car, and they drove off. Marilyn told Joe that not only had Greenson imprisoned her, he'd also encouraged her to break off many of her personal ties, DiMaggio included.

By the time DiMaggio left Los Angeles, having helped Marilyn move some of her new furniture into her Brentwood house, he'd come to thoroughly distrust her psychiatrist. "Even Marilyn began to wonder about Greenson," recalled Joe DiMaggio Jr. "She told me as early as mid-March that she planned to make one more picture and then move back to New York. She'd finally come to share my father's opinion regarding Hollywood — he called it 'a cesspool,' and she termed it 'the first circle of hell.' "

Ongoing surveillance of Monroe by both the Secret Service and the FBI revealed that on March 24, 1962, Monroe and John F. Kennedy spent the night together at Bing Crosby's Palm Desert residence. A photograph of them, located in the FBI files, shows JFK attired in a turtleneck sweater and slacks, while Marilyn has on only a white terry cloth bathrobe. Peter Lawford originally asked Frank Sinatra to host Marilyn and the president at his Palm Springs home. In anticipation of their arrival, Sinatra had spent some $500,000 transforming his estate into the West Coast White House, constructing a series of bungalows for the Secret Service and a heliport to accommodate the executive chopper that would be used to transport Kennedy from the Palm Springs airport to the property.

"A month before the visit," said Peter Lawford, "J. Edgar Hoover informed Bobby Kennedy that the FBI had been made aware of Frank Sinatra's ongoing dealings with leading Mob figures, such as Sam Giancana. I received a phone call from Bobby informing me that they'd decided to have the president stay at Bing Crosby's house rather than Sinatra's. Bobby asked me to pass on this information to Sinatra, which I did. From that day forward Sinatra was *persona non grata* at the Kennedy White House. He blamed me for what happened, and it ended our friendship. He was furious. He got hold of a jackhammer and tore up the heliport outside his property. His last words to me were, 'Why would he stay at Crosby's place? Crosby's a fucking Republican.' "

Despite his growing animosity toward Marilyn's psychiatrist, the month of April turned out relatively well for Joe DiMaggio. He spent several days with Marilyn at her Brentwood house, met with his son one weekend in San Francisco, was paid handsomely to appear at a baseball memorabilia show in Boston, and was invited to lunch at the United Nations with UN Undersecretary General Ralph Bunche. Although the working press had to provide UN security guards with proper identification, when DiMaggio reached the dining room entrance, the guards instantly recognized him. "Come on in, Joe," said one of them, "Dr. Bunche is waiting for you."

The same month proved to be much more problematic for Monroe. In April she attended costume and makeup tests for *Something's Got to Give.* A remake of *My Favorite Wife,* a 1940 comedy starring Cary Grant and Irene Dunne, the never-to-be-completed *Something's Got to Give* was about a shipwrecked woman, thought to be deceased, who returns home after several years only to learn that her husband has remarried.

The ill-fated project was doomed from the start. One of the major problems was that Twentieth Century–Fox began shooting long before having a completed and approved script in hand. The other major problem was Marilyn Monroe herself. "Her chief gripe," reported Whitey Snyder, "was that Fox had given Elizabeth Taylor a million dollars to star in *Cleopatra,* whereas she was being paid one-tenth that amount. She said she should never have disbanded Marilyn Monroe Productions or gotten rid of Milton Greene, and she blamed it all on Arthur Miller. From the beginning, Marilyn had it out for Fox's bosses, all of whom she contended were corrupt. As usual, she was constantly late on the set, arrived high and hung over and unable to recall her lines. To complicate matters, Dr. Ralph Greenson had convinced Fox to hire him in a sort of supervisory capacity to keep Marilyn going. He felt she needed the picture for her own self-esteem. In my opinion, he should never have been directly involved with the project. There seemed to be something strange and phony about Greenson's relationship with Marilyn."

Shortly after production on the film began, Marilyn received an unexpected and highly disturbing note from C. Stanley Gifford, the man she believed to be her birth father. Claiming that he wished to "make amends" for his refusal in the past to acknowledge or meet Monroe, Gifford's brief letter wished her luck on her latest film venture and ended with the words: "From the man you tried to see some ten years ago. God forgive me."

Upon receipt of the card, Marilyn contacted Lotte Goslar and read it to her. "She was in tears," Goslar recalled, "and she kept saying, 'It's too late, much too late.'"

A week later, according to Goslar, Marilyn received a telephone call at Fox from a woman in Palm Springs who claimed to be Stanley Gifford's private nurse. Gifford had suffered a heart attack and wasn't expected to survive. That's the reason he'd sent her the note. He wanted to talk to her before he died. Monroe responded by telling the nurse exactly what she'd been told ten years earlier when she'd approached Gifford: "Please assure the gentleman I have never met him, but if he has anything specific to say to me, he can contact my lawyer. Would you like his number?"

That was the last Marilyn heard from Gifford, and vice versa. As it turned out, Gifford survived his heart attack and outlived his daughter. Their interaction during the filming of *Something's Got to Give* brought to an abrupt halt Marilyn's lifelong search for her real father. It likewise, no doubt, contributed to Marilyn's mounting slag heap of personal problems, earmarked most profoundly by her addictions and difficulties in front of the cameras. Director George Cukor lashed out at Pat Newcomb one day for bringing a bottle of champagne onto the set. "Stop acting like a fucking social director," he yelled, "and start acting like a publicist!" Following a series of arguments with Monroe, who constantly complained that the script kept changing, Cukor sent Darryl Zanuck a memo expressing his disdain for Monroe and her lack of consideration for the cast and crew: "Marilyn is the least professional performer I have ever worked with." To which Zanuck replied: "If I could, I would launch a torpedo from here — aimed directly at her dressing room." Screenwriter Nunnally Johnson sent Henry Weinstein, producer of the picture, a letter complaining that Marilyn Monroe "represents everything that's wrong with Hollywood. She's spoiled silly and drugged out of her mind. I saw some footage yesterday, and she seemed to be moving in slow motion, as if in a trance. It's difficult to watch."

The situation grew progressively worse. Three weeks into production, Marilyn came down with a viral infection and refused to go to work. Peter Levathes, acting head of the studio, dropped in on Monroe at her Brentwood house. He thought she looked and sounded fine. He made an appointment with Mickey Rudin, her attorney, and pointed out that Marilyn had certain contractual obligations, which she wasn't meeting. He told Rudin, "All I ever hear, every single day, is, she's not feeling well, she has a cold, she has a virus, she's under the weather. The point is, she's never on the set, and on those rare occasions when she's around and in front of the cameras, she either massacres her lines or forgets them altogether." Rudin communicated with Ralph Greenson, noting that Levathes had threatened to terminate Marilyn and shut down the production. The psychiatrist "guaranteed" that Marilyn would show up punctually every day and would apologize to the director and producer for her absences. Although Greenson had come to disapprove of Joe DiMaggio's presence in his ex-wife's life, he turned to the ballplayer in an effort to convince Marilyn to resume work on the project. Reluctant to become involved with Twentieth Century–Fox, DiMaggio nevertheless spent two days with her in Brentwood, attempting to raise her spirits.

It was at this stage, following DiMaggio's departure, that Marilyn surprised both Greenson and Cukor by vanishing from Los Angeles and flying to New York for three days on what she termed "a top-secret" mission. The mission entailed singing the "Happy

Birthday Song" to President John F. Kennedy at Madison Square Garden on May 19, 1962, in celebration of his forty-fifth birthday.

It had been Peter Lawford's idea to have Marilyn Monroe sing for the finale of the president's birthday gala, a Democratic Party fund-raiser held before eighteen thousand paying supporters and a television audience numbering in the millions. In Monroe's absence, shooting on *Something's Got to Give* once again ground to a halt. As Marilyn and Peter Lawford flew to New York, Bobby Kennedy telephoned Milton Gould, the chairman of Fox's executive committee, and requested that the studio release Marilyn for several days so she could participate in the festivities. Unaware that Monroe had already departed, Gould said it would be impossible — the film was way behind schedule. Recalling the conversation, Gould noted that RFK called him "a no-good Jew bastard" and hung up on him.

Marilyn had asked fashion designer Jean Louis to create her dress for the occasion. At a cost of $7,000, the couturier had fashioned a skintight, flesh-colored mesh gown studded with rhinestones. Wearing nothing underneath, Marilyn described the garment as "all skin and beads." "The skin was visible," commented Peter Lawford, "but the beads were not." Marilyn personally paid the bill for the gown but was later reimbursed by Bobby

Kennedy, who evidently wrote it off as a "Justice Department expense."

Another payment assumed by RFK went to Mickey Song, a Beverly Hills hairstylist who attended to JFK and RFK whenever one or both visited the West Coast. Song had been flown to New York to cut President Kennedy's hair prior to the Madison Square Garden birthday party. "I saw Marilyn Monroe sitting alone in her Garden dressing room and noticed that while her hair had been preset, it had to be brushed out," said Song. "I asked Bobby Kennedy, whose hair I also cut earlier that day, if Marilyn needed me to attend to her hair. He led me to her and introduced us, though I'd met her previously on several occasions at Hollywood parties. She seemed nervous as I worked on her hair. A few minutes later Bobby returned and said he needed to talk with Marilyn, so I left the room. The next thing I knew, he came barging out of her dressing room and slammed the door behind him. 'I think she needs you again,' he said. And under his breath, he muttered, 'What a bitch!' I went back in. Her hair was totally disheveled. She didn't say anything as I combed it back into place, but it seemed apparent to me that he'd tried to put the make on her and she fought him off. For my bouffant job on Marilyn, Bobby eventually sent me a check for fifty dollars."

Mickey Song further remembered that

Marilyn was drinking heavily, alternating between champagne and vodka, as she waited for her cue. Among the celebrities in the packed house that night were Jack Benny, Henry Fonda, and Ella Fitzgerald. Peter Lawford introduced her. Her gown glittering, she moved slowly in the direction of the spotlight, stopped, looked straight at the president and began to sing her seductive, unmistakably sexual rendition of "Happy Birthday, Mr. President." Ethel Kennedy had joined Bobby in the audience, but Jackie passed the evening at her retreat near Middleburg, Virginia, evidently uninterested in hearing her husband serenaded by the woman who secretly planned to evict her from the White House.

After completing the number, Marilyn launched into a specially written version of "Thanks for the Memory," and then led the audience in a happy birthday chorus. A large cake was wheeled out, and the president soon appeared onstage to cut it. "I can now retire from politics," he joked to the crowd, "having had 'Happy Birthday' sung to me in such a sweet, wholesome way."

With the show over, the party adjourned only long enough for a few of the more notable participants to relocate to a private affair hosted by Arthur Krim, head of United Artists. Still wearing her nearly diaphanous gown, Marilyn was as much a hit in Krim's town house as she'd been at the Garden.

Although the actress had rejected Bobby Kennedy's advances earlier that evening, he hadn't given up. UN ambassador Adlai Stevenson would recall in his autobiography that in order to converse with Marilyn that evening, he'd been "forced to break through the strong defense established by Robert Kennedy, who was dodging around her like a moth around the flame."

Marilyn's escort for the evening was Arthur Miller's father, whom she introduced to both the president and the attorney general. At midnight, she placed Isidore Miller in a taxicab and returned to the party. Later that night, she joined JFK for a private birthday celebration in one of the bedrooms of the family's penthouse suite at the Carlyle. As usual, a Secret Service agent was posted outside the front door of the suite to guard against the possibility of somebody walking in on the couple. An FBI report not released until 2010 revealed a new wrinkle concerning Monroe's dealings with the Kennedys. Apparently in an alcoholic haze, she'd spent an hour in bed with JFK, and then entered a second bedroom and passed the remainder of the night with Robert F. Kennedy, whose aggressive nature and perseverance had obviously paid off. The following day, RFK bragged to Pierre Salinger, the White House press secretary, that he'd finally "bagged Miss Monroe." It was Salinger who disclosed this information to an FBI agent.

Back in Los Angeles, Marilyn went to dinner with Ralph Roberts. "She gave me a detailed account of the birthday bash, but couldn't seem to recall what happened after she and the president reached the Carlyle," said Roberts. "However, I must admit I didn't realize until this particular point in time just how much John F. Kennedy had meant to her. She'd built the affair into a full-blown romantic fantasy. For months she'd been calling the president at the White House, writing him letters, even sending him snippets of her love poetry. But what truly amazed me was her admission that she'd once telephoned Jackie Kennedy. She actually told the First Lady she wanted to marry the president, and apparently Jackie humored her by saying she had no objection and, in fact, had grown weary of her fishbowl existence in the executive mansion. I could well imagine their conversation, both women expressing their thoughts in that whispery, Little Bo Peep voice they shared. Still, I had some serious misgivings about Marilyn. She seemed to have constructed a whole new reality for herself, a magic kingdom in which she — and she alone — reigned supreme."

On May 25, back on the set, Marilyn did a nude swimming pool scene. "It's the only time she seemed to come alive," said George Cukor. On June 1 she celebrated her thirty-sixth birthday by taking Dean Martin's teen-aged son to a Los Angeles Dodgers baseball game and then went to dinner with Frank Sinatra at Trader Vic's. The next morning she came down with a head cold, and again production on the film had to be suspended — but not before the cast threw a small birthday party for Marilyn at the Fox Studio. On June 8, having seen and heard enough, Peter Levathes issued the following public statement: "Marilyn Monroe has been removed from the cast of *Something's Got to Give*. This action was necessary because of Miss Monroe's repeated willful breaches of contract. No justification was given by Miss Monroe for her failure to report for photography on many occasions. The studio has suffered losses through these absences."

Levathes attempted to salvage *Something's Got to Give* by replacing Monroe with actress Lee Remick, but Dean Martin — the male lead — refused to work with anyone other than Marilyn. Levathes offered Martin's role to Robert Mitchum, but Mitchum — a friend to both Monroe and Dean Martin — wasn't interested. With few options available, the studio now sued Monroe for $750,000 in a futile attempt to recover a fraction of its losses. The lawsuit never reached court.

"They ought to sue Elizabeth Taylor, not me," Marilyn told Ralph Roberts. "*Cleopatra* has cost them far more than my stupid little film. But it's easier to blame me for everything. I'm a pushover. Elizabeth Taylor's the Queen of the Nile."

In despair over her ouster from the film, Marilyn turned to Joe DiMaggio for consolation. In spite of his past rages, his hatred of Hollywood and the movie industry, Joe had never turned away from Marilyn. Nor had he ever given up hope of getting back with her on a full-time basis. In anticipation of spending more time with her, he had just resigned his position at Monette. He arrived at Marilyn's Brentwood home and asked her to marry him. He wasn't a billionaire, but he had more than enough money to support them both. He would supplement what he already had by endorsing products and appearing in television commercials. They could still have children — if need be, they could always adopt. In time they could revive Marilyn Monroe Productions, and she could star in a film every year or two, but the films would be of a serious nature, and she would make far more than she currently earned as a "studio slave" — he would see to that.

Marilyn turned him down, though not necessarily forever; she had to think about it. They argued. Joe told her she was killing herself, giving up all potential happiness, sacrificing all normal human emotions, and for what? For the sake of the studio dictators who'd imposed upon her the role of a super sex symbol and little else? "Now they've even got you posing in the nude!" he yelled, before slamming the door behind him.

She later admitted to Ralph Roberts that she'd been high on pot and LSD when Joe proposed to her, but even if she hadn't been, she wouldn't have gone along with it. They had a good thing going now, so why ruin it by getting married again? They would only repeat all the same patterns and make the same mistakes that had befouled their first marriage.

According to Richard Ben Cramer, DiMaggio's biographer, Joe boarded the next flight to New York and headed straight for Toots Shor's. When he recounted his conversation with Marilyn for the saloon keeper's benefit, Toots said something like, "Aw, Joe, what do expect from a whore like that?" DiMaggio told his longtime buddy to go fuck himself. He never spoke to Toots Shor again.

CHAPTER 19

Despite a birthday to remember, and despite the $1 million Marilyn Monroe had helped raise for the Democratic Party that night at Madison Square Garden, John F. Kennedy was done with the actress. Her erratic behavior — her letters, phone calls, and love poems, as well as her call to Jackie — no longer amused him. Too many people, including the Secret Service and FBI, knew of the affair by this time, and while the press in those days didn't peer into the closets (or private lives) of politicians, there were those that did. The Kennedy clan's list of perceived enemies — Fidel Castro, the Mafia, and Jimmy Hoffa, president of the largest union in America, the International Brotherhood of Teamsters, to name a few — was long and getting longer. The president was only too pleased to assign Bobby Kennedy the unpleasant (some might say pleasant) task of getting Marilyn off his back.

Bobby's arrival on the scene came at a

precarious point in Marilyn's career. After Fox fired her from *Something's Got to Give,* she suffered what Dr. Ralph Greenson described as a "deeply paranoid and depressive reaction." She placed some of the blame for her misfortune on George Cukor, stipulating that Cukor, an outspoken and admitted homosexual, had been jealous of her affair with Yves Montand during their joint appearance in *Let's Make Love.* Cukor, she claimed, had himself lusted after Montand despite the fact that the actor left little doubt as to his sexuality.

Against Dr. Greenson's advice, MM turned to Bobby Kennedy for help, asking the attorney general to intervene on her behalf with Fox. RFK discussed the situation with Pierre Salinger and urged him to do what he could. "I didn't know anyone at the studio," said Salinger, "so I contacted Peter Lawford for advice. Peter loved Marilyn. He said she was having trouble and was more dependent than ever on barbiturates and probably ought to be placed in a detoxification unit if she hoped to get back to work. She was doing with RFK what she'd previously done with the president, besieging him with letters and phone calls, which in fact she'd been doing since first meeting him at Peter's house. Jackie's problem had now become Ethel's. In any case, Peter gave me a list of names at Fox. I placed several calls. I have no idea how useful I might've been, but within days negotiations began between Mickey Rudin and Fox about resuming work on the film."

Jeanne Carmen, an actress Monroe first met at the Actors Studio in New York and with whom she established a close friendship after both moved to Los Angeles, happened to see a good deal of Marilyn in 1962. "We were sleeping pill buddies," recalled Carmen. "I wasn't a big drinker, but Marilyn thought nothing of mixing booze and pills, and that's where she got into trouble. We once did cocaine together and wound up bouncing off the walls. Neither of us liked it. We were both chronic insomniacs, and all we wanted to do was fall asleep. We took mostly Seconal and Nembutal, both very potent sleeping pills. They helped me a bit, but they did next to nothing for Marilyn. It amazed me how little her psychiatrist, Dr. Greenson, seemed to help her. Somewhere along the line he decided she was a waif in need of a family, so for a while he had her sleeping over and helping out in the kitchen by peeling potatoes and washing dishes, the same chores she'd performed as a child in the orphanage. During the period I knew Marilyn, she suffered from drastic mood swings. I'm no shrink, but to my mind she was bipolar, a manic-depressive. She saw Greenson practically every day, but I can't say I saw any improvement in her condition. If anything, her condition deteriorated, particularly near the end. I don't believe Greenson had the faintest notion what to do with her other than medicate her to death."

Indeed, the idea seemed to be never to deny Marilyn when she wanted a prescription, because the only thing that would happen is she would procure medication elsewhere and not inform her primary physicians, in this instance Dr. Greenson and Dr. Engelberg. So whenever she asked for a drug, she usually got it. Daniel Greenson, Dr. Greenson's son, noted that treating a celebrity of Marilyn Monroe's magnitude was a complex and often thankless proposition. "She called the shots," he said. "Because she feared not being able to fall asleep, she began medicating herself. If she had a ten-day supply of barbiturates, her tendency was to take them all in a day or two. There wasn't much anyone could do about it. If my father had refused to renew a given prescription, she would've simply turned to somebody else."

The problem was that Marilyn turned to both Greenson *and* Engelberg for prescriptions. Engelberg discussed the procedure he and Greenson followed in attempting to coordinate efforts: "I usually communicated with Dr. Greenson as to her sleeping medication, but I didn't go over it with him if, say, I wanted to give her antibiotics for an infection. Nor would I tell him every time I gave her an injection of liver or vitamins. I also used to inject her with Heparin, a blood thinner which at the time was touted as a 'youth drug' and which helped stave off strokes and heart attacks. There were other exceptions. During the shooting of *Something's Got to Give,* she developed sinus problems and the flu, which I treated without conferring with Dr. Greenson. Near the end of Marilyn's life, there seemed to be a misunderstanding of sorts, and it appears Dr. Greenson and I were simultaneously prescribing sleeping medication for her. I didn't know Dr. Greenson was supplying her with barbiturates at this juncture. Had I known, I obviously wouldn't have given her the same drug. Judging from the volume and variety of drugs in her house at the time of her death, I realized just how little control Dr. Greenson and I had over her. It appears that during her trip to Mexico, where you can procure every and any medication over the counter, she'd picked up a stash of sedatives and barbiturates. After her death, the police confiscated some fifteen bottles of pills from her house."

Another subject that went unspoken between the two physicians was that in early June, two months before her death, Marilyn Monroe began an affair with Hyman Engelberg, adding the doctor's name to a roster of lovers that included John and Bobby Kennedy, Frank Sinatra, and Joe DiMaggio.

Marilyn's liaison with her internist served to further complicate a life that long before had begun to spiral out of control. Dr. Eric Goldberg, a Santa Barbara physician and Engelberg's closest friend, was evidently the only person with whom the internist talked about the affair.

"I'd known Hy for years," said Goldberg. "We used to play tennis together every weekend. I had three sons, and so did he. He treated any number of celebrity patients, among them Rita Hayworth, Burt Lancaster, and Danny Kaye. At the time of his affair with Marilyn, which, by the way, has remained secret until now, Hy was separated from his wife. They eventually divorced, and he remarried. But in mid-1962 he was living alone in a three-bedroom house just off Sunset. I once met Marilyn at his house. On the surface, she seemed to possess everything you would want in a woman, except that she was hooked on prescription drugs. Hy wasn't in love with her, nor was she with him, which I suppose is why the relationship worked. He introduced her to his youngest son, an undergraduate at Columbia University, and one morning they all had breakfast together, which Marilyn prepared. During June and July, Hy saw her almost every day, mostly for medical reasons. He told me she used to complain about pain in her chest, so he began giving her shots of morphine. It occurred to me she might be sleeping with Hy in order to get whatever drugs she wanted, but then again there were any number of physicians in and around Los Angeles who would have been more than glad to prescribe medications for her. After she died, Hy worried that she'd mentioned their affair to friends and that he could lose his medical license. Aside from the affair, there were questions as to the injections and medications he'd given her. What's most bizarre, I suppose, is that she never mentioned the affair to Ralph Greenson. I can't help but wonder what other secrets she kept from her psychiatrist."

Asked to elaborate on his affair with Marilyn, Dr. Engelberg would say only, "It happened. We were both very lonely. Let's just leave it at that."

With negotiations still underway over a new contract for *Something's Got to Give,* the actress continued to publicize the figure known to the world as "Marilyn Monroe," a persona entirely invented, designed, created, and controlled by the former Norma Jeane Baker. During the last week of June, she participated in a three-day shoot with photographer George Barris for *Cosmopolitan.* While in her company, Barris noticed that Marilyn would lapse into an occasional depression, then bounce back to her former, more jovial self. In a serious frame of mind, she told Barris she wanted to have children but didn't feel she could raise a child properly so long as she remained alone.

She did two photo sessions with Bert Stern for *Vogue.* Stern had set up a makeshift studio at the Bel Air Hotel, supplying Marilyn with a case of Dom Pérignon and several bottles of vodka. After several hours of conventional shots, Marilyn asked Stern if he wanted to shoot her in the nude. She disrobed and donned a see-through bed jacket. Babs Simpson, *Vogue*'s photo editor, took one look at Monroe and said, "Oh, no! I don't like that." And Marilyn countered, "Well, I do."

As she assumed a suggestive pose, Marilyn said, "How's this for thirty-six?" Stern didn't know if she was referring to her breasts or her age.

"I liked her . . . and I was also very attracted to her — like most guys," admitted Stern. "She was very natural in a way that's hard to explain. And she had a quality — like she was *willing to be yours.* She gave you the feeling it was okay to jump in a car and drive off with her."

Pat Newcomb had arranged and attended the *Cosmopolitan* and *Vogue* photo feature shoots. In her typically overgenerous manner, Marilyn rewarded Newcomb with an array of offerings: a new car, a black mink coat, and the emerald earrings Frank Sinatra had once given her. Newcomb had also set up an interview for Marilyn with *Life,* to be conducted by Richard Meryman.

"We did it in two parts," said Meryman. "We met at her Brentwood house on July 4 and then again about ten days later. Marilyn asked to have the questions in advance. Although she'd prepared for the interview, her answers seemed spontaneous. I sensed she gave the interview to rearrange an image of herself she didn't like. She spoke from the heart. She was real. She was bright and businesslike. At one point during our July 4 interview, the telephone rang. Pat Newcomb, who was present the entire time, answered the phone. It was Joe DiMaggio. 'Tell him to call back,' said Marilyn.

"During our second interview, she seemed weary, less relaxed, more on edge. Her mood had changed a good deal from our first meeting. Where before she'd been energetic and positive, she now seemed sad and ill at ease. She complained about being alone in the world. One of her themes throughout our two sessions was the fickle nature of fame — she had it today, but would it be there for her tomorrow? Or as she put it, 'Fame may go by and — So long I've had you, Fame.' "

Richard Meryman's Q and A with Marilyn turned out to be the last interview she ever gave. It appeared in the August 3, 1962, issue of *Life.* She died the following day.

■ ■ ■ ■

During the first week of July, Joe DiMaggio Jr., on leave from Camp Pendleton, his Marine base in San Diego, spent the afternoon with Marilyn at home in Brentwood. He told her his mother and her companion, Ralph Peck, had opened a supper club, Charcoal Charlie's, outside Palm Springs. She sang, and he accompanied her on the piano. Joey couldn't bring himself to visit the place. He went on to discuss Pam, his girlfriend, and said he was thinking of marrying her. Marilyn told him that sometimes getting married merely made matters more complicated.

"I wondered when she said that," remarked Joey, "if she had herself and my father in mind. I mentioned that I found him a bit more relaxed now that he was no longer working for Monette. I asked Marilyn if she knew he'd put together a number of scrapbooks devoted to her, containing articles and photographs, including one scrapbook dealing solely with their wedding. I also told her I'd discovered he kept garbage bags and pillowcases full of cash in his San Francisco home. 'He's been doing that for years,' said Marilyn. 'He doesn't trust banks. He distrusts them almost as much as he distrusts Twentieth Century–Fox.' "

Marilyn showed Joey a Western Union telegram his father had sent her on her thirty-sixth birthday, which read: "Happy Birthday — Hope today and future years bring you sunny skies and all your heart desires. As ever, Joe." Marilyn liked the telegram because it was simple yet eloquent.

Before leaving, Joey asked how Marilyn's negotiations were going with Fox. "Those bastards!" she said. "I've made millions for them over the years, and this is how they thank me — by letting me go. They're lucky I'm even willing to negotiate with them."

Marilyn reminded Joey of an angry young child. "I told her I was sure in the end it would all work out," he said. "She walked me out of the house and gave me her usual warm hug. I'd driven to Brentwood from Camp Pendleton in the car Marilyn gave me. She followed me to the car and gave me another hug. 'Call me later to let me know you arrived safely,' she whispered. She turned, and I watched her walk back into the house. I didn't realize it at the time, of course, but I never saw Marilyn again. She died about a month later."

Jeanne Carmen met Joe DiMaggio only once or twice but recalled thinking that while he may not have made a good husband for Marilyn, no one cared more for her. He was always, both before and after their divorce, her most devoted friend. "When they first met," said Carmen, "Marilyn had yet to prove herself as an actress, whereas Joe's baseball-playing days were behind him. I'm convinced that had she lived, they would've at some point remarried. And it would probably have been a much more successful union the second time around."

Carmen noted that over the last two months of her life, Marilyn seemed despondent at times but never to the point where she became reclusive or showed any signs of giving up. "She remained active," said Marilyn's friend. "She talked a lot about prospective film projects. She was thinking of doing a musical with the songs of Jule Styne and had planned to see Styne in New York in mid-August to discuss the project. She also wanted to play Lady Macbeth in a movie version of Shakespeare's play. And she was still floating the idea of playing Jean Harlow in a bio flick, an idea she'd been kicking around for some time. She and Sidney Skolsky drove to Indio, past Palm Springs, to meet Jean Harlow's mother. Mama Jean said Marilyn was 'just like my baby.' The comment pleased Marilyn no end. I think she considered herself a reincarnation of Jean Harlow, destined to depart at an early age. I'll never forget the night Whitey Snyder came to her house for dinner, and she said to him, 'Promise me that if something happens to me, nobody must touch my face but you. Promise me you'll do my makeup, so I'll look my best when I leave.' "

Beyond the prospect of a new film venture, Marilyn engaged in activities such as yoga and tai chi (meditation) lessons, which she took at home with a private instructor while listening to the music of Bach and Vivaldi. She ate dinner, often alone, at La Scala. She took walks with Maf along the beach at Santa Monica or in Barrington Park, where she invariably paused to watch children romp in a playground. She went to Renna's place — called Madame Renna's — in Beverly Hills for facial massages with Dr. G. W. Campbell. Ralph Roberts would appear at her house every evening to give her a body massage. She would leave the kitchen door unlocked so he wouldn't have to deal with Eunice Murray. Apparently Eunice caught him sneaking into the house one night and reported him to Dr. Greenson, who berated Marilyn: "I thought we agreed you weren't going to see Ralph Roberts any more — how can I help you if you don't listen to me?" For once Marilyn told Greenson off. Whether he liked it or not, there were several men in her life she wasn't willing to discard, and one of them was Ralph Roberts. 'The other two that immediately come to mind,' she told him, 'are Frank Sinatra and Joe DiMaggio.' "

According to Jeanne Carmen, Marilyn

seemed most depressed following her sessions with Dr. Greenson. "I'd occasionally pick her up at his home after a session," she said, "and her beautiful blue-gray eyes would invariably be filled with tears. And it wasn't because she'd experienced some great psychiatric catharsis or awakening. Yet when Greenson went away on a European vacation with his wife, Marilyn couldn't deal with it. She and Greenson had worked out some weird ploy whereby one of the pieces in a chess set she'd bought in Mexico earlier that year supposedly came to represent her psychiatrist, and in his absence she carried the chess piece around with her wherever she went; appropriately enough, it was the white knight. She also had a copy of the children's book *The Little Engine That Could,* which Greenson's daughter had given her to instill confidence. Unfortunately, she couldn't cope without her shrink. So they reached him in Switzerland and asked him to return. Because he left while she was still involved with *Something's Got to Give,* Marilyn blamed him for many of her troubles on and off the set; he, in turn, held her responsible for making him cut short his vacation."

Lotte Goslar spent early July in New York, where she'd gone to speak to publishers about the possibility of penning a book on acting. "Marilyn had offered me the use of her East Fifty-Seventh Street apartment," she recalled, "but I decided to stay at the Chelsea Hotel instead. While there, I received a letter from Marilyn in which she said Joe DiMaggio had sent her a surprise package. Inside the package were two items: a new nightgown and a pair of his pajamas. 'I think he's trying to tell me something,' Marilyn wrote. Enclosed with the letter was a poem she'd just written. Her friend Norman Rosten, whom I'd met through Marilyn, told me that poetry was her way of saying difficult things to herself. A theme that ran through her body of poems had to do with Marilyn becoming one with nature. . . . And now, in death, she'd returned to nature, become one with the universe."

Soon after his son saw her, Joe DiMaggio arrived in Brentwood to spend a few days with Marilyn. During his visit, they shared simple dinners at home and only once went out to eat. After dinner Marilyn would brew tea for Joe, and they would watch a bit of television. They rented bikes and rode on San Vicente Boulevard in the direction of the ocean. They went shopping together. He accompanied her, as he had in former days, to Saks Fifth Avenue and Jax, both in Beverly Hills, to buy clothes. She purchased cashmere sweaters, a half dozen blouses, two evening dresses, and a pair of stilettos. That night she modeled the stilettos, *sans* apparel, just for Joe in the privacy of her bedroom.

Joe escorted Ralph Greenson and Marilyn when she went to see Dr. Michael Gurdin, a well-known plastic surgeon, to explore the possibility of some minor facial work. DiMaggio then took her to attorney Mickey Rudin's office to discuss a revision of the will she'd executed the year before in New York with Aaron Frosch. The actress had left a sizable portion of her estate to Lee and Paula Strasberg, and while she didn't want to excise them from the document, she did want to reduce and reapportion their present bequest. Rudin suggested they table the discussion until early August. ("Let's face it, Marilyn, it's not as if you're going to drop dead tomorrow," he said.) The attorney later admitted that Ralph Greenson, his brother-in-law, had indiscreetly suggested to him that Monroe was "gradually losing touch with reality." Rudin wondered whether a new last testament would stand up if it were challenged in probate court. He made no mention of his reservations to either Monroe or DiMaggio. Instead, he told them he thought his negotiations with Fox, on Marilyn's behalf, were going better than expected. He felt they were planning to reshoot *Something's Got to Give* and that Fox would almost certainly offer Marilyn an increase in salary.

Although Joe DiMaggio had ended his employment with Monette, he'd promised to make several appearances for the company at the end of July. Before leaving Marilyn, and with few expectations, he once again "popped the question," asking her to marry him. To his utter surprise and immense delight, he heard her say "Yes."

When he reached New York, Joe told George Solotaire that Marilyn had told him she was tired of Hollywood, tired of the studio creeps, tired of Ralph Greenson, tired of Eunice Murray, and, yes, maybe it was time to start over again. She was finally ready to make a change. After all, what was more important in life than happiness? Her career and her life to date — full as they were with mistake after mistake — had afforded her little in the way of joy. And when she thought about it, she realized that all the years of therapy and psychoanalysis had done virtually nothing for her. Thanks to her own devices, she knew now who was important to her and who wasn't, who cared about her and who didn't. And Joe cared. She'd always known that but hadn't always wanted to admit it. But now, finally, once and for all, she realized that Joe was her man. More than anything she wanted to be with him, grow old with him, have children with him, and be his wife. Together they would make right everything that had previously gone wrong. Joe would accomplish what nobody else could: he would help her conquer her addictions; he would steer her career, or what remained of it, in the right direction, and he would protect and cloister her from all the negative forces that threatened to do her in. In short, he would make her whole, make her complete.

The complexity inherent in Marilyn's private life, the chaos within a mind that struggled for clarity, remained unresolved despite her stated intention to remarry Joe DiMaggio. For reasons she herself probably couldn't fathom or explain, she was still sleeping with her personal physician. She and Frank Sinatra were even now occasional lovers. From time to time, there were others, including a Los Angeles cab driver in whose taxi she found herself one afternoon and whom she invited home for lunch because "he looked hungry." Furthermore, he resembled a young Clark Gable, which was apparently enough of an endorsement to land him a spot in Monroe's bed.

And then there was Bobby Kennedy, who'd taken it upon himself to divert the actress's attention away from his brother the president and onto himself. Instead of cutting off Marilyn, Bobby only drew her deeper into his family's orbit. Smitten by her, and perhaps feeling sorry for her, he encouraged her to communicate with him. She did, often chatting with Angie Novello, his private secretary, when the attorney general wasn't available.

But when she succeeded in reaching him, they would sometimes talk for hours. It didn't seem to disturb Bobby in the slightest that the movie star's phone had been bugged and that transcripts of their conversations were being turned over to any number of interested parties, including J. Edgar Hoover.

"To John Kennedy, Marilyn was just another fuck," contended Jeanne Carmen. "I doubt he ever really cared for or about her. Bobby had a reputation as a cutthroat politician — a real rattlesnake, when it came down to it — but in my opinion he seemed much more sensitive and compassionate than JFK. For whatever combination of reasons, Bobby truly fell for Marilyn. I'm not saying he was in love with her, but in his own fashion he was enamored of her. As for Marilyn, whereas she'd previously fantasized about marrying JFK and becoming First Lady, she now fantasized about marrying Bobby and *eventually* becoming First Lady, a fantasy RFK encouraged by telling MM, in a moment of passion or perhaps weakness that he would *love* to be married to her. It was common knowledge that Bobby was being groomed to take over after his brother's second term in office. And after Bobby, there was Teddy. These were the Kennedys, and that was the game plan."

Jeanne Carmen wasn't alone in feeling that Robert Kennedy had come to inhabit Marilyn's fantasies during her last summer. A journalist friend of hers, W. J. Weatherby of the British newspaper the *Manchester Guardian,* remembered her telling him that she might get married again — no, not to Joe DiMaggio; rather, someone in politics, a Washington insider. He'd asked her to marry him. She couldn't divulge the person's name, but he was important and powerful.

Meanwhile, late in July, with Joe DiMaggio safely ensconced at Monette Company headquarters in Virginia, Bobby Kennedy flew to Los Angeles to attend a party at Peter and Pat Lawford's beach house. Marilyn had last seen him there on June 27, when the Lawfords gave a luncheon to celebrate RFK's book *The Enemy Within,* which had just been made into a motion picture. On that occasion, Bobby had brought along his wife but nevertheless managed to spend several hours alone with Marilyn that evening. This time he came alone, without Ethel. Chuck Pick, a parking lot attendant by day and a bartender by night, worked the bar that evening at the Lawford residence. "The minute I arrived," said Pick, "a Secret Service agent took me aside and issued a curious warning: 'You have eyes, but you can't see; you have ears, but you can't hear; and you have a mouth, but you can't speak. You may see things here tonight, but you have to remember to keep your trap shut.' Other than the usual array of celebrities that one would expect to find at such a gathering, nothing seemed particularly unusual — that is, until around ten at night when Marilyn Monroe showed up. She was two hours late.

"Marilyn had a few drinks and socialized with everyone for an hour or so, at which point she and Robert Kennedy walked out the door together, hand in hand, and vanished into the night. When they left, so did the Secret Service agent who'd spoken to me earlier in the evening. I found out they went back to Monroe's house in Brentwood — Bobby and Marilyn in a Cadillac convertible owned by Bill Simon, chief of the Los Angeles FBI office; RFK's Secret Service escort in a separate car directly behind theirs."

Bobby and Marilyn spent the night together. The following morning, Jeanne Carmen joined them for a hot breakfast of oatmeal and cheese omelets prepared by Eunice Murray. "I figured Mrs. Murray would report back to Dr. Greenson about Bobby, and all hell would break loose," said Carmen. "Then again, I don't think Marilyn cared any longer what the sinister Dr. Greenson thought. As demonstrated by Marilyn's reaction when he told her not to see Ralph Roberts, it seemed pretty evident he'd lost his hold over her. She saw him at this time primarily as an enabler, a supplier of drugs. Dr. Hyman Engelberg filled a similar role.

"Years after Marilyn's death, I heard a rumor that she and Engelberg might have been romantically involved, which didn't surprise me. She saw a great deal of him that summer. He gave her a series of what Marilyn claimed were multivitamin injections, though, frankly, I never bought that explanation. I believe he was giving her liquid Nembutal and Amytal intermingled with other substances. He reminded me of President Kennedy's physician, Dr. Max Jacobson — Dr. Feelgood — who traveled everywhere with Kennedy and saw him regularly in the White House. Jacobson injected JFK with meta-amphetamines and porcupine piss, or something along that order. Engelberg had become Marilyn's Dr. Feelgood. Dr. Lee Siegel, Fox's Dr. Feelgood, supplemented Engelberg's injections by giving Marilyn shots of his own."

After breakfast, as Jeanne Carmen remembered it, an argument broke out between Bobby and Marilyn, when he came across a journal she'd been keeping, which contained notes on conversations she'd had with JFK and him. "It wasn't the so-called little red diary that supposedly disappeared after Marilyn's death," said Carmen. "In fact, there was no little red diary. I'd been to Marilyn's house dozens and dozens of times and never saw anything that even remotely resembled a little red diary. In 1963, with the press all abuzz about this supposed diary of Marilyn's, I asked Ralph Roberts if he'd ever come across such an item. Nobody was closer to Monroe than Roberts. He assured me he'd seen lots of journals and notebooks in her possession but never a little red diary. And no single notebook was devoted only to the Kennedys. Her notebooks were filled with notations of all sorts: poems, aphorisms, fragmented thoughts, bits of conversation, lists of all kinds. Bobby saw one or two paragraphs on his brother and assumed the worst. He grabbed the notebook and threw it on the floor. 'Get rid of this!' he shouted. I assume this was the moment Bobby started to realize just how dangerous the relationship might really be for him and his career."

Despite Bobby's sudden awareness that he was susceptible to the possibility of a scandal were he to be discovered in a compromising relationship with Marilyn (or anyone else, for that matter), he seemed determined to continue the affair, even to the extent that he was willing to falsify his logbook schedule in order to spend time with the movie star. His schedule for July 19, for example, has him back in Washington (and then Hyannis Port), whereas he actually spent the afternoon driving around Malibu with Marilyn and Jeanne Carmen.

"We put Marilyn in a black wig and baseball cap," said Carmen. "She had a fake goatee that belonged to one of her actor friends, so we put it on Bobby and gave him a baseball cap as well. I don't know how, but he somehow got rid of his Secret Service detail, after which we clambered into the Cadillac and drove to a nude beach, past Pepperdine [University]. Once there, we walked by the water. We kept our clothes on. Nobody recognized RFK or Marilyn. Later we drove back to Marilyn's house. I left, and the two of them spent a few more hours together before Bobby returned to Peter and Pat Lawford's place."

One of the oddities of the RFK-MM fling was that while neither the press nor the public at large seemed aware of it, the Secret Service, the Mafia, Jimmy Hoffa and the Teamsters, the FBI and even the CIA knew practically everything. The FBI reports of that period were rampant with references to Marilyn's involvement with both Kennedys. At least some of the information on the two affairs was developed by way of multiple taps on Monroe's phone. Several of the involved agencies also seem to have bugged Marilyn's Brentwood home as well as Peter Lawford's. The FBI reportedly used a surveillance operations expert Bernie Spindel to do its dirty work, aided by a former private investigator named Fred Otash. As a precaution against anyone breaking into her house to plant a hidden mic, Marilyn kept changing the locks on her doors. Other than Eunice Murray, the only person with keys to the residence was Joe DiMaggio. One might wonder what would have become of Robert Kennedy had DiMaggio paid a surprise visit and found the attorney general in bed with the actress.

One of the more explicit FBI reports to wind up in J. Edgar Hoover's hands was filed in October 1964, more than two years after Monroe's death. The report, pertaining to an undated party that took place at Peter Lawford's house, read as follows: "During the period of time that Robert Kennedy was having his sex affair with Marilyn Monroe, on one occasion a sex party was conducted at which several other persons were present. A tape recording was secretly made and is in the possession of a Los Angeles private detective agency. A certified copy of the recording has been made. All voices on the tape, including Kennedy's and Monroe's, are identifiable."

Others who were well aware of Bobby's fling with Monroe included select members of President Kennedy's White House staff. Historian Arthur Schlesinger, a speechwriter for JFK, later wrote what has come to be regarded as Robert F. Kennedy's definitive biography. When asked why the biography failed to mention RFK's affair with Monroe, Schlesinger pointed out that as a loyal friend to the family, he didn't wish to cause more anguish than they'd already endured. "That's not to say that it didn't happen," Schlesinger added. "It did happen. Bobby was human. He enjoyed a stiff drink now and then, and he liked attractive women. He indulged that side of his personality primarily when he traveled — and in his position as attorney general, he had to travel a good deal."

The evening of July 21, Joe DiMaggio drove Marilyn home from Cedars of Lebanon after yet another surgical procedure, performed by Dr. Leon Krohn, to alleviate some of the symptoms linked to her chronic endometriosis. Following the procedure, DiMaggio asked the physician if Marilyn could still have children. "It's possible," responded Krohn, "but not probable."

For better or worse, children or no children, Joe was determined to do whatever it took to convince Marilyn to commit to a mutually convenient wedding date. Before returning to the East Coast to complete his obligation to Monette, he once again broached the subject of marriage. Less enthusiastic than she'd been in their previous discussion but probably not eager to argue with Joe, Marilyn suggested he pick the time and place. He told Marilyn he wanted to marry her at Los Angeles city hall on August 8. He ordered food and champagne for a small reception to be held at Marilyn's house following the ceremony. Through his New York travel agent, he reserved two round-trip, first-class airplane tickets from Los Angeles to Rome. Besides Rome, they would honeymoon in Venice, Florence, and Sicily. Joe had always wanted to take Marilyn to Italy and show her the region of his parents' birth — and now he finally could.

That, at any rate, might have been one ending to the saga. There were other possibilities as well. But the ending that finally did evolve may well have been inevitable and most probably had been set in motion long before Marilyn first met Joe DiMaggio in mid-March 1952. The seeds of her slowly developing self-destruction had originated in a traumatic and loveless childhood marked most profoundly by a schizophrenic mother, an endless stream of indifferent foster families, a prisonlike orphanage, and the uncertainty associated with a pattern of continuing and constant abandonment on the part of nearly everyone she'd ever known and cared about. Her heightened sense of abandonment would once again come back to haunt her. Following her latest rendezvous with Bobby Kennedy, it became clear to the actress that something was terribly wrong.

That summer, Pierre Salinger saw the attorney general at the Kennedy compound in Massachusetts. "After a family dinner," said

Salinger, "Bobby invited me into his study for coffee, cognac, and an illegally obtained Cuban cigar. He knew I was familiar with the entire Marilyn Monroe mess, starting with Jack, and he wanted my advice. He'd recently seen her and discovered a notebook in her house with some scribblings in it on the Kennedys. And in addition, she was calling him all the time, at all hours of the day and night. He'd thought it over, and he realized he'd perhaps made a mistake, gone too far. Originally, he'd wanted to help her because of Jack, but now he wanted to bow out — gracefully, if possible."

Salinger recommended that for starters Bobby would do well to change his private telephone number.

"I've already done that," said RFK.

"Well, then, why not just call her up, and tell her the truth?"

"Why don't you call her for me?" said Kennedy.

"If you're not going to call her yourself," said Salinger, "then your best bet has to be Peter Lawford. He and Marilyn are great pals. He's known her for years. He'll know what to say."

It therefore fell on Peter Lawford, as it so often did, to clean up the mess left behind by one or another of the Kennedy brothers. "Pat invited Marilyn over for dinner," Lawford recalled. "We plied her with booze to make it easier on everyone. We blamed the breakup on Ethel. We told Marilyn she knew about the affair, which she probably did, and that she'd threatened to divorce Bobby. 'But then that's perfect,' Marilyn interjected. 'Bobby promised he'd divorce Ethel and marry me. So it works out perfectly.' I pointed out that Bobby was first and foremost a politician. After Jack, the presidential torch would be passed to Bobby, and a divorce would be the kiss of death. He'd never win the election. Marilyn blew up. 'He asked me to marry him and have his children,' she persisted. 'If he and Jack think they can pass me around like a football and then jilt me, they're sadly mistaken. I'm not one of those broads they bring into the White House for their daily swimming pool orgies.' The more she drank, the angrier she became. 'The Kennedys use you, and when they're done, they dispose of you like so much rubbish. Your former buddy Francis Sinatra warned me about them, but I didn't listen. He was right. And if the Kennedys think I'm going away, they're wrong.' "

Because Marilyn had put away so much alcohol, Peter thought it would be better for her to spend the night. He and Pat helped her into the guest bedroom. Peter woke up very early the next morning and found their guest in one of Pat's robes perched on the balcony staring into the pool below. "Are you all right?" Lawford asked her. She was crying. He led her into the house and prepared breakfast, and then he and Pat consoled her for hours. She was, as Lawford noted, "completely down on herself, talked about how ugly she felt, how worthless, how used and abused." Then she reiterated what she'd said the night before. She wasn't going away. She wasn't going to surrender. And then she said something that alarmed Peter.

Marilyn had decided to hold a press conference. She would tell the nation all about Jack and Bobby Kennedy — their extramarital affairs, their empty promises, and the way they used people and then discarded them. She had reams of documentation to support her charges, from correspondence to tape recordings. Jean Kennedy Smith had written to her, acknowledging the affair with her brother Bobby. She had all sorts of notes and letters on the same subject from Peter's wife. And then she had tapes of herself with the attorney general that would prove more than a little embarrassing, were they to be played. When Peter warned her that such a scandal could possibly bring down the government and hurt the country, Marilyn told him it could only help the country to know what its leaders were up to in their spare time.

"They're not going to fuck with me!" she vowed.

. . . .

Back in Brentwood, Marilyn's emotional tirade ran the gamut from hysterical weeping to uncontrollable rage. Like a child suffering a tantrum, she threw breakable objects against a wall — mirrors, plates, drinking glasses, anything she could lay her hands on. She spent hours spewing venom on the recording device she used for her free-association tapes for Dr. Greenson. Unable to sleep, she contacted Dr. Margaret Hohenberg, her former psychiatrist, currently residing in Haifa, Israel. They'd spoken several times earlier in the summer. In addition to the Kennedys, Marilyn complained to Hohenberg about Dr. Greenson. He'd tried to control her, cut her off from everyone she knew. He was a possessive, tyrannical figure, who could succeed as a therapist only in a place like Hollywood. She'd barely finished talking to Dr. Hohenberg when the phone rang. It was Milton Greene, whom she hadn't heard from in years. "I heard you're going through some difficult times," he said. "Do you want me to come out there?" "Yeah," responded Marilyn. "I can only stay a few days," said Greene, "because I have a photo assignment in Paris." It was all arranged, but then Marilyn called him back. "Never mind, I'm okay for the moment," she said. "You go

543

to Paris and then fly to LA. We'll be able to spend more time together." She concluded the conversation by telling her former business partner that she planned on moving back to New York. "I'm sick of Hollywood, and Hollywood's sick of me," she said.

Surprisingly, Monroe now turned to Mickey Song, the hairstylist who'd been present at Madison Square Garden the evening of President Kennedy's birthday gala. "I felt happy to hear from Marilyn, although I wasn't quite sure what she wanted," said Song. "She asked me over for a drink, and I thought maybe she wanted me to become her full-time hairstylist. Jazz musician Hank Jones happened to be visiting me, so I asked Marilyn if he could come as well. She didn't mind. She knew him because he'd accompanied her on the piano when she sang 'Happy Birthday' to JFK. So we drove to her house and found her in a state of despair."

Monroe wanted to talk about the Kennedys. As a member of their West Coast entourage, Song presumably knew where most of the bodies were buried. Marilyn asked for the names of other Hollywood actresses with whom the Kennedy brothers had been romantically linked.

"I told her I was privy to the same rumors as everybody else," said Song. "She didn't believe me, because she asked why I went out of my way to protect the Kennedys.

Didn't I feel used by them? They used everyone, she said, and I was no exception. I told her I didn't feel used. On the contrary, they'd afforded me opportunities I wouldn't otherwise have had, such as a trip to the White House to cut the president's hair before a state dinner when his regular barber was out of town. I had the impression that Marilyn felt emotionally abused by Jack and Bobby and was trying to dig up dirt on them. She interrogated me for an hour or so, then turned to Hank Jones and began interrogating him. After a while, he said to her, 'I don't know what the Kennedys did to you, but you ought to let it go. Life's too short.' "

Neither Song nor Jones realized that Marilyn had secretly taped their conversation. "I learned that she'd hired a private investigator to install a hidden recording device in both her bedroom and living room. She'd amassed an entire inventory of tapes containing conversations with nearly everyone, including Bobby Kennedy. It's illegal to do that in California. After she died, Peter Lawford got hold of the tapes and presumably destroyed them."

Peter Lawford had been placed in an unwelcome and untenable position of middleman between Marilyn and the Kennedys. Related to the Kennedy clan by marriage, he also considered himself one of Monroe's closest and most stalwart friends. Nevertheless, concerned about her threat to hold a press conference in which she planned to divulge details of her love affairs with the president and the attorney general, Lawford felt he had no choice but to call Bobby Kennedy and discuss the matter with him. "I didn't know if my own phone was bugged," said Lawford, "so I called from a public phone booth. Bobby was alarmed by what I told him. He finally realized the potential danger he and his brother faced having become involved with an exceedingly famous but thoroughly unstable woman. He advised me to phone her shrink, who would surely be able to quiet her down. So I called Dr. Greenson.

"Marilyn had already informed him as to her curt dismissal by RFK. She'd placed numerous phone calls to him at the Justice Department, none of which he'd returned. The problem was that she'd constructed an entire romantic fantasy in her mind, which initially involved the president; after Bobby entered the picture, she made him the focus of her fantasy. In her disoriented state, she had difficulty discerning the difference between fantasy and reality. What worried Greenson was that in the past, Marilyn often made suicide threats and would fake a suicide attempt in order to gain sympathy. The one person Greenson felt could truly help Marilyn was Joe DiMaggio, but because the situation centered on Marilyn's imagined desire to marry Bobby Kennedy, he couldn't bring himself to involve DiMaggio."

An event that ordinarily would have elevated Marilyn's mood took place in July 1962. An exuberant Mickey Rudin contacted her with what he considered wonderful news: Peter Levathes had revived Monroe's contract with Fox, offering to double her previous salary and agreeing to restart shooting on *Something's Got to Give.* Rudin subsequently told Ralph Greenson about the offer, and Greenson relayed the information to Peter Lawford.

"I went to Marilyn's house to congratulate her in person," said Lawford. "She looked pretty grim. All she could talk about were the Kennedys. So I told her I was going to Cal-Neva Lodge at Lake Tahoe for the weekend. I invited her along thinking some peace and quiet and a change in scenery might cheer her up. 'We'll celebrate your new contract,' I said. She brightened a bit. 'Thanks, Peter,' she replied. 'You're a good man, and there aren't many like you.' "

CHAPTER 20

Peace and quiet were not commodities in great supply at the Cal-Neva, a resort and gambling casino that attracted the Rat Pack, the Mafia, and an assortment of high rollers and heavy drinkers. Before departing Los Angeles, Marilyn received a hypodermic injection courtesy of Dr. Hyman Engelberg and a fresh supply of barbiturates and sedatives as prescribed by Dr. Greenson. Besides the new supply, Marilyn had stocked her suitcase with an arsenal of pharmaceuticals taken from her medicine cabinet. She'd been taking pills for so long, she told a fellow resort guest, that only high doses had any effect.

Marilyn had spent a day at Cal-Neva with the Lawfords earlier in the month and had swallowed enough pills to knock herself out. She'd left her telephone line open to the resort switchboard, and when the operator heard her labored breathing, she located the Lawfords, who rushed to the room to find

Marilyn unconscious on the floor next to the bed. Peter and Pat alternated cups of coffee with walks around the room until Monroe regained her senses. Frank Sinatra flew her back to Los Angeles that night in his private plane.

Joe DiMaggio had heard about the earlier Cal-Neva incident and blamed Sinatra and Skinny D'Amato, who'd left the 500 Club in Atlantic City to manage Cal-Neva, for plying Marilyn with alcohol. When Inez Melson, MM's business manager, apprised Joe of Marilyn's departure for the Lake Tahoe gambling resort, he made immediate arrangements to follow her there. To avoid a confrontation with Sinatra, he checked into the nearby Silver Crest Motor Hotel and surprised Marilyn when he walked into the Cal-Neva dining room, where she was seated with the Lawfords.

"We were eating dinner, and in marched Joe DiMaggio," said Peter Lawford. "It was the first time in a long time I'd seen Marilyn crack a big smile. She leaped out of her chair and embraced DiMaggio for what must have been a good five minutes. To be honest, Pat and I were delighted to see him because it took the onus of responsibility for her well-being out of our hands. DiMaggio spent the night with her in one of the bungalows on the property. He had some business to attend to on Saturday afternoon and disappeared for several hours, which was when Marilyn again became very despondent and testy. She started drinking and taking pills. She also renewed her threat to 'get even' with the Kennedys. I took this to mean she still planned to give a press conference. She quieted down only when DiMaggio returned. We spent Sunday morning, July 29, by the swimming pool. Sam Giancana came by with a few assistant hoods, if I can call them that. He knew DiMaggio, and the two of them chatted for a while. After they departed, Marilyn said something that in retrospect seemed rather prophetic. She talked about growing old and wasn't sure she wanted to go through it. 'What's worse than an aging sex symbol?' she asked. 'Everything — breasts, belly, bottom — begins to sag.' "

That Sunday night, Joe DiMaggio accompanied Marilyn and the Lawfords back to Los Angeles before continuing on to San Francisco, still secure in his conviction that he and Marilyn would be remarried on August 8. "Marilyn never uttered a word to me concerning her intention to rewed Joe DiMaggio," remarked Peter Lawford. "I heard about it after she died. I have to believe this was DiMaggio's fantasy, not Marilyn's. Her fantasy resided in the hope that Bobby Kennedy would change his mind, and *they* would walk down the aisle together. And if that didn't happen, she intended to bring him down. To preclude this eventuality, Pat and I were determined to stick as close to Marilyn as possible."

On July 30 the Lawfords joined Marilyn and Pat Newcomb for dinner at La Scala. At another table, across the room, sat a New York publicist named Connie Stanville and Billy Travilla, Monroe's former fashion designer. "Billy and I were good friends," said Stanville. "We would have dinner together whenever I found myself on the coast. So we were dining at La Scala when I spotted this woman on the opposite side of the restaurant. She looked very thin and wore no makeup. 'Isn't that Marilyn Monroe?' I asked. Billy gazed in the woman's direction and said, 'I think it is.' When we finished our meal, we went over to her table. It was Marilyn, all right, but she didn't look well. In fact, she looked stoned and glassy eyed. She stared at Billy but obviously didn't recognize him. He asked her how she was doing, and she smiled but said nothing. After a minute or two, she asked, 'Billy, is that you?' We left the restaurant and headed for the street. Billy seemed hurt and upset. He couldn't believe she hadn't recognized him. They'd been very close at one point. In fact, they'd had a brief affair. He called me the next day and said he was going to write her a nasty letter. Marilyn died a few days later. Billy called me again. 'Thank God I didn't write that letter,' he said. 'Thank God!' "

In the late afternoon of August 1, Marilyn called Ralph Roberts and asked him to take her to Largo, a Los Angeles nightspot with a strip club on one side of the establishment and a gay bar on the other. "Largo was a bit sleazy," said Roberts, "but it was unique in that it catered to both heterosexuals and gays. You had a lot of straight men watching the young female strippers on the club side, and a whole gay crowd — men and women — packed into an adjacent bar. The bar had a jukebox and a small dance floor. The men danced with men, the women with women. A soundproof wall separated the bar from the strip club.

"I picked up Marilyn at her house and learned that Jeanne Carmen would be joining us. Marilyn gave me a drink and poured herself one as well. We stepped outside into the garden, which was illuminated by a floodlight. She told me she'd been to a shop on Santa Monica Boulevard in West Hollywood, where she'd acquired a few items of furniture and a wall hanging depicting Adam and Eve in the Garden of Eden. From her local nursery she'd also purchased three more citrus trees and a half dozen rose bushes that were supposed to be delivered on August 4. I found this a bit odd in light of the fact that she kept telling me she intended to leave Los

Angeles and move back to New York."

By this time, Jeanne Carmen had arrived, and the three of them set off for Largo. "En route," continued Roberts, "Jeanne started talking about Robert Kennedy, which I didn't think was a great idea. She said Bobby and Marilyn had frequently engaged in phone sex. 'Can't you just see the attorney general jerking his chain while Marilyn talked him through the sex act?' To change the subject, I asked Marilyn about Joe DiMaggio. She said he and his brothers Vince and Dom had agreed to participate in an Old Timers' charity baseball game in San Francisco on August 4 and that he'd be joining her again in Los Angeles a day later. To which Jeanne said, 'Yeah, but he bugged your phone just like the rest of them.' 'If that's true,' responded Marilyn, 'it's because he wants to protect me. Listen, if it weren't for Joe, I'd probably have killed myself years ago.' "

Those were Marilyn's last coherent words that evening. When they reached Largo, Marilyn — in her usual disguise — headed straight for the bar, ordered three bottles of champagne, handed one each to Ralph and Jeanne, chugalugged the third herself, ordered another, grabbed Jeanne's hand, and hit the dance floor.

"I spent the better part of the night," said Roberts, "standing at the bar, declining offers to dance from a variety of men in leather and chains. When I drove Marilyn home at three in the morning, her eyes were vacant. She looked like a zombie. She was drunk and drugged. The sight of her in that woeful state, as she wobbled out of the car and into her house, saddened and haunted me. After that night, we spoke on the phone once or twice, but I never saw Marilyn again."

That summer, Marlon Brando and Marilyn communicated by telephone every few days. In his autobiography, *Songs My Mother Taught Me*, Brando claims they often spoke for hours. They frequently discussed the prospect of doing a film together. Another favorite subject was Lee Strasberg — both actors agreed he'd used them to further his own reputation. Brando and Monroe conversed for the last time in August, when she called to invite him over for dinner together with his great pal Wally Cox. Cox, a cast member of *Something's Got to Give,* had established a separate friendship with Marilyn. Brando told her he and Wally had a previous engagement but that he would call her the following week to set something up. "Fine," she said. He noted that she didn't sound depressed. For that matter, she sounded healthier emotionally than she'd sounded in months.

She also called Dr. Leon Krohn, her gynecologist, and asked him over for dinner. He accepted, but after hanging up, she called him back and said she wanted to have him to dinner the same night as Marlon Brando — she wanted the two to meet. She told Krohn she'd call him back the following week.

That evening, she ate dinner by herself at La Scala. When she returned home, she called Norman Rosten and Kurt Lamprecht, both in New York. She told each of them that she and Joe DiMaggio were probably going to marry again. "I wondered," said Lamprecht, "if this was simply some passing romantic notion, or whether it would really come to pass. What was predictable about Marilyn Monroe is that she was totally unpredictable."

Norman Rosten, with whom she spoke for more than thirty minutes, thought she sounded high on drugs. She prattled on and on, barely pausing for a breath, skipping from one subject to another, repeatedly returning to Joe DiMaggio and the topic of marriage. Monroe and Rosten had once made a deal that if either one ever felt like jumping off a bridge, he or she would first notify the other. Rosten sensed no such urgency in Marilyn's voice, only perhaps a bit of forced joy.

Next Marilyn called Lotte Goslar. "She sounded extremely positive at first," said Goslar. "She had all sorts of plans in the works. First of all, there was her new house. She'd never owned a house before, and she loved furnishing and decorating it. Then there was

Something's Got to Give, which would soon resume production with Marilyn once again in the lead role. And Jack Benny, on whose television show she'd once appeared, had asked her to join him in a monthlong Las Vegas revue that would net her nearly $1 million. She still wanted to visit Russia and was now thinking of going to China and Japan as well. She was reading Harper Lee's *To Kill a Mockingbird.* She'd just bought an Italian cookbook so she could learn to prepare deep-dish pizza for Joe DiMaggio. They were seriously considering the possibility of getting remarried, so much so that she'd gone ahead and ordered a wedding dress from Jean Louis, the same designer who'd fashioned the gown she wore at Madison Square Garden the night of President Kennedy's birthday shindig. She wanted to know what I thought of the idea. I assured her I was all for it. I always had been. Of all the men she'd known, he remained the one who loved her the most and was most capable of providing her with an emotional anchor. And she, in turn, understood him. She maintained a good sense of humor about him. I remember she gave him a record album of the Great Caruso performing a selection of arias, which he never unwrapped. 'Joe,' she kidded him, 'you're the only Italian I've ever met who doesn't love opera.' 'I love you,' he responded, 'and you're more than enough for me.'

"My conversation with Marilyn ended on an ominous note. Before marrying Joe, she vowed to hold a press conference in which she would *out* the Kennedys, expose them for what they were — a pair of womanizers, users and abusers. I told her I'd support whatever she chose to do, though I personally felt it was a mistake. What possible benefit could she derive from publicly humiliating the Kennedys? I had no idea, of course, that this was to be our final conversation. In retrospect, I realized Marilyn had a long and complicated history of feigned suicide attempts. She was like the boy who cried 'wolf' one too many times. She had a death wish but didn't want to die. And in the end, not even Joe DiMaggio could save her. Nobody could."

On Friday, August 3, Peter Lawford again went to dinner with Marilyn and Pat Newcomb. Pat Lawford had departed for Hyannis Port the day before. Over dinner the actress continued her obsessive rant about Bobby Kennedy, complaining that he hadn't even had the common decency to apologize for his actions. Although he tried, Peter Lawford wasn't able to assuage his dinner companion's feelings. By the end of the meal, she was practically screaming.

At home later, unable to sleep, Marilyn resolved to speak to Bobby, even if it meant instigating the conversation herself. She phoned Peter, and he told her the attorney general was scheduled to be in San Francisco that weekend before giving an address there on Monday to a meeting of the American Bar Association. Noting the coincidence of Kennedy's being in the same town as Joe DiMaggio, Marilyn asked where RFK would be staying. Lawford didn't know, but he thought his wife might, and he gave Marilyn Pat's number at the Kennedy compound in Massachusetts. The movie star called. Pat Lawford told her to try to reach Bobby at San Francisco's St. Francis Hotel.

Marilyn left several messages for RFK at the St. Francis, which is where a lawyers' group had booked rooms for the attorney general, his wife, and four of their children. But the Kennedy family was staying at the ranch of John Bates, a wealthy attorney (and president of the California Bar Association) who lived in Gilroy, some eighty miles south of San Francisco. Marilyn at last heard back from Bobby; after a brief and somewhat caustic conversation, he agreed to see her the following day.

Marilyn had demanded a full-scale, face-to-face explanation from her lover as to why she'd been abandoned. Bobby would now give it to her. Early Saturday morning, August 4, he flew to Los Angeles. From the airport he took a helicopter to the Twentieth Century–Fox lot, where Peter Lawford picked him up and drove him back to his house.

At eleven thirty, Lawford called Marilyn to say that he and Bobby would be at her place no later than two in the afternoon. It had already been a busy morning for Monroe. At eight in the morning, Pat Newcomb, having spent the night in the guest bedroom at the Brentwood house, drove Marilyn to Dr. Greenson's home for a ninety-minute therapy session. The actress complained that Newcomb had "slept like a baby," while she'd suffered her usual bout of insomnia. Overwrought because of her lack of sleep and Robert Kennedy's impending visit, Marilyn convinced her psychiatrist to renew several of her barbiturate prescriptions, including one for chloral hydrate as well as another for Nembutal. She made no mention of the fact that on July 25, Fox's Dr. Lee Siegel had given her two prescriptions for Nembutal, neither of which she'd filled as yet. Alarmed by Marilyn's current state of mind, Greenson also called Dr. Engelberg and suggested he see the patient. Engelberg, who'd visited with (and injected) her the day before, was waiting for her when she returned home. Under the impression that Marilyn had run out of barbiturates, Engelberg administered a combination vitamin-barbiturate injection and wrote her a prescription for twenty-five additional Nembutal. When later asked by authorities why he'd given her a prescription for Nembutal without notifying Greenson, Dr. Engelberg replied that he'd been having problems with his estranged wife and hadn't had time to report back to Monroe's psychiatrist. Over the years, Engelberg's version of events continually changed. The only explanation he failed to provide for his overt willingness to overmedicate the movie star was that he had, like so many other men, fallen victim to her charms.

Pat Newcomb, her throat suddenly sore, departed Marilyn's home shortly after Dr. Engelberg's arrival. When Engelberg left, Lawrence Schiller, a photographer who'd worked with Marilyn on *Something's Got to Give,* drove by and gave the actress photo stills from the unfinished film, a number of which appeared in Norman Mailer's 1973 biography of Monroe. Eunice Murray, scheduled to sleep over on Saturday night (Dr. Greenson insisted that Monroe was never to be left alone), greeted Schiller and then drove to the pharmacy to fill the various prescriptions Marilyn had collected from her three physicians. When she returned, she fielded a call from Isidore Miller, who wanted to speak to his former daughter-in-law. He'd spoken to her two days earlier, and Marilyn had assured him, "Dad, I feel fine." In response to his August 4 call, Mrs. Murray told Isidore that Marilyn would have to call him back. She never did. Mrs. Murray was quick to notice that in her absence Marilyn had downed half a bottle of champagne and several Nembutal tablets from an old prescription. A major dilemma in the management of Marilyn's self-medication regimen was that she often forgot how many pills she'd previously taken and would simply take them again — and again.

Bobby Kennedy and Peter Lawford arrived at Marilyn's house at two in the afternoon. "In anticipation of our arrival," recalled Lawford, "Marilyn had set out a buffet consisting of guacamole, stuffed mushrooms, Greek olives, and Swedish meatballs, plus a chilled magnum of bubbly. I poured myself a glass and wandered out to the swimming pool so Marilyn and Bobby could talk. Within minutes, I heard shouting. I returned to the kitchen, where they were having it out. Bobby maintained he was going to leave and return with me to my house. Marilyn insisted he spend the rest of the day alone with her."

They argued back and forth for a good ten minutes, Marilyn — semipolluted and high on drugs — becoming more and more hysterical. At the height of her anger, she allowed how first thing Monday morning she was going to call a press conference and reveal the details of the treatment she'd suffered at the hands of the Kennedy brothers. At this point, Bobby Kennedy became livid. He told her in no uncertain terms that she would have to leave both Jack and him alone — no more telephone calls, no letters, no threats, nothing. They didn't want to hear from her again.

"He would've probably said a lot more," remarked Lawford, "had I not prewarned him that she might be using a hidden tape recorder. As it is, she went batshit. She absolutely lost it, screaming obscenities and heaving the contents of her half-filled glass of champagne at Bobby, but drenching me instead. I'd moved in close to Bobby in case I had to separate them, and Marilyn's drink splattered against my face rather than his. Marilyn apologized and handed me a napkin. Bobby was already halfway out the door. I caught up to him. After we drove off, RFK suggested we contact Marilyn's psychiatrist — maybe he could help her. So I pulled into a service station and called Dr. Greenson from a public phone booth. I described the scene that had just taken place. Greenson thanked me and said he'd drive over to see Marilyn."

Bobby Kennedy said little as Lawford drove in the direction of his Santa Monica beach house. "Needless to say, he wasn't a happy camper," observed Lawford. "I don't think he thought Marilyn would go through with her press conference threat, but Bobby wasn't the kind of guy who liked to lose control of a situation. 'Well, nobody can say I didn't try,' he ventured. 'She's crazy — it's tragic.' Indeed, by the end, Marilyn had slid into a psychiatric pit. She'd always been afraid of winding up like her schizophrenic mother. And in a sense, that's what was happening.

"As for Bobby, once we reached my house, he made a telephone call, and a government car picked him up a few minutes later. So far as I know, he flew back to San Francisco, because Monday morning he gave his little talk before the bar association. Once the press started nosing around, John Bates, at whose ranch he stayed, swore up and down that Bobby had never left his place and barely knew Marilyn Monroe. Nobody believed him."

Eunice Murray opened the door for Ralph Greenson at four in the afternoon. He found Marilyn in far worse shape than she'd been that morning. He attributed her despondency in part to the interaction of the medications in her system in addition to the train wreck of the near violent confrontation with Robert Kennedy.

Ralph Roberts called Marilyn's house at about four thirty in the afternoon. "Dr. Greenson answered," said Roberts. "I asked to speak with Marilyn. 'Who's calling?' he asked, as if he didn't recognize my voice by now. I identified myself. 'Ralph,' he said, 'this is Dr. Greenson. Marilyn is not here at the moment, and I don't know when she'll be back.' It made no sense. What would Greenson be doing in her house if she wasn't around?"

Greenson stayed with Marilyn until five and then departed to attend a dinner party with his wife. Before he left, he suggested to Eunice Murray that she take Marilyn for a drive along the Pacific Coast Highway. It would relax her. They drove around for an hour, and when they returned, the phone rang. It was Peter Lawford. Apparently suffering an attack of conscience, he wondered how Marilyn was doing. "Better," she said. Did she want to come to his place for dinner? He'd send out for Mexican food and maybe ask a few friends to join them, perhaps play a little poker.

"Is Bobby Kennedy still with you?" she asked.

"He left," Lawford replied. "I'm all alone."

Marilyn thanked Peter for the dinner invitation but told him she felt tired. "I think I'll eat a sandwich, take my pills, and try to sleep," she said.

As soon as she'd hung up with Lawford, Marilyn's phone rang again. It was Joe DiMaggio Jr. calling from his marine base in San Diego. "I told Marilyn I'd broken my engagement to Pamela," he recalled. "She seemed delighted to hear it. She never liked the girl and suggested I was too young to get

564

married. 'But you were only sixteen when you first got married,' I reminded her. 'Yeah — and divorced before you could blink an eye,' she answered. I thought she sounded a bit spacey, but nothing out of the ordinary — not for her, at any rate. She didn't sound depressed. On the other hand, I later realized she would've done and said almost anything to protect me, to prevent me from seeing her at her worst.

"The one subject that didn't come up in our conversation was the possibility that she and my father might remarry. I never mentioned it, and neither did she. I don't know what she had in mind; whether she intended to go through with it or not. I don't think she herself knew what she intended to do. That's Marilyn for you: fey, capricious, unpredictable. And when you get down to it, those were the very qualities that my father loved about her. He was stiff, regimented, and set in his ways; she was elusive, unmanageable, a creature from another realm.

"Our conversation lasted about fifteen minutes. Had I known what she was about to do to herself, I would've kept her on the phone forever."

At approximately seven o'clock, Peter Lawford called Milt Ebbins, his business manager.

"I'd flown with Marilyn, Pat Newcomb, and Peter from Los Angeles to New York in May when she sang 'Happy Birthday, Mr.

President' at Madison Square Garden," said Ebbins. "Peter introduced her that evening with the words 'Mr. President, I give you the *late* Marilyn Monroe.' He meant she'd been delayed coming onstage, but in retrospect it takes on a much darker meaning. In any event, I knew all about her and the Kennedy boys and how they'd shamelessly exploited her. I wasn't surprised to hear what had transpired when Robert Kennedy went over there to deliver the final kiss-off. Peter and I spoke for a few minutes and made plans to get together the following day. Then, about an hour later, he called me back. He said Marilyn had just phoned. She appeared to be in bad shape, slurring her words and whatnot. She sounded a million miles away. And that's when she made that now classic little farewell speech of hers. 'Say good-bye to Pat, say good-bye to the president, say good-bye to yourself because you've been a good guy.' Then her line went dead."

Peter Lawford wanted Milt Ebbins to call Marilyn to make sure she was okay. He gave Ebbins her phone number. Ebbins called. The line was busy. Fifteen minutes later, he tried again. Busy. He asked the telephone operator to check the line. The operator reported that Monroe's phone appeared to be out of order. Ebbins got back in touch with Lawford and explained that he hadn't been able to get through. Alarmed by the possibility that something had happened to Marilyn, Lawford told Ebbins he'd drive to her house and look in on her. Ebbins stopped him by suggesting that he — Ebbins — contact Mickey Rudin, Marilyn's lawyer. When he reached Rudin, the attorney said to Ebbins, "Tell Peter to stay put. I'll check it out and get back to you."

"As I understand it," claimed Ebbins, "Rudin had seen Ralph Greenson, his brother-in-law, earlier that day, and Greenson had been quite concerned about Marilyn. For his part, Rudin was convinced that Marilyn was a very sick girl: totally insane, for that matter. He felt Greenson had done everything he possibly could to help her and could do no more. In any case, Rudin had a second private telephone number for Marilyn's house. He dialed it, and Eunice Murray picked up. She said Marilyn appeared to be fine. Murray could hear the radio on in her bedroom, and under the doorway she could see that the light hadn't been turned off. She'd probably fallen asleep and, as was later discovered, dropped her Princess phone on the floor. It happened all the time. Rudin asked Murray to enter the bedroom to make certain Marilyn was asleep. Murray said she'd tried to get into the bedroom a few minutes earlier, but the door was locked from within.

"Does she usually lock her door?" asked Rudin.

"No," responded Murray. "Not usually, but she does on occasion."

Rudin later expressed regret that he hadn't probed deeper, but under the circumstances, he thought MM had merely fallen asleep. He called back Milt Ebbins and then went out for dinner with his wife. Ebbins phoned Peter Lawford. "Maybe you ought to drive over there after all," he suggested. Lawford said he would wait until the next day and then go to see her.

In the end, it was Eunice Murray who felt most uneasy about Marilyn. Waking up after a few hours of fitful sleep, she went back to Marilyn's bedroom. Nothing had changed. The radio and light were still on, and the door remained locked. She knocked at the door and called Marilyn's name. No answer. She went outside and peered through a bedroom window. Marilyn unfailingly drew her blinds upon retiring, but to Murray's surprise, they were wide open. The actress lay naked and motionless atop her bed, an arm extended, her eyes shut, mouth agape. Her position and appearance startled Murray. She returned to the house and immediately called Ralph Greenson, who'd returned home hours earlier. Something seemed terribly amiss with Marilyn, she told him, but she didn't know exactly what. Greenson phoned Hyman Engelberg. Apologizing for the lateness of the hour — it was one thirty in the morning — Greenson quickly explained the reason for his call. Twenty minutes later, the two physicians stood in front of the entrance to Marilyn Monroe's house.

"Eunice Murray let us in," said Dr. Engelberg. "Because Marilyn's bedroom door was locked, we grabbed a poker from the living room fireplace, walked outside, broke her bedroom window, undid the latch, lifted the window, and climbed into the room. Marilyn was sprawled across the bed. We were obviously too late, but we worked on her for more than an hour trying somehow to bring her back to life. I estimated she'd been dead since nine or ten p.m. Afterward we just sat there, silent and sullen. We were stunned. I have no idea how much time elapsed. Then we talked a little, and that's when it emerged she'd received sleeping medication from both of us. But even if we hadn't both medicated her with Nembutal, there were enough pill bottles in her medicine cabinet and on her night table to have killed a herd of cattle. The police confiscated no fewer than fifteen bottles of tranquilizers, sedatives, and sleeping pills from her house following her death, among them Seconal and chloral hydrate, both of which she probably procured during her visit to Mexico earlier that year. Still, I can't say I wasn't worried about covering my ass. Had Marilyn died ten years later, when authorities began paying attention to overdoses and their causes, Dr. Greenson and I could well have ended up together in a jail cell, our medical licenses revoked, our careers ruined."

At three in the morning, Ralph Greenson phoned Mickey Rudin and gave him the news. Marilyn Monroe was dead, the victim of an apparent suicide. Rudin climbed out of bed, dressed, and drove to Marilyn's home, arriving at approximately the same time as Arthur Jacobs, head of the publicity firm that represented Marilyn. Rudin had called Jacobs earlier that evening, reaching him in the middle of a concert at the Hollywood Bowl. Hearing that Marilyn might be in trouble, Jacobs had left the concert and gone home to await further word. Now, like the others, he was staring at Marilyn's lifeless body. Pat Newcomb, who worked for Jacobs, had likewise been notified and arrived at Monroe's home shortly after four in the morning.

"When I got there," recalled Mickey Rudin, "Romey Greenson took me aside and whispered, 'Engelberg gave her a prescription I didn't know about.' I didn't want to get in the middle of it, so I kept my mouth shut. Mrs. Murray looked exhausted. She was doing the laundry. I couldn't figure out why. I guessed it was Marilyn's bedding and underclothes from the day before. I asked Dr. Engelberg whether anyone had called the police. Nobody had done that, so I asked him to place the call, which he did."

Jack Clemmons, a sergeant with the West Los Angeles branch of the LAPD, was the first police officer to arrive on the scene, setting foot in Marilyn's Brentwood home at 4:50 a.m. Like Hyman Engelberg, he discerned that the actress had been dead since the evening hours of August 4. He started asking questions — he wanted to know why they'd waited so long before contacting the police.

"We felt we had to first get clearance from Twentieth Century–Fox's publicity department," responded Greenson.

"The cop shot Dr. Greenson an unbelieving glance," said Hyman Engelberg. "I mean, this bloke was a regular Sherlock Holmes. He had it all figured out. Not that Greenson's explanation was true or made any sense, but this fellow had already determined that Marilyn hadn't died by her own hand. In the days, weeks, and months that followed, he never deviated from that opinion, telling anyone who'd listen that Marilyn Monroe had been killed, that her corpse had been taken from her bedroom, then returned several hours later. This theory, propounded by any number of conspiracy buffs, finally brought forth an ambulance driver who claimed he'd been summoned to the Monroe residence and had carted Marilyn's body off into the night. Mind you, not a shred of evidence, not a scintilla, supported any of this. It was pure conjecture. The cop was eventually dismissed by the Los Angeles Police Department for continuing to hawk his mawkish tale. I have no clue what became of the ambulance driver. I do know that an entire mythology was created around Marilyn's death, part of which had to do with the so-called little red diary, which supposedly contained all sorts of state secrets that had been conveyed to Marilyn by the Kennedys. We were told by the myth makers that Bobby Kennedy himself somehow got hold of the diary and disposed of it by dumping it in the Potomac."

According to Dr. Engelberg, the five-hour autopsy performed on Monroe later that day — August 5 — did little to establish the exact cause of death. Thomas Noguchi, otherwise known as "the coroner to the stars," conducted the autopsy. Surprisingly, he found no trace of barbiturates in Marilyn's stomach lining or digestive tract and reported no evidence of needle puncture wounds, despite the fact that Dr. Engelberg had given her three separate injections over the last four days of her life. Calling Monroe's death "a probable suicide," Noguchi was widely criticized for having conducted an incomplete and inconclusive autopsy of Monroe, including the issuance of a merely partial toxicological report. Most notable was his failure to test Marilyn's small intestine to determine the presence of barbiturates and alcohol. Nor did it help that an entire set of Marilyn's tissue slides disappeared at some point during the autopsy, making it even more difficult to determine a definitive cause of death.

"There's no question that Marilyn killed herself," said Peter Lawford. "But as with the assassination of John F. Kennedy in 1963, there were those that couldn't accept the obvious. There had to be some other, more sinister, and convoluted explanation. Lee Harvey Oswald, a virtual nobody, couldn't possibly have killed the president of the United States without help from some higher authority. In Marilyn's case, the most popular alternative theme had it that Bobby Kennedy hired a couple of hit men to dispose of his former lover because of her threat to hold a press conference wherein she would reveal the salacious details of their affair as well as her tryst with the president. So what! There were dozens of women who could've made more or less the same claim. It was clear to anyone with half a brain that Marilyn Monroe, at age thirty-six, had inadvertently taken her own life."

Joe DiMaggio didn't disappoint. On the afternoon of August 4, the day he and his two brothers took part in an Old Timers' charity baseball game in San Francisco, the forty-seven-year-old former star center fielder for the New York Yankees thrilled thirty thousand spectators by belting a soaring home run into the left-field bleachers. After the game, the Yanks, having sponsored the event, presented the Clipper with a Wittnauer wristwatch inscribed with his name. That evening, Joe, Lefty O'Doul and O'Doul's stepson, Jimmy, plus a couple of Lefty's pals, went out to dinner and then on to the 365 Club, best known for its comely chorus line of showgirls. Aware of DiMaggio's plans to remarry Marilyn Monroe, Lefty O'Doul said to him, "Think of tonight as your bachelor party."

Regretting that he hadn't called Marilyn that night, Joe retired shortly after two in the morning. Five hours later, the phone rang in his Beach Street home. Dr. Hyman Engelberg was calling from Marilyn's Brentwood residence. The connection was poor, but DiMaggio made out the words "a terrible accident" and "Marilyn's dead, I'm sorry."

Not yet in shock, DiMaggio called Inez Melson. Marilyn's business manager had just heard the news from Mickey Rudin and was about to call Joe when he called her. After speaking with Melson, DiMaggio phoned Harry Hall and asked his old friend to pick him up at the airport in Los Angeles. He'd try to catch the nine o'clock United Airlines flight in the morning.

"To be honest," said Mickey Rudin, "none

574

of us knew what to do. I contacted Aaron Frosch in New York, but he didn't know what to do either. Marilyn's mother was locked away in a mental hospital, so we couldn't turn to her. I called Inez Melson and got a phone number in Florida for Berniece Miracle, Marilyn's half sister, but she wasn't around. Ultimately we took the cowards' way out: we turned to Joe DiMaggio."

Harry Hall picked Joe up at the airport at ten o'clock and drove him to the Los Angeles County Morgue, where he and Inez Melson officially identified Marilyn's body. He signed the forms to have the body released for autopsy purposes, after which it would be transported to the mortuary at Westwood Memorial Park Cemetery, where Marilyn often indicated she wanted to be interred after her death. Hall then drove Joe to the Miramar Hotel. Checking into suite 1035, DiMaggio locked the door behind him and called his son. Joe Jr. arrived at the Miramar in the early afternoon. He found his father seated on the bed, his shoulders "stooped with grief." As he sat there, said Joey, "a sound came out of him, an inhuman sound, almost like the roar of a lion. He then bent over and started to weep in deep gulps and gasps. We were alone at the time. Harry Hall had gone out to buy some booze. He returned with a couple of bottles of scotch and vodka. My father stopped crying, but he refused to drink. In addition, he refused to speak to the press. They kept calling the hotel for a comment. He instructed the front desk manager to hold his calls, except for Inez Melson and Berniece Miracle. Burying Marilyn would prove to be the most difficult thing my father ever had to do."

Joe sent Berniece Miracle a telegram, requesting permission to make the final funeral arrangements. He wanted a small, simple, very private service for Marilyn, with "none of the usual Hollywood crowd." Berniece agreed and granted him power of attorney to carry out his plan. Later that day, Joe, Joe Jr., and Harry Hall drove out to Monroe's Brentwood house. The police were still there. "It was terribly depressing, what with all of Marilyn's books, phonograph records, clothes, and furs still in place, as if she'd merely gone to the corner to buy a newspaper," recalled Joey. "Maf, her little dog, eventually wound up with Frank Sinatra's secretary. After looking around, we headed for Marilyn's bedroom and located some of her correspondence and personal papers. My father rifled through the bundle, pausing here and there to read this or that. I have no idea what he was looking for. I don't think he knew, either."

Joe's face suddenly brightened. He'd come across a short letter Marilyn had recently written to him but never mailed: "Dear Joe,

576

If I can only succeed in making you happy — I will have succeeded in the biggest and most difficult thing there is — that is to make *one person completely happy.* Your happiness means my happiness. Marilyn." DiMaggio neatly folded the handwritten note and slipped it into a pocket.

Berniece Miracle arrived in Los Angeles the following afternoon, Monday, August 6, and took a cab to the Miramar, where she, Joe, and Inez Melson went over DiMaggio's list of funeral guests. They then issued a statement to the press, which read in part: "Last rites for Marilyn Monroe must of great necessity be as private as possible so that she can go to her final resting place in the quiet she always sought." On Tuesday morning, Berniece and Inez Melson met with Eunice Murray at Marilyn's home to select an appropriate burial gown for the actress. From her wardrobe closet they chose a chic, long-sleeved, apple green Pucci gown that Marilyn had last worn in February, while visiting Mexico.

That same evening, Whitey Snyder and his wife, Marjorie, arrived at the Westwood Memorial Park mortuary, where Marilyn's body was being kept. After Whitey's wife dressed the actress in the green gown selected for the somber occasion, Whitey began applying makeup, gradually transforming Marilyn's death mask into a glowing presence.

Agnes Flanagan came in to work on Marilyn's hair. Assessing the damage done to the deceased's scalp during the autopsy, she opted for a hand-styled blond wig similar in appearance to the hairdo worn by Marilyn in her most recent films.

"Joe DiMaggio sat in the cool, dark room and quietly watched as the three of us attended to Marilyn," said Whitey Snyder. "He simply stared at Marilyn's face, his body bent slightly forward toward her, his hands clasped tightly in his lap. He didn't move. We finished our work about eleven at night and left the mortuary. Joe remained behind. Because of her funeral on Wednesday, August 8, I decided to return to the mortuary in the early morning to retouch Marilyn's face. Joe was still there, in the same spot, having obviously spent the night alone with Marilyn as she lay in her open, bronze casket lined with champagne-colored satin. Lost in a trance, he barely noticed me when I came in. As I was about to leave, he said softly, 'Thanks, Whitey — I'm certain you know that you were always one of Marilyn's favorites.' "

At ten in the morning, Harry Hall drove Joe back to the Miramar, so he could shower, shave, and dress for the funeral, scheduled to begin at one o'clock at Westwood Memorial Park Cemetery. DiMaggio had engaged the Reverend A. J. Soldan to conduct a nondenominational service, together with a reading of the Twenty-third Psalm. Joe had asked Carl Sandburg to deliver the eulogy, but the writer had fallen ill, and although he later penned a *Look* magazine tribute to the actress, it was Lee Strasberg who composed and presented the eulogy.

Joe and Joe Jr. rode to Westwood Memorial Cemetery in a mortuary limousine. Joey wore his marine dress uniform, while Joe had on a charcoal gray suit. Joe Jr. suddenly noticed that his father was crying again. Without a word, Joe reached out and clutched his son's hand. He held it until they reached the cemetery. Thinking back on the event, Joey reflected that he and his dad had never been closer.

Besides Joe and Joe Jr., the guest list included Lee and Paula Strasberg, Inez Melson, Berniece Miracle, Eunice Murray, Mr. and Mrs. Whitey Snyder, Agnes Flanagan, Mickey Rudin, Aaron Frosch, Ralph Roberts, Anne and Mary Karger, Sydney Guilaroff, the Greensons (Ralph, Hildi, Joan, and Dan), George Solotaire, and Lotte Goslar.

In total, thirty-one mourners attended Marilyn Monroe's funeral. Dr. Hyman Engelberg had been invited but opted not to go. "I meant no disrespect, and it had nothing to do with our affair," he said. "I simply wanted to mourn Marilyn's death in private and in my own way."

George Solotaire had originally planned on

flying from New York to Los Angeles on August 7 in order to serve as best man at Joe and Marilyn's on-again, off-again wedding ceremony. "That was certainly one of the sadder aspects of Marilyn's death," claimed Robert Solotaire, George's son. "Joe had spoken to my Dad about getting remarried on August 8. As it turned out, that was the day of Marilyn's funeral. Joe loved Marilyn beyond anyone's imagination. He was totally distraught. I recall my dad telling me that somebody showed Joe an August 7 copy of a *Los Angeles Times* interview with Peter Lawford in which the actor lambasted DiMaggio for not allowing Marilyn's Hollywood pals to attend the funeral. Joe had an absolute shit-fit. He said, 'Sinatra and the others, including those goddamn low-life bastards the Kennedys, killed Marilyn. That faggot Peter Lawford also had a hand in it. If he or any of those fucking Kennedys turn up at Marilyn's funeral, I'll bash in their faces. All of those sons of bitches killed Marilyn.' The truth of the matter is that Joe never fully recognized the degree and extent to which Marilyn was addicted to booze and pharmaceuticals. In the long run, that's what killed her — not the Kennedys."

For their part, the Kennedys couldn't distance themselves far enough from Monroe's death. The only comment offered by any member of the family came from the

First Lady. Asked by a reporter what she thought of MM, Jacqueline Kennedy responded, "There will never be another Marilyn Monroe, but there doesn't need to be because she will go on eternally."

Reverend Soldan conducted the first part of Marilyn Monroe's funeral service inside the Westwood Memorial Park Chapel. "Marilyn's casket lay open," said Lotte Goslar, "and Marilyn looked at peace. As private a man as he happened to be, Joe DiMaggio made no effort to masquerade his emotions. He broke down, crying openly during the service, and truly my heart went out to him. His son also cried. It seems almost trite to say that with Marilyn's death, Joe DiMaggio died as well. Her unintentional suicide took two lives."

The service, as stark and poignant as DiMaggio had envisioned it, ended with Lee Strasberg's eulogy, which began: "Marilyn Monroe was a legend. In her own lifetime she created a myth of what a poor girl from a deprived background could attain. For the entire world she became a symbol of the eternal feminine. But I have no words to describe the myth and the legend. I did not know this Marilyn Monroe . . ."

As the guests filed out of the chapel and into the bright California sunlight, Joe DiMaggio approached Marilyn's casket. He knelt beside it and kissed Marilyn's lips for the last time, then placed three long-stemmed red roses in her folded hands. Although no direct source is cited, Richard Ben Cramer writes in his DiMaggio biography that Joe's final words to Marilyn were "I love you, I love you, I love you."

The casket, now shut, was carried two hundred yards from the chapel to crypt number 24 amidst a tranquil setting of grass and trees, an oasis in the center of a jumble of steel-and-cement high-rise office buildings. Throngs of onlookers lined the stone walls that ran along the edge of the cemetery. There was some running and shouting, even some laughter and the sound of transistor radios. A contingent of young, burly policemen stood guard along the interior of the wall. A mountain of flowers from all over the world was piled high in front of the vaultlike crypt. No bouquet was larger or more impressive than Joe DiMaggio's heart-shaped arrangement of roses. A half dozen cemetery workers attired in black lifted the casket and slid it into place. The crypt was closed and locked. From beginning to end, Marilyn Monroe's funeral lasted less than thirty minutes.

The mourners, among them Joe and his son, left soon after, as did the cemetery workers and the police. Now the crowd that had gathered behind the surrounding walls descended and headed straight for Marilyn's crypt. Surging forward like a swarm of locusts, they grabbed each and every flower, tearing them off the mountain until not a single blossom remained. Watching the carnage from afar, Joe DiMaggio surmised that maybe Marilyn would have enjoyed the spectacle, just as she'd adored the adulation of thousands of American servicemen when she performed for them in Korea during their honeymoon in early 1954. The problem, DiMaggio later told his son, was that what Marilyn needed was less adulation and more of what is real.

To avoid the press, if for no other reason, Joe DiMaggio decided to leave the country. On Friday evening, August 10, he joined Harry Hall and Harry's crony Sugar Brown on a ten-day road trip to Mexico. On their way out of town, the trio stopped off at Westwood Memorial Park Cemetery, where Joe went over a few of the thousands of condolence cards and telegrams that had poured into the cemetery office during the past two days, along with hundreds of fresh bouquets of flowers. Joe arranged with the office manager to have Inez Melson come in and pick up the cards and telegrams. Given what had taken place after Marilyn's funeral, he authorized the cemetery to donate the flowers to nursing homes and hospitals in the area.

While Harry and Sugar returned to the car

to wait for him, Joe walked out to the crypt for a good-bye visit with his beloved. The cemetery had closed for the night, and Joe had Marilyn all to himself. He'd already made plans with a nearby florist to deliver fresh roses to the crypt twice a week for years to come. He'd also ordered a bench to be made and installed in front of the crypt so that visitors could sit and soak it all in.

In the gathering dark, with only a sliver of moon in the sky, Joe stayed only for a minute. Overcome by sadness, he vowed never to return. It was too upsetting for him.

Before rejoining his friends in the car, Joe stopped back in the cemetery office. He told the office manager he had one final request. He wanted to pay the cemetery to have a plaque of white marble permanently affixed to crypt number 24, and it should read simply, "MARILYN MONROE, 1926–1962." The cemetery consented, and the plaque was attached to the crypt. With the passage of time, the white marble gradually turned gray.

CHAPTER 21

Never for a moment did Joe DiMaggio consider the possibility that Marilyn Monroe's death had been an intentional act. Nor, as so many conspiracy buffs wanted to believe, that she was a murder victim. She had simply miscalculated, forgotten the number of pills she'd already consumed when, unable to sleep, she decided to take more medication. She had done it before — not once, not twice, but on a number of occasions. The potential for something going drastically awry had always existed. It could happen to almost anyone. Depressed and confused, perhaps somewhat inebriated, Marilyn had taken one tablet too many. Only this time, unlike others, there was nobody around to save her.

What distressed DiMaggio wasn't so much the *way* Marilyn died — he could somehow rationalize her multiple addictions. Nor was it even the individuals he held indirectly responsible for her death: the Kennedys, Frank Sinatra, Peter Lawford, the bosses and leeches at Twentieth Century–Fox who'd used and abused her. Rather, he was distraught over the medical supervision she'd received in the final months and weeks of her life. According to invoices received by Inez Melson (after MM's death), Marilyn had consulted with Dr. Greenson twenty-seven times over a span of thirty-five days (July 1 to August 4); she'd seen Dr. Engelberg on fifteen separate occasions during the same period. DiMaggio concluded, not unjustifiably, that Marilyn's fame had served to seduce both physicians, rendering them incapable of saying no to their star patient.

In search of answers, DiMaggio eventually contacted Dr. Marianne Kris, Marilyn's therapist prior to Dr. Ralph Greenson. Joe wanted to know if Kris felt Marilyn had been well served by Greenson and Engelberg. In response, Kris insisted that "under difficult circumstances" the two doctors had "done their best." DiMaggio had his doubts. If a coroner's inquest and grand jury investigation had taken place, he told Kris, Greenson and Engelberg would both have had to account for their questionable dealings with the actress. "I doubt they'd still be in business," he said. "Greenson all but kidnapped Marilyn, and Engelberg gave her injections of God-knows-what. And what took them so long to notify the police the night Marilyn died? What was that all about?"

Dr. Kris agreed with at least one of DiMaggio's contentions. There ought to have been an official investigation into Marilyn's death. It would have cut short all that speculation as to who or what contributed to Marilyn's end: all the chatter about hit men, enemas, and executions. It would have provided ample evidence that Marilyn, whether accidentally or on purpose, had been her own assassin.

Following Marilyn's death, after returning to New York from Mexico, Joe DiMaggio gained entrance to her Manhattan apartment in order to retrieve some of his own personal belongings, including a blue shoe box that contained a half dozen of his love letters to Monroe. The one item he missed was a crucifix that had belonged to his mother. While still in the apartment, he came across several hypodermic syringes, three vials containing some kind of powder, and other drug paraphernalia. The discovery upset DiMaggio, though he'd never known Marilyn to use hard drugs. He suspected she might have been keeping the powder and syringes for one of her friends, possibly Montgomery Clift.

"Marilyn didn't disclose everything to me," DiMaggio told George Solotaire, "but I seriously doubt she resorted to illegal drugs, with the possible exception of an occasional joint. She sometimes did pot when she got depressed. It didn't help much. If anything, she became even more depressed. And when she became depressed, she tended to withdraw. She'd go into that darkened bedroom of hers in New York and stay in there for days. She was moodier than anyone I ever knew. She'd say, 'I feel blue today.' She used the word *blue* to describe how she felt, and it was the darkest shade of blue you could possibly imagine. On the other hand, I laughed more and harder with Marilyn than I ever have with anyone. She would rebound from her dark moods as easily as she fell into them. A week before she died, she said to me, 'Things are looking up. I feel I'm just getting started.' And then that damn funeral!"

George Solotaire had last spoken with Monroe a month or so before she died. In keeping with her habit of late-night calls, she phoned him around midnight (three o'clock in the morning, New York time) and chatted with him for more than an hour. Much of their conversation centered on Joe DiMaggio. "I've known Joe for more than ten years," she said. "I guess I know him as well as it's possible to know him. The point is, I don't know if I really know him at all. I don't know if anybody knows him, or if he even knows himself."

Joe DiMaggio's best friend felt certain that whatever else one might conclude about MM's liaison with Joe, it was by far the most sexually stimulating and satisfying relationship she'd ever had. "Above all," said George Solotaire, "they enjoyed each other physically. We all know that over the years Marilyn had numerous affairs. Going to bed with a man was her way of saying thank you. It didn't mean much to her. That wasn't the case with respect to Joe. That part of their relationship continued long after their divorce and in a sense never ended."

As if more proof were needed of Marilyn's sexual awakening, particularly at the hands of Joe DiMaggio, one of the stream-of-consciousness tapes she made for Dr. Greenson touched precisely on this subject. "I could count on one hand the number of orgasms I had in previous years," she ventured. "But of late I've had lots of orgasms — not only one but two and three with a man who takes his time. I never cried so hard as I did afterwards. It was because of all the years I had so few of them. What wasted years!"

If Marilyn Monroe's death sealed Joe DiMaggio's fate and solitary state forever, it had an equally devastating effect on the life and career of Dr. Ralph Greenson. Haunted by the sight of Marilyn nude in bed, alone, at night, her bedroom lights ablaze, bedroom door locked, forty to fifty Nembutal tablets in her system, Greenson never succeeded in putting Marilyn's death behind him. Lambasted by press and public alike, as well as by the majority of his colleagues, Greenson at first attempted to justify his unorthodox psychiatric approach to Marilyn by writing an article for the *Medical Tribune,* which he began the day after Marilyn's death and completed several weeks later: "My particular method of treatment for this particular woman was, I thought, essential at that time. But it failed. She died."

Anna Freud, one of Greenson's few supporters, wrote to him from London on August 6, 1962, two days after Marilyn's death, to say how sorry she was. "I know exactly how you feel," she wrote, "because I had exactly the same thing happen with a patient of mine." She went on to say that she believed that sometimes psychiatry was inadequate to the task of fixing "wounded psyches."

On August 20, in response to Anna Freud's letter, Greenson wrote: "I cared about her, and she was my patient. . . . I had hopes for her and I thought she was making progress. And now she's dead and I realize that all my knowledge and desire and strength were not enough."

Dom DiMaggio recalled hearing from his brother several weeks after Marilyn's death. "Joe had invited Dr. Greenson and the doctor's family to Marilyn's funeral," said Dom, "but in truth they were no longer on decent terms. Joe had come to the realization that Greenson's therapy sessions and technique had done Marilyn more harm than good, and he regretted not having done more to encourage Marilyn to find another shrink. He spread the word on Greenson, telling everyone what an unprofessional creep he turned out to be. When Greenson heard what Joe was saying about him, he retaliated. He told a reporter that Joe and Marilyn were ill suited and that she would have been better off staying with Arthur Miller, who at least satisfied her intellectual curiosity."

Formerly regarded as one of the country's leading psychoanalysts and therapists, Ralph Greenson's reputation plummeted following Marilyn Monroe's death. In late August 1962, hidden behind a newly grown full beard, Greenson departed for New York, where he visited with Dr. Kris and underwent his own series of therapy sessions with Dr. Max Schur, a colleague and old friend. Depressed and disillusioned, Greenson returned to Los Angeles two months later. His troubles continued to mount until, in 1970, another patient, thirty-five-year-old actress Inger Stevens, who looked like Monroe, also committed suicide. Increasingly Greenson began to miss appointments with his remaining patients. He suffered bouts of aphasia, where he lost his ability to speak or comprehend, and he sought refuge from the outside world behind the locked doors of his study. In essence, he became another person.

"It seemed as though he wanted to escape from himself," said Hyman Engelberg. His friendships waned, and he became something of a recluse. I saw less and less of him as time went on, partially, I suppose, because I left the medical offices we shared and moved to a new address. A frail and broken man, haunted by his failed efforts to save Marilyn Monroe, Ralph Greenson died in 1979. Frankly, I don't think there's anything that anyone, including Ralph Greenson, could have done to rescue Marilyn. One way or the other, she had made up her mind by this juncture to end her life."

On September 15, 1962, a little more than a month after Marilyn's death, Rebecca Miller was born to Arthur and Inge Morath Miller, whom the playwright had married following his divorce from Marilyn Monroe. Still conflicted and embittered over their divorce, Arthur Miller later told Christopher Bigsby, his biographer, that he hadn't been able to mourn Marilyn when she died; it was twenty years after her death before he could cry at the thought of her death.

On first hearing of his former wife's demise, Arthur Miller wrote to Joe Rauh, his longtime attorney: "I guess you're as stunned as I've been about Marilyn. It's still hard to accept although I'd always worried that she'd step over the line. I don't think she meant to. And that's even more terrible." Miller later gave an interview to the *New York Post* in which he seemed to contradict what he'd written earlier to Joe Rauh. According to the *Post* interview, Miller wasn't at all "shocked" by Monroe's death. "It had to happen," said Miller. "I don't know when or how, but it was inevitable."

In 1966 Arthur and Inge Miller had a second child, a son named Daniel. Because the child suffered from Down syndrome, and because the Millers weren't able to care for the child, they placed him in an institution. "As I heard it," reported Norman Mailer, "Inge Morath often visited the child, whereas Arthur never visited, never so much as mentioned his son. That's who Arthur Miller was. He couldn't deal with problematic situations. Nor could he deal with people who had problems, which is why he couldn't handle Marilyn Monroe. She was too much for him. She frightened the hell out of him."

Marilyn Monroe's will was admitted to probate on October 30, 1962. The actress left $100,000 in a trust fund for her mother, the annual interest from which (approximately $5,000) would be used for Gladys Baker's maintenance and upkeep in a mental institution. Clearly, mental illness had been on Marilyn's mind during the last year of her life. To their immense surprise, she left

$20,000 to Dr. Hohenberg and $10,000 to Dr. Kris; she also left Anna Freud $10,000 to continue her work with troubled children. Xenia Chekhov, the widow of Michael Chekhov, Marilyn's drama coach, received $2,500 per year for the remainder of her life. Marilyn bequeathed $10,000 to her half sister Berniece Miracle. She left the Rostens $5,000 to be used for the college education of Patricia Rosten, their daughter. There were other bequests of varying amounts, but the bulk of the Monroe estate (including all of Marilyn's personal possessions) went to Lee and Paula Strasberg, presumably to be used for their ongoing work with the Actors Studio.

In the last months of her life, Marilyn had expressed an unmistakable desire to excise the Strasbergs from her will, primarily because she had grown apart from them and had never fully forgiven them for their involvement in having her placed in the Payne Whitney Psychiatric Clinic in New York. Having heard Marilyn's lament, Inez Melson, her former business manager, contested the will on the grounds that when it was written, Marilyn had been under the direct influence of Lee Strasberg. Melson's claim was eventually dismissed. The situation concerning the Strasbergs and Marilyn Monroe's last will and testament became increasingly controversial. Paula Strasberg died in 1966 at age fifty-seven. A year later, Lee Strasberg married

Anna Mizrahi, a television actress from Venezuela who happened to be thirty-eight years younger than her newlywed husband. When Lee Strasberg died in 1982, Anna inherited everything, including the Monroe trademark and everything connected to it. Anna Strasberg never met Marilyn Monroe, yet she became extraordinarily wealthy as a result of MM's legacy.

More than two years after Marilyn Monroe's death, wealthy businessman Louis Wolfson sponsored a social function in San Francisco to which he invited his old pal Joe DiMaggio as well as Sam Yorty, mayor of Los Angeles from 1961 to 1973. "Yorty, a baseball fanatic, had always wanted to meet DiMaggio," recalled Wolfson. "So I introduced them at the party, and the two of them went off into a corner to talk. Apparently Yorty told Joe he'd read all the police reports, and there was no question but that on the last day of her life Marilyn received a visit from Bobby Kennedy. I'm not certain if Joe knew about the visit, because he didn't like to talk about Marilyn. I do know he loathed the Kennedy family. I can vouch for the fact that he shed no tears when JFK got assassinated. I saw Joe the day after the assassination of President Kennedy. 'The bastard got what he deserved,' he snarled. I guess if I'd been in Joe's shoes, I might have felt the same way."

Louis Wolfson remembered a DiMaggio-RFK incident that took place in the mid-1960s: "Robert Kennedy was guest of honor at the annual New York Yankees Old Timers' Day game. Had DiMaggio known that RFK would be there, I'm certain he wouldn't have participated. Joe assured me he didn't know until he found himself on a reception line with the other old-timers, and here comes Bobby Kennedy walking along, shaking every old-timer's hand one by one. When he reaches DiMaggio, there's no one there. Joe had stepped off the line and turned his back on Kennedy. I don't know how many people picked up on it. 'What's the big fucking deal?' I said to him afterward. 'Shake his hand and be done with it.' And he says, 'I wouldn't shake that little prick's hand for all the money in the world.' "

According to an FBI report dated February 15, 1965, Joe DiMaggio offered to pay $25,000 to a pair of unnamed mobsters for a two-minute pornographic film showing a "young" Marilyn Monroe (at nineteen or twenty) performing a sexual act with an unidentified male figure.

"The report turned out to be accurate," said Dom DiMaggio. "My brother acquired the film with money that had been given him by one or another of his wealthy buddies. He showed me the film, but I can honestly say I don't know if it was Marilyn or not. It looked like her, but who knows? I didn't know her at that age. Given the possibility that it was Marilyn in the film, Joe was taking no chances. He wasn't about to let her name get dragged through the mud, particularly when she wasn't able to defend herself. After showing me the film, he got out a pair of scissors and cut it into shreds."

If Joe DiMaggio hadn't been as well known as he was — one of the most recognizable men in the country — he could have readily passed for a banker, chief executive officer of a major corporation, or an investment broker. His tall frame impeccably tailored, fingernails manicured, every one of his gray hairs in place, he looked like anything but the son of a struggling, craggy-faced fisherman from "the old country." Yet the demise of Marilyn Monroe — *his* Marilyn — had left him joyless.

"We would be relaxing in the office or in an airport lounge, sometimes in the midst of a conversation," reported DiMaggio's attorney and constant companion Morris Engelberg, "when suddenly his head would droop. When I asked him what was the matter, he picked up his head, looked right at me, and said, 'Don't you know, Morris, don't you know?'" Even at times when he should have been feeling exhilarated, such as when he was receiving an award or enjoying his family, the sadness would rob him of all pleasure.

Joe DiMaggio was not a man of complex sensibilities and in fact had a rather dour, literal way of taking in the world. Years later, after DiMaggio died, singer-songwriter Paul Simon reported, in an article he wrote, that when he met Joe DiMaggio for the first time, the two had only one thing to talk about. "What I don't understand," Simon quotes DiMaggio as saying, "is why you ask where I've gone. I just did a Mr. Coffee commercial, I'm a spokesman for Bowery Savings Bank, and I haven't gone anywhere." In fact, Simon was making no attempt to address the metaphorical value of using Joe DiMaggio, whose larger-than-life presence had been in some ways an illusion. Appearing on *The Dick Cavett Show,* Simon himself averred that he was actually a bigger fan of Mickey Mantle and had chosen Joe DiMaggio's name by default only because Mantle's didn't have enough syllables.

The only thing that truly interested Joe after Marilyn's death was making money. He was very naïve about the process, but he was meticulous about his image, and, luckily for him, Madison Avenue liked it. In 1972 Joe signed on to be the spokesman for the Bowery Savings Bank of New York City, and even when the bank was in danger of being seized by the FDIC (Federal Deposit Insurance

Corporation), Joe's commanding presence gave them the air of stability and solvency. Nobody was more surprised than Joe was to find that he was good at this spokesperson job. He had always shied away from cameras and had hated anyone invading his privacy, but he learned the scripts that were written for him, and he delivered his lines like he truly believed in the Bowery Bank. Joe seemed to be the perfect gentleman to ask, "Is there anyone who couldn't use a bundle of cash?" He stayed with the bank until 1992.

Joe never learned to completely trust his ability to work in front of the camera very much, and when Vincent Marotta, the president of Mr. Coffee, called him, having gotten his number from a mutual friend in Cleveland, to ask Joe to represent the new coffee maker company in 1972, DiMaggio's impulse was to run away. "I rang Joe up on a Saturday morning," Marotta told Linda Wertheimer on NPR in 2005. "It was about eleven; I shall never forget this. He answered the phone, and I told him who I was, and, of course, he said, 'What's the name of that product?' And I said, 'Mr. Coffee. You haven't heard of it, Mr. DiMaggio, 'cause it's brand new.' And he said, 'Well, I have heard of it. Yes, I was playing in a golf tournament last week. I won one as a prize.' " Joe then turned him down flat. The next day, however, Marotta flew to California and called DiMaggio once again.

"This time when he answered the phone, he said, 'Well, hi! How you doing? How's the weather there?' He had a whole different attitude." The two had lunch in San Francisco's Fairmont Hotel, and DiMaggio listened, impressing Marotta with his choice of broiled salmon, and when the lunch was over, Marotta said, "He put out his hand and shook hands. He said, 'I'm going to go with you.' That was it. And he ended up being with me almost fifteen years."

Though Joe was never much of a coffee drinker — because of his ulcer, he preferred tea and Sanka, which was decaffeinated — people believed that he was the owner of the company, and they would come to him with their complaints, in which case he would tell them to write to Marotta's office. The relationship with Mr. Coffee ended abruptly in 1987, when the company added elements to his contract that he had not approved.

Not long afterward, DiMaggio was offered a sizable amount of money to lend his name to a chain to be called DiMaggio Cucina Italian restaurants, which one of the owners of Famous Ray's Pizza planned to open all across North America. According to Morris Engelberg, they made two critical mistakes. First, when they invited Joe in for the meeting, the restaurant was packed with people who obviously expected Joe DiMaggio to be there, and Joe did not like being the unwitting main attraction. The other mistake was not warning the guests to stay away from the subject of Marilyn Monroe.

One of the pizza-eating guests asked Joe, "How was Marilyn?" and another asked his companion Martha Lee if she was Marilyn Monroe's daughter. Joe was silent for the entire meeting, and when he left, he was in a deep funk. Even though it would have been very painful for him to turn down the kind of money he had been offered, Joe decided to walk away from the deal altogether.

In 1989 the Loma Prieta earthquake, a quake of 7.1 magnitude, overwhelmed the greater San Francisco and Monterey Bay areas, the largest earthquake to hit the San Francisco area since 1906. The event lasted only about twenty seconds, but it did massive damage that extended into a focal depth of eleven miles (typical focal depths are four to six miles), leaving homes in ruin and even disrupting service on the Oakland Bay Bridge. Joe DiMaggio's house at 2150 Beach Street was unharmed, but stories circulated about Joe vacating the home carrying garbage bags filled with cash in the amount of some $600,000.

The slugger had driven his friend Sam Spear's car to Candlestick Park for a World Series game that day, and he had not made arrangements with the Giants for parking. "So we had to park in the Hunters Point

Shipyard dirt lot," Spear explained. Reporters said that Joe left by limo as soon as there was a rumor of tremors, but Spear corrected that inaccuracy. "We didn't park in the players' lot, and Joe didn't leave in a limo. He left in my Buick." Says writer Ben Cramer, "As to the six hundred thousand dollars — not true. Joe didn't have anywhere near that amount of cash, and even if he did, he was very conscious of interest offered by the banks, and that money was important to him. Sam Spear, as far as I know the only eyewitness to the scene, confirmed my suspicions. 'He didn't have any bags in his hands. Absolutely not. He was in there only for a few minutes. He was wearing a sport jacket, and if he had any cash, there is just so much room in a pocket.' " Even though the house was undamaged, the aftershocks were still threatening, so Joe spent the night at Spear's home.

Besides money, Joe DiMaggio had only one other passion that eased the pain of living without Marilyn: his work with the South Broward County Memorial Hospital that led to creating the Joe DiMaggio Children's Hospital in Hollywood, Florida, where Joe kept the home he had bought for his retirement.

In 1992, administrators at Memorial were wracking their brains for ways to beef up services and facilities in their 144-bed children's wing, when someone suggested that they try to get a celebrity sponsor. Chief executive Frank Sacco came up with Joe DiMaggio's name. "We asked him because he's a hero, and he's here, and we knew he loves children," Sacco said. "He goes beyond baseball. He's an American hero." It went against DiMaggio's nature to let the hospital use his name. He was, after all, a man who treasured his privacy in an almost obsessive way, and giving them his name would certainly compromise the barrier he had carefully constructed between himself and the public. "He forced himself to endure — sometimes grudgingly — the attention of adoring adults at charity events that helped raise millions for his namesake hospital," reported Bob LaMendola, health reporter for the *South Florida Sun-Sentinel*. The hospital benefited from Joe's participation. With Joe DiMaggio on its board, the hospital could all of a sudden raise $600,000 in a single day, $3 million in a year. Sacco said, "He helped the hospital land big donations — up to five hundred thousand — by going to private lunches with prospective donors, even though he didn't like such affairs."

According to LaMendola, right up until the last year of his life, when he was too sick to travel anymore, "DiMaggio made monthly visits to the children's hospital, stopping at children's bedsides and bringing bears at Christmas — all without publicity. He rejected the idea of inviting the news media."

The hospital remains Joe DiMaggio's living legacy, and thousands of children have been treated, regardless of their circumstances. The hospital's credo is a phrase that DiMaggio coined early on. He suggested they adopt as a slogan "Whether rich or poor, no child will ever be turned away." Today the motto appears above the entrance to the Joe DiMaggio Children's Wing, in the lobby, in the building elevators, and on all its promotional materials.

Nothing could fill the void that Marilyn's death had left in the Yankee Clipper's heart, however, and her absence seemed to cause him more pain as years went on. In 1991 DiMaggio served as grand marshal of the Orange Bowl Parade on New Year's Eve, and Morris Engelberg accompanied him in the parade. After it was over, around ten at night, Engelberg took DiMaggio out to eat at the Deli Den and then pleaded that Joe come back to his place to ring in the New Year. "It doesn't mean anything to me," said DiMaggio. "It's just another night." Engelberg drove DiMaggio home and then watched him walk through the lobby of his building, stooped and fragile, displaying his "bad head," as Engelberg called it, the moody look his friend would get whenever he let Marilyn Monroe into his thoughts.

As far as Engelberg could tell, Monroe was the one person in life that DiMaggio had truly loved, particularly since DiMaggio had a special fondness for underdogs and blondes but had also created what Buzz Bissinger called, in his 2000 *Vanity Fair* piece "For Love of Joe DiMaggio," a "trail of relationships chopped off as if with the stroke of an ever sharpened knife because of distrust, or suspicion, or failure to obey the rules of DiMaggio."

CHAPTER 22

As Joe DiMaggio aged, he became more embittered by the loss of Marilyn Monroe, and he pushed further and further away from the people who wanted to be close to him. As writer David Halberstam once observed, "He lived a very, very lonely life for a long time." DiMaggio had a definitive mistrust of people, and no one was immune from his scorn, just as no one was assured of lifelong friendship or devotion. Over the years, Joe grew ever warier that his so-called friends were capitalizing on his name and profiting at his expense.

Through the 1990s, he began frequenting New York again in ways he had not been doing in many years, and he seemed, to some of the people who knew him, to be tiring at least somewhat of Morris Engelberg and was seeking relationships on the East Coast. Other pals speculated that he went to New York to get away from business, and he kept his visits under wraps, staying at the New York apartment of friends Dick and Kathy Burke and frequenting an Irish pub in Atlantic City as much as any restaurant in NYC. He often had lunch with cartoonist Bill Gallo, and Gallo frequently mentioned DiMaggio in his column, which didn't bother the Clipper because DiMaggio said he could tell Gallo didn't want anything from him.

He was bored with Florida and California, and he established a new version of the kind of roundtable he had had at Toots Shor's years before, this one called the Bat Pack, a group started by his podiatrist Rock G. Positano, who had treated him for a heel spur on his right foot. Writer Elisabeth Bumiller reported that "Dr. Positano strapped up DiMaggio's foot, fitted him with an arch support, and gradually built a retinue of four or five guys . . . who ate dinner with DiMaggio and reveled in his orbit when the legend visited New York."

The rules that Joltin' Joe imposed on his family and friends were demanding and strict, and any deviation from them would lead to suspension of all communication. Perhaps because he came late to Joe's life, Positano remained close to Joe to the end, and the podiatrist was more than willing to adhere to DiMaggio's rules of conduct. On one occasion, Positano arrived for dinner with Joe and his granddaughters, Kathie and Paula, at Coco Pazzo in the city, wearing a cashmere shirt and blazer, which constituted a violation of the Clipper's commandments on proper attire in the presence of women. When the young women excused themselves to go to the bathroom, Joe instructed Positano to excuse himself as soon as they returned; Rock was to say that he had received an emergency call, and then he should go to his office, where he could don a proper shirt and tie before he returned. Aware that failure to do so would mean expulsion from the inner circle, Positano did just what he was told, and when he reappeared at the restaurant, Joe announced, "Okay. Now we can have dinner."

Positano understood how hard a friend needed to work just to remain friends with Joe. "He was one of the warmest, sincerest people you'll ever meet in your life," Positano said, "but it wasn't easy being part of Joe's inner circle. There was always a tremendous responsibility and stress, because so few were allowed in. You couldn't even bring a friend to dinner without clearing it with Joe first." The worst offense anyone could commit was the mention of Marilyn Monroe. "Nobody mentioned Marilyn," said his friend Gene Schoor, the journalist who wrote a definitive biography about Yogi Berra. "If they did, they were dead from then on. Period."

After DiMaggio's death in 1999, Rock Positano was the person that Morris Engelberg, as executor of DiMaggio's will, entrusted with the task of organizing a memorial service in New York.

The entire DiMaggio clan had always seemed close, but there were seeds of discord even in their youth, and the parents' deaths (Giuseppe's in 1949, and Rosalie's in 1951) marked the beginning of a shift in loyalties, after which there was less and less incentive to keep sibling relationships intact as time went on. The oldest DiMaggio brother, Tom, told a reporter before Marilyn's death that while he might not be rich or well known, he felt sure that Joe was jealous of what he did have, which included a satisfying life with his wife and children.

Everyone in the family, especially Joe, was truly devastated by the death of brother Michael, a tragedy that facilitated Joe's decision to marry MM, but it did nothing to shore up the relationships Joe had with his siblings. Joe played alongside Vince and Dom on the San Francisco Seals baseball team, but he soon surpassed both the younger and the older brother and became a star. Vince was content to stay with San Francisco and was also convinced that he was far more fortunate than Joe would ever be because of his happy family. Dom, who played for the Boston Red Sox for many years, always found that his famous brother perpetually overshadowed him, but he learned to live with it. Joe, however, never entirely trusted that Dom wasn't jealous or forever trying to get something from him.

When Joe DiMaggio lived in San Francisco after MM's death, he lived with his sister Marie in a house he had bought for his parents while he was playing for the Yankees. Marie kept house and did basic bookkeeping for him, signing checks for his corporation and opening his mail. Morris Engelberg remembered her as "one of the sweetest, sweetest ladies I had ever met." Most of the time, he said, "she would be sitting at the kitchen table, drinking coffee and smoking cigarettes." At some point, Joe suspected that she was stealing from him items that he had been given as gifts. He stripped her of her bookkeeping duties and instructed Engelberg to cut her out of his will, even though she was already in her eighties. When she died in 1996, DiMaggio did not even attend her funeral. One day Engelberg visited Joe and asked casually, "How's Marie doing?" "She died a couple months ago," DiMaggio replied tonelessly. Engelberg searched his friend's face for some sign of emotion but found none.

Vince moved away, and the situation between Joe and Dom became increasingly combative. They would go months without exchanging a word, stabbing each other with cold silences, and no one knew why. Dom

610

would show up for games or at dinners where he knew Joe was sure to be, and Joe surmised that Dom was trying to steal the spotlight, and that would set him off. Dom was better with money than Joe was, amassing a fortune in what appeared to Joe to be a ridiculously easy manner. He sold the building where the family restaurant had once been, for example, and made a fortune, and his every investment seemed to pay off in the biggest possible way. Joe was clearly angered by his little brother's success and resented it openly.

The brothers fought about their sisters. Dom advocated on Marie's behalf, which irritated Joe, and when others sympathized with Dom, that irritated him further and made him take it out on Dom. When their sister Mamie got sick, Joe was not the least bit interested in helping out, but Dom frequently flew cross-country to look after her until he could get her into a nursing home. Of course, Dom resented Joe for putting him in that position, but Joe, too, was equally miffed. He felt that Dom's heroics had made him look bad, and he could not forgive his brother for "shaming" him.

In addition, there was a split between the brothers that resulted from a failure in the US Mail. Dom was invited to a charity event but didn't get the invitation and therefore never showed up; Joe was furious and would not entertain any suggestion of clemency. For a long time after that, neither brother spoke to the other, but mostly it was Joe who would not speak with Dom. When push came to shove, Dom was always willing to forgive. It was Dom who delivered the eulogy at Joe's funeral, and their mutual friend Joe Nacchio proclaimed, "Dominic was a good brother, and he was a good brother to the end."

Joe DiMaggio wouldn't speak to Ted Williams, had no time for Mickey Mantle, ostracized several presidents, and found reasons to get out of having to interact with anyone he had the slightest criticism against — especially anyone who had, in his estimation, done him the slightest wrong. He even very nearly severed his relationship with Morris Engelberg, who was the most loyal of all his friends and followers, responsible for having won contracts that provided DiMaggio with a financially comfortable old age.

Joe was once at a baseball card show in Atlantic City and insisted that Engelberg join him. The attorney had just had eye surgery and was unable to fly, but because he had been summoned, he took a train from Florida to Philadelphia and then had himself driven by car to Atlantic City. Joe was not impressed with the lengths to which his friend, whom he would only introduce to others as his lawyer, had gone to be there with him; at one point, he went so far as to slap Engelberg's hand for not handing over memorabilia quickly enough for him to sign, prompting Engelberg to get up and leave. In this case, the Clipper came as close as he ever did to an apology. "Sometimes these shows piss me off," he said, and Engelberg forgave him.

Of all Joe DiMaggio's failures with people, the one that hurt him the most was the complete collapse of any association with Joe DiMaggio Jr., his only child, who once told a reporter proudly, "My lifestyle is diametrically opposed to my father's." For his part, Joe Sr. hardly wanted to discuss his son. Said baseball memorabilia collector Barry Halper, DiMaggio's friend of twenty-seven years, "There were two subjects that were taboo with Joe: Marilyn Monroe and Joe Jr. In all the years I knew him, he never said a word about either one. You just knew not to ask."

Morris Engelberg said that Joe DiMaggio's heart was broken only twice in his life: once by Marilyn Monroe and then by his son. A photograph taken by Robert Solotaire in 1952 shows father and son sharing a smiling, carefree moment at a beach in the water with a surfboard, but all Joe Jr. remembered when asked about his dad was that "we were from different planets."

Big Joe referred to Little Joe as "my boy," never by name, never as his son, long after "my boy" reached manhood. When Little Joe was well into his fifties, Morris Engelberg offered to entice him to Florida, where he could be watched closely in an effort to keep him from drugs and alcohol. "You don't know my boy," DiMaggio responded. "You're barking up the wrong tree. It would be a waste of your time." Engelberg often spoke to Big Joe about reconciling with Little Joe, but the senior DiMaggio's response was always the same: "My boy is a bum." The "boy" was a grandfather by then, and even though DiMaggio had tried to help his son financially, he refused to give him the only thing that DiMaggio Junior really wanted, which was respect. Joe couldn't give that, even though his declaration that his boy was a bum was often followed by a sheepish addendum, "But he's a good boy." If Joey had heard even that much approval, he might have been content.

"I never knew my father," Joe Jr. told Larry King in the late 1960s. "My parents were divorced when I was little, and I was sent away to private school, and my father was totally missing from my childhood . . . We were on the cover of the first issue of *Sport* magazine when it came out in 1949, my father and I, me wearing a little number five jersey. I was driven to the photo session, we had our picture taken, and I was driven back. My father and I didn't say two words.

"I cursed the name Joe DiMaggio Jr. At Yale, I played football — I deliberately avoided baseball — but when I ran out on the field and they announced my name, you could hear the crowd murmur . . . When I decided to leave college and join the marines, I called my father to tell him. You call your father when you make that sort of decision. So I told him, and he said, 'The marines are a good thing.' And there was nothing more for us to say to each other."

Joe Junior did remember being something like close to his father once in his life: in the car on the way to MM's funeral. He said his father had always gone on loving Monroe, and since he loved her too, they had shared that bond, but it didn't last.

The elder DiMaggio had formed a close relationship with Joe Jr.'s wife, Sue, and was, in his own eyes, at least, an ideal grandfather to her daughters, Paula and Kathie, whom Joe Jr. had adopted. He even moved the family to the Bay Area from Massachusetts so they could be closer to him. DiMaggio was very critical of his son's failure to be a good father. "My kid never put his head to anything," he said.

After the divorce, Joe Sr. kept close to the girls and their mother and remained devoted to them. In fact, sometimes he was too involved in their lives, especially his favorite, Paula's, and he would try to control them, telling them where to go to school, whom to befriend, and eventually whom they could and could not date. He regularly sent money for clothes and school supplies and the like. He footed the bill for Kathie's degree from the University of California, and he bought and maintained a condominium for Paula while he paid for her to attend beauty school. But although he went out of his way to remain connected to Sue's daughters, DiMaggio grew further and further apart from his son.

After returning to California, Joe Jr. got into a social group that revolved around drugs. "Speed," said his ex-wife Sue. "He loved speed." He would leave Sue and the kids for days at a time to explore and experience the drug scene in San Francisco, and he could not understand why Sue would not follow him there. He began to beat her. "It was very embarrassing, and I didn't want anyone to know," Sue would say. "I thought it was my fault." When she left him, Joe Jr. seemed unperturbed, finding no problem attracting plenty of female companions. The drugs caused him a nearly fatal automobile accident, jail time, and the loss of every job he ever took on, which angered and mortified his father.

Joe Sr. tried to help, but since he couldn't be available emotionally, his help was mostly financial. He put up the funds for Joey to establish a polyurethane factory, and then, when that failed, he bought his son a very expensive truck so that the younger man could go into the trucking business. Joe Jr. proceeded to wreck the truck, and then he set off on what his father called his hobo adventures. He didn't even bother trying to make telephone contact, as no connection to his father seemed to matter to the son, who spent his time drinking wine or beer with other itinerant drinkers and bikers, while he collected welfare checks in addition to the money his father regularly sent. Joe Sr., who had had the highest expectations of Joe Jr.'s opportunity to attend Yale, never understood his son's flagrant disregard for real work and could not forgive the way "my boy" squandered everything his father gave him or did for him. For his part, Joe Jr. felt that his father had long since rejected him.

A particularly poignant episode happened in the Napa Valley long after Joe Jr. had begun to go gray. Joe Sr. and his friend Sam Spear would often take rides into wine country, and Joe would insist on going through Martinez, a town where Joe had grown up and Joey was said to be living. After many failed attempts, the father spotted the son walking in town, dressed shabbily and looking wan and starving. "Pull over, pull over. There's Joey," DiMaggio ordered Spear. Then he called to his son, "Joey! Joey! Joey!" Without so much as slowing his walk, the younger DiMaggio shouted back, "You don't know me. You don't know who I am. Leave me alone." The father was embarrassed and forlorn, but he didn't want to talk about the incident. He didn't have the words for the way he felt or the way Joey had disappointed him yet again. And Joey took it in, adding yet another failure to the many he had already accrued.

By then, Joe Jr. had been homeless or quasi homeless for some years. "He was a trouble-maker," his cousin Joe's (Vince's son) wife, Marina, said of him. "But I miss him." Tooth-less, scruffy, and vagrant, Joey drifted around the Martinez area, refusing to accept rides, refusing to hold down a job, wandering rather pointlessly but insisting, "I'm fine. Thank you very much." Joe Nacchio, who was one of Joe Sr.'s best-educated, most perceptive, and sensitive friends, described Joe Jr.: "His choice of words was above the ordinary person's. He was sensible and logical, and he talked with a great deal of reason." Knowing that his son was a well-educated do-nothing with bad teeth and poor health infuriated the father even more. Joe Sr. bought his son new teeth and begged him to get cleaned up, but the son didn't like wearing the false teeth and was more likely to use them as a weapon to throw at someone with whom he was angry than as they were intended.

In the mid-1990s, Joe Jr. contented himself with doing odd jobs until he went to work for

Mike Fernandez, a DiMaggio cousin, who owned a junkyard in Bay Point. Joey loved working at the junkyard and soon moved into a trailer that had been discarded there. Later, Fernandez fixed up a bungalow on the property, and Joe Jr. moved in — until he felt crowded by reporters asking too many questions about his father, who was dying by then. He moved to another junkyard in another town not far away.

Marina DiMaggio said of Joe Jr., "He was a con artist. He could con you out of anything." When his father lay dying, the television tabloid news show *Inside Edition* offered the son $15,000 to be interviewed about his relationship to Joe Sr. Junior took the money and conned the producers, carefully avoiding the issues they were most interested in discussing, which included anything remotely related to Joe Sr.'s personal life and the reason that the famous ballplayer's son was in such dire straits. "What is Joe DiMaggio's son supposed to do?" he chided the interviewer. "I'm free . . . just a free spirit. No commitments. The first of the month rolls around, and I have no payments to make."

Joey was invited to collaborate on a damning tell-all book with an author who saw an opportunity to cash in on DiMaggio's dark side, but Joey refused to participate. That was at least one thing Joe Sr. could be proud about. "My boy is loyal," he said. "He wouldn't talk, even for a million dollars." Money was never something that interested Joe DiMaggio Jr. The only reason, he once admitted to Mike Fernandez, that he took the money from *Inside Edition* at all was so he could, on his own, buy dentures that actually fit him.

DiMaggio Jr. was a lost soul, but, according to Morris Engelberg, he was a "warm, gentle person, and, as everyone said, articulate and bright." Unlike his father, Joey was demonstrative and openly affectionate toward those he liked, and he knew more about sports trivia — especially basketball statistics and factoids — than most people. He never got his teeth right, however. One of Engelberg's last memories of the Clipper's son was a visit they both made to Mama Mia's, a popular Italian restaurant in Hollywood, Florida, after Joe Sr.'s death. Owner Joe Franco observed that when Junior entered, "He had no teeth and was wearing thongs and a ponytail. "He ordered a huge meal but spent most of his time at his table drinking several beers. He barely touched his knife and fork and had the food wrapped to go." Engelberg learned later that Joey was embarrassed to eat in public because he believed that his false teeth failed to "work well."

In the *Inside Edition* interview, Junior explained why he hadn't run to his father's bedside when he was taken ill. "You know, I never got the words 'Come now.' Or I'd have been there in a flash. I love him, and just all of the things that are felt between people but never said. When he wants me there, I'll be there."

By March 1998, Joe DiMaggio had begun to notice that he seemed to be without energy for things he always liked to do, but it wasn't till the end of the year before he finally got the attention his ailment needed. He was unable to eat the food he loved, was easily tired and weak, and he coughed incessantly. The loss of appetite seemed fairly predictable, given his advanced age of eighty-four, but he had also begun to cough up blood and foul-looking phlegm, and that was shocking. He'd had a pacemaker implanted the preceding March, and he figured the coughing had something to do with the three packs of cigarettes he smoked each day. There had been a similar instance in 1992 that had amounted to no cause for alarm, and, besides, he had a year full of appointments and promises to keep.

In September, as the '98 baseball season was coming to a close, DiMaggio had two major commitments that no physical ailments could keep him from honoring. The National Italian American Sports Hall of Fame unveiled a statue of the slugger in Chicago's newly minted Piazza DiMaggio and feted him with a dinner in his honor. The next morning, he rang the opening bell at the Chicago Board of Trade. He was running a fever, feeling every bit of his eighty-four years, but he was where he was scheduled to be.

After the three-day agenda of ceremonies, Joe had to fly back to New York, where he was to be honored at Yankee Stadium upon arrival. George Steinbrenner sent a car to pick Joe up at LaGuardia Airport, and though Joe was feeling poorly, his color gray and his posture sagging, after a cup of coffee with the Yankees owner in the private box, Joe embarked on Joe DiMaggio Day, which turned out to be a difficult if fond farewell to Yankee Stadium and New York City.

A security snafu kept DiMaggio waiting in the sun-drenched bullpen for far too long, and by the time the tribute got under way, the Clipper was in a lather. "I don't need this crap," he declared. "I want to get out of here." Engelberg reminded the champ that before the announcement that the day would be known as Joe DiMaggio Day, only eighteen thousand tickets had been sold; by the time Joe was on the verge of collapse in the dugout, the stadium had sold out all of its fifty-six thousand seats. The attorney went on to disclose a secret Steinbrenner had been holding on to in order to surprise Joe at midfield: he'd had replicas made of the eight World Series rings that had been stolen from the slugger's hotel room years before and was about to present them in front of fifty-six thousand delighted fans. In the end, as he always did, Joe DiMaggio rose to the occasion, overcame the extreme discomfort caused by his illness, age, and the blazing sun, and he thrilled the assembly with his warm smile and his grateful wave. His speech was true to form: simple and short. He thanked the fans for their kind ovation and the Yankees for the gifts and the day, and then he quoted Lou Gehrig, who, he said, was "one of the greatest baseball players of all time," saying, "I am the luckiest man on the face of the earth to be here today and to have had the opportunity to play for the greatest franchise in sports history, the New York Yankees. New York," he went on, "thank you for the best thirteen years of my life. God bless you all."

The next day Joe DiMaggio left New York City, never to return.

Upon his arrival in Florida, Joe visited his pulmonary specialist Dr. Aaron Neuhaus, and he soon learned that an X-ray had detected an odious white spot on his lung, a spot that was eventually identified as tuberculosis and then complicated by the additional diagnosis of pneumonia. Joe was admitted to the hospital. When none of the treatments gave DiMaggio any relief, and his condition continued to deteriorate, Neuhaus ran more tests and found advanced-stage lung cancer. A protracted fight with the various complications of the illness ensued, and the Clipper was not released from his confinement for ninety-nine days.

At first, when Joe entered the hospital for the surgery to remove and assess the cancer, he instructed Morris Engelberg, who kept an unceasing vigil through the several stages of DiMaggio's illness, to censor all reports about his condition. He was adamant that his granddaughters be protected from concern, that his friends and family have no reason for pity, that his baseball colleagues lose no respect, that the Yankees be undeterred from their race for the pennant and the World Championship. He had checked into the hospital under a pseudonym so that the press would be kept away from the hospital as well as from him and his close circle. When it became impossible to keep the truth from Paula and Kathie, the young women flew to his side and did not leave. When Dom, his only remaining sibling, learned through the grapevine that DiMaggio was ill, he came, and since Joltin' Joe was far too ill to object, the rift between the brothers was tentatively called off.

DiMaggio defied all the odds. When the surgeon Dr. Luis Ansanza emerged from the operation, Engelberg reported, it was clear that the Clipper was done for. He explained that a tumor had been removed, but that the cancer had spread to locations in the lungs that were inoperable. Joe DiMaggio's death seemed imminent.

But Joltin' Joe was not ready to leave. He survived several crises — his lungs collapsed, he contracted serious infections and hospital-borne illnesses, his heart failed, and he became disoriented — but he fought on. Word leaked to the press, and a barrage of nosy reporters soon pressed in on the staff and other patients as well as on Joe and his small entourage. A security guard had to be hired, and a psychiatrist was engaged along with round-the-clock protection by hospital staff and others. But he rallied.

George Steinbrenner came to visit Joe in the hospital. Nervous about seeing Joe fragile and weakened by illness, Steinbrenner fretted about what he would say, how he would react to the Clipper, but he needn't have worried. When Steinbrenner arrived, DiMaggio was sitting up in bed, his trachea tube removed for the occasion, holding a baseball. They discussed the Yankees owner's plans to trade players. Steinbrenner wanted to acquire veteran pitching star Roger Clemens, saying, "He's the Michael Jordan of baseball!" The Clipper lobbied for keeping left-hander David Wells. "David Wells is a big Yankees fan," DiMaggio argued. "He knows about Babe

Ruth. He even has a gut like Babe." Engelberg, who was with the two in the hospital room, reported that the meeting was "a tonic for DiMaggio's morale. He talked about it for days."

In January, in defiance of all the predictions to the contrary, DiMaggio left the hospital and went home to his house on Waterside Lane, in Harbor Islands, Florida. Though DiMaggio's doctors expected him to expire quickly once he left the hospital, Engelberg had equipped the house to make it as much like an intensive care unit as possible without extinguishing the comforts of home. Joe loved the view from his windows of the Intercoastal Waterway, and he had pushed Engelberg to get the doctors to release him so that he might return there. Whether he knew he was dying was a matter of concern to all who knew him, but no one knew for sure. Engelberg was afraid that the knowledge that he had reached the end would plunge his friend into a depression that would speed the inevitable, and he was determined to keep Joe around as long as he could. He also knew that DiMaggio's fragile mental state must be protected by keeping the old man stimulated with activities, responsibilities, and commitments.

Once home, Joe insisted on being well groomed and hidden from view. Engelberg planted ficus trees to create a wall around the house, shielding its occupant from peering eyes of neighbors and strangers alike. Engelberg hired DeJan Pesut to be DiMaggio's security guard, cook, shopper, maintenance supervisor, and companion, and Pesut was able to move him gently about while his nurses kept him dressed, manicured, trimmed, and clean shaven. Though DiMaggio was not inclined to eat very much, Pesut insisted on using his Croatian skills to cook authentic Mediterranean food Italian style. The staff kept a library of Western movies and boxing bouts so that whenever there was nothing he wanted to watch on television, he could choose from any of dozens of alternate options.

News of DiMaggio's confinement reached his multitudinous admirers, and cards and letters began to flow daily into his home in amazing numbers, from statesmen, politicians, celebrity actors, athletes, and especially from his fans. The letters kept the Clipper busy and comforted, as did the constant presence of Engelberg, the granddaughters, and the handful of others he was willing to see. But his strength continued to fail, and even the task of signing baseballs, which was once effortless for him, became overwhelmingly exhausting. At one point, Joe said to his friend, "Morris, soon Marilyn and I will be together again. Up there."

■ ■ ■ ■

On March 2, 1999, George Steinbrenner visited the Clipper and spent the afternoon reminiscing and arguing again about some of Steinbrenner's managerial choices and discussing the upcoming Yankees season. Steinbrenner told DiMaggio he expected Joltin' Joe to throw out the first ball when the season opened the following month, but Joe didn't commit himself. When Steinbrenner left, it was clear that the visit had been a great elixir for the retired Yankee, and Engelberg encouraged Joe to allow him to invite other friends to visit. Some of those summoned were able to get to DiMaggio in time. Other of Joe's friends were emotionally unable to face his death, and still others were disinterested; some, like Barry Halper, were refused entry by DiMaggio himself. Morris Engelberg and granddaughters Paula and Kathie did not stray from Joe's side for more than a few minutes at a time, and while Dom and his brother were not speaking to each other again, Dom and his wife, Emily, were steadfast and resolute in their determination to be near Joe. In the middle of the first week of March, Engelberg consulted with Joe's family, and they decided it was time to call hospice in.

Javier Ribe, a registered nurse with the

nearest hospice, was assigned the job of easing Joe DiMaggio into death. Ribe visited every day to assess the Clipper's condition, and he instructed the family that no matter what time of the day or night death seemed imminent, they were to call him. He wanted to be the one to be there to call the funeral director and make the final arrangements. On the third day, Dom and his grandnieces called in a priest so that Joe might receive last rites. No call was made to Joe DiMaggio Jr.

On Saturday, March 6, the family and Engelberg realized that the end was surely near, when DiMaggio could not be roused even to watch the fight televised on HBO. By Sunday morning, DiMaggio was in a deep coma, barely hovering between life and death. That day was Engelberg's birthday, and the friend hoped desperately that the old man would live until the day had passed. Dom, never one to be ultrasensitive to his brother, sat by Joe's bed and spoke openly about funeral arrangements, which enraged Engelberg, who asked Dom to leave. The younger brother didn't argue with Engelberg but gathered his belongings and left for a prearranged meeting with a business associate.

By this time, Joe's oldest friend, Joe Nacchio, had returned from a trip to Panama and had joined the vigil at DiMaggio's bedside. Engelberg, knowing how important the World

Series rings had been to DiMaggio, forced the '36 Series ring, which Joe had asked him to protect, onto the Clipper's swollen finger. Engelberg, Javier Ribe, Kathie, Paula and her husband, Jim Hamra, held Joe's hands and feet, weeping openly, knowing they could not hold him back from death but hoping to ease his journey to the other side.

Moments after midnight on March 8, Joe rallied. His trachea tube had been removed, and he cleared his throat feebly. In a voice that none of the assembled family and friends recognized, Joe said, "I'll finally get to see Marilyn again." Seconds later, he was gone, but everyone there had heard his last words with absolute clarity.

Joseph Paul DiMaggio, the Yankee Clipper died in the first hour of Monday, March 8, 1999.

After the funeral home van had carried off Joltin' Joe's body to be prepared for burial, his trusted friend and attorney sat at his desk and penned a press release to be disseminated among the news media. Then, after months of rarely leaving his best friend's side, the fifty-nine-year-old lawyer broke down emotionally, contemplating the weeks that had just passed. "I was consoled that Joe died peacefully," Engelberg reflected. "He went the way he lived his life and played baseball: with dignity and with class, *la bella figura* to the last. He had a clean shave, his hair was combed, and his nails were manicured. The French doors facing the Intercoastal were open, and a cool breeze was blowing in."

Major League Baseball chartered a plane to carry Joe DiMaggio's body, accompanied by Baseball Commissioner Bud Selig, Dom and Emily DiMaggio, and American League President Gene Budig, back to San Francisco. The funeral was held in the same church where Joe and Dorothy had been married, and where many DiMaggio family events had been consecrated. Yet even before the plane touched down, the controversy surrounding the funeral service had begun.

Kathie and Paula were adamant that DiMaggio's wishes be honored and that, with the exception of Joe Nacchio and Morris Engelberg, only family be allowed to attend. As Evelyn Nieves wrote in the *New York Times,* "Even though he was one of the most famous men of this century, DiMaggio's funeral this morning at SS. Peter and Paul Roman Catholic Church . . . was astonishingly small, devoid of the celebrities of his vanishing era."

Though George Steinbrenner and baseball luminaries such as Yogi Berra, Phil Rizzuto, and Reggie Jackson wanted to be there, none was invited. "They said they wanted it to be family," reported Rev. Armand Oliveri, who presided over the service; "and that was about it."

As the preparations were nearing completion, Joe Nacchio insisted that Joey Jr. be contacted, saying it would serve as a "fitting tribute and a mark of respect for his father." Junior had called at least a couple times during Joe's illness to find out how the old man was, but he had made no attempt to get to the dying Clipper. "Just give my regards to my father and tell him that I love him," he told Engelberg. But as the funeral approached, no one was sure what Joe Jr. might or might not know, as no one knew where he was or what his situation might be. Dom DiMaggio wanted to hire professional pallbearers, but Nacchio and Engelberg disagreed, and Engelberg, who was Joe's legal representative, decreed that pallbearers would include Joe's brother Vince's grandsons, Joe Nacchio, Morris Engelberg, and, if they could locate him, Joe DiMaggio Jr. Dom DiMaggio disagreed about finding Joe Jr. "You're wasting your time," he said. "He's nothing more than a bum, and he won't come."

But Joseph DiMaggio Jr. did come to his father's funeral, and he was a pallbearer. After driving for hours about Northern California, Engelberg and Nacchio located Joe Jr. under a car, doing maintenance work, somewhere outside of Pittsburg, California, looking every bit as he had once described himself: "diametrically opposed" to his father. Nacchio told him Joe would have wanted his son to be at his funeral. "He loved you, you know," Nacchio told Joey. "I loved my father too," he replied. "I'll be there."

Nacchio gave Junior $400 to "get cleaned up and buy appropriate clothing" for the funeral, and the family warned that Nacchio had probably been conned. "He's a manipulator," vowed Cousin Joe. But Nacchio had absolute faith that the son would be there to accompany the father's casket into the church and to his final resting place, and Joseph DiMaggio Jr. did not disappoint.

Joey arrived at the funeral in a white limo and emerged wearing a new, well-pressed, and tailored three-button suit and shiny shoes. His hair, though still in a ponytail, was clean and carefully controlled, and his hands were scrubbed to pristine softness with manicured and polished nails. He entered the arena of his long-neglected family with warmth and exuberance, and he greeted them all as though he had never been apart, as though they had always been close-knit and loving. Jim Hamra, Paula's husband, was very taken with the way Joe Jr. handled himself that day. "He stood there, off to the side of the room, shoulders back, head up, studying the people as if he was figuring out who he knew and who he didn't know. He then worked the room, hugging some people, shaking hands with some, and he seemed completely at ease."

All was forgiven. Joseph DiMaggio Jr. had come home to his papa.

AFTERWORD

Five months after Joe DiMaggio's death, his son Joe DiMaggio Jr. died of an asthma-induced heart attack in Northern California, ending, finally, a two-decade struggle with alcohol, drug abuse, and homelessness. After his death at the age of fifty-seven, a cousin, Maria Amato Goodman, said of him, "He had a brilliant mind. He was one of the intelligentsia. But he lived in the shadow of his father and could not rise above that." Unlike his father, the son went to eternity without pomp and circumstance. No church service attended his leaving, and no richness of mourners paid their respects. Joe Jr. was simply cremated, and his ashes were scattered at sea. "He marched to a different drummer," Amato said of him. "He was sensitive to the people close to him. He was not a bad boy. He was confused about a lot of issues in his life."

Perhaps the deep sensitivity, the superior intellect, the marching to his own beat were what so endeared Joe Jr. to Marilyn Monroe, who adored him. It was their love for the free-spirited Monroe that proved the only commonality between father and son, and one likes to think that perhaps in death, somewhere on the other side, they have all found one another and have made peace at last.

ACKNOWLEDGMENTS

The family of C. David Heymann (1945–2012) gratefully acknowledges the efforts of the many researchers and interviewers and the assistance Heymann and they received from archival and library staffs in gathering the information needed for the writing of *Joe and Marilyn,* his final project. Those who agreed to be interviewed for this project are also gratefully acknowledged; they are named on a chapter-by-chapter basis in the chapter notes section of this book.

Special gratitude is extended to Mel Berger, Heymann's literary agent at William Morris Entertainment, for his encouragement and guidance as well as to his assistants Graham Jaenicke, Hadley Franklin, and William Lo-Turco. Equal indebtedness is due Emily Bestler, Heymann's editor at Emily Bestler Books — an imprint of Atria Books, at Simon & Schuster — for her unwavering faith in the book, as well as special thanks to Caroline Porter, her editorial assistant, and Megan

Reid, her assistant editor. The photographs that appear in this book were gathered and organized by Jane Tucker. Thanks are also due Heymann's invaluable chief researcher, Helen Valles, who was instrumental in gathering, organizing, and collating reams of research material for the author. Victoria Carrion provided much-needed bookkeeping services, and Mark Padnos, a librarian in the City University system, contributed as Heymann's research assistant and compiled the bibliography. And thanks to senior editorial assistant/pinch hitter Carla Stockton, without whom completion of this book would not have been possible.

Finally, C. David Heymann's wife, Beatrice, would like to add a personal note of thanks to all those who helped her see this project to completion, and she wishes to acknowledge the love, devotion, and partnership she shared with her husband. She extends, as well, a special thanks to the loyal readers of C. David Heymann's books; their devotion enabled him to have a career in writing, a life he loved.

NOTES

Chapter 1
Chapter 1 relies on interviews conducted with Dom DiMaggio, Norman Mailer, William Ryan, Robert Solotaire, now called George Solotaire. (All references to George S. in this chapter are from the Robert Solotaire interview.)

"fed on sexual candy": Norman Mailer interview. Also, Mailer uses this term in his bio of MM: *Marilyn, A Biography.*
"I felt as if I were stuck to the flypaper," Joe told Marilyn: Dom DiMaggio provided many of the details from Joe's youth in his interview.

Chapter 2
Chapter 2 relies on interviews conducted with Tim Jeffries, Robert Solotaire, Shelley Winters.

"Your friend struck out": Jill Isaacs, "Starlet Marries the Slugger: Nine Months of Tur-

moil," *Los Angeles Times,* March 9, 1999, p. 4.

One afternoon Joe joined Frank Sinatra for lunch at the Polo Lounge: The encounter between DiMaggio and the autograph seeker was overheard by then busboy Tim Jeffries.

"He has a big name": Richard Ben Cramer, *Joe DiMaggio: The Hero's Life,* p. 23.

"We're like a good double-play combination": Randall Riese and Neal Hitchens, *The Unabridged Marilyn: Her Life from A to Z,* p. 122.

Truman Capote: Author interview with Lester Persky, close friend of Capote's. Marilyn Monroe also admitted her prostitution to newspaper columnist Earl Wilson. (See Wilson papers at Indiana Library, Department of Special Collections.)

"the unforgivable sin" of posing: Riese and Hitchens, *Unabridged Marilyn,* pp. 70–71.

"You don't have to be part of it": Marilyn Monroe with Ben Hecht, *My Story.* All dialogue that follows is from the same source.

Richard Ben Cramer: Cramer, *Hero's Life,* p. 328.

"If I die": ibid., p. 326.

"she'd taped a note to her abdomen": Lois W. Banner, *MM Personal: From the Private Archive of Marilyn Monroe,* p. 177.

"all those vultures": JD would repeat the advice he gave MM to George and Robert Solotaire.

Chapter 3
Chapter 3 relies on interviews with Barbara Anthony, William Davies, Dr. Rose Fromm, Beebe Goddard, Dr. Judd Marmor, Susan Ryder.

"One of my patients": Dr. Judd Marmor interview. Marmor's papers are currently housed at UCLA (special collections) but as of 2011 had not yet been available to the public. It is not clear if they contained any notations on Marmor's dealings with Monroe. There seems to be no record of Marilyn Monroe's visits with Marmor in his papers at UCLA.
The doctor's name was Rose Fromm: Dr. Rose Fromm interview. Dr. Fromm kept notes on her meeting with MM, and these notes were made available to the author.
Roxanne Smith (pseudonym).
At age twenty, Jim Dougherty: Riese and Hitchens, *Unabridged Marilyn,* pp. 193–94.
she started to meet: ibid., p. 154.
"I never knew Marilyn Monroe": Hollywood Couples: Marilyn Monroe and Joe DiMaggio, DVD, 2005.

Chapter 4

Chapter 4 relies on interviews with Truman Capote, Bill Dickey, Dom DiMaggio, Emerald Duffy, Tommy Henrich, Eleanor James, Dario Lodigiani, Phil Rizzuto, Robert Solotaire, Richard Widmark.

"You'd have been better off with Joan Crawford": Fred Lawrence Guiles, *Legend: The Life of Marilyn Monroe,* p. 195.

claimed Joyce M. Hadley: Joyce M. Hadley, *Dorothy Arnold: Joe DiMaggio's First Wife,* pp. 52–58.

Del Prado Hotel: ibid., p. 62.

They spent Christmas: ibid., pp. 69–70.

Roger Kahn: Roger Kahn, *Joe & Marilyn: A Memory of Love.*

Dorothy hired a private investigator: Hadley, *Dorothy Arnold,* p. 77.

divorce papers: Superior Court of the State of California and the County of Los Angeles.

Richard Ben Cramer: Cramer, *Hero's Life,* pp. 333–34.

Chapter 5

Chapter 5 relies on interviews with Art Buchwald, Truman Capote, Dom DiMaggio, Joe DiMaggio Jr., Dario Lodigiani, Lester Persky, Sam Peters, Jane Russell, Robert Solotaire.

The first thing he did: Cramer, *Hero's Life,* p. 334.

Dorothy claimed she knew: There was a series of articles in a variety of magazines, beginning November 10, 1952, chronicling the legal showdown between Joe DiMaggio and Dorothy Arnold.

Judge Elmer Doyle: Superior Court in the State of California and the County of Los Angeles.

single: Robert F. Slatzer, *The Marilyn Files.*

"Good night, slugger": Jane Ellen Wayne, *Marilyn's Men: The Private Life of Marilyn Monroe,* p. 67.

second spat: Cramer, *Hero's Life,* p. 336.

on Christmas Eve: Donald Spoto, *Marilyn Monroe: The Biography,* p. 235.

Early one morning: June DiMaggio, *Marilyn, Joe & Me: June DiMaggio Tells It Like It Was,* pp. 64–68.

They shoved off: ibid., pp. 80–85.

Chapter 6

Chapter 6 relies on interviews with Paul Black, Bernie Kanter, Joe DiMaggio Jr., George Millman, Doris Lilly, Amy Lipps, Robert Solotaire, Shelley Winters.

Allan "Whitey" Snyder: All references in this chapter to Snyder are from an author interview with Snyder; cf. Snyder interview with Donald Spoto, July 22, 1992, at Marjorie Hendrick Library, Los Angeles.

"wanted to be an artist, not an erotic freak": Anthony Summers, *Goddess: The Secret Lives of Marilyn Monroe,* p. 51.

"Marilyn's the biggest thing": Riese and Hitchens, *Unabridged Marilyn,* p. 108.

"Café de Paris": See also James Haspiel, *Young Marilyn: Becoming the Legend,* p. 84. Haspiel, having interviewed 20th Century–Fox costume designer Billy Travilla, describes a similar scene, also at the Café de Paris.

Ned Wynn: Ned Wynn, *We Will Always Live in Beverly Hills: Growing up Crazy in Hollywood,* p. 80.

Rumpelmayer's: Interviews; cf. Morris Engelberg, *DiMaggio: Setting the Record Straight,* p. 195.

Baja California: Joe Jr. interview; cf. Robert Huber, "Joe DiMaggio Jr. Would Appreciate It If You'd Leave Him the Hell Alone," *Esquire.* June 1, 1999, p. 82; cf. Engelberg, *Setting the Record Straight,* pp. 191–96.

Chapter 7

Chapter 7 relies on interviews with Truman Capote, Dom DiMaggio, Lotte Goslar, Hugh Hefner, Whitey Snyder, Robert Solotaire.

"Joltin' Joe DiMaggio": Whitey Snyder interview; cf. Cramer, *Hero's Life,* p. 148.

members of his staff: Michelle Morgan, *Marilyn Monroe: Private and Disclosed,* p. 134.

Joe's thirty-ninth birthday: Summers, *Goddess:* p. 140.

Alice Hoffman: Morgan, Private and Disclosed, p. 135.

In his autobiography: Elia Kazan, *Elia Kazan: A Life,* pp. 453–54.

"womanly woman": Wayne, p. 112.

"I met a man tonight": Summers, *Goddess,* p. 56.

"Bewitch them": Christopher Bigsby, *Arthur Miller, 1915–1962,* p. 497.

"As you probably read": Letter from MM to Arthur Miller, January 7, 1954, confidential source.

Chapter 8
Chapter 8 relies on interviews with Dom DiMaggio, Joe DiMaggio Jr., Lotte Goslar, Robert Solotaire, Whitey Snyder.

Marilyn looked "radiant": Spoto, *Monroe: The Biography,* p. 261.

"I finally did it": Summers, *Goddess:* p. 92.

as a gesture of good: Spoto, *Monroe: The Biography,* p. 261.

"marriage is now my main career": Kahn, *A Memory of Love,* p. 255.

"We're not going shopping": ibid.

George H. Waple: See George H. Waple Papers, US Army Military History Institute. Waple also penned an autobiography, *Country Boy Gone Soldiering,* Airleaf Press, pp.

178–80.

"Dad": the Joe DiMaggio Collection at Public Auction, Item 866.

Sidney Skolsky: Lena Pepitone and William Stadiem, *Marilyn Monroe Confidential: An Intimate Personal Account,* p. 55.

she knew it was chic: Marilyn Monroe: In Her Own Words, p. 46.

abstract, impersonal concepts: Kazan, *A Life,* p. 403.

substantial raise: Cramer, *Hero's Life,* p. 362.

Chapter 9

Chapter 9 relies on interviews with Joe DiMaggio Jr., Lotte Goslar, Jim Haspiel, Evelyn Keyes, Hal Schaefer, Whitey Snyder, Robert Solotaire.

"I don't resent": Cramer, *Hero's Life,* p. 366.

"mob-connected fixers": Cramer, pp. 314, 405–6, 415–16, 419.

"It's ridiculous": Riese and Hitchens, *Unabridged Marilyn,* p. 287.

became so perturbed: Jerome Charyn, *Joe DiMaggio: The Center Fielder's Vigil,* p. 89.

"Dear Joe, I know I was wrong!": Joe DiMaggio Collection at Public Auction, #884.

"We used a friend's apartment": Hal Schaefer interview; cf. Summers, *Goddess,* pp. 109–110.

"dopey blonde": Susan Strasberg, *Marilyn and Me: Sisters, Rivals, Friends.*

"We went to the Palm": Robert Solotaire interview; cf. Engelberg, *Setting the Record Straight,* p. 250.

He had "the look of death": Charyn, *Center Fielder's Vigil,* pp. 90–91.

"Why are you calling me?": Lotte Goslar interview; cf. Charyn, *Center Fielder's Vigil,* p. 91.

Donald Spoto: Spoto, *Monroe: The Biography,* p. 291.

In response to a barrage of questions: ibid.

"I voluntarily gave up": UPI press release, October 27, 1954.

An intriguing footnote: interview with clerk of court, Los Angeles Superior Court, Los Angeles, CA, May 2010.

"If I get hit": Cramer, *Hero's Life,* pp. 370–71.

Roy Craft: Bigsby, *Arthur Miller, 1915–1962,* p. 300.

Chapter 10
Chapter 10 relies on interviews with and conducted by Truman Capote, Dom DiMaggio, Joe DiMaggio Jr., Jane Duffy, Amy Greene, Iselin Simon, Whitey Snyder, Robert Solotaire, Donald Spoto, Susan Strasberg.

Marilyn first met Greene: Spoto, *Monroe: The Biography,* p. 158

Marilyn Monroe Productions: Riese and Hitchens, *Unabridged Marilyn,* pp. 307–10.

press got wind: Dom DiMaggio interview; cf.

Spoto, *Monroe: The Biography,* p. 306.

"DiMaggio must have driven": David Cataneo, *I Remember Joe DiMaggio: Personal Memories of the Yankee Clipper by the People Who Knew Him Best,* p. 98.

to avoid being critical: Completed auction archives, Hunt Auctions, 2003.

"I saw that": Riese and Hitchens, *Unabridged Marilyn,* p. 501.

"For Dr. H—": Marilyn Monroe: *Fragments: Poems, Intimate Notes, Letters,* ed. Stanley Buchthal and Bernard Comment, p. 77.

Marilyn demonstrated: Steven Poser, *The Misfit* (ebook).

Harry Freud: Klaus Kamholz and Peter Swales, "Marilyn Monroe and Psychiatry," *Profil,* July 1992.

"People took advantage": Summers, *Goddess,* p. 129.

"A Beautiful Child": Truman Capote, *A Capote Reader,* pp. 578–89.

In his 1994 autobiography: Riese and Hitchens, *Unabridged Marilyn,* p. 164.

Chapter 11

Chapter 11 relies on interviews with Paul Baer, Gregg Sherwood Dodge, Lotte Goslar, Jim Haspiel, Suzanne McShane, Liz Renay, Liz Rohey, Robert Solotaire, Susan Strasberg, Ruth Warwick.

"There's no reason": JD letter to MM, June 24, 1955, confidential source.

"I no longer knew": Arthur Miller, *Timebends,* p. 356.

"He seemed rather desperate": Earl Wilson *Notebook,* Indiana University Library, Manuscript Division.

Horace Stoneham: Jeffrey Lyons, *Stories My Father Told Me: Notes from "The Lyons Den,"* p. 110.

"heart-throb": Cramer, *Hero's Life,* p. 505.

Liz Renay: Liz Renay interview; cf. Darwin Porter, *Hollywood Babylon: It's Back,* pp. 144–45.

Sir Cedric Hardwicke: Lyons, *Stories My Father Told Me,* p. 111.

Lee Meriwether: Cramer, *Hero's Life,* pp. 376–78.

Chapter 12

Chapter 12 relies on interviews with Cindy Adams, Maury Allen, Paul Baer, Saul Bellow, Joe DiMaggio Jr., Lotte Goslar, Kurt Lamprecht, Iselin Simon, Robert Solotaire, Susan Strasberg.

"When I tell": Riese and Hitchens, *Unabridged Marilyn,* p. 275.

"Why the hell": Joshua Logan, *Movie Stars, Real People, and Me,* pp. 111–12.

she made herself indispensable: ibid.

Lee Strasberg: Cindy Adams, *Lee Strasberg:*

The Imperfect Genius of the Actors Studio, pp. 269–72.

Maury Allen: Cramer, *Hero's Life,* pp. 374–75.

"I guess I was": Claire Booth Luce, "What Really Killed Marilyn Monroe," *Life.* August 7, 1964, p. 68.

"A good marriage": Marilyn Monroe: Fragments, ed. Buchthal and Comment, p. 219.

flirted with him: Joan's Show — a one-woman show at the Acorn Theater, August 2011.

"Why didn't you": Logan, *Movie Stars,* pp. 113–14.

"It was something about": Bigsby, *Arthur Miller, 1915–1962,* p. 588.

"always been deeply": Sam Kashner, "Marilyn and Her Monsters," *Vanity Fair,* November 2010, p. 110ff.

Paula Fichtl: Luciano Mecacci, *Freudian Slips: The Casualties of Psychoanalysis from the Wolf Man to Marilyn Monroe,* p. 9.

"When she left me": Kamholz and Swales, "Marilyn Monroe and Psychiatry."

"a garnet-colored velvet gown": Jeffrey Meyers, *The Genius and the Goddess: Arthur Miller and Marilyn Monroe,* p. 141.

"George, sweetie": confidential source.

Chapter 13

Chapter 13 relies on interviews with Rupert Allan, Paul Baer, Truman Capote, Joshua Greene Jr., Kurt Lamprecht, Lena Pepitone, Delos Smith, Susan Strasberg.

"sophisticated enough": Meyers, *The Genius and the Goddess,* p. 103.

"extraordinary child": Bigsby, *Arthur Miller, 1915–1962,* p. 507.

"My company wasn't": Meyers, *The Genius and the Goddess,* p. 167.

According to Amy Greene: Marie Clayton, *Marilyn Monroe: Unseen Archives,* p. 237.

Patricia Rosten: The Patricia Rosten section is based on interviews and correspondence with Rosten, today Patricia Rosten Filan, and her essay "Patricia Rosten on Marilyn," from the anthology *Close-Ups: Intimate Profiles of Movie Stars by Their Costars, Directors, Screenwriters, and Friends,* ed. Danny Peary.

"I am so concerned": Sam Kashner, "Marilyn and Her Monsters," p. 110ff.

Ernest Hemingway: Lyons, *Stories My Father Told Me,* p. 111.

Lola Mason: Cramer, *Hero's Life,* p. 376.

"A man and a woman": Summers, *Goddess,* p. 172.

"The very idea": Donald H. Wolfe, *The Last Days of Marilyn Monroe,* pp. 307–8.

John Strasberg: John Strasberg, *Accidentally on Purpose: Reflections on Life, Acting, and the Nine Natural Laws of Creativity,* pp. 21–22. In addition to reading his memoir, the author attempted to interview J.S., who declined to be interviewed.

refreshments had been served: Inez Melson, to Marilyn Monroe, December 5, 1954, confidential source.

Chapter 14
Chapter 14 relies on interviews with Paul Baer and Joe DiMaggio Jr.

Thanksgiving break: Cramer, *Hero's Life,* pp. 385–87.
5-5-5: Charyn, *Center Fielder's Vigil,* p. 102.
V. H. Monette: Cramer, *Hero's Life,* p. 401.

Chapter 15
Chapter 15 relies on interviews with Rupert Allan, Art Buchwald, Dom DiMaggio, Patricia Rosten Filan, Zsa Zsa Gabor, Lotte Goslar, Bernie Kamber, Lena Pepitone, Rob Saduski, Whitey Snyder, Robert Solotaire, Donald Spoto, Susan Strasberg, Jack Tilden.

"I'd love": Bigsby, *Arthur Miller, 1915–1962,* p. 604.
"Help, help, help": Kashner, "Marilyn and Her Monsters," p. 110ff.
"Had you, dear Arthur": Tony Curtis, *Tony Curtis: The Autobiography,* p. 162.
a British journalist: confidential source.
"My first meeting": Riese and Hitchens, *Unabridged Marilyn,* p. 315.
"Marilyn is a simple girl": ibid., pp. 317–18.

Chapter 16

Chapter 16 relies on interviews with Paul Baer, Truman Capote, Nancy Dickerson, Joe DiMaggio Jr., Kurt Lamprecht, Peter Lawford, Ralph Roberts, Lena Pepitone, Whitey Snyder, George Smathers, Dr. Milton Wexler, John White.

Monroe's addictions: Bigbsy, *Arthur Miller, 1915–1962,* p. 651.
Paula answered: ibid., p. 626.
Last Year: Poser, *The Misfit* (ebook).
"Oh Paula": Kashner, "Marilyn and Her Monsters," p. 110ff.
"I could not place": Miller, *Timebends,* p. 306.

Chapter 17

Chapter 17 relies on interviews with Paul Baer, Hans Bickel, Joey Bishop, Joe DiMaggio Jr., Peter Lawford, Mickey Mantle, Lena Pepitone, Janet Ramos, Ralph Roberts, Hal Schaefer, Earl Wilson.

therapy sessions: Greenson's patient notes.
seven-page letter: letter from Marilyn to Greenson in Greenson Archives at UCLA.
"Dr. Kris has had me put": Spoto, *Monroe: The Biography,* p. 364.
"Leave the lady alone": Cramer, *Hero's Life,* p. 396.
Miller had taken: Bigsby, *Arthur Miller, 1915– 1962,* p. 518.

Sinatra: Much of the information about Sinatra throughout comes from Riese and Hitchens, *Unabridged Marilyn.*

"Dear Dad Darling": Marilyn Monroe telegram to JD, Completed Auction Archive #27, 2003.

she felt happy: Ralph Roberts interview; cf. *Marilyn's Last Words: Her Secret Tapes and Mysterious Death,* p. 205.

"I love you, Joe": telegram from MM to JD, January 1, 1962. Confidential source.

Chapter 18

Chapter 18 relies on interviews with Joan Braden, Joe DiMaggio Jr., Lotte Goslar, Sidney Guilaroff, Peter Lawford, Ralph Roberts, Pierre Salinger, Whitey Snyder, Robert Solotaire, Mickey Song, Donald Spoto.

financial situation: Banner, *MM Personal,* p. 290. Banner's figures differ slightly from those derived from current author.

12305: Gary Vitacco-Robles, *Cursum Perficio: Marilyn Monroe's Brentwood Hacienda — The Story of Her Final Months.* pp. 16–20.

"like a young girl": Norman Rosten, *Marilyn: An Untold Story,* p. 107.

"she never came back": Cramer, *Hero's Life,* p. 406.

"Come on in": Lyons, *Stories My Father Told Me,* p. 111.

"From the man": Riese and Hitchens, *Un-*

abridged Marilyn, p. 175.

lashed out at: Peter Harry Brown and Patte B. Barham, *Marilyn: The Last Take,* p. 186.

"a no-good Jew bastard" and hung up on him: C. David Heymann, *RFK: A Candid Biography of Robert F. Kennedy,* p. 307.

Chapter 19

Chapter 19 relies on interviews with Jeanne Carmen, Joe DiMaggio Jr., Dr. Hyman Engelberg, Amy Greene, Daniel Greenson, Lotte Goslar, Peter Lawford, Richard Meryman, Chuck Pick, Ralph Roberts, Pierre Salinger, Arthur Schlesinger, George Solotaire, Mickey Song, Donald Spoto, Bert Stern.

"deeply paranoid": Dr. Ralph Greenson Archives, UCLA.

Dr. Eric Goldberg: a pseudonym. The Santa Barbara physician, now in his nineties, wishes to remain anonymous.

Chapter 20

Chapter 20 relies on interviews with Joe DiMaggio Jr., Milt Ebbins, Dr. Hyman Engelberg, Lotte Goslar, Kurt Lamprecht, Peter Lawford, Ralph Roberts, Mickey Rudin, Whitey Snyder, Robert Solotaire, Donald Spoto, Connie Stanville.

Norman Rosten: Cramer, *Hero's Life,* p. 364.

"I'd moved in": In an interview with the author, Peter Lawford originally claimed that Marilyn threatened RFK with a kitchen knife; he then revised the anecdote to indicate instead that she threw a glass of champagne at him.

"To be honest": Mickey Rudin interview; cf. Cramer, *Hero's Life,* pp. 411–14.

"Dear Joe": Gulies: *Legend,* p. 274.

"Last rites": Cramer, *Hero's Life,* p. 417.

"Marilyn Monroe was a legend": New York Times, August 9, 1962.

"I love you, I love you, I love you": Cramer, *The Hero's Life.*

The problem: Joe DiMaggio also seems to have discussed this subject with Lotte Goslar, who conveyed the quote to the author, as did Joe DiMaggio Jr.

Chapters 21 and 22

Chapter 21 relies on interviews with Dom DiMaggio, Joe DiMaggio Jr., Dr. Hyman Engelberg, Norman Mailer, Robert Solotaire, Louis Wolfson. Chapter 22 relies on material gleaned from the sources listed below.

several hypodermic: Summers, *Goddess,* p. 147.

"I could count": confidential source.

"It had to happen": Arthur Miller quoted in the *New York Post,* September 15, 1962.

Vincent Marotta: Linda Wertheimer interview.

According to Morris Engelberg: This and most of the quotes in this section are from Engelberg, *Setting the Record Straight.*

writer Ben Cramer: This and the anecdotes that follow are from Cramer, *Hero's Life.*

Chief executive Frank Sacco: Bob LaMendola, "Joltin' Joe," *South Florida Sun Sentinel,* March 9, 1999, p. 1A.

"very, very lonely life for a long time": Buzz Bissinger, "For Love of DiMaggio," *Vanity Fair,* September 2000, pp. 362–376.

"we were from different planets": This and other quotations from Joe DiMaggio Jr. come from Larry King interview with Joe DiMaggio Jr. on CNN.

"You know, I never got the words": Greg Garber, "Joe DiMaggio Jr.: In the Shadows," *Seattle Times,* March 21, 1999, p. D-3.

through still in a ponytail: Richard Jerome, "Joe DiMaggio: The Quiet Man," *People,* March 29, 1999, p. 110–113.

BIBLIOGRAPHY

Adam, V. *The Marilyn Encyclopedia.* New York: Overlook Press, 1999.

Adams, Cindy. *Lee Strasberg: The Imperfect Genius of the Actors Studio.* Garden City, NY: Doubleday, 1980.

Adams, Joey. *Here's to the Friars: The Heart of Show Business.* New York: Crown, 1976.

Adomites, Paul, ed. *Cooperstown Baseball's Hall of Famers.* Lincolnwood, IL: Publications International, 1999.

Allen, Maury. *Where Have You Gone, Joe DiMaggio: The Story of America's Last Hero.* New York: E. P. Dutton, 1975.

Anderson, Janice. *Marilyn Monroe.* UK: Skegness, LIN, 1991.

Appel, Marty. *Now Pitching for the Yankees: Spinning the News for Mickey, Reggie and George.* Kingston, NY: Sport Media, 2003.

Bacall, Lauren. *Lauren Bacall by Myself.* New York: Knopf, 1979.

Bacon, James. *Hollywood Is a Four-Letter Town.* New York: Avory, 1976.

Baker, Carroll. *Baby Doll: An Autobiography.* New York: Arbor House, 1983.

Banner, Lois W. *MM Personal: From the Private Archive of Marilyn Monroe.* Photographs by Mark Anderson. New York: Abrams, 2010.

Barris, George. *Marilyn: Her Life in Her Own Words: Marilyn Monroe's Revealing Last Words and Photographs.* Secaucus, NJ: Carol, 1995.

Barven, Marilyn. *Screen Greats No. 4.* Milburn Smith, ed. New York: Barven, 1971.

Bell, Simon, et al. *Who's Had Who.* New York: Warner Books, 1990.

Bellow, Saul. *Letters.* Benjamin Taylor, ed. New York: Viking, 2010.

Berle, Milton, with Haskel Frankel. *Milton Berle: An Autobiography.* New York: Applause Theatre & Cinema Books, 2002.

Bernard, Susan. *Marilyn: Intimate Exposures.* Los Angeles: Playboy Press, 2011.

Berra, Yogi, with Dave Kaplan. *Ten Rings: My Championship Seasons.* New York: William Morrow, 2003.

Berthelson, Detler. *Alltag bei Familie Freud: die Erinnerungen der Paula Fichtl.* Hamburg, Germany: Hoffmann und Campe Verlag, 1987.

Bigsby, C. W. L. *Arthur Miller, 1915–1962.* Cambridge, MA: Harvard University Press, 2009.

Bissinger, Buzz. "For Love of DiMaggio," *Vanity Fair,* September 2000.

Blackwell, Earl. *Earl Blackwell's Celebrity Register.* New York: Simon & Schuster, 1973.

———. *Earl Blackwell's Celebrity Register.* Towson, MD: Times, 1986.

Boorstin, Daniel J. *The Image: A Guide to Pseudo-Events in America.* New York: Atheneum, 1972.

Bosworth, Patricia. *Montgomery Clift: A Biography.* New York and London: Harcourt Brace Jovanovich, 1978.

Brando, Marlon, with Robert Lindsay. *Brando: Songs My Mother Taught Me.* New York: Random House, 1994.

"Brilliant Stardom and Personal Tragedy Punctuated the Life of Marilyn Monroe." *New York Times,* August 6, 1962.

Bronaugh, Robert Brett. *The Celebrity Birthday Book.* Middle Village, NY: J. David, 1981.

Bronner, Edwin. *The Encyclopedia of the American Theatre, 1900–1975.* San Diego: A. S. Barnes, 1980.

Brown, David. *Let Me Entertain You.* New York: William Morrow, 1990.

Brown, Les. *The New York Times Encyclopedia of Television.* New York: Times Books, 1977.

Brown, Peter Harry. *Kim Novak: Reluctant Goddess.* New York: St. Martin's Press, 1986.

Brown, Peter Harry, and Patte B. Barham. *Marilyn: The Last Take.* New York: E. P. Dutton, 1992.

Buchthal, Stanley, and Bernard Comment, eds. *Marilyn Monroe: Fragments, Poems, Intimate Notes, Letters.* New York: Farrar, Straus, and Giroux, 2010.

Bumiller, Elizabeth. "Late to DiMaggio Orbit, but Staging Send-Off." *New York Times,* April 23, 1999.

Cataneo, David. *I Remember Joe DiMaggio: Personal Memories of the Yankee Clipper by the People Who Knew Him Best.* Nashville: Cumberland House, 2001.

Capell, Frank A. *The Strange Death of Marilyn Monroe.* Zarepath, NJ: Herald of Freedom, 1964.

Capote, Truman. *A Capote Reader.* New York: Random House, 1987.

————. *Music for Chameleons: New Writing.* New York: Random House, 1980.

Carpozi Jr., George. *Marilyn Monroe: "Her Own Story."* New York: Bellmont, 1961.

Cassini, Igor, with Jeanne Molli. *I'd Do It All Over Again.* New York: G. P. Putnam's Sons, 1977.

Cassini, Igor. *In My Own Fashion: An Autobiography.* New York: Simon & Schuster, 1987.

Charyn, Jerome. *Joe DiMaggio: The Center Fielder's Vigil.* New Haven, CT: Yale University Press, 2011.

Clark, Colin. *My Week with Marilyn.* New York: Weinstein Books, 2011.

———. *The Prince, the Showgirl, and Me: Six Months on the Set with Marilyn and Olivier.* New York: St. Martin's Press, 1996.

Clarke, Gerald. *Capote: A Biography.* New York: Simon & Schuster, 1988.

Clayton, Marie. *Marilyn Monroe: Unseen Archives.* Bath, England: Paragon, 2009.

Collier, Peter, et al. *The Kennedys: An American Drama.* New York: Summit Books, 1984.

Conover, David. *Finding Marilyn.* New York: Grosset & Dunlap, 1981.

Considine, Bob. *Toots.* New York: Meredith Press, 1969.

Considine, Shaun. *Bette and Joan: The Divine Feud.* New York: E. P. Dutton, 1989.

Conway, Michael. *The Films of Marilyn Monroe.* New York: Citadel Press, 1964.

Coward, Noel. *The Noel Coward Diaries.* Graham Payn and Sheridan Morley, eds. Boston: Little, Brown, 1985.

Cramer, Richard Ben. *Joe DiMaggio: The Hero's Life.* New York: Simon & Schuster, 2000.

Cunningham, Ernest W. *The Ultimate Marilyn.* Los Angeles: Renaissance Books, 1998.

Curti, Carlo. *Skouras, King of Fox Studios.* Los Angeles: Holloway House, 1967.

Curtis, Tony. *American Prince: A Memoir.* New

York: Harmony Books, 2008.

Curtis, Tony, with Mark A. Vieira. *The Making of* Some Like It Hot: *My Memories of Marilyn Monroe and the Classic American Movie.* Hoboken, NJ: John Wiley & Sons, 2009.

Curtis, Tony, and Barry Paris. *Tony Curtis: The Autobiography.* New York: William Morrow, 1993.

Dalton, David. *James Dean, American Icon.* Photo editor, Ron Cayen. New York: St. Martin's Press, 1984.

————. *James Dean, The Mutant King: A Biography.* New York: St. Martin's Press, 1974.

David, Lester, and Jhan Robbins. *Richard & Elizabeth.* New York: Funk & Wagnalls, 1977.

de Dienes, André. *Marilyn.* New York: Barnes & Noble, 2007.

————. *Marilyn, Mon Amour: The Private Album of André de Dienes, Her Preferred Photographer.* New York: St. Martin's Press, 1985.

DeGregorio, George. *Joe DiMaggio: An Informal Biography.* New York: Stein and Day, 1981.

Dick, Bernard F. *Billy Wilder.* Boston: Twayne, 1980.

DiMaggio, Dom. *Real Grass, Real Heroes: Baseball's Historic 1941 Season.* New York: Kensington, 1990.

DiMaggio, Joe, with Richard Whittingham. *The DiMaggio Albums: Selection from the Public and Private Collections Celebrating the Baseball Career of Joe DiMaggio.* New York: G. P. Putnam's Sons, 1989.

DiMaggio, Joe. *Lucky to Be a Yankee.* New York: Grosset & Dunlap, 1957.

DiMaggio, June. *Marilyn, Joe & Me: June DiMaggio Tells It Like It Was.* Roseville, CA: Penmarin Books, 2006.

Doug, Warren. *The Reluctant Movie Queen.* New York: St. Martin's Press, 1981.

Dougherty, James E. *The Secret Happiness of Marilyn Monroe.* Chicago: Playboy Press, 1976.

————. *To Norma Jeane with Love, Jimmie.* Chesterfield, MO: Beach House Books, 1997.

Dunleavy, Steve. *Those Wild, Wild Kennedy Boys.* Reported by Stephen Dunleavy and Peter Brennan. New York: Pinnacle Books, 1976.

Dunn, Herb. *Joe DiMaggio, Young Sports Hero.* New York: Aladdin Paperbacks, 1999.

Durso, Joseph. *DiMaggio: The Last American Knight.* New York: Little, Brown, 1995.

Dwight, Eleanor. *Diana Vreeland.* New York: Harper Collins, 2002.

Edwards, Anne. *The Grimaldis of Monaco.* New York: William Morrow, 1992.

————. *Judy Garland: A Biography.* New York:

Simon & Schuster, 1975.

————. *Vivien Leigh: A Biography.* New York: Simon & Schuster, 1977.

Eells, George. *Robert Mitchum: A Biography.* New York: F. Watts, 1984.

Engelberg, Morris. *DiMaggio: Setting the Record Straight.* St. Paul, MN: MBI, 2003.

Farber, Stephen. *Hollywood on the Couch: A Candid Look at the Overheated Love Affair Between Psychiatrists and Moviemakers.* New York: William Morrow, 1993.

Fein, Irving A. *Jack Benny: An Intimate Biography.* New York: G. P. Putnam's Sons, 1976.

Franklin, Joe, and Laurie Palmer. *The Marilyn Monroe Story.* New York: R. Field; Greenberg trade distributors, 1953.

Freedland, Michael. *Jane Fonda: A Biography.* New York: St. Martin's Press, 1988.

Freud, Anna. "Beating Fantasies and Daydreams (1922)" in *The Writings of Anna Freud,* vol. 1. New York: International Universities Press, 1974.

Freud, Sigmund. *The Selected Letters.* New York: Basic Books, 1960.

Frommer, Harvey. *The New York Yankee Encyclopedia.* New York: Macmillan, 1997.

Gabler, Neal. *Winchell: Gossip, Power and the Culture of Celebrity.* New York: Knopf, 1994.

Garber, Greg. "Joe DiMaggio Jr.: In the Shadows," *Seattle Times.* March 21, 1999.

Gatti, Arthur. *The Kennedy Curse.* Chicago:

Regnery, 1976.

Gentry, Curt. *J. Edgar Hoover: The Man and the Secrets.* New York: Norton, 1991.

Giancana, Sam. *Double Cross: The Explosive, Inside Story of the Mobsters Who Controlled America.* New York: Warner Books, 1992.

Giesler, Jerry, as told to Peter Martin. *The Jerry Giesler Story.* New York: Simon & Schuster, 1960.

Glatzer, Jenna. *The Marilyn Monroe Treasures.* New York: Metro Books, 2008.

Godfrey, Lionel. *Paul Newman, Superstar: A Critical Biography.* New York: St. Martin's Press, 1978.

Good, David F., and Ruth Wodak, eds. *From World War to Waldheim: Culture and Politics in Austria and the United States.* New York and Oxford: Berghahn, 1999.

Goode, James. *The Story of* The Misfits. Indianapolis: Bobbs-Merrill, 1963.

Goslar, Lotte. *What's So Funny: Sketches from My Life.* Australia: Harwood Academic, 1998.

Gottfried, Martin. *Arthur Miller: His Life and Work.* Cambridge, MA: Da Capo Press, 2003.

Graham, Sheilah. *Hollywood Revisited: A Fiftieth Anniversary Celebration.* New York: St. Martin's, 1985.

Greenberg, Harvey R. *Screen Memories: Hollywood Cinema on the Psychoanalytic*

Couch. New York: Columbia University Press, 1993.

Greenson, Ralph R. Archives, UCLA Library System, Los Angeles.

―――. *Explorations in Psychoanalysis*. New York: International Universities Press, 1978.

―――. *The Technique and Practice in Psychoanalysis*. London: Hogarth Press, 1967.

Gregory, Adela, with Milo Speriglio. *Crypt 33: The Saga of Marilyn Monroe — The Final Word*. Secaucus, NJ: Carol, 1993.

Greif, Martin. *The Gay Book of Days: An Evocatively Illustrated Who's Who of Who Is, Was, May Have Been, Probably Was, and Almost Certainly Seems to Have Been Gay During the Past 5,000 Years*. London: W. H. Allen: Comet, 1982.

Griffith, Richard, and Arthur Mayer. *The Movies: The Sixty-Year Story of the World of Hollywood and Its Effect on America from Pre-Nickelodeon Days to the Present*. New York: Bonanza Books, 1957.

Grobel, Lawrence. *Conversations with Capote*. New York and Scarborough, Ontario: New American Library, 1985.

―――. *The Hustons*. New York: C. Scribner's Sons, 1989.

Grosskurth, Phyllis. *Melanie Klein: Her World and Her Work*. Cambridge, MA: Harvard University Press, 1987.

Guilaroff, Sydney, as told to Cathy Griffin.

Crowning Glory: Reflections of Hollywood's Favorite Confidant. Introduction by Angela Lansbury. Santa Monica, CA: General, 1996.

Guild, Leo. *Zanuck, Hollywood's Last Tycoon.* Los Angeles: Holloway House, 1970.

Guiles, Fred Lawrence. *Legend: The Life of Marilyn Monroe.* New York: Stein and Day, 1984.

————. *Norma Jean: The Life of Marilyn Monroe.* New York: McGraw-Hill, 1969.

Hadley, Joyce M. *Dorothy Arnold: Joe DiMaggio's First Wife.* Oak Park, IL: Chauncey Park Press, 1993.

Hamblett, Charles. *Who Killed Marilyn Monroe? Or, Cage to Catch Our Dreams.* London: Leslie Frewin, 1966.

Harris, Warren G. *The Other Marilyn: A Biography of Marilyn Miller.* New York: Arbor House, 1985.

Haspiel, James. *Marilyn: The Ultimate Look at the Legend.* New York: Henry Holt, 1991.

————. *Young Marilyn: Becoming the Legend.* New York: Hyperion, 1994.

Herndon, Venable. *James Dean: A Short Life.* Garden City, NY: Doubleday, 1974.

Hersh, Seymour M. *The Dark Side of Camelot.* New York: Little, Brown, 1997.

Heymann, C. David. *The Georgetown Ladies' Social Club: Power, Passion, and Politics in the Nation's Capital.* New York: Atria Books, 2003.

———. *Liz: An Intimate Biography of Elizabeth Taylor.* New York: Atria Books, 1995.

———. *RFK: A Candid Biography of Robert F. Kennedy.* New York: E. P. Dutton, 1998.

———. *A Woman Named Jackie: An Intimate Biography of Jacqueline Bouvier Kennedy Onassis.* New York: Carol, 1994.

Hirschhorn, Clive. *Gene Kelly: A Biography.* New York: St. Martin's Press, 1984.

Hollywood Couples: Marilyn Monroe and Joe DiMaggio, DVD, 2005.

Hougan, Jim. *Spooks: The Haunting of America: The Private Use of Secret Agents.* New York: William Morrow, 1978.

Houseman, John. *Front and Center.* New York: Simon & Schuster, 1979.

Hoyt, Edwin Palmer. *Marilyn, the Tragic Venus.* New York: Duell, Sloan and Pearce, 1965.

Huber, Robert. "Joe DiMaggio Jr. Would Appreciate It If You'd Leave Him the Hell Alone," *Esquire.* June 1, 1999.

Hudson, James A. *The Mysterious Death of Marilyn Monroe.* New York: Voilant Books, 1968.

Huston, John. *An Open Book.* New York: Da Capo Press, 1994.

Images of Marilyn. Bath, BA1, 1HE, England, 2008.

Isaacs, Jill. "Starlet Marries Slugger: Nine Months of Turmoil." *Los Angeles Times.* March 9, 1999.

Israel, Lee. *Kilgallen.* New York: Delacorte Press, 1979.

Jacke, Andreas. *Marilyn Monroe und die Psychoanalyse.* Giessen, Germany: Psychosozial-Verlag, 2005.

Jacoby, Russell. *The Repression of Psychoanalysis: Otto Fenichel and the Political Freudians.* New York: Basic Books, 1983.

James, Ann. *The Kennedy Scandals & Tragedies.* Lincolnwood, IL: Publications International, 1991.

Jerome, Richard. "Joe DiMaggio: The Quiet Man." *People,* March 29, 1999.

The Joe DiMaggio Collection at Public Auction. New York: Hunt Auctions, 2006.

Johnson, Nora. *Flashback: Nora Johnson on Nunnally Johnson.* New York: Doubleday, 1979.

Josefsberg, Milt. *The Jack Benny Show.* New Rochelle, NY: Arlington House, 1977.

Jung, C. G. "Psychic Conflicts in a Child (1910)" in *Collected Works,* vol. 17. London: Routledge & Kegan Paul, 1954.

Kael, Pauline. *Reeling.* Boston: Little, Brown, 1976.

Kahn, Roger. *Joe & Marilyn: A Memory of Love.* New York: William Morrow, 1986.

Kamholz, Klaus, and Peter Swales. "Marilyn

Monroe and Psychiatry." *Profil.* July, 1992.

Kaplan, James. *Frank: The Voice.* New York: Doubleday, 2010.

Kashner, Sam. "Marilyn and Her Monsters," *Vanity Fair,* November 2010, p. 110.

Kashner, Sam, and Nancy Schoenberger. *Furious Love: Elizabeth Taylor, Richard Burton, and the Marriage of the Century.* New York: HarperCollins, 2010.

Katz, Ephraim. *The Film Encyclopedia.* New York: Harper & Row, 1979.

Kazan, Elia. *Elia Kazan: A Life.* New York: Alfred A. Knopf, 1988.

Kelley, Kitty. *Elizabeth, The Last Star.* New York: Simon & Schuster, 1981.

————. *His Way: The Unauthorized Biography of Frank Sinatra.* Toronto and New York: Bantam Press, 1986.

Kennedy, Jacqueline. *Jacqueline Kennedy: Historic Conversations on Life with John F. Kennedy. Interviews with Arthur M. Schlesinger, Jr.,1964.* Foreword by Caroline Kennedy. Introduction by Michael Beschloss. New York: Hyperion, 2011.

Kenneth. *Kenneth's Complete Book on Hair.* Joan Rattner Heilman, ed.; Cornelia Smith, ill. Garden City, NY: Doubleday, 1972.

Keyes, Evelyn. *Scarlett O'Hara's Younger Sister: My Lively Life in and out of Hollywood.* Secaucus, NJ: L. Stuart, 1977.

Klein, Melanie. *The Writings of Melanie Klein.*

London: Hogarth Press and the Institute of Psycho-Analysis, 1975.

Knight, Timothy. *Marilyn Monroe in the Movies: A Retrospective.* New York: Metro Books, 2009.

Kobal, John, ed. *Marilyn Monroe: A Life on Film.* Introduction by David Robinson. London and New York: Hamlyn, 1983.

Kreisman, Jerold Jay. *I Hate You, Don't Leave Me: Understanding the Borderline Personality.* New York: Avon Books, 1989.

Lacey, Robert. *Grace.* New York: G. P. Putnam's Sons, 1994.

LaGuardia, Robert. *Monty: A Biography of Montgomery Clift.* New York: Arbor House, 1977.

LaMendola, Bob. "Joltin' Joe." *South Florida Sun-Sentinel,* March 9, 1999.

Lawford, May, Lady. *"Bitch!": The Autobiography of Lady Lawford.* Brookline Village, MA: Branden, 1986.

Lawford, Patricia Seaton, with Ted Schwarz. *The Peter Lawford Story: Life with the Kennedys, Monroe, and the Rat Pack.* New York: Carroll & Graf, 1988.

Leamer, Laurence. *The Kennedy Women: The Saga of an American Family.* New York: Villard, 1994.

Learning, Barbara. *Marilyn Monroe.* New York: Crown, 1998.

———. *Orson Welles: A Biography.* New York:

Penguin, 1989.

Leavy, Jane. *The Last Boy: Mickey Mantle and the End of America's Childhood.* New York: Harper, 2010.

Leigh, Janet. *There Really Was a Hollywood.* Garden City, NY: Doubleday, 1984.

Lemboum, Hans Jorgen. *Diary of a Lover of Marilyn Monroe.* Trans. by Hallberg Hallmundsson. New York: Arbor House, 1979.

Lerman, Leo. *The Grand Surprise: The Journals of Leo Lerman.* Stephen Pascal, ed. New York: Alfred A. Knopf, 2007.

Levy, Shawn. *Rat Pack Confidential: Frank, Dean, Sammy, Peter, Joey, and the Last Great Showbiz Party.* New York: Doubleday, 1998.

Linet, Beverly. *Susan Hayward: Portrait of a Survivor.* New York: Atheneum, 1980.

Lloyd, Ann, and Graham Fuller, eds. *The Illustrated Who's Who of the Cinema.* Arnold Desser, consultant editor. New York: Macmillan, 1983.

Logan, Joshua. *Movie Stars, Real People, and Me.* New York: Dell, 1978.

Luce, Claire Booth. "What Really Killed Marilyn Monroe," *Life.* August 7, 1964.

Lyons, Jeffrey. *Stories My Father Told Me: Notes from "The Lyons Den."* New York: Abbeville Press, 2011.

Madden, Bill. *Steinbrenner: The Last Lion of Baseball.* New York: HarperCollins, 2010.

Mailer, Norman. *Marilyn, A Biography.* New York: Grosset & Dunlap, 1973.

————. *Of Women and Their Elegance.* New York: Simon & Schuster, 1980.

Mann, May. *Jayne Mansfield: A Biography.* London: Abelard-Schuman, 1974.

Manso, Peter. *Brando: The Biography.* New York: Hyperion, 1994.

————. *Mailer: His Life and Times.* New York: Simon & Schuster, 1985.

Mark, Kenneth S. *Star Stats: Who's Who in Hollywood.* Los Angeles: Price Stern Sloan, 1979.

Marshall, David. *The DD Group: An Online Investigation into the Death of Marilyn Monroe.* iUniverse, 2005.

Martin, Pete. *Will Acting Spoil Marilyn Monroe?* Garden City, NY: Doubleday, 1956.

Martin, Ralph G. *A Hero for Our Time: An Intimate Story of the Kennedy Years.* New York: Macmillan, 1983.

Marx, Arthur. *The Nine Lives of Mickey Rooney.* New York: Stein and Day, 1986.

Masters, George. *The Masters Way to Beauty.* New York: E. P. Dutton, 1977.

McBride, Joseph, ed. *Focus on Howard Hawks.* Englewood Cliffs, NJ: Prentice Hall, 1972.

McDonough, Yona Zeldis, ed. *All the Available Light: A Marilyn Monroe Reader.* New York: Simon & Schuster/Touchstone, 2002.

McIntosh, William Currie. *The Private Cary*

Grant. London: Sidgwick & Jackson, 1983.

Mecacci, Luciano. *Freudian Slips: The Casualties of Psychoanalysis from the Wolf Man to Marilyn Monroe.* Isle of Lewis, Scotland: Vagabond Voices, 2009.

Mellen, Joan. *Marilyn Monroe.* New York: Pyramid, 1973.

Meyers, Jeffrey. *Gary Cooper: American Hero.* New York: William Morrow, 1998.

———. *The Genius and the Goddess: Arthur Miller and Marilyn Monroe.* Urbana and Chicago: University of Illinois Press, 2009.

Miller, Arthur. *After the Fall: A Play in Two Acts.* New York: Viking Press, 1964.

———. *Timebends: A Life.* New York: Penguin Books, 1995.

Miller, Arthur. Interview in the *New York Post.* September 15, 1962.

Miracle, Berniece Baker, with Mona Rae Miracle. *My Sister Marilyn: A Memoir of Marilyn Monroe.* Chapel Hill, NC: Algonquin Books of Chapel Hill, 1994.

Monroe, Marilyn, with Ben Hecht. *My Story.* New York: Stein and Day, 1974.

Montalban, Manuel Vazquez. *El hermano pequeño.* Barcelona, Spain: Planeta, 1994.

Moore, Jack B. *Joe DiMaggio, Baseball's Yankee Clipper.* New York: Praeger, 1987.

Moore, Robin. *Marilyn & Joe DiMaggio.* New York: Manor Books, 1977.

Morelle, Joe. *Brando: The Unauthorized Biog-*

raphy. New York: Crown, 1973.

Morgan, Michelle. *Marilyn Monroe: Private and Disclosed.* New York: Carroll & Graf, 2007.

Mosley, Leonard. *Zanuck: The Rise and Fall of Hollywood's Last Tycoon.* London: Granada, 1984.

Moss, Leonard. *Arthur Miller.* New York: Twayne, 1967.

Munn, Michael. *Hollywood Rogues.* New York: St. Martin's, 1991.

Murray, Eunice, with Rose Shade. *Marilyn, the Last Months.* New York: Pyramid Books, 1975.

Nelson, Nancy. *Evenings with Cary Grant: Recollections in His Own Words and by Those Who Knew Him Best.* New York: William Morrow, 1991.

Noguchi, Thomas T. *Coroner to the Stars.* London: Corgi Books, 1984.

Oates, Joyce Carol. *Blonde: A Novel.* New York: Echo Press, 2000.

Okrent, Daniel. *Baseball Anecdotes.* New York and Oxford: Oxford University Press, 1989.

Olivier, Laurence. *Confessions of an Actor: An Autobiography.* New York: Simon & Schuster, 1982.

Oppenheimer, Joel. *Marilyn Lives!* New York: Delilah Books, 1981.

Pack, Robert. *Edward Bennett Williams for the*

Defense. New York: Harper & Row, 1983.

Parish, James Robert. *The Fox Girls.* New Rochelle, NY: Arlington House, 1972.

Peary, Danny, ed. *Close-Ups: Intimate Profiles of Movie Stars by Their Co-Stars, Directors, Screenwriters, and Friends.* New York: Workman, 1978.

Pepitone, Lena, and William Stadiem. *Marilyn Monroe Confidential: An Intimate Personal Account.* New York: Simon & Schuster, 1979.

Persico, Joseph E. *Edward R. Murrow: An American Original.* New York: McGraw-Hill, 1988.

Pitts, Michael R. *Hollywood on Record: The Film Star's Discography.* Metuchen, NJ: Scarecrow Press, 1978.

Plimpton, George. *Truman Capote: In Which Various Friends, Enemies, Acquaintances, and Detractors Recall His Turbulent Career.* New York: Nan A. Talese, Doubleday, 1997.

Porter, Darwin. *Hollywood Babylon: It's Back.* Staten Island, NY: Blood Moon Productions, 2008.

———. *Hollywood Babylon Strikes Again.* Staten Island, NY: Blood Moon Productions, 2010.

Poser, Steven. *The Misfit* (ebook). New York: RosettaBooks, 2011.

Renay, Liz. *My First 2000 Men.* Fort Lee, NJ: Barricade Books, 1992.

Riegert, Ray. *Hidden San Francisco and Northern California: Including Napa, Sonoma, Mendocino, Santa Cruz, Monterey, Yosemite, and Lake Tahoe.* San Francisco: Ulysses Press, 1984.

Riese, Randall, and Neal Hitchens. *The Unabridged Marilyn: Her Life from A to Z.* New York: Congdon & Weed, 1987.

Roberts, Glenys. *Bardot: A Personal Biography.* London: Sidgwick & Jackson, 1984.

Robertson, Patrick. *Movie Facts and Feats: A Guinness Record Book.* New York: Sterling, 1980.

Robyns, Gwen. *Princess Grace.* New York: McKay, 1976.

Rollyson Jr., Carl E. *Marilyn Monroe: A Life of the Actress.* Ann Arbor, MI: UMI Research Press, 1986.

Romero, Gerry. *Sinatra's Women.* New York: Manor Books, 1976.

Rooney, Mickey. *Life Is Too Short.* New York: Villard Books, 1991.

Rosen, Marjorie. *Popcorn Venus: Women, Movies & the American Dream.* New York: Coward, McCann & Geoghegan, 1973.

Rosten, Norman. *Marilyn: An Untold Story.* New York: New American Library, 1973.

Russell, Jane. *Jane Russell: My Paths and My Detours.* New York: F. Watts, 1985.

Russo, Vito. *Celluloid Closet: Homosexuality in the Movies.* New York: Harper & Row, 1981.

Sands, Frederick. *The Divine Garbo.* New York: Grosset & Dunlap, 1979.

Saxton, Martha. *Jayne Mansfield and the American Fifties.* Boston: Houghton Mifflin, 1975.

Schickel, Richard. *Elia Kazan: A Biography.* New York: HarperCollins, 2005.

Schlesinger Jr., Arthur M. *Journals, 1952–2000.* Edited by Andrew Schlesinger and Stephen Schlesinger. New York: Penguin Press, 2007.

Schneider, Michel. *Marilyn Dernières Séances.* Rome and Paris: Grosset, 2006.

Sciacca, Tony. *Who Killed Marilyn.* New York: Manor Books, 1976.

Scott, Henry, E. *Shocking True Story: The Rise and Fall of* Confidential, *"America's Most Scandalous Scandal Magazine."* New York: Pantheon Books, 2010.

Selsman, Michael. *All Is Vanity: Memoirs of a Hollywood Operative.* Los Angeles: New World Digital, 2009.

Shaw, Sam. *Marilyn Monroe in the Camera Eye.* London: Hamlyn, 1979.

———. *Marilyn Monroe as the Girl. The Candid Picture — Story of "The Seven Year Itch."* Foreword by George Axelrod. New York: Ballantine Books, 1955.

Shaw, Sam, and Norman Rosten. *Marilyn Among Friends.* London: Bloomsbury, 1987.

Sheppard, Dick. *Elizabeth: The Life and Career of Elizabeth Taylor.* Garden City, NY: Doubleday, 1974.

Shevey, Sandra. *The Marilyn Scandal: Her True Life Revealed by Those Who Knew Her.* New York: William Morrow, 1987.

Shipman, David. *The Great Movie Stars: The Golden Years.* New York: Hill and Wang, 1979.

Signoret, Simone. *Nostalgia Isn't What It Used to Be.* New York: Penguin Books, 1979.

Silverman, Stephen M. *The Fox That Got Away: The Last Days of the Zanuck Dynasty at Twentieth Century–Fox.* Secaucus, NJ: Lyle Stuart, 1988.

Sinatra, Barbara, with Wendy Holden. *Lady Blue Eyes: My Life With Frank.* New York: Crown Archetypes, 2011.

Skinner, John Walter. *Who's Who on the Screen.* Worthing, England: Madeleine Productions, 1983.

Skolsky, Sidney. *Don't Get Me Wrong — I Love Hollywood.* New York: G. P. Putnam's Sons, 1975.

Slatzer, Robert F. *The Life and Curious Death of Marilyn Monroe.* New York: Pinnacle Books, 1974.

———. *The Marilyn Files.* New York: S.P.I. Books, 1994.

Smith, Ella. *Starring Miss Barbara Stanwyck.* New York: Crown, 1974.

Smith, Matthew. *Marilyn's Last Words: Her Secret Tapes and Mysterious Death.* New York: Carroll & Graf, 2004.

Spada, James, with George Zeno. *Monroe, Her Life in Pictures.* Garden City, NY: Doubleday, 1982.

Spada, James. *Peter Lawford: The Man Who Kept the Secrets.* New York: Bantam Books, 1991.

Speriglio, Milo. *The Marilyn Conspiracy.* New York: Pocket Books, 1986.

————. *Marilyn Monroe, Murder Cover-up.* Van Nuys, CA: Seville, 1982.

Spoto, Donald. *Marilyn Monroe: The Biography.* London: Arrow, 1974.

Springer, John Shipman, and Jack D. Hamilton. *They Had Faces Then: Annabella to Zorina: The Superstars, Stars, and Starlets of the 1930's.* Secaucus, NJ: Citadel Press, 1974.

Steinberg, Cobbett. *Film Facts.* New York: Facts on File, 1980.

Steinem, Gloria. *Marilyn.* New York: MJF Books, 1986.

Stern, Bert. *The Last Sitting.* Milan: Electa; New York: distributed by Random House, 2006.

Stine, Whitney. *Stars & Star Handlers: The Business of Show.* Santa Monica, CA: Roundtable, 1985.

Stout, Glenn. *DiMaggio: An Illustrated Life.*

Dick Johnson, ed. New York: Walker, 1995.

Strasberg, John. *Accidentally on Purpose: Reflections on Life, Acting, and the Nine Natural Laws of Creativity.* New York and London: Applause Books, 1996.

Strasberg, Lee. *The Lee Strasberg Notes.* Lola Cohen, ed. London and New York: Routledge, 2010.

Strasberg, Susan. *Bittersweet.* New York: G. P. Putnam's Sons, 1980.

————. *Marilyn and Me: Sisters, Rivals, Friends.* New York: Warner Books, 1992.

Stuart, Sandra Lee. *The Pink Palace: Behind Closed Doors at the Beverly Hills Hotel.* Secaucus, NJ: L. Stuart, 1978.

Sullivan, George. *Sluggers: Twenty-Seven of Baseball's Greatest.* New York: Atheneum, 1991.

Summers, Anthony. *Goddess: The Secret Lives of Marilyn Monroe.* A chapter has been added to the original text. New York: New American Library, 1986.

————. *Official and Confidential: The Secret Life of J. Edgar Hoover.* New York: G. P. Putnam's Sons, 1993.

————. *Goddess: The Secret Lives of Marilyn Monroe.* London: V. Gollanz, 1985.

Talese, Gay. *The Gay Talese Reader: Portraits & Encounters.* Introduction by Barbara Lounsberry. New York: Walker, 2003.

Taraborrelli, J. Randy. *Sinatra: Behind the Leg-*

end. Secaucus, NJ: Carol, 1997.

————. *The Secret Life of Marilyn Monroe.* New York and Boston: Grand Central, 2009.

Taylor, Roger G. *Marilyn in Art.* London: Elm Tree, 1984.

————. *Marilyn Monroe In Her Own Words.* New York: Delilah/Putnam, 1983.

Thomas, Bob. *King Cohn: The Life and Times of Harry Cohn.* New York: G. P. Putnam's Sons, 1967.

Thomas, Evan. *The Man to See: Edward Bennett Williams — Ultimate Insider; Legendary Trial Lawyer.* New York: Simon & Schuster, 1991.

————. *Robert Kennedy: His Life.* New York: Simon & Schuster, 2000.

Thurman, Judith. *Isak Dinesen: The Life of a Storyteller.* New York: St. Martin's Press, 1982.

Todd Jr., Michael, and Susan McCarthy Todd. *A Valuable Property: The Life Story of Michael Todd.* New York: Arbor House, 1983.

Tornabene, Lyn. *Long Live the King: An Autobiography of Clark Gable.* New York: G. P. Putnam's Sons, 1976.

Tosches, Nick. *Dino: Living High in the Dirty Business of Dreams.* New York: Doubleday, 1992.

Tracy, Kathleen. *The Everything Jacqueline*

Kennedy Onassis Book: A Portrait of an American Icon. Avon, MA: Adams Media, 2008.

Truitt, Evelyn Mack. *Who Was on Screen.* New York: Bowker, 1984.

Tynan, Kathleen. *The Life of Kenneth Tynan.* New York: William Morrow, 1987.

Van Meter, Jonathan. *The Last Good Time: Skinny D'Amato, the Notorious 500 Club, and the Rise and Fall of Atlantic City.* New York: Crown, 2003.

Vickers, Hugo. *Cecil Beaton: A Biography.* Boston: Little, Brown 1985.

Vitacco-Robles, Gary. *Cursum Perficio: Marilyn Monroe's Brentwood Hacienda — The Story of Her Final Months.* New York: Writers Club Press, 1999.

Wagenknecht, Edward, ed. *Marilyn Monroe: A Composite View.* Philadelphia: Chilton Books, 1969.

Walker, Alexander. *The Celluloid Sacrifice: Aspects of Sex in the Movies.* London: Joseph, 1966.

Wallace, Irving, Amy Wallace, David Wallechinsky, and Sylvia Wallace. *The Intimate Sex Lives of Famous People.* New York: Delacorte Press, 1981.

Wallis, Brian. *Marilyn, August 1953: The Last Look Photos by John Vachon.* Afterword by John Grafton. Mineola, NY: Calla Editions; Newton Abbot; David & Charles [distributor], 2010.

Waple, George H. *Country Boy Gone Soldiering.* Princeton, NJ: Xlibris, 1998.

Wasson, Sam. *Fifth Avenue, 5 A.M: Audrey Hepburn, Breakfast at Tiffany's, and the Dawn of the Modern Woman.* New York: Harper Studio, 2010.

Wayne, Jane Ellen. *Grace Kelly's Men: The Romantic Life of Princess Grace Kelly.* New York: St. Martin's Press, 1991.

————. *Marilyn's Men: The Private Life of Marilyn Monroe.* London: Robson Books, 1992.

Weathersby, William J. *Conversations with Marilyn.* New York: Mason/Chortey, 1976.

Weiland, Dennis. *Arthur Miller.* New York: Grove Press, 1961.

Wertheimer, Linda. Interview with Vincent Marotta, National Public Radio, October 29, 2005.

Who's Who of American Women: A Biographical Dictionary of Notable Living American Women. Chicago: Marquis Who's Who, 1958/59.

Wilkerson, Tichi, and Marcia Borie. *The Hollywood Reporter: The Golden Years.* New York: Arlington House, 1984.

Williams, Edward Bennett. *One Man's Freedom.* Introduction by Eugene V. Rostow. New York: Atheneum, 1962.

Wilson, Earl. *Hot Times: True Tales of Hollywood and Broadway.* Chicago: Contemporary Books, 1984.

————. *The Show Business Nobody Knows.* Chicago: Cowles, 1971.

Wilson, Liz. "Marilyn Monroe Interview." *American Weekly.* September 25, 1955.

Winters, Shelley. *Shelley: Also Known as Shirley.* New York: William Morrow, 1980.

————. *Shelley II: The Middle of My Century.* New York: Simon & Schuster, 1989.

Wolfe, Donald H. *The Assassination of Marilyn Monroe.* London: Warner Books, 1999.

————. *The Last Days of Marilyn Monroe.* New York: William Morrow, 1998.

Wynn, Ned. *We Will Always Live in Beverly Hills: Growing Up Crazy in Hollywood.* New York: William Morrow, 1990.

Yellin, Emily. *Our Mothers' War: American Women at Home and at the Front During World War II.* New York: Free Press, 2004.

Young-Bruehl, Elisabeth. *Anna Freud.* New Haven, CT: Yale University Press, 1988.

Zeffirelli, Franco. *Zeffirelli: The Autobiography of Franco Zeffirelli.* New York: Weidenfeld & Nicolson, 1986.

Zolotow, Maurice. *Billy Wilder in Hollywood.* New York: G. P. Putnam's Sons, 1977.

————. *Marilyn Monroe.* New York: Bantam Books, 1960.

————. Interview with David March. *Milwaukee Sentinel.* October 23, 1953.

ABOUT THE AUTHOR

C. David Heymann (1945-2012) is the author of several *New York Times* bestselling biographies, including *Bobby and Jackie, American Legacy, The Georgetown Ladies' Social Club,* and *RFK: A Candid Biography of Robert F. Kennedy.*